Exploring Disability
A Sociological Introduction
Second Edition

Colin Barnes and Geof Mercer

LIS LIBRARY

Date	Fund
19/1/11	Q

Order No

216954 x

University of Chester

KU-736-914

polity

Copyright © Colin Barnes and Geof Mercer 2010

The right of Colin Barnes and Geof Mercer to be identified as Authors of this Work has been asserted in accordance with the UK Copyright, Designs and Patents Act 1988.

First published in 2010 by Polity Press

Polity Press
65 Bridge Street
Cambridge CB2 1UR, UK

Polity Press
350 Main Street
Malden, MA 02148, USA

All rights reserved. Except for the quotation of short passages for the purpose of criticism and review, no part of this publication may be reproduced, stored in a retrieval system, or transmitted, in any form or by any means, electronic, mechanical, photocopying, recording or otherwise, without the prior permission of the publisher.

ISBN-13: 978-0-7456-3485-2 (hardback)
ISBN-13: 978-0-7456-3486-9 (paperback)

A catalogue record for this book is available from the British Library.

Typeset in 10.5 on 13 pt Swift
by Servis Filmsetting Ltd, Stockport, Cheshire
Printed and bound in Great Britain by the MPG Books Group

The publisher has used its best endeavours to ensure that the URLs for external websites referred to in this book are correct and active at the time of going to press. However, the publisher has no responsibility for the websites and can make no guarantee that a site will remain live or that the content is or will remain appropriate.

Every effort has been made to trace all copyright holders, but if any have been inadvertently overlooked the publisher will be pleased to include any necessary credits in any subsequent reprint or edition.

For further information on Polity, visit our website: www.politybooks.com

Contents

Preface to the Second Edition

IN the first edition of *Exploring Disability* (Barnes, Mercer and Shakespeare, 1999) we highlighted the extraordinary politicization of disability, particularly since the 1960s. Campaigns by disabled people and their organizations challenged the dominant view of 'chronic illness and disability' and its overwhelming preoccupation with an individual's functional limitations and perceived 'abnormalities', whether in mind or body. In contrast, disabled activists redirected attention to the importance of the diverse social, cultural, economic and political barriers to inclusion in everyday life experienced by many people with impairments. Increasingly, these protests have gathered support from disabled people around the world.

The campaigns have also made a growing impression on governments and disability policy. High-profile concerns include poverty and employment, cultural representations, disability rights, user involvement in services, anti-discrimination legislation, euthanasia and genetics. At the same time, contributions to academic theorizing and researching disability have drawn on a broader range of disciplinary influences, besides attracting more mainstream recognition. This is evident in the remarkable growth in books and journal articles on disability across the humanities, education, law and the social sciences. One direct consequence has been the emergence of a distinctive subject area of 'disability studies' in universities and colleges.

This burgeoning interest in disability issues warranted more than the basic revisions and updating already required to a volume published ten years ago. Most notably, two chapters have been written specifically for this edition. The first considers recent developments in genetics and their implications for people with accredited impairments and long-term illness conditions. The second additional chapter focuses on the expanding literature on disability and impairment in poorer or underdeveloped countries.

We hope that this second edition offers an up-to-date, wide-ranging and critical review of key issues and debates relevant to sociological studies of disability.

Acknowledgements

We recognize the inspiration of the many disabled individuals and their allies who have, over the years, struggled to put disability on the political agenda, without whom this book would not have been written.

Those readers familiar with the first edition of *Exploring Disability* will note that Tom Shakespeare no longer appears as a co-author. He participated in some of the early discussions, but felt unable to devote the time necessary to preparing this second edition because of his commitments to other writing and research projects. We want to record our thanks for his support.

Finally, we are grateful to the following organizations for permission to reprint the following material: Figure 2.1: The World Health Organization for figure in WHO (1980, p. 30) *International Classification of Impairments, Disabilities and Handicaps*, Geneva: World Health Organization; Figure 2.3: The World Health Organization for figure in WHO (2001, p. 18) *International Classification of Functioning, Disability and Health*, Geneva: World Health Organization; Table 5.1: Edward Elgar Publishing for Table 2.1 in K. Vleminckx and J. Berghman (2001) Social Exclusion and the Welfare State: an Overview of Conceptual Issues and Implications. In D. G. Mayes, J. Berghman and R. Salais (eds), *Social Exclusion and European Policy*, Cheltenham: Edward Elgar; Figure 5.3: The Cabinet Office for Table 2.1 in Cabinet Office (2005) *Improving the Life Chances of Disabled People: Final Report*, London: The Cabinet Office. (Available at: http://www.strategy.gov.uk/downloads/workareas/disability/disabilityreport/index.htm); Figure 6.1: The Open University Press for Table 2 in S. M. Peace, L. A. Kellaher and D. M. Willcocks (1997) *Re-evaluating Residential Care*, Buckingham: Open University Press; Figure 10.1: The Department for International Development for Figure 2 (Poverty and Disability – a vicious circle) in Department for International Development (DfID) (2000) *Disability, Poverty and Development*, London: DfID. (Available at: http://www.dfid.gov.uk/Documents/publications/disabilitypovertydevelopment.pdf).

CHAPTER 1

Introduction: Analysing Disability

IN Western industrialized societies, 'disability' is widely regarded as an individual failing and a personal tragedy. This is confirmed by its pre-eminent medical diagnosis in terms of individual pathology, and associated deficits, abnormalities and functional limitations. Crucially, these difficulties become both the explanations for the wide-ranging social disadvantages and dependence and the justification for routine intervention in disabled people's lives by health and social welfare professionals. This approach is further confirmed in public attitudes towards the 'victims' that emphasize 'imaginative concern, mawkish sentimentality, indifference, rejection and hostility' (Thomas, 1982, p. 4).

In the 1960s, disabled activists in North America, Scandinavia and Western Europe initiated campaigns against this disability orthodoxy. The goal was to shift public and policy attention away from its overwhelming preoccupation with individual 'incapacity' as the source of their dependency and marginalization. Instead, the spotlight was directed onto the role of 'disabling barriers' (social, economic, cultural and political) in excluding disabled people from participation in mainstream society and denying their citizenship rights (Finkelstein, 1980; DeJong, 1981).

The academic community was relatively slow to attribute any significance to disabled people's political actions, let alone to recognize the potential of social analyses of disability. 'There were no disjunctures between the dominant cultural narrative of disability and the academic narrative. They supported and defended each other' (Linton, 1998a, p. 1). It was not until the 1990s that a trend towards rethinking disability gathered momentum. This is evident in the sustained growth in monographs, edited collections and specialist journals, which warranted claims of a distinct field of 'disability studies', with specialist university programmes appearing around the world. Moreover, contributions have expanded across the social sciences, education, law and the humanities (for example, Butler and Parr, 1999; Gleeson, 1999; Albrecht et al., 2001; Longmore and Omansky,

2001; Stiker, 1999; Breslin and Yee, 2002; Snyder et al., 2002; Borsay, 2005; Tremain, 2005a; Goodley and Lawthom, 2006; Pothier and Devlin, 2006; Florian, 2007).

The aim of this book is to explore key issues and themes in developing a sociology of disability, while drawing on insights from other (social science) disciplines. In this introductory chapter we prepare the ground by, first, tracing the grass-roots origins of critical responses to the dominant 'personal tragedy' approach and the instigation of a new 'disability politics' to challenge conventional theory and practice. Second, we outline key parameters for sociological analyses of disability, and the diversity in theoretical perspectives and the contrasting implications for studying disability. We conclude with an overview and rationale of the central issues examined in subsequent chapters.

Grass-roots mobilization

A significant stimulus to recent academic and policy debates on disability has been the politicization of disabled people. Groups of disabled people have set up their own organizations with an overtly political agenda to campaign against discrimination and for greater inclusion in mainstream society. While there had been important instances of protest by groups of disabled people earlier in the twentieth century, it was the rise of the American Independent Living Movement (ILM) in the 1970s that first attracted international awareness of the politicization of disability and the possibilities for collective action (Bowe, 1978; Longmore and Omansky, 2001). In Europe, disabled people prompted a variety of innovative projects, such as accessible housing in Sweden (Brattgard, 1974; Grunewald, 1974) and the Het Dorp community in the Netherlands (Zola, 1982).

The exponents of this new disability politics embarked on 'a struggle for both self-determination and self-definition' (Longmore and Omansky, 2001, p. 8). Historically, disabled people have been 'isolated, incarcerated, observed, written about, operated on, instructed, implanted, regulated, treated, institutionalized, and controlled to a degree probably unequal to that experienced by any other minority group' (Davis, 1997, p. 1). Disabled people now highlighted their everyday familiarity with social and environmental barriers, restricted life chances, and negative cultural representations. This required a re-evaluation of their individual and collective support needs and rights. It encompassed a critique of the regulation of disabled people's everyday lives by a diverse group of health and welfare professionals. Disability activists did not deny the positive potential of appropriate medical and allied intervention. Rather, they challenged those professional experts who equated disability solely with functional limitations and concentrated service provision on individual rehabilitation and adjustment.

Needless to say, disabled people's campaigns demonstrated the influence of contrasting national and historical contexts, such as the role of the welfare state in disability policy. In the USA, for example, the primary spur to political activity was the characterization of disabled people as a minority group who were denied basic civil rights and equal opportunities. This emulated protest movements by black people and women (Zola, 1983; Hahn, 1985; Linton 1998a). In the UK, activists favoured an interpretation of disability as a form of social oppression or exclusion encountered by people with impairments. This underscored arguments for radical social change rather than piecemeal reforms as the means for overturning the disabling (capitalist) society (Finkelstein, 1980; Oliver, 1983).

Notwithstanding these differences, the new disability politics identified a distinctive set of policy objectives for improving disabled people's life chances. These ranged from civil/citizenship rights, independent living in the community and equal access in the built environment, to mainstreaming education, employment and leisure opportunities. Such campaigns generated increasing interest around the world. In 1981, Disabled Peoples' International (DPI), an international umbrella for organizations controlled and run by disabled people, was formed. A decade later, 4,000 delegates from over 120 countries attended its third world congress in 1992 (DPI, 1992).

A range of important initiatives emerged at the international level (Albrecht et al., 2001; Barton, 2001; Barnes and Mercer, 2005a, 2005b). The United Nations (UN) introduced measures on the rights of disabled people, notably the General Assembly's Declaration on the Rights of Disabled People in 1975. It nominated 1981 the International Year of Disabled Persons and proclaimed 1983–92 as the Decade of Disabled Persons. Disabled people's protests also helped persuade the World Health Organization (WHO) to replace the *International Classification of Impairments, Disabilities and Handicaps (ICIDH)* (WHO, 1980) with the *International Classification of Functioning, Disability and Health* (shortened to *ICF*), which sought to incorporate medical and social approaches (WHO, 2001a). Governments in North America, Europe and Australasia responded with policies to improve disabled people's everyday lives, recognize the rights of disabled people, and introduce anti-discrimination legislation (Clear, 2000; Bickenbach, 2001a; CEC, 2003; Doyle, 2008).

However, an individual, medicalized perspective exercises an enduring influence around the world on public and policy debates about disabled people's support needs, as in 'special education' and segregated/sheltered employment options (Longmore and Omansky, 2001; Ratzka, 2003; Morris, 2004). The slow progress of disabled people's campaigns sparked renewed discussion about the aims and strategies of disability politics around equality and inclusion, identity and representation, citizenship and human rights.

Sociological perspectives

How then might sociological analyses contribute to understanding disability and its changing political and policy profile? In his celebrated essay on the sociological imagination, C. Wright Mills (1970) argued that the discipline has a particular contribution to make to social and political analyses by encouraging critical reflection on seemingly 'personal troubles'. These affect individuals and their social relations with others but are more appropriately understood as 'public issues' linked to social institutions and society more generally (ibid., p. 14). Hence, the sociological interest in reviewing the connections between individual experiences and biography and wider historical and political circumstances:

> Deeply immersed in our daily routines, though, we hardly ever pause to think about the meaning of what we have gone through; even less often have we the opportunity to compare our private experience with the fate of others, to see the *social* in the *individual*, the *general* in the *particular*; this is precisely what sociologists can do for us. We would expect them to show how our individual *biographies* intertwine with the *history* we share with fellow human beings. (Bauman, 1990, p. 10, *emphasis in original*)

As an illustration, the failure of a disabled individual to obtain paid employment is widely explained in terms of individual shortcomings. However, if the unemployment rate for disabled people is much higher than that of the rest of the population, an alternative account might be more persuasive. One suggestion would be that the disabled population generally experiences exclusion from the workplace because of structural factors or discrimination. This moves the explanation from the individual level to collective social disadvantage, and a different set of policy responses.

This illustrates a fundamental sociological theme of the value of reassessing familiar or common-sense ways of thinking and behaving. 'The fascination of sociology lies in the fact that its perspective makes us see in a new light the very world in which we have lived all our lives' (Berger, 1963, p. 21). Apparently 'natural' attitudes, institutions, processes and structures are regarded as contingent on social factors and contexts, while sustained and modified by human action.

The aim is not to replace 'error' with incontestable 'truth', but rather to engage in critical reflection to improve our understanding of the social world (Bauman, 1990).

Additionally, comparative studies of disability illustrate the diverse understandings of disability that exist outside British (and Western) society. It is equally necessary to recover the 'world we have lost' to examine how and why attitudes and practices towards disability vary historically. Moreover, 'Sociology cannot be a neutral intellectual endeavour, indifferent to the practical consequences of its analysis for those whose conduct forms its object of study' (Giddens, 1982a, p. vii). Instead, social inquiry should draw on the comparative and historical standpoints to produce a 'critique of existing forms of society' and prompt an awareness of 'alternative futures' (Giddens, 1982b, p. 26).

From this basic statement of intent, a number of themes dominate theoretical debates in sociology:

> Firstly, sociology is concerned to understand the meaning of social action, that is the subjective perspective, emotions and feelings of human agents as social individuals. Secondly, sociology is concerned with the relationship between agency and structure. Sociology attempts to explore the relationship between human action and the structural determination of social relations by certain constraining elements which in general we can describe as power relations. Third, classical sociology has been organised around the problem of social order, that is the question of social integration through the presence of consensus and constraint in human life. Quite simply, sociology is concerned with the ultimate question of 'How is society possible?' Finally, sociology is about the analysis of the social processes and circumstances which constantly disrupt and disorganise the fragile order of social relations and social exchange. We can summarise this problem as the question of social inequality, because it is through an analysis of the unequal distribution of power (in terms of class, status and power) that we can begin to understand the de-stabilisation of social relations and social systems through organised conflict and individual resistance. (Turner, 1995, p. 3)

To understand the social world, it is necessary to explore people's subjective 'definition of the situation' and their attempts to navigate its inherent uncertainties and dilemmas. A central assumption underpinning social action is that human beings are creative in that they have a capacity for choice or 'agency', but are still constrained to some degree in what they think and do. This has led to considerable variation in assessments of the relative importance of agency and structure. Some accounts emphasize structural factors and stress how behaviour and attitudes have their bases in the social circumstances and the social groups to which people belong. Other approaches represent social interaction as far less 'determined'.

Another major area of debate in classical sociology is the basis of social order and the sources and containment of potential disruption. Social order is often fragile, with diverse and competing interests, so that accounts have polarized in how far they represent social life and its underlying structures and processes as characterized more by consensus or conflict. A consensus approach assumes that social stability is maintained because of the effectiveness of socialization, so that people generally accept the benefits of co-operation and the legitimacy of political regulation. In contrast, from a conflict perspective, society is distinguished by power inequalities, with diverse and frequently antagonistic material and other concerns.

This raises further questions about the main forms of social control, power and regulation. Typically, dominant social groups seek ways to perpetuate and enhance their privileged position and to secure the compliance of subordinate groups, whether by overt use of power and authority or through more covert influence and manipulation, perhaps by generating a set of ideas (ideology) that reflect and sustain the position of a social group. Over recent decades, increased significance has been accorded to 'ideological domination', hegemony and the generation of 'willing consent', which potentially deflects attention away from structural (class) inequalities (Gramsci, 1971, 1985). At the same time, it is important to investigate how dominant groups are destabilized and new ideologies become the basis for collective resistance and mobilization.

This literature links with another major sociological topic: the extent and character of social inequalities and exclusion. A vital question is how socially defined groups (based typically in industrialized societies on social class) are located differently in respect of power and status. It is illustrated by empirical studies in such areas as income, education and the labour market. Over recent years, the preoccupation with social class inequalities has been displaced as a result of criticism that sociologists have ignored or disregarded the significance of other lines of social divisions, based, for example, on age, gender and ethnicity.

Levels of analysis

A next step is to translate these broad sociological themes into a widely used conceptual framework that differentiates, at least for analytical purposes, between micro-individual, meso-social group or institutional, and macro-societal levels of inquiry (Turner, 1995; Layder, 1997).

At the micro-level, there is a range of interactionist and interpretative perspectives, including symbolic interactionism (relations between the individual and society that focus on symbolic processes of communication), phenomenology (the interpretation of the everyday activities and routines people employ to give meaning to social life) and ethnomethodology (how people produce or make sense of the everyday world and its taken-for-granted aspects). For instance, 'experiential' approaches examine how meanings emerge from, and are modified through, interaction. An associated issue is how individual self-identity links with everyday routines and changes over time and between social contexts. The study of face-to-face interaction spans less formal contexts, such as the family and household, to more organized settings such as the workplace, residential institutions and encounters with professional experts. Most micro-level approaches stress that interaction is part of a negotiated and emergent, rather than fixed or determined, social process.

The meso-level spotlight is on social institutions, roles and norms, along with the potential links across levels. This has encouraged studies of impairment, disability and the disabled body as the product of social and cultural practices, and how specific conditions or attributes such as 'mental illness' or 'mental handicap' are 'stigmatized' (see chapter 3). A core focus is the separation of 'normal' and 'deviant' behaviour and attitudes. This labelling entails a social judgement, with definitions and meanings contested and liable to vary over time and between societies and cultures (Becker, 1963). A related focus includes the activities and impact of specialized, bureaucratic institutions (in such areas as health, education and welfare).

The macro-level comprises the overall societal organization of systems, including the state, economy and social policy. These subjects are explored by a diverse group of structuralist and systems approaches, such as functionalism and neo-Marxism. Among the latter group, materialist and political economy analyses have been very influential in their portrayal of the relationship between capitalism, power and patterns of inequality. A minority group (or groups) has access to disproportionate power, economic resources and knowledge. A specific focus is the relationship between dominant groups and the role of the state and how far it helps to sustain the power, status and material rewards of specific groups, the medical profession among them. A parallel literature identifies significant shifts towards a post-modern society and culture. This is highlighted by trends in industrialized societies towards greater diversity, including new lines of social fragmentation and a growing pluralism in cultural allegiances.

A notable, recent ferment in social theory has been driven by debates within social constructionism. There was a rejection of modernist 'grand narratives' stretching back to the Enlightenment period in the late eighteenth century. Instead, shifting social and cultural conditions heralded a new post-modern era, with a distinctive 'cultural turn' in social theory (Lyotard, 1984). Post-structuralists (such as Jacques Derrida and Michel Foucault) broke with assumptions of a single, progressively evolving reality or truth and traditional authority and hierarchies of knowledge, while stressing multiple realities, discontinuity and difference (Burr, 1996). This presents a sharp contrast to orthodox approaches to the 'social construction of reality' in which ideas and practices are externalized and accepted at the 'common-sense' level (Berger and Luckmann, 1967). In different ways, the ethnomethodological and post-structuralist literatures stress the importance of language in social interaction and in 'shaping social order' (Jaworski and Coupland, 1999, p. 3). The post-structuralist literature draws heavily on Michel Foucault's (1965, 1976, 1980) analysis of the interrelationship between knowledge and power. This emphasizes a distinctive view of power as subject-creating and a source of self- rather than external regulation, as well as how discourses generate rather than reflect social reality.

The fervour for post-structuralism has generated renewed interest in critical realism, with a distinctive ontological stance (on the character of social reality). It shares a materialist focus and assumption that phenomena exist irrespective of whether we have knowledge of them or linguistic concepts to describe them. Its epistemological position (theory of knowledge) is that what we know must not be confused with what actually exists (ontology) – a view attributed to post-structuralism. Moreover, 'mind-independent generative structures' and a range of non-observable causal mechanisms have an impact on social life irrespective of whether their existence is 'known' (Bhaskar, 1998). This has important implications in contradicting post-structural accounts of human bodies and impairment.

Understanding disability requires analyses of experiences at the individual level, the social construction and creation of disability and 'middle-range' theorizing, together with broader analyses of societal power and social inequalities. Yet, while most sociologists distinguish several levels at which sociological analysis operates, these are not discrete areas in everyday practice. Additionally, strategic concepts, such as power, span more than one level.

Social analyses applied to disability

Initially, disabled people's campaigns around disability generated little academic curiosity, whether in the social sciences or the humanities. There were occasional references to the social disadvantages and environmental barriers affecting disabled people (Blaxter, 1976; Safilios-Rothschild, 1976), but relatively few attempts to reconsider existing theoretical accounts and go beyond individual, biologically based explanations (Bogdan and Biklen, 1977; DeJong, 1979a). Indeed, it was a few disabled academics with close links to disabled people's political campaigns – such as Irving Zola (1982) in America and Vic Finkelstein (1980) and Mike Oliver (1983) in the UK – who proved most influential in raising the profile of disability for a social science audience.

In the 1970s, there were two main points of entry for disability into academic debates: first, through the examination of social problems; and, second, via studies of 'chronic illness and disability' by medical sociologists. In America, in particular, there was a long-established tradition of studying the social problems associated with industriali- zation and urbanization such as poverty, crime, drug use and family breakdown (Gouldner, 1970). Social problems were widely described as a discrepancy between what is and what people think ought to be (Merton, 1966). In textbooks on social problems, this standard menu of topics was increasingly complemented by a chapter on 'mental disorder' and sometimes 'mental handicap' (Merton and Nisbet, 1966; Neubeck, 1979). This literature sought explanations of the social origins and trajectory of social problems as well as likely policy remedies.

A new brand of constructionist accounts presented the foremost challenge to this realist approach by moving the spotlight from the search for underlying structural causes to people's subjective under- standings of social problems. That said, from an ethnomethodological perspective, the crucial analytical issue is not whether there is an objective basis to social problems but how these are constituted as important (or not) by individuals (Garfinkel, 1967; Spector and Kitsuse, 1977). Besides this, 'strict' constructionists did not see it as their role to inform social movement practice in seeking social change or evalu- ating the accuracy of claims-makers' arguments (Holstein and Miller, 1993).

Another major source of theorizing and research on disability emanated from sociological studies of 'chronic illness and disabil- ity'. Talcott Parsons's (1951) functionalist investigation of illness as a social status as much as a biophysical condition highlighted the sick role and doctor–patient encounters. This heralded a shift away from a 'medical model' of health and illness and towards analysing 'disabil- ity' as a form of social deviance. An interactionist literature focused on the social processes of labelling and the problems of living with a 'stigmatized' condition (Becker, 1963; Goffman, 1963; Scheff, 1966). On a related tack, interpretive approaches gained prominence, stress- ing the 'insider's view' of long-term illness and impairment and the impact on social relationships, sense of self and identity (Edgerton, 1967; Strauss, 1975).

The traditional sociological focus on social inequalities, primarily those rooted in social class, endured into the 1970s. At that time, criticism of the neglect of other social divisions, notably those located in gender, ethnicity and 'race', opened up new lines of theorizing and research. Yet, it was not until the 1990s that investigations of the form and extent of socio-economic disadvantages and inequalities facing disabled people began to attract noticeable academic attention. Familiar social inequality themes emerge, such as whether material and normative divisions are related to disability; how far disability produces a distinctive, collective identity; and how far, and in what ways, disability interacts with or mediates other lines of social division.

The academic literature largely ignored or disputed the social barriers approach promoted by disabled people's organizations, with disability redefined as a form of social oppression. Radical disability theorists roundly condemned the sociological and social policy literature for not breaking with the traditional functional limitations perspective (Oliver, 1990). More recently, social theory has taken new directions, especially in the humanities and cultural studies, with interdisciplinary approaches flourishing. Post-structuralist analyses of competing discourses exerted a growing influence (Foucault, 1980). In the case of disability, a biomedical discourse achieved pre-eminence in the production by specific practitioners and institutions of 'welfare subjects', their needs and management. In turn, competing discourses, such as those advanced by disabled activists, are 'problematized' and deconstructed. At the same time, there is a much greater willingness to acknowledge that disability raises significant normative and ethical issues of general public concern, from social justice to the quality and meaning of life (Corker and Shakespeare, 2002; Snyder et al., 2002; Williams, 2003; Tremain, 2005a; Davis, 2006; Snyder and Mitchell, 2006).

Our preference is for a socio-political approach that incorporates the understandings and priorities of disabled people. Despite our differences with some of the mainstream academic approaches, there are also opportunities worth exploring for a cross-fertilization of ideas in theorizing and researching disability (Barnes and Mercer, 1996, 2003; Scambler, 2004; Thomas, 2007). Potential areas include the experience of disability, and its variation across social contexts and groups; the social processes by which perceived impairments become the basis for disablement; how people with impairments are dealt with by professional (and other) agencies of social control; and the political economy of the structural conditions and policy responses which produce impairment and sustain disability, including suggested qualitative shifts to industrial capitalism and subsequent developments, to a late modern if not post-modern society.

A brief word on terminology

It is now widely accepted that the language and concepts we use influence and reflect our understanding of the social world. This standpoint informs campaigns against prejudicial attitudes and stereotypes from a diverse range of disadvantaged groups, including women, minority ethnic groups, older people, lesbians and gay men. Equally, where impairment is defined in negative terms, this reinforces disparaging attitudes, with disabled people pitied and patronized as tragic victims.

In the English-speaking world, terms such as 'cripple', 'spastic' and 'mongol' lost their original technical meaning and became terms of abuse. Yet, as the translation of impairment and disability illustrates, there is not always an exact equivalent in other languages. Thus, the term 'handicap' now has oppressive connotations in English-speaking countries because of its historical association with begging and charity or reduced capacity, although this is not always the case in other languages. For example, Disabled Peoples' International (DPI) initially adopted the terms 'disability' and 'handicap' (DPI, 1982; Driedger, 1989), emulating the World Health Organization's *ICIDH* (WHO, 1980). A decade later DPI Europe opted instead to use 'impairment' and 'disability' (DPI, 1994).

While recognizing that choice of terminology is very contentious, even among those identifying as disabled people, in this book we follow (with some qualifications) the terminology agreed in 1981 at its inception by the British Council (of Organizations) of Disabled People (BCODP) – since 2006 renamed the UK Disabled People's Council (UKDPC). This differentiates 'impairment', as a medically classified biophysiological condition, from 'disability', which denotes the social disadvantage experienced by people with an accredited impairment. As a result, we avoid the phrase 'people with disabilities' (except in quotations from others) because it both blurs the conceptual division between impairment and disability and implies that impairment defines an individual's identity. Similarly, we steer clear of words that depersonalize individuals, such as 'the deaf' or 'the mad'. What is at issue is far more than a choice of words but the most appropriate way to understand and contest disability.

Overview of the book

The starting point in chapter 2 is contrasting historical views of disability. This provides a necessary context to a review of the main approaches to disability at the present time. These comprise the individualized, or 'socio-medical', classification of 'impairments, disabilities and handicaps' (WHO, 1980); a social model of disability advanced by activists in Britain (Oliver, 1983, 1990); and recent attempts to synthesize these competing accounts by the WHO (2001a).

The medical sociology literature on 'chronic illness' that contains the traditional location for studies of 'disability' is considered in chapter 3. A pre-eminent interactionist and phenomenological emphasis on experiential accounts of illness often downplays the impact of structural factors, or 'disabling barriers'. Other issues overlap more immediately with social model preoccupations, ranging from the medicalization of social problems and professional dominance to newer (post-structuralist) themes, particularly Michel Foucault's (1965, 1976) distinctive discourse analysis and social constructionism, in respect of both the 'disabled body' and 'madness'.

Chapter 4 traces the emergence of attempts to theorize disability, underlining the competing arguments over structural or materialist accounts compared with those rooted in individual experience. It examines calls for 'bringing impairment back in' as well as the relative absence of studies of other important social divisions affecting the lives of disabled people, including gender, minority ethnic status, and 'race', age and sexuality. Additionally, this chapter discusses the relationship between sociological studies of 'chronic illness and disability', along with the application of post-structuralist analyses to disability and arguments for an embodied approach to disability. This raises fundamental questions about the direction and status of 'social model' theorizing and its disregard for analyses of 'impairment effects'.

Chapter 5 documents the materialization of disability policy with the rise of the welfare state since the mid-twentieth century. It traces the various social, economic, political and cultural barriers confronting disabled people and the impact of accelerating the privatization and commodification of welfare and support. The systematic exclusion of disabled people is discussed in terms of key institutions of contemporary society, such as education, employment and the labour market, and the built environment. These aspects are also addressed in chapter 6, particularly the role of social welfare policy in the lives of disabled people. A central interest is the critique advanced by disabled people's organizations of 'care' and 'dependency' and the promotion of 'independent living', with its underpinning of specific support needs and the policies that best advance this goal, such as direct payments and user-controlled services.

The next two chapters illustrate the changing political and cultural contexts of disability. Chapter 7 begins with an evaluation of the social forces precipitating the arrival of the disabled people's movement over recent decades and subsequently explores the arguments, both theoretical and empirical, surrounding its role as a catalyst for meaningful social change in light of the apparent recent adoption of socio-political solutions to the problem of disability by politicians and policy-makers in many societies. Chapter 8 explores the role of culture, media and leisure in the social construction of disability and the significance of disability culture and arts in forging a positive disabled identity.

Chapter 9 appraises the concerns, contradictions and moral dilemmas for advocates and supporters of a disability rights agenda triggered by eugenic and euthanasia-type solutions to perceived impairments and long-term health conditions, including the Human Genome Project, within Western societies. The issues surrounding the moral justification for prenatal screening, selective abortion and 'mercy killing' are set within recent developments in biomedical technology, medical ethics, rising costs of health and welfare provision, ageing populations, and the pursuit of bodily perfection.

Finally, chapter 10 examines understandings and experiences of disability and impairment in poorer, underdeveloped societies and the implications of transferring Western-oriented approaches. It highlights the interrelationship between economic development, poverty, impairment and disability. Further attention is given to the 'internationalization' of disability and the growing involvement of supranational agencies, governments and non-governmental organizations (NGOs). This is mirrored by the politicization of disabled people and their organizations, together with the emergence of a disability rights agenda and schemes to promote inclusion.

CHAPTER
2

Competing Models and Approaches

THE individual, medicalized approach embedded in modern Western industrialized societies equates 'disability' with a professionally diagnosed condition characterized primarily by functional limitations. This underpins a policy emphasis on medical rehabilitation and allied service provision. An individual's 'disability', as viewed through the prism of a personal tragedy, is the fundamental reason for their social exclusion. Alternative interpretations attracted only occasional public or policy attention and had a minimal impact on public service provision. It was not until the 1960s, amidst wider social and economic upheavals, that campaigns organized by disabled people outlined a serious challenge to the orthodoxy surrounding disability.

This chapter begins by tracing the socio-historical origins of the established orthodoxy: the individual or medical approach to disability. What are its main contemporary features and why have disability theorists identified it with a 'personal tragedy' approach? The next section traces the development of alternative accounts by groups of disabled people. In America, the rise of the Independent Living Movement generated a new 'paradigm of disability' (DeJong, 1979a), while in the United Kingdom an emphasis on the social barriers to inclusion took root. A more detailed discussion then follows of the elaboration of this critique into a social model of disability (Finkelstein, 1980, 1991, 1993a; Oliver, 1983, 1990). The final section considers attempts to integrate specific aspects of the medical and social options, as illustrated by the World Health Organization's 'biopsychosocial' model (WHO, 2001a). Its 'environmental turn' is echoed in Nordic debates that stress a 'relational' approach to disability (Gustavsson, 2004).

Socio-historical perspectives

It has become commonplace to disavow early historical studies of disability. Most criticism highlights the lack of theoretical analysis and adequate empirical grounding, as well as the pervasive claims of a steady, if uneven, growth of liberal and humanitarian policies and service provision with the rise of modern, industrial societies (Winzer, 1993; Gleeson, 1997; Bredberg, 1999). The literature is replete with examples of cruel and extraordinary attitudes and practices. Recent research has produced a much more complex picture of what was considered an impairment and how this was evaluated, and the identification of disabled people as a separate social group (Stiker, 1999). Studies document the considerable variation historically and cross-culturally in both patterns and perceptions of impairment and disability and appropriate local policy responses. Hence, it is important to locate attitudes and practices within a specific social context and to examine the interaction of diverse economic-material, cultural and political factors.

For so much of recorded history, the commonality of disease, infirmity and death, widespread poverty and violence has given a harsh reality to everyday life. Only a small privileged few were perhaps able to avoid their full impact. Thus, in ancient Greece and Rome: 'Most of the chronically deformed and disabled had to support themselves either by begging or by claiming the indulgence of a well-to-do relative' (Garland, 1995, p. 44), while people with perceived 'abnormalities' were widely devalued and openly derided (ibid., pp. 73–86). On occasion, contemporaries justified discrimination on economic grounds, but more typically accounts drew on dominant cultural values, with practices such as infanticide attributed to the negative religious omens of the birth of an 'abnormal' child (Stiker, 1999). It was important to appease or deflect the possible threat to social order.

Even so, while religious beliefs were central to ancient societies, their prescriptions regarding impairment exhibited considerable diversity. Judaism regarded many impairments and diseases as a sign of wrongdoing, uncleanliness and ungodliness that provided a justification for separating individuals from the rest of the society. Leviticus (21: 16–20), in the Old Testament of the Bible, catalogues a variety of impairments which precluded the possessor from participating in religious rituals – a crooked nose, sores, a missing limb, leprosy and skin diseases, and crushed testicles. Yet Judaism also prohibited infanticide of newborn children with an impairment and emphasized the importance of providing 'charity' for the 'sick' and less well-off. This ambivalence was replicated in the reactions of the early Christian Church, although again impairment and many other unexpected happenings were widely regarded as a punishment for sin or attributed to the 'forces of evil' (Stiker, 1999). Again, medieval society's 'astonishing sensibility' (Bloch, 1965, p. 73) to the supernatural extended to the potency of a range of demonic forces, revealed in the demise of individuals with 'disordered' minds and the denunciation of visibly impaired infants as 'changelings' – the Devil's substitutes for human children, and the result of their mother's embrace of sorcery and witchcraft (Haffter, 1968). The disabled child 'became a shameful stigma in the eyes of society and a reason for isolation, ostracism and even persecution' (ibid., p. 61). Similarly, in everyday social interaction, specific impairments were routine targets for popular jokes and denigration. Even so, poorer sections of the population and other marginal social group, bore the brunt of such hostility towards 'abnormality'.

Notwithstanding such potential for public hostility, everyone, including those regarded as sick or infirm, was expected to contribute as much as possible to the household and local economy so that these were self-sufficient (Botelho, 2004). Those individuals not supported by their families had to rely on the haphazard benefits of charity and alms-giving for subsistence. By the sixteenth century in England, the combination of a decline in the wealth and power of the Church and a perception of a growing vagrant population as a result of plagues, poor harvests and immigration from Ireland and Wales threatened social stability, with a rising demand for charity and poor relief (Stone, 1985). The English Poor Law of 1601 sought to consolidate existing practices into a national system paid for by local rates. Yet there was considerable unevenness and arbitrariness in identifying those individuals regarded as legitimately unable to work and deemed part of the 'deserving' poor.

The possibilities of locating ideas and practices towards disability within broader socio-historical trends are illustrated by Norbert Elias's (1978) detailed analysis of the 'civilizing process' in which people learn to revise their perceptions of repugnance and shame and restraint in social relationships. His comparison of medieval and eighteenth-century European court societies illustrates how public manners and body control became targets for 'improvement', ranging from eating and drinking to farting, spitting, blowing one's nose, and urinating and defecating in public. Historically, the increasing emphasis on 'external' surveillance helped to transform self-control into a mark of social esteem. Yet, conversely, unruly bodies became a sign of animality and a rationale for the spatial segregation of increasing numbers of disabled people. This encompassed a general individualization of the body as a self-contained and controlled entity (Shilling, 1993).

Industrialized societies

Through the eighteenth century there was an intensification of the commercialization of land and agriculture and a marked rise

in industrialization and urbanization. These had significant consequences for community and family life and institutions. As far
as disabled people were concerned, the speed of factory work, or
working to the rhythms of machinery, often undertaking complex,
dextrous tasks, coupled with its regimented discipline, formed 'a
highly unfavourable change from the slower, more self-determined
methods of work into which many handicapped people had been
integrated' (Ryan and Thomas, 1980, p. 101). What might be ignored
or tolerated in the slower and more flexible pattern of agricultural or
domestic production became a source of friction and lost income, if
not a threat to survival, within the new industrial system.

As yet, there was no distinct social group identified as comprising
disabled people, just as there were competing cosmologies surveying
the bases and possible remedies for disease, illness and impairment
(Jewson, 1976). There was an increased categorization of 'sick and
infirm' people as a social problem – marginalized by the economic
system and socially dependent. In Britain, amidst concerns that the
poor laws were not coping with the increased demand for assistance
and considerable local variation in provision, legislative reforms in
1834 emphasized national standards, denial of relief outside an institution, and setting support at low levels to deter claimants. A variety
of institutional 'solutions' were being promoted to contain the rising
number of 'casualties' of the 'far-reaching changes in work and family
life' (Ryan and Thomas, 1980, p. 101).

In Britain, the 'aged and infirm' comprised one of the main categories in the new workhouse population. There was also an upward
trend in incarcerating people defined as 'defectives', including people
with visual, hearing or communication impairments and epilepsy.
One of the most high-profile attempts to confine problem groups
underscored the growth of asylums for those diagnosed as 'mad'
(Scull, 1984). The institutionalized population rose substantially
through the nineteenth century, from three to thirty per 10,000 (Scull,
1979). The inmate population in 'medical handicap' institutions also
expanded significantly into the twentieth century. The rise of Social
Darwinism offered fresh justification for 'intellectual' divisions and
hierarchies based on the 'survival of the fittest'. Those categorized
as 'subnormal' inspired fears of moral collapse, with resumptions of
close links to sexual and criminal deviance (Ryan and Thomas, 1980).
Additionally, the introduction of diagnostic labels such as 'Mongolian
idiot' suggested that 'mental deficiency' constituted a potential racial
threat to civilized society.

A notable development affecting notions of disability stemmed
from the consolidation of an orthodox, state-legitimated medical
profession, with a distinctive scientific knowledge and practice, based

in residential sites ranging from hospitals to asylums. Through the nineteenth century, the medical profession took the lead in colonizing impairment by providing a comprehensive system of regulation and surveillance from diagnosis to treatment, based on its claim to scientific knowledge. Medical knowledge determined the boundaries between 'normal' and 'abnormal' individuals, the sane and insane, healthy and sick people. These categories were continually being redrawn, with new diseases and impairments identified. There was an associated expansion in the number of medical specialisms, as in the fields of 'mental illness' and 'mental handicap', with a growing separation of the 'lunatic' and 'idiot' asylums. More recently, rehabilitative medicine has become more prominent, along with a growth in allied professional groups. Furthermore, there was a rise in activity by charitable organizations directed at the social problems associated with the dependency of particular groups of disabled people.

In the first half of the twentieth century, the growth of segregated, residential institutions continued apace. The live-in solution was particularly significant for the high number of children with impairments, with many common childhood diseases carrying a significant risk of impairment if not death. In a period of minimal social welfare provision, poorer families found it very difficult to meet the high medical costs and support required by a disabled child (Humphries and Gordon, 1992). There was also a widening impact of the medical profession's authority on policies towards disabled people, from the broad legitimation of an individual's claim to sickness and impairment. However, how far this translated into social and welfare benefits remained a contested area and, in general, a low priority for governments and public alike. The result was an uneasy trade-off between humanitarian and economic factors (Blaxter, 1976; Borsay, 2005).

The individual or medical model of 'disability'

By the late nineteenth century, the individual approach to disability located in medical knowledge was widely accepted in Western industrialized societies. It focused on bodily 'abnormality', disorder or deficiency and how this 'causes' functional limitation or 'disability'. For example, people with quadriplegia lack the use of their arms and are therefore unable to wash or dress without assistance. The foundations are laid by professional diagnosis, treatment and the measurement of recovery, although the distinctive character of 'chronic' conditions highlights rehabilitation rather than 'cure'. The authority of scientific medicine extends to allied health professionals, such as physiotherapists and occupational therapists, as well as psychologists and educationalists. While also described as a medical model, more strictly it is 'an individual model of disability of which medicalization is one significant component' (Oliver, 1996a, p. 31).

It was not until the mid-twentieth century that legislation used the generic term 'disabled' – defined in the 1948 National Assistance Act as covering 'the blind, the partially sighted, the deaf, the hard of hearing, and the general classes of the physically handicapped'. The administrative task of setting precise (impairment) eligibility criteria for welfare benefits and social services concentrated on the extent of an individual's physical 'abnormality' or 'loss' and its translation into a specific level of incapacity. Even in the 1960s, the British National Insurance Benefit Regulations advised that the loss of fingers and a leg amputated below the knee constituted a 50 per cent disability, while that of three fingers and the amputation of a foot or the loss of an eye translated into a 30 per cent rating (Sainsbury, 1973, pp. 26–7). However, this largely mechanistic approach to the effects of impairment was attracting growing censure from policy-makers, social researchers and disabled people alike.

This prompted a shift to more explicit assessment and measurement of an individual's functional limitations in performing everyday tasks (Jefferys et al., 1969). The first national survey was undertaken by the Office of Population Censuses and Surveys (OPCS) in the late 1960s (Harris et al., 1971a, 1971b). It utilized a threefold distinction between

- *impairment*: 'lacking part or all of a limb, or having a defective limb, organ or mechanism of the body'
- *disablement*: 'the loss or reduction of functional ability'
- *handicap*: 'the disadvantage or restriction of activity caused by disability' (Harris et al., 1971a, p. 2).

The measurement of the level of handicap was based on a series of questions about an individual's ability to undertake key personal activities such as toileting, eating and drinking, and doing up zips and buttons.

Over time, the definition of impairment ('disability') has been widened to encompass 'anatomical, physiological or psychological abnormality or loss', such as those without an arm or a leg, or who are 'blind, or deaf or paralysed', as well as chronic conditions that interfere with 'physiological or psychological' processes, such as arthritis, epilepsy and schizophrenia (Townsend, 1979, p. 686). There were continuing efforts to produce more valid and reliable measures of an individual's ability to perform key personal activities. The early focus on physical capacity was complemented by research into the service requirements of people with perceived 'mental' and 'intellectual' impairments (Herz et al., 1977; Meltzer et al., 2000).

Internationally, the most influential contribution has been the World Health Organization's *International Classification of Impairments, Disabilities and Handicaps (ICIDH)* (WHO, 1980). This taxonomy was designed to complement the *International Classification of Disease* (WHO, 1976) by moving beyond acute conditions and the simple causal sequence 'etiology → pathology → manifestation' (WHO, 1980, p. 10, where the last stage consisted of an outcome measure of degree of recovery following medical treatment. It demonstrates many similarities with the OPCS scheme in the definition of its central components:

- *impairment*: 'any loss or abnormality of psychological, physiological or anatomical structure or function' (ibid., p. 27)
- *disability*: 'any restriction or lack (resulting from an impairment) of ability to perform an activity in the manner or within the range considered normal for a human being' (ibid., p. 28)
- *handicap*: 'a disadvantage for a given individual, resulting from an impairment or a disability that limits or prevents the fulfilment of a role that is normal (depending on age, sex, social and cultural factors) for that individual' (ibid., p. 29).

Impairment covers those parts or systems of the body that do not work properly, and 'disability' centres on the (functional) activities that an individual cannot accomplish. The *ICIDH* represented a break from the traditional medical model by its inclusion of social 'handicap'. The first OPCS survey demonstrated the growing attention of social researchers to the impact of impairment/disability on valued social roles and relationships (Harris et al., 1971a, 1971b). This is substantially extended in the *ICIDH* coding classification to encompass, for example, socio-economic disadvantages or 'economic self-sufficiency' (Bury, 2000a, p. 1074). Consequently, exponents of the *ICIDH* asserted its distinctive credentials as a 'socio-medical model' (Bury, 1996, 1997).

The overall disablement process is represented in terms of a causal chain between separate but linked linear states (figure 2.1).

These discussions leading to the *ICIDH* also influenced the second OPCS national study of disability in Britain in the 1980s. It examined functional limitations in nine fields:

- reaching and stretching
- dexterity
- seeing
- hearing
- personal care.
- continence
- communication
- locomotion behaviour
- intellectual functioning

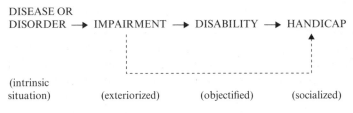

Source: WHO (1980, p. 30).

Figure 2.1   The process of disablement

On the basis of performance across these areas, the OPCS research-ers constructed an overall measure of 'disability' with ten levels of severity. This echoes policy approaches in other Western societies. For instance, the Americans with Disabilities Act of 1990 defines 'dis-ability' as an 'impairment that substantially limits one or more of the major life activities', with 'normal' functioning again the yardstick.

The OPCS surveys in the 1980s were undertaken with a sample of disabled adults and children who lived in either 'communal estab-lishments' or private households. The 'entry criteria' were widened in comparison with its earlier study (Harris et al., 1971a) to take in people with a 'mental illness and handicap' and those with 'less severe' impairments (Martin et al., 1988). As a consequence, the esti-mated number of disabled adults in Great Britain (England, Scotland and Wales) doubled to 6.2 million, equivalent to 14.2 per cent of the total population. More consistently, both surveys reported that a majority of this disabled population was over sixty years of age and contained a higher proportion of women than men. Increasing age was also closely associated with 'severity of disability'. Overall, almost a third of the disabled population was ranked in the two 'least severe' categories.

More recent data from the General Household Survey (figure 2.2), based on a different measure – a self-classifying head count of people with a 'limiting long-standing' condition – indicate an increase to nearly 12 million people, or around 19 per cent of the total popula-tion (Cabinet Office, 2005). The United States Census Bureau (Brault, 2008) identifies a similar proportion, 18.7 per cent, of the population in 2005, although this represented a slight decline from 1992, when 19.4 per cent of Americans reported a 'disability'. Additionally, both national surveys relate impairment to a wide range of social disadvan-tages, for example, in employment and transport.

However, the diverse ways in which these surveys are designed and implemented internationally suggest considerable caution when comparing data on the size and composition of the disabled popula-tion, as well as trends over time. Measures change, while the collection

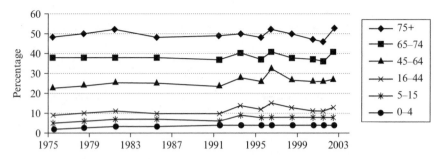

Source: Cabinet Office (2005, (p. 55)).

Figure 2.2   Percentage of the UK population who reported limiting long-standing
illness or disability, by age

and presentation of information on impairment/disability also vary
between countries. These contrasts weaken, if not undermine, the
reliability of historical and international comparisons (Fujiura and
Rutkowski-Kmitta, 2001; Mbogoni, 2003; Eide and Loeb, 2006).

The attempts to operationalize the individual/medical model highlight major difficulties in its underlying theoretical basis and policy
implications. Key tenets of the medical model include '(1) the definition of disease as deviation from normal biological functioning; (2)
the doctrine of specific etiology; (3) the concept of generic diseases,
that is, the universality of a disease taxonomy; and (4) the scientific
neutrality of medicine' (Mishler, 1981, p. 3). Yet each of these has been
disputed by social scientists. For example, the definition of disease
(and impairment) as a deviation from a 'normal' biological state raises
the question: 'Does normal refer to an ideal standard or to the average
value of a population characteristic?' (ibid., p. 4). Spectacles are a necessary aid for many with a visual impairment, but they have become
so widely used that few regard them as a mark of 'abnormality'.
Furthermore, the apparently objective designation of an individual as
'not normal' may contain a value judgement on that person's social
worth, most obviously with labels such as 'mental illness' and 'mental
handicap'.

Additionally, there has been growing recognition within medicine
of the impact of social factors and relationships on the origins and
trajectory of impairment and illness (Armstrong, 1983). This diverges
from the traditional assumption, illustrated in the OPCS and *ICIDH*
definitions, that 'impairment' is the underlying cause of 'disability' and/or 'handicap'. The orthodox assumption has been that the
primary solution to 'chronic illness and disability' rests with medical
intervention and allied (physical and psychological) rehabilitation.
Conversely, the environment is represented as 'neutral', with little
elaboration of alternative explanations for social 'handicap'. This

downplays the potential of social policy reforms and of legislation to guarantee disabled people full citizenship rights. The disabled person is expected to make the best of their diminished circumstances and concentrate their expectations on individual adjustment and coping strategies, with appropriate professional direction (Finkelstein, 1993a, 1993b).

The individualistic approach is further exemplified by psychological studies of the individual adaptation and adjustment to impairment (perhaps following a stroke) and the 'loss' of bodily function, such as a limb amputation (Parkes, 1975). In the case of a severe spinal injury, a staged process of personal adaptation and accommodation, akin to the grieving process of bereavement, is suggested (Weller and Miller, 1977). The initial reaction of *shock* and horror is followed by *denial* or despair that any recovery is possible, leading to *anger* at others, and finally to *depression* as a necessary preliminary to coming to terms with their diminished circumstances. This fifth stage, termed 'acceptance' or 'adjustment', may not be reached until one or two years later. This psychosocial journey has been widely applied, for example, in counselling those who acquire a hearing impairment (Wilson, 2003) and in charting the experiences of disabled children forced into a segregated 'special' school (Minde et al., 1972), as well as to parents coming to terms with having a disabled child (Sapey, 2004).

Critics complain that this representation of the accommodation to loss is 'too facile' and 'idealized' (Albrecht, 1992, p. 74). The stages are not always evident or followed sequentially. Again, progress is defined and measured by professionally determined criteria and interests. Those who stray from this prescribed script – for example, by not being as depressed as predicted – run the risk of being regarded as in a state of denial and in need of further psychological guidance and counselling (Oliver, 1995; Reeve, 2000; S. Wilson, 2003). The individual's own experiences and priorities are given short shrift, and 'unrealistic' hopes and ambitions are constrained (Alaszewski et al., 2004; Sapey, 2004). In the case of individuals with a spinal cord injury, rehabilitation professionals persist with the goal of helping them to walk again (Seymour, 1998), although individuals may prioritize the inclusive opportunities provided by technological aids and equipment such as wheelchairs (Tremblay, 1996).

Too often, psychological approaches individualize disability and are barely distinguishable from a standard medical approach (Finkelstein and French, 1993; Shakespeare and Watson, 1997). They downgrade the lived experience of disabled people and fail to locate the individual–professional encounter within a wider social context. However, there is a well-established socio-psychological interest in adjustment to physical and mental impairment (Hamilton, 1950;

Barker et al., 1953) that distances itself from an overly medicalized approach. Beatrice Wright's text on the psychology of 'physical disability' emphasizes the influence of the social environment, or 'the ways of behaving prescribed by society' (1960, p. 3), and argues that 'impairment' is not a sufficient condition for social 'handicap' (ibid., p. 9). More recent contributions indicate a growing polarization within psychology of individual and social (psychological) models of disability (Olkin and Pledger, 2003). Dan Goodley and Rebecca Lawthom, for example, advocate a 'community psychology' perspective that owes more to sociology than psychology insofar as it entails 'a counter hegemony to mainstream psychology's individualism; an inter-disciplinary context that brings together politics, sociology, social policy, health and social welfare' (2006, p. 8).

However, disability theorists derided the dominant approach as the 'product of the "psychological imagination" constructed on a bedrock of "non-disabled" assumptions of what it is like to experience impairment' (Oliver, 1996b, p. 21). In a similar vein, psychological contributions are criticized for ignoring the existence of professional stereotypes, 'prejudice and discrimination (physical and social barriers)' while pursuing a 'normalizing and pathologizing perspective' (Shakespeare and Watson, 1997, p. 296). A contrast is drawn with feminist analyses of sexism that identify the individual consequences of collective oppression but look beyond the individual in seeking to understand 'the mechanisms of that oppression' (Abberley, 1993, p. 108).

In summary, the central thrust of the individual model is to cast disability as a personal tragedy where the person with an impairment has a health or social problem that must be prevented, treated or cured: 'the assumption is, in health terms, that disability is a pathology and, in welfare terms, that disability is a social problem . . . To have a disability is to have "something wrong with you"' (Oliver, 1996b, p. 30).

Looking beyond individual solutions

The rise of disabled people's campaigns in America and Europe contained common elements, such as challenging their social and economic exclusion and exposing the ways in which medical rehabilitation and social welfare professionals stressed their functional and other limitations and general dependency, leading to widespread segregation in residential settings. In the United States, protest action was encouraged by a general political context that stressed civil rights and equal opportunities, as well as specific factors such as the return of a significant number of disabled veterans from the

Vietnam War (Safilios-Rothschild, 1976; DeJong, 1979b). In contrast, in Western European and Scandinavian countries, the emphasis was less on civil rights and more on campaigns to influence political parties and policy-makers to enhance state welfare entitlements and service support.

The Independent Living Movement (ILM)

The few academic accounts of the ILM in America stressed the novelty of disabled people's critique. Most notably, it was characterized as akin to a new 'paradigm of disability', epitomized by its campaigns for self-help, consumerism, de-medicalization, de-institutionalization, 'mainstreaming' and 'normalization' (DeJong, 1979b, 1981). This placed the ILM squarely within central political and philosophical traditions and values of capitalist America, namely, 'consumer sovereignty, individualism, self-reliance, economic and political freedom' (Williams, 1984b, p. 1004). The 'free-market pluralist ideology' stressed the enhanced opportunities to pursue a radical consumerist agenda. Notwithstanding disabled people's general experience of structural disadvantage in the economic and political marketplace, the ILM espoused the ambitions of those who wanted to be part of the 'American economic-political system' (DeJong, 1979a, p. 46).

The reliance on medical rehabilitation to the exclusion of change in other areas attracted considerable criticism. This underscored a central aim of the ILM to overturn professional dominance and bureaucratic inertia, which militated against radical policy change. The ILM sought innovative ways of countering the impact of professional dominance and institutionalization in disabled people's lives. This was reinforced by antagonism towards the 'monopolistic stranglehold of state controlled human service organizations' (DeJong, 1979a, p. 47). The new paradigm of independent living also placed a high emphasis on locating disabled people's social exclusion not in their bodies but in negative environmental influences.

The radical programme of the ILM made a great impression on disabled people around the world, not least among disabled activists in Europe (Evans, 1993). However, it was recognized that the ILM philosophy and analysis did not necessarily translate easily from the individualist culture of the United States to those countries where disadvantaged groups looked to state-sponsored welfare systems to address manifest economic and social inequalities. Some social scientists, such as Gareth Williams, argued that the ILM analysis is based on a dubious sociological and political conception of 'an abstract individual battling against a sanitised environment' (1984b, p. 1009). Thus, in practice, liberal market capitalism encourages a bidding war for scarce resources. Action by disadvantaged groups will favour at best a relatively small minority. Indeed, the ILM gained more support among young, well-educated, middle-class white Americans with physical impairments, rather than among the mass of poorer and often retired disabled people. Additionally, while DeJong (1979a, p. 56) accepts the ILM goal of a de-regulated 'attendant care' (personal assistant) market as a progressive move, others echoed C. Wright Mills's (1970, p. 37) trepidation that hopes for free and equal access to economic opportunities in a capitalist society are a 'fairy tale'.

European commentators on the ILM paradigm of disability also expressed reservations about its attachment to a 'behavioural ecology' that risks reducing social actors from active agents to a mere 'cultural dupe' (Williams, 1984b, p. 1006). It underplays issues of power, 'social structure and human agency' (ibid., p. 1008), as well as the 'mediating effects of the symbols and contexts of social life' (ibid., p. 1009), which may be enabling or constraining. In contrast, Williams commends a 'move from an individualist to a relational model that posits an autonomous but social being in a political context rather than an abstract individual battling against a sanitised environment' (ibid.).

Yet, the politicization of disability also fed into an established line of analysis in American politics, with disabled people conceptualized as a 'disadvantaged' or 'minority' group akin to black and minority ethnic people (Albrecht, 1976; Safilios-Rothschild, 1976). Membership signifies an imposed second-class, or deviant, position and a denial of 'majority status' rights, but also a sense of common identity and grievance that sustains political protest. The American political scientist Harlan Hahn (1986, 2002) argues that the growing perception of disabled people as a 'new minority group' confronting prejudice and discrimination heralded a direct challenge to the individual model or 'functional limitations' approach that underpins traditional medical rehabilitation and social policies.

Medical definitions of 'disability' identified 'authoritative' criteria for distinguishing between the 'deserving' and 'undeserving' poor in industrializing societies (Stone, 1985). In America, they were integral to late eighteenth- and nineteenth-century compensation programmes directed at disabled ex-soldiers and workers. Nevertheless, for Hahn, the medical preoccupation with the functional consequences of impairment amounted to a 'cultural invention' (1986, p. 131), whereby individually based 'deficiencies' are accentuated and then used to justify professionally orchestrated 'rehabilitation' programmes. It ignored broader economic policies that created and sustained higher levels of unemployment among disabled people, as well as employer bias against the recruitment of workers with impairments. Hahn suggests such policies contain specific disadvantages for disabled workers while failing to address the general needs of a 'post-industrial society'. They place an exaggerated emphasis on training for low-grade, 'entry level' jobs and manual labour. This inhibits disabled people from 'upgrading their skills' for the type of work increasingly available in a technically advanced service sector economy (Hahn, 1986, 2002).

The implication is that minority group politics encourages radical policy options to overcome the social inequalities experienced by disabled people. While all minorities are 'striving to improve their status in society', disabled people, unlike other groups are still experiencing 'the residual effects of medical concepts' (Hahn, 2002, p. 137). Most noticeably, despite protest action and the introduction of successive legislative measures such as the 1990 Americans with Disabilities Act to secure equal rights for disabled people, US courts still adhere to a traditional 'functional limitations' perspective. Nevertheless, Hahn argues that disabled people have little alternative but to continue the active struggle for civil rights.

Critics of the minority group approach have expressed concerns that disabled people risk becoming one more special interest group competing for attention in a pluralist system of political bargaining. Others have questioned whether their campaigns go far enough in confronting the major organizing structures and values of a disabling society (Liggett, 1988). Hahn maintains that, 'in a fundamental sense, the ultimate origins of the problems facing disabled citizens probably can be traced to the nature of economic systems' (1986, p. 133). However, the minority group approach may militate against detailed analysis of the changing and contrasting forms of disability across industrial capitalist societies, or of the interrelationship between disability and other lines of social division.

Challenging the 'disabling society' – a British perspective

The new ways of thinking about disability in Britain, as in America, had their roots in the climate of social and political protest that emerged in the 1960s. These translated into specific campaigns for greater autonomy and control by disabled people in residential institutions (Finkelstein, 1991) and for a comprehensive disability income and new living options (Oliver and Zarb, 1989).

One of the first books to challenge the 'able-bodied' orthodoxy on disability in the UK was *Stigma: The experience of disability*, edited by Paul Hunt (1966a), a disabled activist. It comprises twelve personal accounts of disability from six disabled women and six disabled men, none of whom was an academic. They were chosen by Hunt from over sixty responses to a letter published in several national newspapers and magazines requesting contributions. His aim was to avoid 'sentimental autobiography' or 'preoccupation with the medical and practical details of a particular affliction'. In his chapter, Hunt argues that 'the problem of disability lies not only in the impairment of function and its effects on us individually but more importantly in our relationship with "normal" people' (1966b, p.146). Disabled people 'are set apart from the ordinary' in ways which see them as posing a direct 'challenge' to commonly held social values by appearing 'unfortunate, useless, different, oppressed and sick' (ibid.).

The perception of disabled people as 'unfortunate' arises because they are unable to 'enjoy' the social and material benefits of modern living. These include the opportunity for marriage, parenthood, social status, independence and freedom, employment, 'a house and a car – these things and plenty more may be denied us' (Hunt, 1966b, p. 147). When, despite these deprivations, disabled individuals appear happy, they are lauded for their 'exceptional courage'. Apart from devaluing other disabled people who may not have the same response to their situation, this encourages non-disabled people to see disablement as a 'personal tragedy'.

The description of disabled people as 'useless' arises because they are deemed unable to contribute to the 'economic good of the community'. This marks them out as 'abnormal' and 'different' or as members of a 'minority group' analogous to other oppressed groups, such as black or gay people. Moreover, 'people's shocked reactions to the "obvious deviant" stimulates their own deepest fears and difficulties, their failure to accept themselves as they really are, and the other person simply as "other" ' (Hunt, 1966b, p. 152). This underpins the 'prejudice which expresses itself in discrimination and even *oppression*' (ibid., *emphasis in original*), akin, for example, to those minorities who experience racism. The last element in disabled people's 'challenge' to 'able bodied' values is that they are 'sick, suffering, diseased, in pain' – in short, they represent everything that the 'normal world' most fears: 'tragedy, loss, dark, and the unknown' (ibid., pp. 155–6).

Hunt acknowledges the 'vast differences' between disabled people and other 'downtrodden' groups (1966b, p. 156), with the conscious and unconscious association of a 'sick' body and mind with a sense of evil. Nevertheless, disabled people are 'becoming presumptuous' and rejecting 'all the myths and superstitions that have surrounded us' (ibid., p. 157). He detects the beginnings of a growing collective consciousness: 'We are challenging society to take account of us, to listen to what we have to say, to acknowledge us as an integral part of society itself. We do not want ourselves, or anyone else, treated as second class citizens, and put away out of sight and mind' (ibid., p. 158).

As Peter Townsend argues in his foreword to Hunt's volume, the inequalities experienced by disabled people 'reflect a much deeper problem of a distortion of the structure and value-system of society' (1966, p. vi). With disabled people set apart by their 'incapacity' and 'unproductiveness', they are relegated to the bottom of the social hierarchy. Townsend wonders about the appropriate political response: 'Is it possible to secure real gains for those who are disabled without calling for a reconstruction of society and schooling new attitudes in the entire population?' (ibid.). For Hunt and his co-contributors, the aim was to break free from a system 'dominated by condescension and patronage on the one hand and inferiority or deference on the other' (ibid., p. viii). These arguments underpin the demand for a new approach to social equality, one that sustains 'more equal and less discriminatory social relationships' (ibid.).

In the UK, a number of groups of disabled people were formed to explore an alternative approach. Among these was the Liberation Network of Disabled People (LNDP), which produced its own magazine, *In From the Cold*, containing political commentary and personal experiences of exclusion and discrimination (Campbell and Oliver, 1996). Another small group of disabled activists, including Paul Hunt and Vic Finkelstein, established the Union of the Physically Impaired Against Segregation (UPIAS) in 1974. The designation as a 'union' announced its political intentions. Their 'manifesto' – *Fundamental Principles of Disability* (UPIAS, 1976a) – criticized organizations controlled by non-disabled 'experts' for their failure to address the social barriers central to disabled people's exclusion from mainstream economic and social activity and their lack of accountability to the disabled community. This has exerted a major influence on the disabled people's movement and disability theorizing in the UK (Oliver, 1983, 1996a).

The social model of disability

During the 1970s and 1980s, disabled activists and their organizations in Europe and North America became increasingly vocal in their dismissal of the individual, medicalized model of disability and its psychological and social welfare implications. Reflecting on their experiences of discrimination, disabled people focused on the organization of society rather than individual functional limitations or differences. Modern society failed to recognize or accommodate the human diversity associated with impairment (Oliver, 1983; Zola, 1983).

UPIAS made a fundamental distinction between impairment and

disability. The medical definition of impairment is broadly accepted as an individual attribute, but the meaning of disability is radically reinterpreted:

- *impairment*: 'lacking part or all of a limb, or having a defective limb, organ or mechanism of the body'
- *disability*: 'the disadvantage or restriction of activity caused by a contemporary social organization which takes no or little account of people who have physical impairments and thus excludes them from participation in the mainstream of social activities' (UPIAS, 1976a, p. 14).

Subsequently, the restriction to 'physical impairments' was dropped to incorporate all impairments: 'In the broadest sense, the social model of disability is about nothing more complicated than a clear focus on the economic, environmental and cultural barriers encountered by people who are viewed by others as having some form of impairment – whether physical, mental or intellectual' (Oliver, 2004, p. 21).

This social model approach breaks the traditional causal link between impairment and disability. The 'reality' of impairment is not denied, but it is not necessarily a sufficient condition of disability. Instead, the spotlight shifts to how far, and in what ways, society restricts opportunities to engage in mainstream economic and social activities and renders people with impairments more or less dependent. In what has become the defining statement, *Fundamental Principles* argues that: 'In our view it is society which disables physically impaired people. Disability is something imposed on top of our impairments by the way we are unnecessarily isolated and excluded from full participation in society. Disabled people are therefore an oppressed group in society' (UPIAS, 1976a, p. 14). Overall, disability is 'the outcome of an oppressive relationship between people with . . . impairments and the rest of society' (Finkelstein, 1980, p. 47). This asserted the significance of common interests and experiences of oppression and concentrated on those areas that might be changed by collective political action and social change.

The clear distinction drawn between impairment and disability replicates a division between the biological and social domains. On that basis, Oliver asserts that 'disablement has nothing to do with the body' (1990, p. 45) and that the 'social model is not an attempt to deal with the personal restrictions of impairment but the social barriers of disability' (1996a, p. 38).

> The achievement of the disability movement has been to break the link between our bodies and our social situation, and to focus on the

real cause of disability, i.e. discrimination and prejudice. To mention biology, to admit pain, to confront our impairments, has been to risk the oppressors seizing on evidence that disability is 'really' about the physical limitation after all. (Shakespeare, 1992, p. 40)

The rationale for the social model separation of impairment and disability was 'pragmatic' (Oliver, 1996a, p. 38), and this 'does not deny that some illnesses may have disabling consequences and many disabled people have illnesses at various points in their lives' (ibid., pp. 35–6). However, this points to major difficulties in disentangling the circumstances under which specific illnesses are 'disabling' or not (Thomas, 1999).

Nevertheless, the architects of the social model mostly resisted studies of the experience and impact of impairment on the grounds that these would not advance the understanding of disability, but were more likely to reinforce a personal tragedy orientation and so undermine a radical disability politics (Finkelstein, 1996, 2002). The UPIAS view was that, 'at the personal level we may talk about acquiring an impairment being a personal tragedy, but at the social level we should talk about the restrictions that we face are, and should be interpreted as, a crime' (Finkelstein, 2001a, p. 2).

UPIAS reserved some of its most scathing remarks for the ways in which non-disabled experts exercised a harmful influence over the everyday lives of disabled people:

We reject also the whole idea of 'experts' and professionals holding forth on how we should accept our disabilities, or giving learned lectures about the 'psychology' of impairment. We already know what it feels like to be poor, isolated, segregated, done good to, stared at, and talked down to – far better than any able bodied expert. We as a Union are not interested in descriptions of how awful it is to be disabled. What we *are* interested in is the ways of *changing our conditions of life*. (UPIAS, 1976b, pp. 4–5, *emphasis in original*)

As an illustration, Finkelstein (1999) explored ways of emulating initiatives by user-led organizations to build alternative service support to institutional 'care'. He bemoaned the descent of professions allied to medicine into performing bureaucratic, task-oriented activities that undermine the basic aim of providing services that empower clients. He argues instead for a new type of professional to support disabled people's efforts to achieve independent lives – what he terms 'Professions Allied to the Community' (PACs). Others have stressed the value of recruiting more disabled people into professional ranks, as well as extending existing initiatives to generate 'anti-oppressive' practice (French and Swain, 2001).

In his codification of UPIAS's (1976a, 1976b) statements on disability, Mike Oliver differentiated 'personal tragedy' from 'social oppression' theory – that is, an individual/medical from a social model approach. Quite simply, 'personal tragedy theory has served to individualize the problems of disability and hence to leave social and economic structures untouched' (Oliver, 1986, p. 16). This parallels sociological criticism of the extension of professional intervention into areas not hitherto regarded as relevant to its knowledge base (Zola, 1972; Strong, 1979b) (see chapter 3). The medicalization of disability raises immediate concerns, because 'disability is not measles' (Rioux and Bach, 1994). Nevertheless, the social model emphasis on overcoming social barriers to inclusion does not extend to blanket opposition to medical treatment for impairment or long-term illness.

The ways in which the social model approach differs from that of the individual model are illustrated by Mike Oliver (1990, pp 7–8). He compares questions devised by OPCS from an individual perspective in the 1980s with his own reinterpretations based on a social barriers perspective – as the following selection illustrates:

- *OPCS: 'Are your difficulties in understanding people mainly due to a hearing problem?'*
- Oliver: 'Are your difficulties in understanding people mainly due to their inability to communicate with you?'

- *OPCS: 'Does your health problem/disability prevent you from going out as often or as far as you would like?'*
- Oliver: 'What is it about the local environment that makes it difficult for you to get about in your neighbourhood?'

- *OPCS: 'Does your health problem/disability affect your work in any way at present?'*
- Oliver: 'Do you have problems at work because of the physical environment or the attitudes of others?'

- *OPCS: 'Does your health problem/disability mean that you need to live with relatives or someone else who can help or look after you?'*
- Oliver: 'Are community services so poor that you need to rely on relatives or someone else to provide you with the right level of personal assistance?'

- *OPCS: 'Does your present accommodation have any adaptations because of your health problem/disability?'*
- Oliver: 'Did the poor design of your house mean that you had to have it adapted to suit your needs?'

Oliver's suggestion is that the OPCS items, as with the *ICIDH*, do not allow those questioned to consider or indicate how far, if at all, social and environmental barriers are part of their everyday experience.

This reinforces the near total reliance on a functional limitations approach to disability in the collection of official statistics and governmental research. Indeed, it is only since the 1990s that research funding agencies (including government departments) have responded to calls from disabled people's organizations to sponsor studies of disability (instead of the consequences of impairment). The task of critical disability research is to examine the character and extent of social exclusion and disadvantages facing disabled people, and across different social contexts, as well as the impact of shifts in disability policy towards social barriers – for example, from rehabilitation to an integrated living support system (Finkelstein, 1991, 1993b).

Social modellists further stress the close links between theorizing and researching disability and associated political action. They call for openly partisan and politically committed research that promotes citizenship rights, equal opportunities and inclusion. The central objective is phrased in terms of striving for social justice, to enhance disabled people's autonomy over their lives rather than out of a compassionate concern for their 'personal tragedy' (Rioux and Bach, 1994). This extended to wider claims about the ways in which participatory and, more particularly, emancipatory research methodologies embody a radical alternative to mainstream contributions – not simply in their political goals but also in their procedures by placing disabled people in control (Oliver, 1992; Barnes and Mercer, 1997). The aim is to draw disabled people into the process of designing, conducting and disseminating disability research so as to facilitate debate on the personal tragedy approach and possible alternatives.

> The importance of the social model of disability is that, as a model providing an alternative understanding of the experience and reality of disability, it has given disabled people a basis on which to organize themselves collectively. Using the social model as a basis for explanation, disabled people have been drawing attention to the real problems of disability: the barriers they face; the patronizing attitude they have to deal with; the low expectations that are invested in them; and the limited options available to them. (Swain et al., 2003, p. 24)

Notwithstanding these ambitions, the social model is a simplified representation of a complex social reality, distinguished by its fundamental separation of impairment and disability. It is not a 'substitute for social theory'. 'The social model does not explain what disability is. For an explanation we would need a social theory of disability' (Finkelstein, 2001b, p. 11). It offers a fundamental alternative to the individual model that poses a very different set of research questions, most particularly: 'What is the nature of disability? What causes it? How is it experienced?' (Oliver, 1996b, p. 29). This includes reflection on other social approaches to disability. Precisely because it is a model, it should be judged on its capacity to stimulate a more comprehensive social *theory* (explanations and understandings) of disability and to facilitate socio-political changes that enhance the life chances of disabled people.

Early disability research inspired by a social model account concentrated on structural explanations of the social and material conditions experienced by disabled people in the family, education, income and financial support, employment, housing, transport and the built environment (Barnes, 1991). This was considered central both to building explanations of how far, and in what ways, 'society disables' people with impairments and to analysing the structures and processes associated with social oppression and discrimination, whether at the level of social policy and the state or in everyday social interaction. Key contributors to the development of a social model approach strongly favoured a 'materialist' or 'social creation' strategy over an 'idealist' account that prioritized cultural values and representations (Finkelstein, 1980; Oliver, 1990). Notwithstanding this emphasis on the social oppression of disabled people, an associated priority is to examine the circumstances in which disabled people resist and challenge orthodox ideas and practices.

While the social model, as elaborated by UPIAS, has been proclaimed as 'the big idea' of the disabled people's movement in Britain, it has been subjected to a range of criticism from service providers, policy-makers and academic social scientists, as well as from some disabled people who are perhaps otherwise generally supportive of the new disability politics. At this juncture, we briefly outline some of the main areas of debate among writers on disability, while leaving more detailed discussion to subsequent chapters.

The significance of separating impairment and disability in *Fundamental Principles* triggered a variety of questions on the grounds that it wrongly diminishes the significance of impairment, whether in terms of theorizing disability or as a reflection of disabled people's everyday lives. The social model was further questioned for its own form of reductionism, based on what Carol Thomas argues is a misreading of the original UPIAS formulation, that 'all restrictions of activity experienced by people with impairment are caused by social barriers' (1999, p. 42).

Disabled feminists in particular led calls to 'bring impairment back in' to theorizing disability on the grounds that disabled people do not typically differentiate impairment and disability, and that the 'personal is political', in contrast to the public domain assumptions that permeate the social model (Morris, 1991; Crow, 1996). It appeared that the social model disregard for the personal experience of impairment replicated the general 'malestream' dismissal of private compared to public life:

> there is a tendency within the social model of disability to deny the experience of our own bodies, insisting that our physical differences and restrictions are *entirely* socially created. While environmental barriers and social attitudes are a crucial part of our experience of disability – and do indeed disable us – to suggest that this is all there is to it is to deny the personal experience of physical or intellectual restrictions, of illness, of the fear of dying. (Morris, 1991, p. 10; *emphasis in original*)

It is these experiences of impairment and disability that distinguish a disabled from a non-disabled person.

Moreover, some argue that it is wrong to presume that all activity restrictions experienced by individuals with an impairment have a social basis and are therefore amenable to eradication by social changes. Hence, specific impairments will continue to exclude some individuals from some areas of life (Crow, 1992; French, 1993; Shakespeare, 2006). This means it is not possible in the foreseeable future to eliminate all activity restrictions by social intervention.

> I believe that some of the most profound problems experienced by people with certain impairments are difficult, if not impossible, to solve by social manipulation. Viewing a mobility problem as caused by the presence of steps rather than by the inability to walk is easy to comprehend. . . . However, various profound social problems that I encounter as a visually impaired person, which impinge upon my life far more than indecipherable notices or the lack of bleeper crossings, are more difficult to regard as entirely socially produced or amenable to social action. (French, 1993, p. 17)

Sally French cites as examples her inability to recognize people only a short distance away, being 'nearly blinded' in sunlight, and not always being able to understand non-verbal cues in social interaction. Similar points are raised in the (medical) sociology literature on 'chronic illness and disability' and the social body (Barnes and Mercer, 1996; Thomas, 2007).

Reliance on a medical interpretation of impairment has also generated strong objections. For example, a significant proportion of those designated as having a hearing impairment and whose first language is sign language reject this biomedical categorization and identify instead as Deaf people, who are members of a unique linguistic and cultural group (Ladd, 1988). Similar dissent has been expressed by people with the label of learning difficulties (Goodley, 2000) and mental health system users or survivors (Beresford, 2000, 2002). How far who 'qualifies' as having a specific impairment and as a disabled person remains a contentious issue. Again the different social locations, experiences and support requirements of specific groups are not fully recognized in social model debates, as Peter

Beresford (2005) suggests when outlining a 'social model of madness and distress'. An associated criticism is that specific groups are marginalized within the disabled people's movement by the social model's accentuation of disability as an influence on an individual's status and self-identity over other social locations such as social class, gender and ethnicity.

Debates on disability now routinely acknowledge the influence of social model thinking. What is particularly striking is its impact on current policies across a diverse range of organizations, including central to local governments, charities and voluntary agencies. Indeed, some disabled activists and disability theorists have been unsure whether this has always been a positive development (Oliver, 2004). At the same time, attacks by social scientists on the social model have multiplied (Bury, 1997; Williams, 1999; G. Williams, 2001), with additional criticism 'from within' (Shakespeare and Watson, 2001; Shakespeare, 2006). This highlights the importance of exploring the very contrasting interpretations of the social model. A strong dose of caution is obligatory: 'Sadly a lot of people have come to think of the social model of disability as if it were an explanation, definition or theory and many people use the model in a rather sterile formalistic way' (Finkelstein, 2001b, p. 6). Again, the social model must not be overloaded with unrealistic expectations:

> The social model is not about showing that every dysfunction in our bodies can be compensated for by a gadget, or good design, so that everybody can work an 8-hour day and play badminton in the evenings. It's a way of demonstrating that everyone – even someone who has no movement, no sensory function and who is going to die tomorrow – has the right to a certain standard of living and to be treated with respect. (Vasey, 1992a, p. 44)

The biopsychosocial model of disability

Continuing censure of the *ICIDH* (WHO, 1980), on both conceptual and practical grounds, by mainstream researchers, policy-makers and organizations of disabled people led the WHO to plan its revision. The team responsible began their discussions in 1993, and *ICIDH2*, or the *International Classification of Functioning, Disability and Health (ICF)* (WHO, 2001a), as it became known, was finally endorsed by WHO member states in 2001. It was also adopted by the United Nations and incorporated in *Standard Rules on the Equalization of Opportunities for Persons with Disabilities* (UN, 1993).

The WHO development team confirmed the Western scientific medical model as the foundation for classifying, measuring and

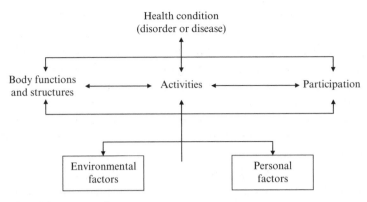

Health condition
(disorder or disease)

Body functions
and structures   ←→   Activities   ←→   Participation

Environmental
factors

Personal
factors

Source: WHO (2001a, p. 18).

Figure 2.3   Interaction between the components of *ICF*

treating biophysiological conditions. However, they accepted dissent with the *ICIDH*'s 'consequences of disease' orientation and its linear (causal) sequence from impairments through 'disabilities' to social 'handicaps'. They agreed with critics from disabled people's organizations that this diverted interest away from examining 'environmental' influences or 'social barriers' (Bickenbach et al., 1999, p. 1176). At the same time, the social model was condemned as neither 'operationalizable' nor amenable to empirical research and validation (ibid., p. 1178).

The team's discussions led to an attempted 'synthesis' of the medical and social approaches in a 'biopsychosocial model'. The *ICF* comprised a classification of 'components of health' (WHO, 2001a, p. 4) rather than of disease, with the aim of establishing 'a coherent view of different perspectives of health from a biological, individual and social perspective' (ibid., p. 20). It confirmed the ambition of universal application, and promised 'a unified and standard language and framework for the description of health and health-related states' (ibid., p. 3).

Similar to the *ICIDH*, the ICF identifies three levels of human functioning: 'at the level of the body or body part, the whole person, and the whole person in a social context' (WHO, 2002, p. 10). It distinguishes (see figure 2.3) body functions and structures (impairments), both 'physical' and 'mental'; activities and participation; and 'contextual factors', which comprise 'environmental' and 'personal' factors. The coding scheme allows either positive/facilitating or negative/barrier outcomes, thus generating a large number of potential categories for data classification.

'Activity' is defined as the execution of a task (based on a clinical assessment in a standardized environment), while 'participation' covers a more 'social' aspect equated with capacity and actual performance (in real-life situations). In practice, this distinction between 'individual' versus 'social' perspectives deviates relatively little from the *ICIDH* formulation, and raises similar doubts because of competing interpretations of these terms by key 'players' such as professionals and disabled people, as well as across societies. Extra qualifiers of 'capacity' and 'performance' differentiate between an individual's ability to undertake a task or action, with or without 'assistive devices or personal assistance' (WHO, 2001a, p. 15).

The contextual (environmental and personal) factors refer to the 'complete background of an individual's life and living'. 'Environmental factors make up the physical, social and attitudinal environment in which people live and conduct their lives' (WHO, 2001a, p. 16). They span the individual (e.g. home, workplace and school) and societal levels (formal and informal social structures and services, such as climate and terrain, transportation systems, government policies, and ideologies). How far these indicators act as barriers or facilitators is based on individual self-reports. Again, different theoretical and methodological concerns will influence the choice of coding options of key dimensions such as 'support and relationships' (ibid., pp. 187–88) and attitudes that 'influence behaviour and social life at all levels' (ibid., p. 190).

Another feature of the *ICF* is the range of 'personal factors' enumerated, which indicates the scale of the task facing researchers and policy-makers:

> gender, race, age, other health conditions, fitness, lifestyle, habits, upbringing, coping styles, social background, education, profession, past and current experience (past life events and concurrent events), overall behaviour pattern and character style, individual psychological assets and other characteristics, all or any of which may play a role in disability at any level. (WHO, 2001a, p. 17)

However, 'assessment is left to the user, if needed' (ibid., p. 19). Aside from the contentious definition of the 'personal' domain, the exclusion of such factors would undermine the broad-based ambitions of the biopsychosocial model.

Despite changes in terminology, the *ICF* retains some obvious similarities with the *ICIDH*. Its association of impairment with a 'significant variation from the statistical norm' (WHO, 2001a, p. 221), raises similar criticism to that directed at its predecessor because it ignores the extent to which identifying and labelling deviations as illness or impairment are social processes, liable to vary between social groups and societies and over time. Again, an individual's capacity and performance are assessed against those of an individual without a similar health condition (disease, disorder or injury, etc.) (ibid., p. 15). The *ICF* also employs a much broader definition of disability that includes restrictions at the level of the body (impairment) as well as in social participation more generally.

The WHO team stresses the novelty of the *ICF* definition of disability as the outcome of a 'complex relationship between an individual's health condition and personal factors, and the external factors that represent the circumstances in which the individual lives' (WHO, 2001a, p. 17; Schneidert et al., 2003). This aligns with extensive research literature in the social sciences on the significance of psycho-social factors on health and illness, as well as 'person–environment interactions' in such fields as public health. While the *ICF* recapitulates social model suggestions that the form of disability (and impairment) varies across societal contexts, it ignores interaction between activities and participation, environmental and personal factors. Overall, there is too little discussion of the level and character of cross-level relationships.

The emphasis throughout the *ICF* is on a 'scientific' approach, and its taxonomy is firmly grounded in Western concepts and theories (Finkelstein, 1998; Pfeiffer, 2000; Baylies, 2002). This underscores its universalism, with expectations that concepts and measures are 'transculturally and linguistically applicable' (Bickenbach et al., 1999, p. 1185). While it anticipates a long-term research programme to validate the required measurement tools, ample evidence already exists of significant cultural differences in a 'normal' health status and ascribed 'deviations'. Moreover, the adoption of a standard quantifying approach, with its emphasis on establishing causal relationships between discrete variables, sits uneasily with recent trends towards more qualitative research in health and disability.

Overall, the *ICF* provides a detailed taxonomy to structure data collection but lacks a coherent theory of social action as a new basis for understanding disability. Significantly, its architects promote it as 'an essential tool for identifying and measuring the efficacy and effectiveness of rehabilitation services' (Üstün et al., 2003, p. 567) rather than of wider social exclusion. They incorporate key elements in the medical and social model approaches to disability without presenting a convincing case that the promised synthesis will progress a deeper understanding of disability. Moreover, one of the principal architects of the *ICF*, Jerome E. Bickenbach, has recently cast doubt on its usefulness.

> So, how do we answer questions about who is disabled or the prevalence of disability in a country or region? As a multi-domain, multi-dimensional, interactive and continuous phenomenon (as it is characterized in the ICF), we must specify which impairment domains

qualify, to which degree of severity. Different prevalence rates flow from different decisions. If we are interested in any impairment domain, to any degree of severity, then prevalence is roughly universal – a conclusion of no use to policy makers whatsoever. if we restrict our scope to specific domains and severity levels, then our prevalence results will differ accordingly. *But these decisions cannot be made conceptually or scientifically, they are political. The scientific approach in a word, does not solve the problem the policy analyst needs to solve.* (Bickenbach, 2009, p. 120, *emphasis added*).

Nonetheless the aim of the *ICF* team to produce an alternative to the individual and social model accounts is mirrored by debates across the social sciences. Most notably, academics in the Nordic countries have championed a 'relational' approach to disability that aligns with policy aims to modify the environment to accommodate people with impairments. Its advocates view disability as 'situational rather than an always present essence of the person' (Tøssebro, 2004, p. 4).

'First, disability is a person–environment mismatch or "poor fit" between the individual's capabilities and the demands of the broader societal environment . . . an individual is defined as disabled if a limitation, disease or loss (impairment) causes him or her to experience significant barriers in everyday life. . . . Second, disability is situational or contextual. . . . Third, disability is relative' (Traustadóttir and Kristiansen, 2004, p. 33). This is the basis for a continuum from 'weak' to 'strong' versions of the relational approach (Tøssebro and Kittelsaa, 2004). Its 'weaker' forms comprise variations on the 'human-ecology model' (Tøssebro, 2004, p. 5), while the social model promoted by activists in Britain is described as a 'strong' approach. This presumes – incorrectly, according to some writers (Thomas, 1999, 2007) – that social modellists claim that impairment is a necessary and sufficient condition for disability and disavows situational or relational aspects. However, Jan Tøssebro reiterates criticism of the social model, that it 'overestimates what can be accomplished by environmental changes', particularly in the case of people with 'severe cognitive disabilities' (2004, p. 5).

More widely, the Nordic literature raises important issues for a social theory of disability. An early influence stemmed from Martin Söder's classification of 'essentialist' theoretical approaches into two main strands: individual (clinical/medical model) and contextual (social model) (1999, cited in Gustavsson, 2004). Söder condemns the reductionism of biomedicine along with the 'determinist' character of the social model, whether in its materialist emphasis on disability as 'caused by contemporary social organization' or in constructionist guises that stress language and culture.

This leaves interactionism as the primary stimulus to the

'environmental turn' underpinning the Nordic relational approach. It comprises four distinct sub-types (Gustavsson, 2004). The first adopts a realist perspective towards disability, as with the *ICIDH* and, even more closely, the *ICF*. A second 'relative interactionist' group emulates critical realism, allied to a 'weak' form of constructionism. This treats social reality as multi-levelled, with interaction at each level explained in terms of its own internal mechanisms while recognizing inter-level relationships. A third approach understands interaction in terms of phenomenological systems theory (Michailakis, 2002) and distances itself from the 'naïve realism' (Gustavsson, 2004, p. 65) of the WHO schema. A fourth 'critical interpretation' approach examines disability at different analytical levels, with an emphasis on 'the life world perspective of human meaning-making' (ibid.).

This account helpfully identifies competing social science currents in theorizing and researching disability. Yet broad references to an 'environmental turn', a 'relational' or even a 'human ecology' approach contain an all-embracing positional statement but lack specificity about their theorization or empirical elaboration. There has been little inclination to incorporate either power relations in theorizing disability or a political economy of disability (Tøssebro, 2004, p. 6). Closer analysis of the interaction between individuals with impairments (accepting the contentious character of these terms) and the precise influence of the physical environment, embodied individuals, and psychological, political, legal, cultural and societal factors are important ingredients in theorizing and researching disability. This is a challenge that extends across theoretical approaches not only for adherents of a social model of disability.

Review

The rise of an orthodox, state-legitimated medical profession in Western societies in the nineteenth century confirmed and medicalized an individual or personal tragedy approach to disability. It focused on an individual's functional limitations: how these led to social restrictions. Hence, the primary policy response rested on individual medical treatment and rehabilitation. This approach was subsequently revised, with the introduction of the *International Classification of Impairments, Disabilities and Handicaps* (WHO, 1980), to allow for 'handicapping' social conditions, although the basic causal link to impairment remained intact.

As disabled people embarked on concerted campaigns against their general marginalization and exclusion from mainstream society, they developed an alternative socio-political approach that directed attention to the social and environmental barriers to inclusion. In Britain, the social model of disability offered an incisive alternative to the individual approach. It drew a basic distinction between impairment, defined largely in medical terms, and disability, which represented any exclusionary relationship between people with impairments and the wider society. Most recently, the WHO produced a biopsychosocial approach that is a synthesis of the individual and social models.

This review of competing models demonstrates some of the key issues and themes that will inform a sociological analysis of impairment and disability. A considerable literature already exists in the area of what medical sociologists call 'chronic illness and disability', and this will be examined in more detail in the following chapter.

Sociological Approaches to Chronic Illness and Disability

EARLY exponents of the social barriers model of disability condemned the failure of sociological approaches to health and illness (medical sociology) either 'to challenge the individualization and medicalization of disability' (Oliver, 1996b, p. 18) or to analyse it as a form of social oppression. Mike Oliver attributed this silence to 'the undoubted influence of American sociological theorists such as Parsons, Becker and Goffman' (ibid., p. 19). This chapter argues for recognition of the diversity of theoretical and empirical debates within medical sociology and their potential relevance for critical analyses of disability (and of impairment).

We begin by tracing studies of illness as a social state, particularly as a form of social deviance, starting with Talcott Parsons's (1951) functionalist analysis of the medical system and, more specifically, the sick role. The discussion then considers contributions from contrasting sociological perspectives, starting with labelling and interactionism and the rise to pre-eminence of interpretive accounts in examining the links between the illness experience, social relations and self-identity. A further literature drawing on conflict and neo-Marxist studies concentrated on a political economy of health and sickness, including medical and professional power. Lastly, we review post-structuralist analyses of the embodied character of social theory and competing discourses around 'chronic illness and disability' in an increasingly 'somatic society'.

Functionalism, Parsons and the sick role

Until the 1950s there was little interest in analysing medicine sociologically. Talcott Parsons's *The Social System* (1951) signalled a change in direction in its chapter on modern medicine. His functionalist analysis of social order presumes that the effective operation of the social system rests on individual performance of necessary social roles. Health is defined as a 'normal' and stable state that underpins optimum role capacity, whereas illness is disruptive insofar as it makes a person unproductive and dependent.

For Parsons, the sick role is a way of managing this threat, both to the individual and to the social system. It provides a temporary and conditional status, equivalent to a form of sanctioned social deviance for sick individuals. At its core are two responsibilities/obligations and two rights/entitlements. In terms of responsibilities, first, at the point of feeling ill, the sick person is obliged to obtain medical confirmation and to co-operate with the prescribed treatment regime. Second, the sick person is expected to regard their condition as undesirable. These obligations are complemented by two rights or entitlements: once diagnosed as ill by the doctor, individuals are relieved of their 'normal' social role requirements; additionally, individuals are not held personally at fault for their illness, nor is it anticipated that they will recover simply by 'willpower'. Parsons emphasizes the anticipated resumption of 'normal' social roles and how this is reinforced by the 'stigmatizing of illness' and the 'mobilization of community resources' (1958, p. 177) so as to counter societal fears that individuals resort to 'motivated deviance' (Gerhardt, 1989).

Mutual advantages and shared goals between the patient and physician sustain the sick role. Highly qualified practitioners take the principal decisions about health and illness, while a professional code of ethics further legitimates medical authority. Thus, patients benefit from the 'institutionalized superiority of the professional roles, grounded in responsibility, competence, and occupational concern' (Parsons, 1975, p. 271). Sympathetic commentators, such as Thomas Szasz and Marc Hollender (1956), enlarge this consensual picture into three types of doctor–patient relations: *active–passive*: the doctor does things to a compliant patient; *guidance–co-operation*: the doctor tells the patient what to do and the patient obeys; and *mutual-participation*: where the doctor assists patients to help themselves. This last is most applicable where patients have a long-standing condition, such as diabetes mellitus, and accumulated extensive experiential knowledge of their condition, but medical treatment options are limited.

This characterization of the sick role attracted considerable criticism. Its functionalist location produced an overly benign representation of modern medical practice, and the existence of a universal sick role was widely disputed (Freidson, 1970a; Ehrenreich, 1978). Research indicated that, in 'real-life' situations, its meaning and performance vary across social contexts and are mediated in important ways by a range of social factors, such as social class, gender and ethnicity, and perceptions of individuals' responsibility for their condition and its severity (Freidson, 1970a, 1970b).

Many sociologists claimed that Parsons's sick role amounted to an ideal-typical account based on acute illness. Gene Kassebaum and Barbara Baumann (1965) contend that individuals with a long-term 'chronic' illlness usually retain only a limited 'functional capability', irrespective of their diligence in following medical advice. This results in a loss of income and resources which, in turn, greatly inhibits the chances of recovery. It encouraged suggestions that individuals with a long-term illness enter a distinctive 'impaired role' as their social dependence becomes established (Gordon, 1966; Sieglar and Osmond, 1974). This goes with a loss of 'full human status' and decline into 'second-class citizenship' (Sieglar and Osmond, 1974, p. 116). It closely parallels a 'rehabilitation role' (Safilios-Rothschild, 1970), where the reduced capabilities require continued medical and allied professional intervention and guidance. This 'normalizes' a lower level of role performance and social reintegration.

Labelling perspectives and stigmatization

Dissatisfaction with functionalist theorizing in general, and its emphasis on individuals fitting into fixed social roles, fostered alternative lines of sociological inquiry (Biddle and Thomas, 1966; Gordon, 1966). Approaches that investigated the links between individual attitudes (meaning) and action attracted growing interest. These shifted the sociological spotlight onto social interaction and how individuals make sense of their everyday world (Blumer, 1969). A particular interest in the 1970s and 1980s centred on the social processes whereby some attitudes, attributes and behaviour are categorized as 'deviant' (Rock, 1979; Downes and Rock, 1988).

Labelling approaches

From a labelling perspective, there is no objective basis for defining individual attributes or behaviour as deviant: 'deviance is not a quality of the act a person commits, but rather a consequence of the application by others of rules and sanctions to an "offender" . . . The deviant is one to whom that label has successfully been applied; deviant behaviour is behaviour that people so label' (Becker, 1963, p. 9). This concentrates attention on both the social reaction and the institutions of social control that view specific behaviour, attributes and attitudes as social problems, with often considerable cross-cultural contrasts (Lemert, 1967).

The labelling approach differentiates deviance ranked as 'primary', which carries minimal social consequences, from that denoted as 'secondary', where the individual acquires a new social status and

LIBRARY, UNIVERSITY OF CHESTER

self-identity (Lemert, 1951, 1967). Thomas Scheff develops these points when discussing the social construction of 'mental illness'. He describes this as 'at least in part a social role, and that the societal reaction is usually the most important determinant of entry into that role' (1966, p. 28). The key criterion is 'residual rule-breaking', or behaviour that is considered a contravention of social norms and situationally inappropriate. Typically, most infringements pass off with little comment, and attaching a deviant label such as 'mental illness' is contingent on the relationship between 'symptoms, context and meaning' (ibid., p. 170). The severity of the societal reaction depends on, 'first, the degree, amount and visibility of the rule-breaking; second, the power of the rule-breaker and the social distance between him [sic] and the agents of social control; and finally, the tolerance level of the community, and the availability in the culture of the community of alternative nondeviant roles' (ibid., pp. 96–7). The transition from 'normal' person to 'rule-breaker' often follows the involvement of an official control agent, such as police officer, social worker or physician.

David Rosenhan's study 'On being sane in insane places' vividly illustrates the 'massive role of labelling in psychiatric assessment' (1973, pp. 252–3). He asked eight individuals to present themselves at a local hospital and report that they were hearing voices. This resulted in their admission to a psychiatric ward, in all but one case with a diagnosis of schizophrenia. Rosenhan then instructed these 'pseudopatients' to behave quite 'normally', and not simulate 'any symptoms of abnormality' (ibid., p. 251) but to keep written notes of their experience. Sometimes, psychiatric staff interpreted this 'excessive writing behaviour' and denials of their 'insanity' as continuing confirmation of the patients' medical diagnosis. Overall, the participants experienced substantial difficulties in convincing staff of their sanity and gaining early release, although a significant minority of the other inmates voiced their suspicions. Rosenhan reasoned that the difficulties that even experienced professionals demonstrated in separating the 'sane from the insane' (ibid., p. 257) confirmed the force of social factors on labelling.

These sociological writings overlap with an 'anti-psychiatry' literature, typified by statements from Thomas Szasz (1961), himself a qualified psychiatrist, that mental illness is a 'myth', without a demonstrable physiological cause. He maintained that the psychiatric label is a metaphor for 'problems in living': 'we call people physically ill when their bodily functioning violates certain norms; similarly we call people mentally ill when their personal conduct violates certain ethical, political and social norms' (Szasz, 1970, p. 23). He points to the arbitrary identification of 'mental diseases' in the Americans with Disabilities Act 1990 as evidence that psychiatric 'diagnoses are social constructs, they vary from time to time, and from culture to culture' (Szasz, 1994, p. 36). The professional diagnosis mystifies what is a moral judgement. It sanctions a wide range of coercive actions, including enforced committal to a psychiatric institution. Equally, psychiatric diagnoses are exploited to 'excuse' wrongdoing, evident in much greater resort to the legal defence that clients 'suffered' from 'diminished responsibility' or a 'post-traumatic stress disorder' (Szasz, 1983).

Historically, medicine has played an increasingly central role in providing not just a clinical but also a social marker of a person's difference or deviance, with professional diagnoses such as 'moron', 'retarded' and 'spastic' transformed into lay terms of abuse. Hence, because the attribution of a medical label becomes the basis for a precise form of social control, it is important to examine the processes by which individuals and groups are set apart. For instance, the label of 'mental handicap' is more prevalent in societies that prioritize achievement values over ascribed characteristics, and where education generates new forms of social 'incompetence' in everyday life (Jenkins, 1998; Rapley, 2004). Moreover, those so defined come disproportionately from more disadvantaged groups, with their classification often triggered by social misdemeanours rather than demonstrable biophysiological difference (Dexter, 1958; Kurtz, 1977; Jenkins, 1998).

The ambiguous and arbitrary aspects to determing whether behaviour is deviant or non-deviant highlight the importance of organizational practices and contexts (Kitsuse and Cicourel, 1963). Control agents do not simply identify deviant behaviour but help to produce and sustain it (Goffman, 1961; Kitsuse and Cicourel, 1963; Lemert, 1967). However, the closeness of fit between deviant labels and self-identity is variable, while there are sometimes competing approaches among control agencies over diagnoses, causes and treatments.

Stigma

The implications of unacceptable difference in social interaction is the subject of Erving Goffman's influential study *Stigma* (1963). 'Stigma' refers to those attributes that reduce the bearer 'from a whole and usual person to a tainted, discounted one' (1963, p. 3). It covers 'abominations of the body – the various physical deformities', 'blemishes of individual character' and, in Britain, social class (ibid., pp. 4–5, n. 3). Examples include the 'dwarf, the blind man, the disfigured, the homosexual . . . and the ex-mental patient'. In each case,

'undesired differentness' from 'normals' is the basis for stigmatization, with discrimination ranging from being patronizing and staring
to contempt and open hostility.

Goffman contemplates the response of stigmatized individuals to
their 'spoiled identity'. He distinguishes between the 'discredited',
those with a visible stigma, and the 'discreditable', whose differentness is not immediately apparent. A 'stigma-theory' or 'ideology'
rationalizes an individual's 'inferiority' as 'not quite human', and
is reinforced in everyday interaction by the use of 'specific stigma
terms such as cripple, bastard and moron' (1963, p. 5). The lack of
social approval is also potentially contagious, with close family and
friends liable to 'share some of the discredit' and acquire a 'courtesy
stigma' (ibid., p. 30; Birenbaum, 1970; MacRae, 1999). This presumes
that there is a shared normative system of grading and categorizing
people in (American) society.

Social interaction between 'normals and stigmatized' is described
as 'one of the primal scenes in sociology' where the 'causes and effects
of stigma must be directly confronted by both sides' (Goffman, 1963,
p. 13). Goffman's interest lies in individual attempts to control this
interaction, and the 'presentation of self' (Goffman, 1959). For those
with a visible stigma, the dilemma is how to manage the tension
involved in social encounters and recover their status and identity.
Responses range from corrective surgery (removing skin 'blemishes')
to heroic feats (a blind person learning to ski), although it may also be
possible to exploit the stigmatized condition for 'secondary gain' or as
an excuse for not doing certain things.

In comparison, 'discreditable' individuals are preoccupied with
managing what information 'normals' acquire on their 'differentness'. 'To display or not to display; to tell or not to tell; to let on or not
to let on; to lie or not to lie; and in each case, to whom, how, when
and where' (Goffman, 1963, p. 42). Goffman identifies three main
strategies: passing, covering and withdrawal. 'Passing' is the 'management of undisclosed discrediting information about self' (ibid., p.
42), whether in terms of social information or symbols. 'Covering' is
a dilemma of the 'discredited with tension to manage' (ibid., p. 102),
where the stigma is apparent and efforts are made to ensure it does
not ruin social encounters. 'Withdrawal' entails removal from social
activities with 'normals' altogether. To achieve proper adjustment,
stigmatized individuals must understand how 'normals' see them.
This means that a 'good adjustment' is a 'quality granted to them by
others' (Radley, 1994, p. 158), with expectations that they act cheerful. Stigmatization is also influenced by social characteristics, such
as socio-economic background, gender, age and ethnicity (Freidson,
1970a; Link and Phelan, 2001).

In a parallel account, Fred Davis idenitifies a strategy of 'deviance disavowal' in interaction between individuals with a visible impairment and non-disabled people. This encompasses attempts by disabled people to orchestrate social encounters so as to present themselves as 'merely different physically but not socially deviant' (1961, p. 122). Initial contacts with 'normals' are variously characterized by ambiguity, embarrassment and non-disabled people's ignorance about impairment. Davis argues that the process of 'breaking through' from a 'fictional acceptance' to a 'normalized' relationship (ibid., pp. 127–30) is fraught with difficulties, and that 'breakdown and repair' is a continuing feature of the management of such 'strained' interaction by disabled people. Nevertheless, stigmatized individuals may reach a stage where they no longer feel it necessary to conceal their perceived 'failing' (Goffman, 1963, pp. 101–2).

The process of socialization into 'normal' society provides the foundation for a 'moral career' (Goffman, 1963, pp. 32–40). This varies depending on whether the individual has an 'inborn stigma' or one acquired later in life. People with a congenital impairment will usually be aware from early childhood that others regard them as 'different'. The negative reactions of family and friends, reinforced by experiences such as periods of hospitalization, segregated special education and an inaccessible physical environment, ensure most children become aware of their ascribed 'disabled identity'. Conversely, the child with a hearing impairment raised in a family with other Deaf members often has more positive early experiences. The impact of social barriers, discriminatory attitudes and practices in the outside world is not then fully realized until attempts are made to participate in peer group activities such as socializing, dating and the transition to work. Conversely, those individuals who acquire a stigmatized condition in adulthood are usually more resistant to identifying as a disabled person because of their prior assimilation of a personal tragedy perspective on impairment and disability.

A graphic picture of how those with a long-term medical condition are inculcated into appropriate public and professional expectations is presented in Robert Scott's (1969) study of 'blindness' in America. He describes how people defined as 'medically blind' who attend a specialized rehabilitation ('blind') agency learn to perform a 'blind social role' in everyday social interaction that differs sharply from the attitudes and behaviour of other blind people. Indeed such agencies target their attention on the children and younger adults and ignore the larger proportion of adult and older people who are blind. Agency professionals encourage recruits to assume a stereotypical 'blind role', while punishing those who resist and cling to 'inappropriate' beliefs and behaviour. This renders blind people 'seriously maladjusted to the outside world' (1969, p. 119), with limited expectations of their capabilities. Nonetheless, blindness agencies are constrained by prevailing socio-cultural norms and values as well as economic pressures to adhere to an 'accommodative approach to rehabilitation' (ibid., p. 120). This is confirmed by the divergent policy goals and strategies adopted by socialization agencies in the USA, Britain and Sweden.

Goffman (1961) also appraises another form of enforced identity change, following an individudal's placement in a 'total institution', such as a psychiatric hospital, prison or monastic order. These consolidate the usually separate spheres of work, leisure, eating and sleeping into a single experience of 'batch living' – akin to animal factory farms. On entry, a 'mortification of self' process begins, with the inmate's former life undercut by such strategies as removing their possessions and replacing their clothes with an institutional 'uniform'. The institution carries out a series of 'degradation rituals' designed to induce inmate docility and submissiveness. A devalued identity – as 'mental patient' – is imposed, with suggestions that it becomes an individual's 'master status'. This 'reorganization of the self' is enforced by strict routines and time discipline, while a 'privilege system' rewards appropriate behaviour and punishes wrongdoing to uphold close identification with organizational goals.

This concentration on the social psychological domain and individual stereotyping provides valuable insights into the lives of people with impairments. However, as Goffman acknowledged, this is at the cost of disregarding power relations and structural discrimination, as well as historical shifts in stigma. Again, his representation of stigmatized individuals accentuates the notion of helpless victims, consumed by defensive and anxiety-ridden manoeuvrings (Edgerton, 1967; Gussow and Tracy, 1968; Link and Phelan, 2001; Scambler, 2004). Nevertheless, Goffman (1961) dispenses with this passive stereotype in his portrayal of inmates of psychiatric asylums. He distinguishes three main responses to these coercive regimes: 'conversion', where the patient enthusiastically embraces their new identity; 'colonization', when the regime is basically but unenthusiastically tolerated; and 'withdrawal' or 'intransigence', where the institution's aims are rejected. He identifies instances of an asylum subculture where inmates engage in various 'undercover practices' (1961, p. 299) such as hiding possessions, consuming alcohol, playing poker, and generally 'working the system'.

Sociological studies across a variety of residential settings replicate this portrayal of the crushing impact of 'custodial' regimes on inmates (Townsend, 1962; Jones and Fowles, 1984) and the 'massive uniformity of institutional life' (Booth, 1985, p. 206). They paint a 'grim picture of degradation ceremonies, soulless routines, loss of independence and the gradual weakening of the self-image until it conforms to institutional expectations' (Thomas, 1982, p. 85). Recent scandals in Britain provide continuing evidence of institutional abuse and other shortcomings (CSCI and Health Care Commission, 2006), while research studies indicate the uneven moves towards less regimated 'residential homes' (Peace et al., 1997; Boyle, 2005).

The labelling approach, including studies of stigmatization, and the character of institutional life exerted an important influence on studies of chronic illness and disability, but they also attracted criticism for representing individuals as the largely passive victims of stigma labels. This aspect was captured in the charge that it offered an 'oversocialized picture' (Bury, 1997, p. 138), which downplayed or ignored human agency and the possibility of actively negotiating, and sometimes resisting, the labelling processes. For others, its emphasis on the social construction of prejudice and discrimination needed to be complemented by consideration of structual factors and of the specific interests that benefit from the imposition of 'deviant' labels (Scambler, 2004).

Negotiated and interpretative accounts

The negotiation approach is aligned with interpretive or phenomenological accounts of people making sense of, or constructing, their immediate world. How do individuals 'go about the task of seeing, describing, and explaining order in the world in which they live'? (Bogdan and Taylor, 1975, p. 17). What is the relationship between the meaning of 'chronic illness', its setting and the resources available to those involved? This points to the '*social* and *psychological* issues faced by the chronically ill (and their immediate families)' (Strauss, 1975, p. 7, *emphasis in original*) and how they 'handle the disease and the associated medical regimens' (Strauss et al., 1984, p. 7). The 'unfolding' or long-term trajectory requires a range of health and social service support. This may prove 'disproportionately intrusive' and demands extensive investment of individual work or 'efforts at palliation' besides its costs (ibid., pp. 11–15).

Studies bring out the 'lived experience' of individuals across diverse illness conditions, in terms of both the (physical) 'symptoms' and any 'sense of loneliness, isolation, dependency and stigmatization' generated (S. Williams, 1996, p. 28). An underlying theme is that the acquisition of a long-term illness or impairment lays bare the body's usually unobtrusive and taken-for-granted character. As Juliet Corbin and Anselm Strauss bluntly state: 'To be disabled means your body has failed you' (1991, p. 138). Individuals move from an awareness that 'something is wrong' to negotiate an understanding of what is happening to their bodies and their 'lost self' (Strauss, 1975; Anderson and Bury, 1988; Frank, 1991). Key themes include 'maintaining a sense of order, self-identity and social interaction under conditions of considerable strain' (Bury, 1997, p. 122).

This formed the basis for a 'socio-medical' approach that incorporates a realist approach to medical knowledge with interactionist and interpretive insights:

> First, is the *biographical disruption* brought about by such illness and the initial attempts to deal with the uncertainty it brings; second, there is the *impact of treatment* on everyday life, where this is relevant; and third, is the long-term *adaptation and management* of illness and disability which is undertaken as people respond and try to reconstruct normal life. (Bury, 1997, p. 123, *emphasis in original*)

A further important distinction is drawn between two types of meaning associated with having a chronic illness: first, as 'consequence' and, second, as 'significance' (Bury, 1988). A considerable literature has grown up on the 'consequences' of chronic illness on an individual's activities and relationships. Research across a broad spectrum of conditions shows how very dissimilar symptoms interfere with everyday routines, ranging from self-care and close personal relations to work and leisure. Routine body maintenance activities, such as cleaning one's teeth, washing and going to the toilet, may be completed only with assistance. One widely cited contributor to these debates concludes that long-term illnesses entail 'living a restricted life, existing in social isolation, experiencing discredited definitions of self and becoming a burden' (Charmaz, 1983, p. 170). Changes in physical or cognitive functions, increased dependence on others, and exclusion from valued social activities encourage a reconceptualization of the individual's self-identity.

The underlying assumption is that acquisition of a limiting, long-term illness clashes with taken-for-granted notions of the physical body, an individual's sense of 'normality', and valued aspects of the self and social relationships (Charmaz, 1980, 2000). At its extreme, Robert Murphy relates his experience of illness and 'progressive' quadriplegia to a 'degree of departure from the standard human form' (1987, p. 132). He employs the term 'liminal' to describe the state of 'social suspension' where individuals are 'neither out of society nor wholly in it', without an established role and status, and so 'in partial isolation from society as undefined, ambiguous people' (ibid., p. 131). Murphy's account of his 'progressive' illness conveys a sense of a 'savaged' selfhood (ibid., p. 90) and a 'new, foreign and unwelcome identity' (ibid., p. 109). The reluctance of friends to 'bear witness' to this decline exacerbated his distress (ibid., p. 124).

The sense of 'betrayal' or 'biographical disruption' (Bury, 1982) is particularly acute in a society that values an active and independent individual lifestyle. It continues beyond the onset and diagnosis of chronic illness, to encompass the uncertain trajectory of symptoms between social contexts. Symptoms fluctuate and are sometimes open to contrary meanings, as when the slurred speech or unsteady gait of a person with multiple sclerosis conveys an impression of being drunk or perhaps mentally ill (Robinson, 1988). Nevertheless, confirmation of a medical diagnosis may validate individual apprehension as well as counter potential lay misinterpretation.

The form and impact of medical treatment also potentially influences people's everyday lives (Strauss, 1975). This spans relatively minor alterations and inconvenience through to the more dramatic effects of invasive surgery that devastates social routines and self-image (Herzlich and Pierret, 1987). In the case of ileostomy, the changed body following surgery requires constant and delicate surveillance and regulation, often with the aim of keeping things hidden from others (Kelly, 1992b). Equally, medical technologies and equipment can generate difficult decisions about the direction of one's life: treatments may clash with participation in desired activities, including continuing in paid employment, or require substantial planning and investment of extra time and resources (Locker, 1983).

The preoccupation of individuals with managing symptoms often leads to difficulties in performing 'ordinary' tasks and 'keeping up' with others (Anderson and Bury, 1988). The unpredictability and 'visibility' of symptoms across illness conditions adds a further complication. For instance, Carolyn Wiener details the attempts of individuals with rheumatoid arthritis to manage the impact of symptoms and particularly their uncertain trajectory, marked by flare-ups and remissions. Individuals strive to disguise their illness and 'pass for normal' in order to minimize its negative and stigmatizing consequences (1975, p. 80). There are continuing efforts to make sense of symptoms, given their 'unfolding' character, and to develop strategies to renormalize their everyday lives, such as 'covering up' and 'eliciting help'.

A distinctively interpretative focus examines the process of adaptation to 'chronic illness and disability'. Mike Bury (1997) outlines two main ways of mitigating biographical disruption: first, by constructing an account of what has happened and why, so that it is possible to repair, or in some way incorporate, the threat posed to everyday routines and meanings (Williams, 1984a); and, second, by according the condition some 'legitimacy' – that is, merging it within the individual's changed lifestyle. This encompasses a range of 'problem-based' and 'emotional' approaches to retain a sense of 'competence' (Radley,

1994, p. 148). Alan Radley and Ruth Green elaborate four 'modalities of adjustment' to illness: accommodation, active denial, secondary gain and resignation. These indicate general choices and location in the 'personal experience of illness to changing social situations and relationships' (1987, p. 179), as well as available (social, emotional and financial) resources that vary across social groups, such as social class, age, gender and ethnicity (Radley, 1989; Bury, 1991). While some individuals consolidate or 'normalize' the illness into a new biography, others continue to resist and hold on to their former self (Corbin and Strauss, 1985, 1991).

The 'public' presentation of 'cheerful stoicism' or 'mustn't grumble' attitudes (Cornwell, 1984) often contrasts with 'private' accounts that signal more sensitivity to negative bodily experiences and pain (Charmaz, 1983; Bury 1988, 1991; Sanders et al., 2002). Moreover, the significance of the illness trajectory must be set within a wider social context. Interviews with asymptomatic HIV-positive men imply that this diagnosis reinforces rather than diminishes their bonds as gay people who experience discrimination, although the transition to full-blown AIDS proves more disruptive of individual identity (Carricaburu and Pierret, 1995). Conversely, the term 'biographical disruption' sometimes exaggerates the degree of change (Williams, 2000a), and an alternative such as 'biographical flow' better captures the link between the pre- and post-illness selves (Faircloth et al., 2004). Furthermore, older people may view some conditions, such as arthritis, as part of a 'normal' biographical transition rather than triggering a qualitative shift in self-identity (Pound et al., 1998; Sanders et al., 2002).

Gareth Williams argues that people with arthritis produce 'narrative reconstructions' set within their personal biography and perceived 'causal' factors. This 'is an attempt to reconstitute and repair ruptures between body, self, and world by linking-up and interpreting different aspects of biography in order to realign present and past and self with society' (1984a, p. 197). In contrast to the pessimism of many interpretive accounts, there has been a growing emphasis on how individuals 'fight' their condition and build a 'reconstituted' identity, or the possibility that it acts as a catalyst for 'self-development' and a positive reassessment of an individual's priorities. Even so, this may rebound on individuals who 'fail' to navigate this journey of rediscovery, or who are constrained by their social and material circumstances, including each stage in the life cycle (Strauss et al., 1984; Bury, 1991; Kelly, 1992a; Mathieson and Stam, 1995).

Contemporary narratives emerge from various socio-cultural contexts, such as the changes in morbidity and mortality patterns, greater public information about disease and impairment, and the

impact of medical intervention (Frank, 1995). One suggestion identifies three main forms: 'contingent narratives' that address the
origins of the condition, as well as its management (including any
involvement of health and social services) and the overall impact
on an individual's everyday life; 'moral narratives' that concentrate
on changes – both positive and negative – in self-identity or 'moral
status'; and 'core narratives' that locate the individual's experience
or narrative form within wider socio-cultural values (such as heroic,
tragic and romantic) (Bury, 2001, p. 263).

When meaning is viewed in terms of 'significance', the accent is on
the divergent evaluations of illnesses and impairments across social
groups and cultures. This is a theme graphically expressed in Susan
Sontag's historical review of 'dread diseases' in Western societies,
where she analyses the contrasting symbolism and media images
attached to tuberculosis, cancer and HIV/AIDS. 'It is hardly possible to
take up one's residence in the kingdom of the ill unprejudiced by the
lurid metaphors with which it has been landscaped' (1991, p. 3). As
with other conditions, the importance of meanings varies across the
life cycle and the 'severity' of the condition.

Studies of the experience of epilepsy expose the subtleties in
dealing with negative stereotypes. The process encompasses both
'enacted' stigma or actual discrimination and the sense of 'felt'
stigma driven by the shame and anxiety about anticipated negative
reactions (Scambler and Hopkins, 1986). Parents are particularly
influential in communicating their fears about the 'exposure' of a
child with epilepsy and insist on concealment and avoidance routines
(Scambler, 1989; Gray, 2003). Other research reinforces the picture
of lay responses that range between passive acceptance and active
resistance to disparaging labels, not least among people with learning
difficulties (Taylor and Bogdan, 1989; Booth and Booth, 1994).

In a similar way, some mental health system users reject medical
labels as explanations of their experiences and distress (Beresford
and Wallcraft, 1997; Mulvany, 2000). 'Mental illnesses' vary in their
perceived stigma and sympathy among professional and lay audiences, as well as the willingness of individuals to embrace the label
as part of their identity (Lester and Tritter, 2005). Studies of service
user discourses have identified three 'ideal types': patient, consumer
and survivor (Speed, 2006). These capture distinctive perceptions of
service users and 'mental illness' (Barnes and Shardlow, 1996; McLean,
2000; Crossley and Crossley, 2001). A further issue to consider is 'how
individuals perceive and report what they do in the face of illness
and what they *actually* did' (Pescosolido et al., 1998, p. 277, *emphasis in
original*). In line with the sick role, 'patients' take on the medical diagnosis – 'I am a schizophrenic'. The 'consumer' is less passive and seeks

further information on their diagnosis and treatment options, without departing markedly from medical opinion. The 'survivor' exhibits more resistance to diagnostic labels and service choices – insisting that 'I am a person who hears voices'. This discourse seeks a novel (non-psychiatric) understanding of distress and the means to overcome it.

In its determination to present a negotiated social order, interpretive accounts too often deflect attention away from the links between micro-level attitudes and practices and the wider social structure and power relations. Yet, as Mildred Blaxter illustrates, the lives of individuals with a severe physical impairment are 'fettered and constrained not only by their social environment but also by the two major systems of society with which their lives were structured: the system of medical care and the administrative system of welfare, employment and social security' (1976, pp. 246–7). Examples include a lack of technical aids and adaptations, poor housing, and social services' reliance on informal voluntary support by female relatives. Medical labels and administrative rules further shape lay people's understanding of their problems and potential help-seeking strategies and solutions. This picture of a 'handicapping' environment is echoed in David Locker's study of people with rheumatoid arthritis. Environmental obstacles 'must be negotiated, consuming reserves of time, money and energy . . . or where the effort is such the person decides not to bother and retreats into an enforced passivity. It is also handicapping to the extent it leaves the individual with no option but to rely on the help of others' (1983, p. 90).

Too much interpretive literature has become so absorbed by the 'failing body' and 'personal troubles' that it disregards the social barriers to participation in everyday life. As Gareth Williams acknowledges: 'The oppressive quality of everyday life is indubitable, and the origins of much of this oppression lie in the hostile social environments and disabling barriers that society (politicians, architects, social workers, doctors and others) erects' (2001, p. 135). While some recognize the value of 'reconciling interpretive and structural approaches' (Bury, 1991, p. 464), interpretative accounts too often descend into 'a vortex of subjectivity' by ignoring how disability is 'the product of the complex relationships between individuals, milieux and social structures' (Williams, 1998, p. 242).

Medical and professional dominance

Sociological approaches that focus on power and social conflict have taken the lead in examining the extent and character of medical dominance and how far, and in what ways, the profession acts as an agency of social control, whether on behalf of capitalism or some dominant social (class) group or 'medical-industrial' complex (Waitzkin and Waterman, 1974; Navarro, 1976; Starr, 1982). Studies range across micro-level lay–professional interaction to macro-level analyses of the political power of the medical profession and the 'medicalization' of everyday life.

As an illustration, Nick Jewson (1974, 1976) advances a socio-historical analysis of the interrelationship between the development of industrial capitalism and discrete 'modes of medical production' distinguished by specific forms of medical knowledge, patron–client relations, institutions and division of labour. By the second half of the nineteenth century, an 'orthodox' medical profession supported by state patronage and legislation achieved a pre-eminent position. This established 'scientific medicine' and the biomedical model of health and illness, along with professional and practitioner expertise and authority over patients, as well as competing practitioners and systems of health knowledge. The profession also exerted a major influence on health and social welfare policy-making and implementation (Stone, 1985; De Swaan, 1988).

Overall, medicine became an exemplar of professionalization because of its demonstrated capacity 'to translate one order of scarce resources – specialist knowledge and skills – into another – social and economic rewards' (Larson, 1977, p. xvii). More recently, there have been suggestions that the links between medical and professional dominance, medicalization and modernity are being redrawn, particularly as a consequence of shifts towards 'late capitalism' or a 'post-modern' society.

Professional–lay encounters

Medicine's claim to expertise and ethicality legitimates the hierarchical character of lay–professional encounters incorporated in the Parsonian sick role. In contrast, 'Medical sociologists have commonly emphasized that patients are victims of relational asymmetry, medical sovereignty, and professional exploitation of power' (Måseide, 1991, p. 545). A variety of 'conflict' approaches identified structural obstacles and contradictions to egalitarian lay–professional exchanges (Waitzkin, 1984, 1989). Professional control of the consultation is 'systematic, all pervasive and almost unquestioned' (Strong, 1979a, p. 129). Even so, patients mostly report general satisfaction with their health care, although a significant proportion also complains that their worries and priorities are disregarded (Freidson, 1970a; Bloor and Horobin, 1975).

Social differences further constrain lay–professional relations, particularly disadvantaging working-class patients and people from minority ethnic groups (Jeffery, 1979; Waitzkin, 1984). Similarly, male practitioners employ ascribed roles and stereotypes with female patients (McIntyre, 1977; Foster, 1989). In the case of patients with impairments or conditions that have a poor prognosis or are difficult to treat, professionals appear particularly uncomfortable and find it difficult to communicate information and differentiate between the person's impairment and their presenting symptoms (Zola, 1982; Begum 1996; Salmon and Hall, 2003). Interactionist approaches stress that the professional–lay encounter is more open to negotiation. This places the emphasis on how participants achieve their preferred outcomes, including the strategies employed by medical practitioners, or 'routine work practices', to maintain their authority (Bloor, 1976; Silverman, 1987).

Medical expertise is embedded in particular situational and institutional contexts, with professionals engaged in integrating structure (institutionally based knowledge and competence) and process (the transformation of knowledge and competence into adequate practice) (Måseide, 1991). This can generate certain 'incongruences': medical claims to knowledge sit uneasily with patients' demands for meaningful co-operation; assumptions of professional authority disavow patients' challenges to medical diagnoses or treatment. This is more likely where the categorization of someone as 'sick' has broader implications – such as leaving paid employment (Bellaby, 1990; Pinder, 1996) or keeping a child off school (Prout, 1986; Silverman, 1987). Other research suggests a degree of patient 'negotiation' of the encounter. Thus, Julius Roth's (1963, 1984) study of a TB sanatorium exemplifies how inmates exploit knowledge acquired on key medical markers of their condition to 'bargain' with staff over the timetable for their recuperation and discharge.

Equally, since the 1980s, government policy has increasingly promoted the role of 'consumers' in the health-care sector and encouraged a more 'democratic' encounter between patients and health professionals. Professional discourse has shifted away from a 'doctor-centred' consultation towards a 'meeting between experts' – conceding the role of lay knowledge and involvement. The traditional marginalization of patients has given way to declarations of greater 'openness' in sharing diagnoses and treatment options and a willingness to engage with patient viewpoints (Tuckett et al., 1985; Bissell et al., 2004). Similarly, the growth of a biopsychosocial discourse facilitates transfer of (some) responsibility for health decision-making to the patient (Måseide, 1991). However, whether the move towards shared decision-making constitutes a real or an illusory shift in the balance of power to the patient remains strongly disputed (Armstrong, 2005; Stevenson and Scambler, 2005).

Other threats to professional and medical hegemony have been detected in both the restructuring of the health labour process within late capitalism and the de-skilling of medicine associated with a heightened resort to managerial intervention in the terms, content and rewards of health work (McKinlay and Arches, 1985). Indeed, the demise of the 'golden age of doctoring' over recent decades has been attributed to the continuing 'corporatization' of American medicine (McKinlay and Marceau, 2002). A further challenge to medical dominance stems from the professionalizing ambitions of nurses and midwives, clinical psychologists and allied health practitioners, such as physiotherapists and counsellors, and their incursion into medical territory (Turner, 1987). Yet, these occupational groups remained allied largely to the traditional individual, medicalized approach to chronic illness and disability.

Additionally, the emergence of 'late modernity' has significant implications for existing forms of medical dominance. This stems particularly from the generation of new information and knowledge about social reality, the codification of professional knowledge, and the centrality of social reflexivity and an emancipatory life politics (Giddens, 1991). The certainties of the traditional order are supplanted by greater choice as well as intensifying self-doubt and uncertainty. Medicine is no exception, with some evidence of reduced lay deference to medical authority and more readiness to confront professionals, including a noteworthy rise in medical litigation (Haug, 1988; Dingwall, 1994; Bury, 2008). Yet, scepticism and disillusionment are matched by continuing expectations of new medical cures and treatments, bolstered by public campaigns (Lupton, 1994; Brown and Zavestoski, 2005; Scambler and Kelleher, 2006). There is also a greater willingness to look beyond orthodox medicine for healing knowledge and support, as indicated by the increasing use of complementary and alternative therapies and practitioners.

A typical conclusion in the 1990s was that 'such changes that have occurred look more like uncomfortable adjustments than a major waning of either the medical profession's institutionalized technical autonomy or of their social and cultural authority' (Elston, 1991, pp. 83–4). A decade later, medical dominance continues to be slowly 'redrawn' and contested, but suggestions of its wide-ranging downfall seem exaggerated (Harrison and Ahmad, 2000; Ballard and Elston, 2005).

Medicalization

A major feature of medical dominance is that 'the medical profession has first claim to jurisdiction over the label of illness and anything to which it may be attached, irrespective of its capacity to deal with it effectively' (Freidson, 1970a, p. 251). Such medicalization is an 'insidious and often undramatic phenomenon' (Zola, 1972, p. 487) that results in an escalating number of 'problems in everyday living' (Szasz, 1961) being defined as an illness or disorder that requires biomedical treatment and supervision. Thus, individuals perhaps previously categorized as 'bad' or 'weak' are deemed 'ill' and the targets of medical intervention (Conrad and Schneider, 1980). This professional takeover of moral-social issues has been identified across the life cycle, from pregnancy and childbirth (Oakley, 1980), behavioural problems in children (Conrad, 1975) and ageing (Zola, 1991), through to dying (Clark and Seymour, 1999).

In a polemical attack, Ivan Illich (1975) insisted that the medical profession had inflated its capacity to heal sick people and ignored negative 'iatrogenic' (that is, provider-induced) consequences. Shortcomings occur at three levels: 'clinical' – modern-day treatments are ineffective and harmful; 'social' – lay people become dependent on the health-care system and service providers; and 'structural' – by undermining the human capacity to cope with pain, sickness and death. Indeed, all professions are denigrated as 'disabling' in that they encourage passivity and undermine people's capacity to take responsibility for their own lives (Illich et al., 1977). However, this 'scattergun' attack on industrial societies lacks secure theoretical grounding.

Neo-Marxist accounts underline medicalization as a key dimension in the reproduction of capitalist society that advances private, corporate interests, leading to assertions of an emerging 'medical-industrial complex' (Waitzkin and Waterman, 1974; Navarro, 1976). The medicalization of eligibility criteria for compensation, resources or support aligns with capitalist interests by effectively depoliticizing or individualizing social problems (Waitzkin, 1983, p. 38). Medicine helps to 'pacify the individual with the rewards and benefits of the sick role' (De Swaan, 1989, p. 1169) and 'ameliorates or makes palatable those diswelfares generated by the economic system' (Navarro, 1978, p. 214). It encourages an ideology of 'victim blaming'. In contrast, the social context that encourages behaviour such as alcohol and tobacco consumption for profits and tax revenues is disregarded, along with other potential 'triggers' of sickness related to the pressures of living and working in an 'alienating' society. Drug companies and manufacturers of medical technology and equipment have a direct interest in extending the market for their products. The media have also demonstrated unabated enthusiasm for stories about health risks, new diseases and 'miracle cures'. Not that all writers accept the charge that medicine is necessarily a tool of capitalism: 'Medicine, as an institutional complex, sits uneasily between employer and employee. It is not an unequivocal ally of capital in the social control and reproduction of the labour force' (Bellaby, 1990, p. 60).

A specific application of these themes suggests the 'psychiatriza-tion of life'. This spans 'four interweaving themes: the development of other sites than simply the asylum or hospital; the embrace of social therapies; the growing public awareness of healthy minds; and the growth of voluntary encounters with a variety of psycho-logical experts on "everyday worries"' (Pilgrim and Rogers, 1993, p. 91). Empirical confirmation is exemplified by the extensive pre-scribing of minor tranquillizers, principally by GPs, directed at all manner of social ills, including broken relationships, insomnia, nerves and employment problems. This connects with the emergence of a 'psy-complex' and the proliferation of new occupational groups contributing to mental health work (Ramon, 1985). For example, clinical psychologists have sought to colonize some of the territory held by psychiatry. This includes aligning the profession with the administrative requirements of the state – such as the regulation of child behaviour, and treating people with a label of 'mental illness' or learning difficulties – while entrenching their expertise through state registration (Pilgrim and Treacher, 1992).

> The statistical plotting of a normal curve of distribution for measured intelligence has probably been the single most influential factor in the definition and creation of a category of persons known as the 'mildly mentally retarded'. Before the advent of the bell-shaped curve, the category simply did not exist. (Jenkins, 1998, p. 17)

This exemplifies arguments that late modern society embraces a 'therapeutic culture of the self' (Rose, 1989), and a 'colonization of the lifeworld' (Crossley, 2000) where self-actualization and emotion man-agement are promoted as ongoing personal projects (Giddens, 1991; Shilling, 2003). Individuals are more likely to frame and seek resolu-tion of personal difficulties in terms set by professionals (De Swaan, 1990). Such trends indicate the 'medicalization of underperformance' (Conrad and Potter, 2000) and 'the public's decreased tolerance for mild symptoms and benign problems' (Conrad, 2005, p. 9). A high-profile case is the reported rise in social phobia and anxiety disorders since the 1980s that have attracted fears of a 'cultural epidemic' (Busfield, 1996; Scott, 2006).

However, not all studies concur with this picture of the inexorable advance of the medical interest. For instance, medical involvement in treating alcoholism has been described as more akin to 'reluctant imperialism' (De Swaan, 1989), with intra-professional disputes and a disinclination to exploit medicine's 'organized power' to promote 'the establishment of programs that rely on medical certification' (Stone, 1979, p. 519). More conspicuously, lay pressure from gay and lesbian groups persuaded the American Psychiatric Association in the early 1970s to de-medicalize homosexuality and classify it as a life-style choice, not a disease (Fox, 1977).

There is also evidence of the impact of other important interests, including the state, private-corporate and voluntary sectors, as well as lay self-help groups (Krause, 1977; Conrad and Leiter, 2004). Peter Conrad (1975) traces the medicalization of childhood behavioural difficulties, such as short attention span, restlessness and mood swings, into one of the most diagnosed conditions in Britain and America. Three factors triggered the 'discovery' in the 1950s of hyperkinesis, or 'minimal brain dysfunction' (MBD). First, the impact of pharmaceutical innovation, and specifically the approval of Ritalin for the treatment of children, greatly raised professional and lay expectations; second, the decline in infectious diseases shifted professional and pharmaceutical attention to other disease areas; and, third, heightened government and public interest – ranging from task forces and research funding to greater media exposure (that targeted parents and schoolteachers) – that led to mounting parental pressure-group activity. Furthermore, since the 1990s, an increasing number of adults have acquired an Attention Deficit and Hyperactivity Disorder diagnosis.

Aggressive marketing by corporate interests and professional groups (not all medical), with particular interest from the media and the internet, are all implicated in the emergence of hitherto unknown health problems. These include Alzheimer's disease (Fox, 1989), hormone replacement therapy (Williams and Calnan, 1996), repetitive strain injury (Arksey, 1994, 1998) and chronic fatigue syndrome (Broom and Woodward, 1996). Increasingly, the body is being medicalized 'piece by piece' (Conrad, 2005, p. 8). Individual medical specialisms have assiduously cultivated public demand, often gendered in its focus, for example for cosmetic surgery (Sullivan, 2001). The pharmaceutical and biotechnology industries have taken the lead in identifying health risks and drug solutions, as with depression (Prozac), and Social Anxiety Disorder (Paxil). Most recently, the potential of genomic medicine has triggered widespread professional and lay anticipation (Conrad, 2005; Conrad and Leiter, 2004).

By the 1990s, other interests had emerged as key factors: 'the engines of medicalization have proliferated and are now driven more by commercial and market interests than by professional claims-makers' (Conrad, 2005, p. 10). Others point to the greater influence of allied health professionals, such as psychologists, therapists and counsellors. Yet, their involvement and exposure of new 'health' problems in need of professional rehabilitation replicated many aspects of medicalization. This ranged from the lack of 'hard' evidence of their effectiveness to a failure to diminish the subordination of the 'client' to professional expertise – however much it is repackaged in terms of individual empowerment.

Towards a political economy of medicine and sickness

Since the 1980s, studies of 'late capitalism' have accentuated the globalization and restructuring of the world economy and the impact of neo-liberalism on policy-making. This revived interest in macro-level studies of health policies (Scambler and Higgs, 1999; Scambler, 2002), as well as the influence of social, economic, cultural and political factors on micro-level interaction (Link and Phelan, 2001).

For instance, Richard Parker and Peter Aggleton explore a 'political economy of social exclusion' with a case study of HIV/AIDS. Their analytical framework shifts the analysis of stigma from individual actions and attributes to the 'intersection of culture, power and difference' (2003, p. 17). They argue that the strength and pervasiveness of negative stereotypes, or 'symbolic violence', help legitimize the oppression practised on subordinate groups (ibid., p. 18). Hence, exposing how some illnesses and impairments are stigmatized directs the spotlight on the general structures of dominance. In a parallel approach, Graham Scambler builds on his 'hidden distress model' of epilepsy to scrutinize the material bases of cultural norms of 'imperfection'. Discriminatory practices range from 'normalization' (e.g. suppressing signing among deaf children) to 'social control' (e.g. sedating or confining people diagnosed as mentally ill) (2004, p. 32). This resonates with social model analyses of discriminatory attitudes and practices towards people with impairments (Oliver, 1990).

Parker and Aggleton (2003, p. 19) intimate that there is an 'intensified interaction' between 'traditional' and 'modern' forms of exclusion that opens up fresh possibilities for the social construction of identities (Hall, 1990). They reference Manuel Castells's (1997) distinction between 'three forms and origins of identity building' in the current 'information age' of capitalism: 'legitimizing identity', which is 'introduced by the dominant institutions of society to expand and rationalize their domination *vis-á-vis* social actors'; 'resistance identity', which is 'generated by those actors that are in positions/conditions devalued and/or stigmatized by the logic of domination, thus building trenches of resistance and survival on the basis of principles different from, or opposed to, those permeating the institutions of society'; and 'project identity', where 'social actors, on the basis of whatever cultural materials are available to them, build a new identity that re-defines their position in society and, by so doing, seek the transformation of overall social structure' (1997, pp. 7–8). One notable instance is feminist struggles to overturn patriarchy, and another is disabled people's campaigns against their social exclusion and oppression.

With a policy shift in the last quarter of the twentieth century, leading to welfare state cut-backs and enhanced market competition within the public sector, there has been 'an extension and political honing of legitimizing notions of deviance and stigma' (Scambler 2004, p. 39). The most disadvantaged in the population are held more responsible for their fate. Overall, 'the logic of shame and its relations of stigma have become more volatile with the switch from organised to disorganised capitalism' (ibid., p. 43). Again, the fluidity of post-modern culture facilitates difference and forms of identity politics, although their impact in countering oppression is less clear. This offers an intriguing but underdeveloped account of how the cultural devaluation of people with impairments is related to the intended (or unintended) consequences of 'the system imperatives of the economy and state' (ibid., p. 37). It must also address the impact of disabled people's campaigns on the introduction of anti-discrimination legislation and other measures to promote social inclusion and 'the life chances of disabled people' (Cabinet Office, 2005).

Social origins and patterns in 'chronic illness and disability'

The social and economic origins of ill-health have been a major research issue in sociological and social policy debates. Studies consistently report social patterns in morbidity and mortality related to socio-economic position, with higher levels of limiting long-term illness among the least well-off (Townsend et al., 1992; Graham, 2000; Smith, 2003). Again, adults and children in the poorest households are twice as likely as the rest of the population to be diagnosed with a mental illness (Meltzer et al., 2000, 2002).

Further social patterns in health status are linked to gender and ethnicity. As an illustration, females are more likely to be diagnosed as 'mentally ill' – particularly with one of the neuroses such as depression – with males overrepresented among those with psychotic conditions. Two main explanations have been put forward: the first emphasizes social causation and the impact of women's subordinate position, whether in paid work or the domestic sphere, while the second (labelling) approach highlights the manner in which key gatekeepers to health services, such as GPs and psychiatrists, perceive female patients in stereotypical terms and overdiagnose certain conditions such as neuroses and phobias (Busfield, 1988, 1989).

There are also significant patterns in the relationship between mental health and ethnicity. The disparity between the prevalence and type of mental illness recorded for African-Caribbeans and the rest of the population is a well-established research finding in Britain (Bhugra and Bhui, 1999; Sharpley et al., 2001; McLean et al., 2003; Keating and Robertson, 2004). There is a significant overrepresentation of young, African-Caribbean males among those diagnosed with schizophrenia, with even higher rates for those born in the UK, although they exhibit lower levels of depression and affective disorders (Smaje, 1995; Nazroo, 1997; Sharpley et al., 2001). Additionally, African-Caribbeans' experience of the mental health system sets them apart: they have higher rates of compulsory hospital admissions under the Mental Health Act, overrepresentation in medium and high-security facilities and a greater likelihood of being administered psychotropic medication and forcible treatment, but lower chances of receiving a 'talking therapy' (Bhugra and Bhui, 1999; Keating and Robertson, 2004, p. 440). Further significant differences exist between Asian and African-Caribbean rates of diagnosis, admission to hospital and types of treatment received (Nazroo, 1997; Bhui et al., 2003).

Explanations of differential rates, treatments and outcomes range from genetic, to socio-economic/environmental, through to artefactual (for example, of the measures used), such as unreliable psychiatric diagnoses or measures (Townsend et al., 1992; Graham, 2000). This often involves complex analysis of experiences specific to individual groups. In the case of ethnic minorities in the UK, for example, how far is ill-health attributable to higher levels of stress and unfavourable socio-economic conditions associated with migration? How far is systematic misdiagnosis a factor, whether because of cultural misunderstandings or racism – as evidenced by the much higher resort to 'pseudo' diagnoses, such as 'cannabis psychosis', when dealing with African-Caribbean males (Littlewood and Lipsedge, 1997; Fernando, 2002, 2003)?

This literature has a direct relevance for studies of the social origins of impairment. It underlines the importance of definitions and measures and amply illustrates how the attribution of diagnostic labels, such as 'mental illness', is mediated by various social factors such as the methods by which professionals and organizations process individuals from different social groups. Yet, recognition of the impact of sexism/patriarchy and racism has been slow to extend to research recognition of disablism.

Embodiment and post-structuralism

Post-structuralism has given a novel impetus to theorizing the social production of medical knowledge and the body. In an emerging 'somatic society' (Turner, 1992), the body is viewed as a basic metaphor for social, political and cultural values and unease (Scheper-Hughes and Lock, 1987). Contrary to traditional assumptions that the body is 'natural' or 'pre-social', post-structuralist analyses privilege the cultural level, according the body a social history:

> Not only has it been perceived, interpreted, and represented differently in different epochs, but it has also been lived differently, brought into being within widely dissimilar material cultures, subjected to various technologies and means of control, and incorporated into different rhythms of production and consumption, pleasure and pain. (Gallagher and Laqueur, 1987, p. vii)

A major inspiration is Michel Foucault's (1965, 1979, 1980) analysis of the body as the discursive product of knowledge–power relations and an increasingly crucial site of self-regulation. 'Sociologists support, criticise, collude with, and conspire against those health professionals whose claim to expertise is their sophisticated knowledge of the body – but rarely if ever to question or criticise their biological vision of that body' (Armstrong, 1987, p. 65). Foucauldian theorizing does just that. It 'problematizes' medical knowledge and views medicine as a way of mediating social relations (Arney and Bergen, 1983). It gives precedence to a 'biopolitics' or 'political anatomy' of the body, with its competing and changing discourses. However, it was not until his later writings that Foucault began to acknowledge forms of subjectivity and the possibilities for 'resistance' and 'overcoming'.

The nature of power shifted historically: from a sovereign, single authority exerted over others to self-disciplinary and multiple forms of surveillance and regulation. With the consolidation of liberal democracies, a space opened up between the state and its citizens, allowing novel forms of 'governmentality' (modes of control that stretch beyond the state). The scientific discourse that took root in the late eighteenth and early nineteenth centuries assumed a novel 'medical gaze' on the body, its ills and appropriate treatments (Foucault, 1965, 1976). It was facilitated by the expansion of hospital-based practice and a scientific preoccupation with physical examination and the classification of diseases. While redefining the boundaries of 'normality' in clinical terms, medicine also served a moral function:

> it claimed to ensure the physical vigour and the moral cleanliness of the social body; it promised to eliminate defective individuals,

degenerate and bastardized populations. In the name of biological and
historical urgency, it justified the racisms of the state . . . It grounded
them in 'truth'. (Foucault, 1979, p. 54)

The history of 'madness' demonstrates a number of decisive discursive changes (Foucault, 1980). Before the eighteenth century,
the perceived 'animal' nature of 'madness' justified harsh, physical
treatment and institutional confinement, but psychiatric diagnosis
began to change its focal point to the lack of self-control and the need
for both moral treatment and support and 'looser' forms of power.
Pursuing this analysis into the twentieth century, David Armstrong
(1980) attributes a comparable importance to the disappearance of
'madness' from the medical vocabulary and its replacement by mental
'disorder'. Medical interest expanded from the 'abnormal' population
in the asylum to a 'community gaze' that potentially encompassed
everyone (Armstrong, 1983, p. 67). There was a corresponding 'invention' of the neuroses, which signalled a novel understanding of the
relationship of the individual to the group, and of social control
mechanisms, under the guise of a new 'humanitarianism' (Armstrong,
1980, p. 293).

Historically, sickness and impairment comprised a diverse category of misfortunes typically attributed to 'fate', religious or
mystical forces, and unpreventable (natural) occurrences. The scientific, medical gaze moved from the hospital bedside to screening
the 'worried well' and 'potential patients' in the community, while
the 'patient-centred' discourse of general practice incorporated the
'whole person' and more areas of what had hitherto been regarded
an individual's 'private' life (Armstrong, 1983, 1984). There was a parallel change in medical discourse away from single pathologies and
ultimate causes to a more holistic approach. By the final decades of
the twentieth century, a novel 'risk discourse' took root (Beck, 1992).
The media, and now the internet, have become key sources for disseminating information on potential problems, from environmental
pollution to unhealthy lifestyles.

This indicates an obvious overlap between the medicalization
literature and the promotion of discourses around health lifestyles
and 'looking good' (Crawford, 1977) and the increased emphasis on 'options and choices' in the emerging consumer culture
(Shilling, 1993, p. 3). This 'healthism' spawned, and was stimulated
by, an expanding health, fitness and 'beauty' industry with a range
of pharmaceutical, surgical and technological products and services.
Corporeal criteria became fundamental to social judgements about
an individual's character and worth (Crawford, 1980; Featherstone,
1991). The 'healthism' discourse underscores individual responsibility

for maintaining health and 'well-being', and provides opportunities for new 'technologies of the self':

> These therapies of normality transpose the difficulties inherent in living on to a psychological register; they become not intractable features of desire and frustration but malfunctions of the psychological apparatus that are remediable through the operation of particular techniques. The self is thus opened up, a new continent for exploitation by the entrepreneurs of the psyche, who both offer us an image of a life of maximised intellectual, commercial, sexual or personal fulfilment and assure us that we can achieve it with the assistance of the technicians of subjectivity. (Rose, 1986, pp. 81-2)

The body is surrounded by other possibilities for change: medical technology offers organ replacement and reshaping, while genetics promises possibilities for designing new human beings. Medical rehabilitation looks beyond the traditional concern with vulnerability and dependence to encourage patients to map out new choices and possible changes in their lives (Seymour, 1998), although this discourse is mediated by traditional stereotypes, with an activity orientation rooted in young, male values and lifestyles (Morris, 1989).

Yet as the somatic society idealizes bodies with a specific shape and capacity, so it denigrates weak and 'ungainly' forms. The celebration of 'able-bodied' norms and values effectively devalues disabled people.

> The rise of consumer culture and healthism has resulted in the ageing body and the disabled body becoming sources of great anxiety. A body that does not function 'normally' or appear 'normal', that is confined to a wheel-chair or bed, is both visually and conceptually out-of-place, as evidenced by the lack of public facilities for people with disabilities or the elderly. (Lupton, 1994, p. 38)

Criticism of these post-structuralist analyses and their broad denial of the material body underpins a resurgence of critical realist accounts to bridge the divide between biology and culture (Williams and Bendelow, 1998). An associated motivation is to overcome post-structuralism's scant regard for individual agency and the lived experience of the body/impairment:

> Foucauldian poststructuralism has examined the enormous variety of discourses by which 'bodies' have been produced, categorized, and regulated . . . At the same time, it denies the sensuous materiality of the body in favour of an 'antihumanist' analysis of the discursive ordering of bodily regimes. (Turner, 2001, p. 255)

One consequence of the growth of social constructionism has been to polarize analyses of the body at the *ontological and epistemological* levels (Williams, 1999). Opponents of discourse analyses have mounted a counter-attack on the notion of fluid and fragmented bodies, arguing for an approach that is simultaneously biological and social analytical (Shilling, 1993). An 'embodied' or material-corporeal sociology (S. Williams, 1996) that takes the path of critical realism approaches disability as 'an *emergent* property' located in 'the *interplay* between the biological reality of *physiological impairment, structural conditioning (i.e. enablements/constraints)*, and *socio-cultural interaction/ elaboration*'. This accentuates the 'conscious awareness and critical praxis of social agents' (Williams, 1999, p. 810, *emphasis in original*) in achieving change.

The promise is that critical realism offers a way to put 'minds back into bodies, bodies back into society and society back into the body' (Williams and Bendelow, 1998, p. 3). It emphasizes 'deep underlying structures and mind-independent generative mechanisms' (Williams, 1999, p. 798; 2000b). This understanding of embodiment within sociological studies of health and illness provides a link with calls from within disability studies to examine how far and in what ways 'impairment and chronic illness have direct causative effects on the daily restrictions of activity that constitute disability' (Thomas, 2004a, p. 577). The disabled body and identity have a 'material reality' that is confirmed in wide-ranging social exclusion from mainstream society. In contrast to post-structuralist writings, the intention is to encompass the subjective experience or phenomenology of embodiment while recognizing the power of social discourses in framing how bodies are viewed, as well as the significance of material and cultural contexts (Turner, 2001; Shilling, 2003).

Review

This chapter has outlined the wide-ranging theoretical bases of the medical sociology literature on 'chronic illness and disability'. Medical sociologists do not 'hunt as a pack'. Formative influences centre on Parsons's analysis of the sick role, labelling accounts, and Goffman's writings on 'stigma'. More recently, contrasting theoretical and research perspectives have promoted 'negotiated' and interpretive approaches. There is also a continuing debate about the form and character of professional and medical dominance and medicalization. An emerging enthusiasm for forms of post-structuralism has generated intense exchanges about the sociological merits of social constructionist analyses of medical knowledge and the (disabled) body. This, in turn, has encouraged a resurgence in critical realism.

While acknowledging the diversity in theoretical and research standpoints, across different 'levels' of analysis, the predominant sociological focus has been with experiential accounts of sickness. From this perspective, social model approaches that examine disability as a specific form of social exclusion are ignored or dismissed as simplistic and 'politically motivated' (G. Williams, 1996; S. Williams, 1999) and as 'oversocialized', reductionist, unidimensional and overpoliticized, and little more than 'Marxist labelling' (Bury, 1997, p. 138). Moreover, suggestions of a middle ground – 'between a wounded storyteller and an overly politicised conception' (Bury, 2000b, p. 182) – typically require breaking the link between social inquiry and political action that has so energized social model analyses of disability.

Nevertheless, making the transition from a social model to a social theory of disability will benefit from more detailed examination of the sociological debates on 'chronic illness and disability', from micro-level social interaction and relations to macro-concerns and inter-level linkages. Unfortunately, there has been too little serious engagement by medical sociologists with a social barriers or oppression approach to disability. Yet there are notable exceptions, including Graham Scambler's (2004) application of a political economy approach to 'reframe' analyses of stigma, and Carol Thomas's (1999, 2004a, 2004b, 2007) critical examination of 'disablism' (see chapter 4). The prospects of a robust social theory of disability will be similarly challenged by applying sociological insights to the experience of social barriers, professional dominance and the 'disabled body'. It is to such issues that we turn next with a review of contributions to theorizing key themes within disability studies.

Theories of Disability

CHAPTER

4

A s noted in previous chapters, the foundations of the theorization of the disabling process were firmly laid in the latter half of the twentieth century. One of these was a volume of the US-based *Journal of Social Issues* in 1948 devoted entirely to this subject. Yet it was not until the 1960s that a discernible literature on disability began to appear. The driving force was the politicization of disability by disabled people and their allies in different countries. This involved the growth of the Independent Living Movement (ILM) in the USA, the self-advocacy movement in Sweden, and struggles by disabled people in British residential institutions for greater control of their lives. A range of issues were identified, including the poverty and exclusion experienced by disabled people and their politicization through civil rights and equal opportunities campaigns and social policy responses. These concerns fuelled a sustained critique of individualistic medical orthodoxies that leave the fate of people with accredited impairments and labelled 'disabled' in the hands of medical, rehabilitation and social care professionals.

With the aid of various heuristic devices, among them the concept of independent living, the social model of disability and the relational model of disability, attention turned to the various economic, political and cultural barriers that prevent the vast majority of disabled people achieving a comparable lifestyle to that of their non-disabled peers. But it is important to remember that there are significant differences between these approaches and that, although advocates would argue that these ideas have provided the necessary analytical tools for exposing the institutional discrimination and ensuing disadvantage encountered by disabled people, they are not sociological theories. However, each of these approaches is associated with contrasting emphases within disability theory and therefore reflects to a greater or lesser degree the various theoretical strands within sociology. Consequentially our discussion in this chapter will centre on these perspectives, beginning with analyses of state welfarism, the human service industries and the disability business inspired by the quest for independent living in the USA. Attention then turns to debates surrounding social model-inspired materialist and structural accounts that emphasize a holistic account of the social oppression encountered by disabled people. The final section addresses the post-modernist turn in disability theorizing – in particular, arguments for an embodied approach to disability that encompasses impairment effects and is inspired by the relational model of disability, which embraces many of the insights generated by medical sociologists discussed in the previous chapter.

Welfarism and its discontents

Hitherto, there has been a symbiotic and mutually beneficial relation-ship between the disabled people's movement and the academy in both America and Britain (Barnes et al., 2002). As we shall see later, in many ways the genesis of the ILM was inspired by the campus culture of American universities. It is not surprising, therefore, that American scholars were the first to employ a sociological framework to explore the potential of the paradigmatic shift associated with the concept of independent living, and also that they should centre on the concerns of disabled activists and their organizations – namely, the dependence-creating processes generated by self-serving profes-sional domination and the inept bureaucratic administration of national and state welfare systems and associate organizations and institutions.

Disabled people and the state

Inspired by the growing concern among American and British politi-cians over the rising costs of disability policy during the 1980s, an American political scientist, Deborah A. Stone, provides an analysis of the creation of the disability category by state welfare systems. Although unacknowledged, Stone's account emulates the arguments of Max Weber (1948) in that capitalist development is accompanied by a process of intensifying scientific rationalization and bureaucracy and that social constructions of 'disability' play a key role in the develop-ment of social policy. Through a historical account of social welfare developments in Britain, Germany and America, Stone argues that official definitions of disability are the outcome of the 'fundamental distributive dilemma' that confronts policy-makers charged with the responsibility of managing a 'needs-based' and 'work-based' distributive system. The key question is when perceptions of need should 'supersede other rules as a principle for distribution' (Stone, 1985, p. 18).

The successful resolution of this problem requires rules that are generally socially acceptable and validated and that do not under-mine the primacy of the work system. Hence medicine and the state collude to construct administrative categories, including 'sickness' and 'disability', that entitle those so classified to certain 'privileges and exemptions' (Stone, 1985, p. 21). Among these are welfare pay-ments and not having to work, although Stone acknowledges that people categorized in this way are liable to stigmatization and eco-nomic deprivation. This is because, historically, the state viewed those claiming exemption from the labour market with suspicion. Hence the link between medicine and 'disability' is crucial, as it provides a legitimate mechanism for separating 'genuine' and 'artificial' claims to sickness and impairment. Stone maintains that the disability category was essential to the development of the workforce in early capitalism and remains indispensable 'as an instrument of the state in controlling labour supply' (ibid., p. 179).

Stone's argument furthers the understanding of 'disability' as a distributive category within state welfare bureaucracies. She also demonstrates how the ascription of the disability label is a 'highly political issue' and a social construction which is transformed into a formal administrative category and made 'objective' by its vali-dation by doctors. However, her 'statist' account concentrates on the broad mechanisms and processes which preclude people from participation in the labour market and moves them into the needs-based system, without exploring the wider disabling barriers within both systems encountered by people with impairments. Moreover, Stone is concerned that, by the late twentieth century, the disability category had become too large and too rigid, as the standards for eligibility became more and more detailed. Moreover, once certain groups are included within the disability category they cannot be ejected from it, since they become socialized into their dependent 'disabled' identity – a categorization legitimated by the medical and welfare bureaucracies. This, Stone maintains, has provoked a crisis in disability programmes that may not be subject to categori-cal solutions, as those charged with the responsibility for defining and monitoring the disability category will have to devise 'ever more situations in which people are legitimately needy, until the categories become so large as to engulf the whole' (1985, p. 192). For Mike Oliver, 'if a situation were to occur, where the distributive dilemma was resolved on the basis of need, then this would surely mark the transition from capitalism to socialism as predicted by Marx' (1990, p. 42).

Growth of the human service industries

Another radical break with earlier theorizing on disability was advanced by the German-born American social scientist Wolf Wolfensberger (1989). His analysis was based on the emergence of what he calls a 'post-primary production economy' – a version of 'post-industrial society' – with a projected fall in employment in primary industries (agriculture, fishing and forestry) by the year 2000 to only 10 per cent of the US workforce, compared with a massive increase in employment in the 'human service industries' in the post-1945 period. With other Western industrial economies following suit, this heralds two major problems for global capitalism: first, an uneven distribution of resources, with only a minority of producers responsible for the lion's share of the nation's wealth; and, second, unprecedented levels of unemployment. Wolfensberger maintains that industrial economies have resolved these problems 'largely unconsciously' by keeping food prices and the cost of other essential goods artificially low, creating unproductive employment – examples include the armaments and advertising industries – and by generating a large human services industry whose growth has been based on more and more (disabled) people becoming dependent on an expanding range of health, education and social welfare services.

Wolfensberger focuses on the 'organizational dynamics' of the human service industries, with special reference to professional groups such as teachers, social workers and rehabilitation experts. He draws a contrast between agencies' manifest or stated purposes and their latent or unacknowledged functions. In a 'post-primary production economy', the latent function of human service industries has been to create and sustain large numbers of dependent and devalued people in order to secure employment for others. This is in marked contrast to their stated function, which is to 'cure' or 'rehabilitate' such people to rejoin the community.

It is also notable that Wolfensberger was extremely influential in the early development of the service principle of 'normalization' or, as it subsequently became, 'social role valorization' (Wolfensberger, 1983). The idea of normalization first gained ground in Denmark in the late 1950s and soon spread to other Scandinavian countries. It was the basis for egalitarian initiatives to generate an environment for people with learning difficulties that offered as 'normal' a life as possible, although this did not necessarily mean their removal from segregated institutions (Emerson, 1992).

Several years later, Wolfensberger pronounced his aim to 'North Americanize, sociologize, and universalize the Scandinavian formulations' (Wolfensberger, 1980a, p. 7). While he began by emphasizing 'culturally normative' means and practices, he later adjusted his focus to the impact of discrimination on disabled people and the need to concentrate attention on achieving 'socially valued' roles (Chappell, 1992). He follows labelling and social reaction theory in explaining how people with learning difficulties find themselves locked into a spiral of devaluation. Wolfensberger's suggested alternative is based on strategies and policies which highlight personal competencies and good practices. This is captured in a subsequent shift in emphasis in his writing from a focus on 'normalization' to what he terms 'social role valorization'. This is defined as the 'creation, support, and defence of valued social roles for people who risk devaluation' (Wolfensberger, 1983, p. 234), including 'socially valued life conditions' (Wolfensberger and Thomas, 1983, p. 24).

As noted in chapter 6, Wolfensberger became an enthusiastic advocate of the notion that professionals should encourage and assist disabled people, particularly those with intellectual impairments or 'learning difficulties', to achieve as 'normal' a lifestyle as possible comparable to that of their non-disabled peers. In contrast to earlier fears about professional dominance, such experts are now accorded a central role in 'interpreting' disabled people's socially valued roles and activities. Critics have suggested that, whatever it achieves for disabled people, 'normalization' facilitates professionals' adaptation to new policies on de-institutionalization and community-based service provision. 'Normalization' does not challenge the legitimacy of the professional role in the lives of disabled people but guarantees its continued authority. The whole focus of this approach is on changing disabled people to make them more like 'normal' people rather than challenging that ideal of 'normality'. Moreover, Wolfensberger's technological determinist approach contains little explanation of the historical relationship between industrial capitalism, the state, professions and disability. Thus, it fails to address the interaction between material and cultural forces and how these precipitate, maintain or undermine general approaches to disability or professional policies towards disabled people.

The disability business

An extensive historical analysis of the social construction of disability and the accompanying growth of the rehabilitation industry is provided by Gary Albrecht in *The Disability Business: Rehabilitation in America* (1992). He offers a 'political economy of physical disability and rehabilitation' in the USA which links 'democracy, social legislation and advanced capitalism' (1992, p. 13) and includes an ecological model of disease and impairment 'production, interpretation and treatment' (ibid., p. 39). Albrecht categorizes societies according to their technological-subsistence base into hunting and gathering, pastoral, horticultural, agrarian and industrial (with post-industrial and post-modern stages). Each societal type is characterized by a distinctive set of relations between its biological, physical and cultural environments, among them a unique 'type, incidence, and prevalence of impairment and disability and of social responses to them' (ibid.).

Albrecht's analysis of industrialization in America provides a valuable corrective to accounts that focus exclusively on Western Europe. While there are significant similarities, the parts played by key interests, including the state, the medical profession and private, corporate interests, demonstrate important differences in emphasis (Berkowitz, 1987). Albrecht acknowledges the significance of the medicalization of impairment and disability but stresses how, in a private insurance-dominated health-care system such as that in the USA, people with impairments have become a huge market for the services and products of health and social care agencies and professions. These include aids and equipment, drugs and insurance, training and rehabilitation: 'The disability business focuses on both treating persons with disabilities as raw materials and by commodifying disabilities and rehabilitation goods and services, making them objects of commerce' (Albrecht, 1992, p. 68).

The profit potential of the disability business has led to considerable competition between different fractions of capital or groups within the dominant class. Marta Russell illustrates how, in what she terms the 'money model of disability' (1998, p. 96), the recent expansion of rehabilitation medicine and services, in particular the massive growth in residential (nursing) homes for disabled people, has turned 'entrepreneurial medicine' into a multi-million dollar business. Moreover, Russell maintains that the American state has facilitated the development of private and professional interests without prioritizing public sector or publicly funded services to the same extent as in many European countries.

Clearly, then, from a variety of theoretical starting points these contributions provide a concerted challenge to the traditional medical approach to disability and presented an important stimulus to subsequent debates and contributions. Key issues are raised, among them the relationship between disability and the evolution of industrial society; the role of material and cultural factors in the development of contrasting forms of disability; the professional domination of disability; and the growth of social protest and political struggles by disabled people.

Yet, in comparison with the British literature, the discussion of the deprivations experienced by disabled people is not developed into a coherent theoretical analysis of disability as a form of social and cultural oppression. Instead, the American version of a socio-political approach concentrates on 'disability' as an administrative issue arising out of the interaction between impairments and a range of environmental and socio-economic characteristics such as gender, ethnicity, age and education (Zola, 1994). It was sustained by continuing civil rights struggles to achieve 'majority status' rights and entitlements.

Theories of disability and oppression

Theoretical analyses of disability in Britain, as in America, have their roots in the political activities of disabled people in the late 1960s and 1970s, among them specific campaigns for greater autonomy and control by disabled people in residential institutions (Finkelstein, 1991) and for a comprehensive disability income and new living options (Oliver and Zarb, 1989). In this climate of social and political change the unprecedented politicization of disabled people runs parallel to the formulation of radical social analyses of disability. A paradoxical feature of early North American literature is that it references the changing status of disabled people in other parts of the world, but ignores the debates about developing a social model of disability in Europe or elsewhere. A further contrast is that these analyses were dominated by academic writers, whereas in Europe disabled activists outside academia provided a significant input (Barnes et al., 2002, p. 6).

Moreover, these analyses offer a comprehensive and, in many ways, accessible examination of the economic, political and cultural phenomena that gave rise to, and continue to shape the process of disablement in industrial and post-industrial societies. Yet they are criticized for their failure to address in sufficient depth the impact of these economic and social forces on marginalized groups within the disabled population, such as women and older people with impairments.

Disability as social oppression

A disabled sociologist, Paul Abberley (1987), provided a nuanced theoretical framework for the analysis of disability as social oppression. By drawing upon comparable work by feminists and anti-racist writers (Barrett, 1981; Brittan and Maynard, 1984), he emphasized that a theoretically informed account must acknowledge the historical specificity of the experience of disability (Abberley, 1987, p. 6). He argued that oppression is an all-inclusive concept which is located in hierar-chical social relations and divisions. Historically, biological arguments have been used to justify the oppression of both women and black people. In the nineteenth century, women's 'maternal instincts' were believed to suffer if they were overeducated (Sayers, 1982), and 'scien-tific' evidence was used to suggest that black people were genetically and intellectually inferior to white people (Kevles, 1985).

Notwithstanding, Abberley argues that the biological element in disabled people's oppression – impairment – is far more 'real' than its counterparts for women and other oppressed groups. Unlike sex and skin colour, impairment is often functionally limiting. Consequently, for many disabled people 'the biological difference . . . is itself a part of the oppression' (Abberley, 1987, p. 7), as they are unable to conform to a 'non-disabled' ideal. As a result they may experience 'internalized oppression' (Rieser, 1990), 'low self-esteem' (French, 1993) or 'psycho-emotional dimensions of disability' (Thomas, 1999), which resemble the notion of 'felt stigma' as conceived and employed by medical sociologists (Scambler and Hopkins, 1986) and discussed in the pre-ceding chapter. Therefore, a social oppression theory of disability must address this material rather than socially constructed difference and 'very real inferiority' for at least two reasons. First, it comprises the bedrock upon which conventional views of disability are based. Second, the extent of internalized oppression forms a major barrier to the development of a 'political consciousness among disabled people' (Abberley, 1987, p. 6).

Abberley (1987) argues that a social oppression theory of disability must address several other considerations too: (1), that as a group disabled people experience economic and social deprivation; (2), that these disadvantages are the consequence of a particular ideology (a set of values and beliefs underpinning social practice) or ideologies which justify and perpetuate them; (3), that this situation is neither natural nor inevitable; and, (4), that there must be some beneficiary of this state of affairs. In 'Disabled people and "Normality"' (1993), he explains disabled people's oppression in terms of the material and ideological forces that accompanied capitalist development. Thus, people with impairments are perceived as 'abnormal' and oppressed, because they are denied full participation in the economic and social life of the community and, therefore, citizenship and rights (Abberley, 2002). But unlike Albrecht (1992) or Wolfensberger (1989), Abberley is less specific about who benefits from disabled people's oppression, apart from suggesting that the 'present social order, more accurately, capitalism in particular historical and national forms', emerges the winner (Abberley, 1987, p. 16). He asserts that to enable disabled people to be less dependent runs counter to the whole individualizing process associated with industrial capitalism, in which reward is an outcome of work and social needs are irrelevant to the ultimate distribution of goods and resources.

In his later work (1995, 1996, 2002) Abberley discusses the relationship between oppression, exclusion and work. This is because in contemporary society social policy at the national and international levels is almost exclusively geared to incorporate marginalized groups into the conventional labour market. This work-based model of social membership is also linked to the 'preventative/cure orientated perspective of allopathic medicine and to the specific instrumental logic of genetic engineering, abortion and euthanasia' (Abberley, 2002, p. 135). The nature and complexity of some impairments will inevitably exclude some sections of the disabled population, unlike other oppressed groups, from employment and therefore equal citizenship. This casts doubt on the notion that equality for all is achievable through inclusion in the workforce. With this in mind Abberley calls for the development of a 'new sociology of disablement' that encompasses discussions of impairment that challenge theoretical orthodoxy and 'replaces it with knowledge that arises from the position of the oppressed and seeks to understand that oppression' (ibid., p. 136).

Such an account must take cognizance of the rejection of the 'male' work-based model of social citizenship (Hill Collins, 1990; Lister, 1997) and those who argue that the days of the 'work society' are numbered and that in future societies' sources of identity will reside in future in the 'self active civil society' of a 'second modernity' (Beck, 2000, p. 20). This has prompted calls for a reconfiguration of the meaning of work to include 'illness management' (Corbin and Strauss, 1988), self-operated support schemes, user involvement in service provision, and delivery and cultural activities (Barnes, 2000; Barnes and Mercer, 2005b; Barnes and Roulstone, 2005; Prideaux, et al., 2009).

In the early 1990s the exploration of disability as social oppression was dominated mostly by those of a neo-Marxist or materialist persuasion and was largely uncontested. This challenge came when feminist and post-structuralist perspectives began to have a greater impact on the disability studies literature. Questions emerged regarding the specific circumstances of disabled women (Lonsdale, 1990; Lloyd, 1992; Morris, 1991) disabled members of minority ethnic groups (Begum, 1992; Stuart, 1992), older disabled people (Zarb and Oliver, 1993), disabled lesbians and gay men (Shakespeare et al., 1996; McRuer, 2006), disabled people with 'learning difficulties' (Walmsley, 1997), 'mental health' system users and survivors (Beresford and Wallcraft, 1997) and Deaf people (Corker, 1998).

In *Justice and the Politics of Difference* (1990) an American political theorist, Iris Marion Young, provides an analytical framework which has

the potential to include and compare the social oppression of all sections of the disabled population as well as other marginalized people.
Although she does not write from a disability studies or sociological
standpoint, she shows both how the demand for social justice has
shifted from distributive aims to a wider canvas of decision-making
and division of labour and culture and social group differences
in structuring social relations and oppression. Following Foucault
(1980), she argues that there is not necessarily one easily identified,
oppressive sovereign power. Oppression is not simply coercion by
the state, but structural and endemic to institutional policies and
practices that include the activities of well-meaning individuals in
ordinary interactions – 'in short, the 'normal processes of everyday
life' (Young, 1990, p. 41).

Young identifies five main areas of oppression: exploitation, marginalization, powerlessness, cultural imperialism and violence.
Exploitation is taken from the Marxist theory of class relations in
the 'mode of production' whereby the dominant class accumulates
wealth from the labours of subordinate classes. However, it may not
be possible to profit from an exploited group's labour if, like disabled
people, they are only partially involved in the labour market. But, as
discussed earlier, it has been argued that the social creation of disability in capitalist societies has resulted in the exploitation of people
with accredited impairments by a vast army of workers employed in
the rehabilitation industries (Albrecht, 1992).

Marginalization refers to the systematic removal of a social group
from the mainstream of everyday life. Young terms this the 'most dangerous' form of oppression and a central element of the experience of
disabled people because of the risk of their removal from social life
through their education and accommodation in special institutions.
'Even extermination' is on the agenda, with examples of infanticide and abortion, forced sterilization of women with intellectual
impairments, and Nazi genocide programmes (Young, 1990, p. 53; see
chapter 9). Countervailing social policies provide some recognition of
disabled people's marginalization, but these solutions often lead to
dependency through enforced reliance on state welfare and services.
Powerlessness is linked to exploitation and marginalization and confirms that people have little control over or choice in what to do with
their lives. It is verified by the traditional distinctions between those
with the authority to exercise power, as in the case of professionals,
and those who are not, such as disabled people; they are therefore
vulnerable to exploitation and abuse.

Cultural imperialism is similar to 'ideological hegemony as conceived
by the Italian Marxist Antonio Gramsci (1971, 1985). Ideological
hegemony is achieved by the constant reification of the dominant

group's world view through various discourses and media as 'natural' or common sense. Henceforth, 'able bodied normalcy' is firmly incorporated in everyday thinking and behaviour as a privileged and desirable form of existence. The concept of an 'able' body/mind assumes normative or universal criteria against which all bodies and minds are judged. Those unable or unwilling to meet these standards are deemed deviant or 'other'. It is contentious, however, that contrary views and interests are eradicated thoroughly, or that the dominant culture is internalized completely by oppressed minorities. Alternative cultures survive, though are not always celebrated, and may be the basis for future protest and opposition (see chapter 8).

The defining feature of *violence* takes the form of random physical attacks, sexual assaults or 'mental' harassment, intimidation and ridicule. Such acts are widely experienced by some oppressed groups. In the case of disabled people, sexual abuse, particularly affecting children and women in institutions, has been widespread (Sobsey, 1994; Westcott and Cross, 1996; Rioux et al., 1997). There is also the systematic violence practised on unborn children with impairments through abortion, and the ridicule and disgust shown towards people who 'look different'.

Young's 'five faces of oppression' are not always easily distinguished in practice, but her account provides further insights into how far disability compares and contrasts with other forms of social discrimination. It does not, however, provide a comprehensive theoretical account of the economic or cultural origins of oppression or discrimination.

Capitalism, Industrialization and disability

The foundations of a fully formed materialist account of the origins of the oppression of disabled people was provided in 1980 with the publication of *Attitudes and Disabled People* by a disabled activist and social psychologist and key figure in the Union of the Physically Impaired Against Segregation (UPIAS) and the UK's disabled people's movement, Vic Finkelstein. This is the first attempt at a historical materialist account of disability. Finkelstein analyses disability as a social problem that is linked directly to the changing 'mode of production' – i.e. division of labour and forms of ownership, including political and ideological factors.

Finkelstein identifies three separate, sequential historical stages. In Phase One, the pre-industrial period, economic activity was agrarian or cottage-based. This mode of production and the social relations associated with it did not preclude people with impairments from economic participation. They were nevertheless at the bottom of the social hierarchy, along with 'the poor and unemployed'. Phase Two relates to the onset of industrial capitalism in the nineteenth century in Western Europe and North America. People with accredited impairments were increasingly excluded from paid work on the grounds that they were unable to keep pace with the 'disciplinary power' of the new mechanized, factory-based production system. This exclusion justified the segregation of individuals with impairments, defined as in need of care and supervision, into various residential institutions: 'Phase Two signalled the growth of hospital-based medicine and the creation of large asylums'. The number of disabled people grew and so too did the number of professionals concerned with their care and rehabilitation (Finkelstein, 1980, p. 10). Phase Three is only just taking shape and heralds the struggle for the reintegration of disabled people in society. It corresponds with the emergence of post-industrial society. Developing technology is viewed as facilitating the emancipation of disabled people through work with others to achieve common goals based on general human needs. For Finkelstein, new technology will enable 'the most severely physically impaired people to operate environmental controls which can enable them to live relatively independently in the community' (ibid., p.11).

Finkelstein's analysis has been criticized for offering a 'mechanical' account of relations between the mode of production and people's perceptions and experiences of disability. Technological determinism submerges its Marxist inspiration. The account also overlooks the fact that technology can be both empowering and disempowering. For example, advanced computer systems enable many people with impairments to enter the workforce (Albrecht, 1992). Conversely, other disabled people, particularly those with learning difficulties and those in older age groups, are marginalized by recent technological changes (Roulstone, 1998; Barnes and Mercer, 2003, 2005b; Sheldon, 2004). Technological development is also unevenly distributed. Many people with mobility-related impairments are unable to afford or obtain motorized wheelchairs (Lamb and Layzell, 1994, 1995). The lack of technical aids and equipment is particularly acute in 'developing' countries of the majority world (Stone, 1999a; WHO, 2001b; Priestley, 2001; Barnes and Mercer 2005a; Albert, 2006). Moreover, new technology may simply shift disabled people's dependence from one set of experts to another. Notwithstanding these shortcomings, and the lack of empirical evidence, Finkelstein's account has inspired other disability theorists to explore the historical development of disability.

Mike Oliver's The Politics of Disablement (1990) provides a more compelling account of a materialist history of disability. He argues that definitions of disability and other 'social problems' are related both to economic and social structures and to the central values of specific modes of production. He explains the emergence of the individualistic and medical approach to disability in terms of capitalism's need for a workforce that is physically and intellectually able to conform to the demands of industrialization. But it is not simply the mode of production that precipitated the genesis of the personal tragedy theories of disability, but also the 'mode of thought' and the relationship between the two.

The rise of capitalism brought profound economic changes to the organization of work. This in turn affected social relations and attitudes, both of which had significant implications for family life. These factors, in conjunction with unprecedented population growth, constituted a potential threat to the established social order. It is not that disability arrives with capitalism but, rather, that it takes a specific form – i.e. the personal tragedy model – and social oppression becomes more acute. Feudalism did not prohibit disabled people from participating in the economy, and even if they could not participate fully they could still contribute. Individuals with impairments were considered 'unfortunate and not segregated from the rest of society' (Oliver, 1990, p. 27).

Industrial capitalism established the institution as the principal means of social control. It is manifest in the proliferation of prisons, asylums, workhouses, industrial schools and colonies, and it embodied both 'repressive' (as it 'offered the possibility of forced removal from the community for anyone who refused to conform to the new order') and 'ideological' (as it acted as a visible deterrent to 'those who would not or could not conform') mechanisms of social control (Oliver, 1990, p. 48). The effect was to segregate and isolate disabled people from the mainstream of community life.

Two factors are central to Oliver's account of the role of ideology in the social creation of disability: first, the individualizing tendencies accompanying capitalist development and, most notably, the growth of free market economics and the spread of wage labour; and, second, the medicalization of the means of social control – specifically, the medical profession's rise to prominence within institutions for sick and disabled people which generated notions of an 'able-bodied individual' (Oliver, 1990, p. 79).

Thus, the medical profession was empowered to focus its 'disciplinary gaze' on both acute and chronic conditions and so expand its sphere of influence. Medical interest was extended to include the selection of educational provision for disabled children, the assessment and allocation of work for disabled adults, the determination of eligibility for welfare payments, and the prescription of technical aids and equipment – all of which transformed the lives of disabled people.

Additionally, the nineteenth century witnessed the increasing portrayal of disabled people as deviant, abnormal and different. For Oliver, such negative cultural imagery came to the fore in the nineteenth century and was reinforced by professional discourses on disability as adjustment to tragedy and stigma. As a result:

> [t]hroughout the twentieth century, whether it be in the novel, newspaper stories, television and films disabled people continue to be portrayed as more than or less than human, rarely as ordinary people doing ordinary things. Without a full analysis of images of disability it is not possible to do other than present examples of these images. (Oliver, 1990, p. 61)

Consequently, the personal tragedy view of disability achieved ideological hegemony and has become 'naturalized' as common sense. Notwithstanding that the economic and political upheavals of the 1960s and 1970s, coupled with the welfare cutbacks of the 1980s, helped fuel the politicization of disability and the emergence of the disabled people's movement in the UK and a reassessment of cultural representations of disabled people (see chapter 8).

Clearly, then, Oliver's account locates the creation of disability firmly within the context of the material and ideological changes that accompanied the emergence of industrial capitalism. It presents a sophisticated review of the social creation of dependency and disability, although it has been taken to task by some Marxists for allowing too much ground to cultural factors (Gleeson, 1997). It also offers little analysis of disability in non- or pre-capitalist societies.

An empirically grounded account is provided by an Australian scholar, Brendan Gleeson. In *Geographies of Disability* (1999) he adopts a 'historical geographical materialist' exploration of the social space of disability in feudal England and industrial cities in Australia and Britain in order to focus on the everyday experiences of people with physical impairments. His analysis shows that, while peasants with impairments experienced the same injustices and exploitation encountered by their 'able bodied' peers, they were not structurally oppressed because of them. His detailed analysis of primary data sources of an industrial city – nineteenth-century colonial Melbourne – shows how the rise of progressive commodity relations lessened the ability of disabled people to provide for themselves and their families. The state responded with the widespread incarceration of those deemed unable to contribute – a policy that persisted well into the twentieth century. As a consequence the oppression of disabled people

> is deeply inscribed in the discursive, institutional and material dimensions of cities. These realms of oppression include an inaccessible built environment, landscapes of dependency (i.e., the frameworks of social support provided by state, private and voluntary bodies),

exclusionary modes of consumption and production, and devaluing cultural imagery and public policies. (Gleeson, 1999, p. 11)

A further innovation within Gleeson's analysis is his 'embodied' account of the social construction of abnormality. By employing Marx's theory of nature and political economy (Ollman, 1971), he situates an analysis of 'the body' in his theory of the social origins of disablement. The social oppression of disabled people – disability – is immersed in a complex and uneven historical repression of certain forms of embodiment, capitalist development, and the inability of people with impaired bodies to sell their labour. In capitalism the embodied characteristics of certain individuals disqualify their claims to social legitimacy, and therefore the social construction of 'abnormality is legitimized. The naturalness of impairment is acknowledged, but the naturalization of disablement is rejected. This is not to deny the functional limitations that may accompany impairment, but to affirm that 'Impairment can only be understood concretely – that is to say historically and culturally – through its socialisation as *disability* or some other (less repressive) identity' (Gleeson, 1999, p. 52, *emphasis in original*).

Disability and social divisions

It is notable that hitherto most theories of the oppression of disabled people have assumed a polarization of disabled and non-disabled populations. The initial concentration on disability as a 'master status' (Goffman, 1963) has effectively glossed over the impact of other social divisions and is now widely contested as a false universalism. The presumed homogeneity of disabled people's experience of exclusion has been countered by demands that studies incorporate the interaction of disability with gender (Deegan and Brooks, 1985; Fine and Asch, 1988; Wendell, 1989, 1996, 2005; Morris, 1991, 1996; Thomas, 1999), 'race' and ethnicity (Stuart, 1993; Begum et al., 1994; Ahmad, 2000; Bell, 2006), sexuality (Shakespeare et al., 1996; Tremain, 1996; Gillespie-Sells et al., 1998; McRuer, 2006), age (Zarb and Oliver, 1993; Priestley, 2003) and social class (Jenkins, 1991).

Yet a simple additive response encourages the construction of a misleading league table of oppressions encountered by different sub-groups of disabled people. As Nasa Begum argues, the 'double oppression' of being a disabled woman, for example, yields to the 'triple oppression of being a black disabled woman [who experiences] . . . racism, sexism and handicapism' (1992, pp. 70–1). In practice, these dimensions are interlocking and provide a complex experience of 'simultaneous' rather than separate oppressions. However, it has proven much easier to identify simultaneous oppression and associated responses in theory than in practice. Moreover, in concert with the fragmentation of mainstream feminist theorizing when it began to engage with the differential experiences of women in terms of ethnicity, class and age, women writing about disability have strived to avoid 'bracketing disabled women into one undifferentiated social grouping' (Thomas, 2007, p. 71).

Disability and gender

Some of the earliest attempts to address the experience of impairment and disability focus on its impact on women. In two collections edited by Jo Campling (1979, 1981), the contributors draw attention to the problems faced by disabled women in such key areas as personal relationships, sexuality, motherhood, education, employment and media stereotypes.

An early theorization of the gendered experience of disability was developed by Michelle Fine and Adrienne Asch (1985, 1988). In their analysis of American literature, they argue that disabled men have had relatively more opportunities to oppose the stigma associated with impairment and thus strive to achieve typical male roles. In contrast, '[e]xempted from the 'male' productive role and the 'female' nurturing one, having the glory of neither, disabled women are arguably doubly oppressed' (Fine and Asch, 1988, p. 13). More recently, attempts have been made to recognize a wider set of differences among disabled women, not least with regard to 'race' (Begum, 1992; Vernon, 1999), sexuality (Tremain, 1996) and age (Priestley, 2003).

Empirical evidence from America and Britain confirms the significant degree of social exclusion encountered by disabled women in the labour market (Fine and Asch, 1988; Lonsdale, 1990). Thus, disabled women experience disadvantages that set them apart from both disabled men and non-disabled women – economically, socially and psychologically. As a consequence, disabled women were either ignored in feminist analyses or portrayed as passive victims: 'Perceiving disabled women as childlike, helpless, and victimized, non-disabled feminists have severed them from the sisterhood in an effort to advance more powerful, competent, and appealing female icons' (Fine and Asch, 1988, p. 4). In *Pride Against Prejudice*, Jenny Morris (1991) is equally critical of feminism for its failure to address the experiences of disabled women. While it has fought long and hard to challenge society's rigid gender roles, it embraced the personal tragedy representation of disabled women as incapable of performing 'normal' female roles. From the perspective of disabled women, 'we are prescribed a life of passive dependence. Our neutered sexuality, negative body-image and restricted gender roles are a direct consequence of the processes and procedures which shape the lives of women' (Begum, 1992, p. 81). Disabled women have also been discouraged from becoming mothers on various grounds that often exaggerate risks or deny choice, such as perceived threats to their own health, passing on an impairment to their children, or questioning their capacity to be a 'good mother' (Finger, 1991; C. Thomas, 1997; Wates and Jade, 1999).

Nevertheless, the feminist rallying call that the 'personal is political' has been enthusiastically incorporated into disabled women's writings. This stresses that 'women's everyday reality is informed and shaped by politics and is necessarily political' (hooks, 1984, p. 24). It triggered a growing literature on individual disabled women's stories of living with impairment (Campling, 1981; Deegan and Brooks, 1985; Morris, 1989, 1996; Driedger and Gray, 1992; Abu-Habib, 1997; Thomas, 1999). This consciously set out to overcome what was regarded as an overwhelming focus on disabled men's experiences, such as at work or their sexual concerns, while female sexuality, reproduction and child rearing had been largely ignored. To politicize the personal domain means taking control, 'including the negative parts to the experience' (Morris, 1993a, p. 69). Notably, a smaller but expanding literature has emerged on the gendered experience of disabled men (Gerschick and Miller, 1995; Robertson, 2004; Smith and Sparks, 2004).

Disability, 'race' and ethnicity

'Race' and ethnicity also plays an important part in social and economic positioning – for both disabled and non-disabled people. A similar impact is evident in media representations. It has been argued that a 'black disabled identity' can be understood only within the context of a deeply embedded social exclusion of black people that is 'institutional racism' (Confederation of Indian Organizations, 1987). The extent of this oppression means that 'black' disabled people form 'a discrete minority within a minority' and often face 'exclusion and marginalisation even within disabled communities and the disability movement' (Hill, 1994, p. 74).

Studies of the interaction of different social divisions and processes provide a picture of 'double' or 'multiple' oppression' (Baxter et al. 1990), although Ossie Stuart argues that 'being a black disabled person is not a 'double' experience, but a single one grounded in British racism' (1993, p. 99). He contends that the distinctiveness of black disabled people's oppression is threefold: first, limited or no individuality and identity; second, resource discrimination; and, finally, isolation within black communities and the family (ibid., p. 95).

In Britain, racism is not so much located in 'colour' as widened to cultural and religious differences so that 'black' disabled people are distanced from both anti-racists and the disabled people's movement. This is evident in the absence of 'black' people and members of minority ethnic groups in disabled people's organizations and suggests the need to build a 'distinct and separate black disabled identity' (Stuart, 1993, p. 94). Yet 'black' disabled people are also marginalized within the 'black' community because of their exclusion from employment and leisure activities and their 'inability to attain accepted roles within black communities' (ibid., p. 99). It follows that other minorities within the 'black' disabled community experience further 'unique' forms of simultaneous oppression.

Studies demonstrate how 'race' and minority ethnic status affects how disabled people are treated in education, work, and health and social support services. This leads, according to Nasa Begum, to complex survival strategies and alliances between black disabled people and other oppressed groups. Specific aspects will be prioritized according to the context. Sometimes black disabled people form alliances with other disabled people to challenge disability, while on other occasions they unite with other black people to fight racism: 'The very nature of simultaneous oppression means that as Black Disabled men and women, and Black Disabled lesbians and gay men we cannot identify a single source of oppression to reflect the reality of our lives' (Begum, 1994a, p. 35). It is not possible to 'simply prioritize one aspect of our oppression to the exclusion of others' (ibid.). Yet the notion of 'multiple oppression' is misleading because it separates the many different dimensions to inequality, as if these can be compartmentalized in everyday experience and then added together in an overall balance sheet.

In summary, these studies demonstrate the importance of analysing the complex interplay of oppressions in ways that avoid a simplistic oppressor–oppressed divide and allow scope for agency or resistance:

> The significance of such a model is that, first, it poses a dynamic relationship between the individual, power and structure, its multifacets or many mirrors reflect the fact that social divisions impact on people, single or in groups in different ways, at different times, in different situations. At one or many moments, in one or many places issues of disability may be highlighted; at another moment the inequalities of class may predominate for the same person or group. (Williams, 1992, pp. 214–15)

This focus on the interrelationship of different (simultaneous) lines of oppression exposes the internal fault lines but still leaves open how exclusionary processes operate across social contexts. As Barbara

Fawcett (2000, pp. 52–3) argues, a middle-class, white disabled man challenging a restaurant's lack of accessibility may appear very powerful to a black, non-disabled waitress. Conversely, the same waitress may demand that a white man with learning difficulties leaves the restaurant because his table manners are upsetting non-disabled customers. 'The challenge then becomes to recognize and challenge oppression, whilst fully acknowledging complexity and inter-relational elements' (ibid., p. 53). Or, to put it another way:

> The politics of disablement is about far more than disabled people, it is about challenging oppression in all its forms. Like sexism, racism, heterosexist and all other forms of oppression it is a human creation. It is impossible, therefore, to confront one type of oppression without confronting them all and, of course, the cultural values that created and sustain them. (Barnes, 1996, p. xii)

Disability and the life course

Over recent years the notion of a normative life course (childhood, adolescence, adulthood and old age) has been a key discursive claim within sociology. Its central stages, statuses or transitions are institutionally and culturally produced. Central institutions such as the family, economy and education exercise potentially defining roles. Traditionally in industrial societies, social class was a defining force in people's lives, but its grip has been loosened, creating less certainty in individual or family biographies. This leads to more life-planning and self-monitoring as well as greater fears of risk or failure and conflicting institutional demands (Beck, 1992).

In terms of disability and the life course, it is important to identify the point in the life cycle when impairment is acquired, as the experience of and social responses to disablement vary significantly with age. Researchers have identified three main trajectories or 'disability careers'. First, people whose impairment is diagnosed at birth or in early childhood; second, those who acquire an impairment during adolescence and early adult years, often as a result of an illness or injury; and, third, older people, whose impairment is most often attributed to the ageing process (Barnes, 1990; Jenkins, 1991; Zarb and Oliver, 1993; Bury, 1997).

Building on a materialist perspective, Mark Priestley provides a structural and cultural analysis of the process of disablement from a generational or 'life course' perspective. Focusing on the differing impact of disabling environments and cultures upon the lives of people with accredited impairments at various stages of the life cycle, he argues that both disablement and society's generational system are the products of modernity and the 'social relations of production in industrializing capitalist economies. (Priestley, 2003, p. 196)

Further, Priestley maintains that the escalating process of individuation associated with late capitalism, or post-modernity, has increasingly undermined traditional life-course trajectories in terms of class, gender and generational expectations. This, coupled with the tendency to view social stratification in terms of patterns of consumption and lifestyle choices, has generated a socio-cultural environment in which disabled people and other historically marginalized groups such as children and older people can successfully lay claim to inclusion and equality. However, he warns that by colluding with a generational system that emphasizes the importance of consumerism and lifestyle choices, particularly marginalized groups such as young disabled children and older disabled people at the end of life, may be further displaced from conventional notions of disability and adult status. Thus:

> The task of including all disabled people is essentially the same task as including the very youngest and the very oldest in society. Both challenge us to reformulate our individualistic, adult centred notions of competence and autonomy in a more relational way. (Priestley, 2003, p. 198)

Post-modernism: back to the future?

As noted earlier, during the late 1990s a concerted challenge to the dominance of materialist analyses of disablement came from advocates of post-modernist or post-structuralist perspectives. Particularly evident in the work of North American writers (Wendell, 1989, 1996, 2005; Davis, 1995; Garland-Thomson, 1996, 1997, 2006a, 2006b; Linton, 1998a; Mitchell and Snyder, 1997, 2000, 2001), these approaches require a move away from an emphasis on the primacy of material factors in the creation of disability towards a more nuanced focus on culture, language and discourse.

While the importance of language in the disablement process has been a major concern for disability activists and writers since the 1970s (Oliver, 1990; Barnes, 1992; Linton, 1998a; Swain et al., 2004; Haller et al., 2006), there is now an expanding literature on lay and 'scientific' terminology used to define and categorize people with accredited impairments from writers influenced by the writings of Jacques Derrida and Michel Foucault. Yet, apart from their rejection of the hegemony of the social model and materialism within disability studies, there are many strands within post-modernism to be considered. Advocates are generally opposed to being pigeonholed into singular theoretical categories, favouring instead a more eclectic approach (Thomas, 2007).

Disability, normality and difference

Derrida (1990), for example, is concerned with ways of thinking that formulate and establish the meanings surrounding 'identity' and 'difference'. Meanings are organized through a continuous and dynamic process of interaction that can only be understood through the systematic deconstruction of orthodox assumptions and discourses. Consequentially a key feature of post-modernist writings is the rejection of assumed Cartesian dualisms that proliferate within Enlightenment-inspired theorizing and culturally dominant discourses associated with modernist society. Examples include mind/body, individual/society, normal/abnormal distinctions. It is argued that this type of 'either/or' thinking plays a central role in the social oppression of disabled people. Hence:

> A Derridean perspective on disability would argue that although they are antagonistic, 'normativism' needs disability for its own definition: a person without an impairment can define him/herself as 'normal' only in opposition to that which s/he is not – a person with an impairment. (Corker and Shakespeare, 2002, p. 7)

Moreover, a deconstruction of the concept of normality or 'normalcy' and its discursive impact on societal responses to impairment is provided by Lennard Davis (1995). Drawing on the work of Derrida and Foucault, his analysis of changing cultural responses to impairment provides a useful addition to materialist accounts of the emergence of the disability category discussed earlier. He argues that 'the social processes associated with disabling cultural environments arrived with industrialization' (1995, p. 24) as a new set of discourses and practices. In earlier epochs, perceptions of the human body and mind were visualized against the 'ideal' as represented in art, mythology or imagination. Since an ideal is generally thought of as unattainable, all human beings are by definition imperfect. Hence, before the ideological, political and cultural upheavals of the Enlightenment, people with impairments were not distinguishable as a group, but lived as individuals within the community.

The construction of the 'disabled' individual and group was an inevitable outcome of the displacement of the 'ideal' by the 'normal/abnormal' dichotomy with the use of statistics to bolster medical knowledge and practice. Consequently, the dominant discourses around notions of the 'grotesque' and the ideal body in the Middle Ages were completely overturned by the normalizing gaze of modern science. This established a hierarchical standard for pronouncing some bodies and minds as abnormal and inferior – in terms of appearance and performance. Standards of physical health, mental balance and moral soundness become closely linked, so that defective bodies and minds were associated with 'degeneracy' (Young, 1990).

Post-structuralist accounts have also sought to analyse how the categories of 'impairment' and 'disability' are being constantly rewritten as part of a wider politics of the body. An attempt to generate an embodied notion of disability is evident in the work of Rosemarie Garland-Thomson. In *Extraordinary Bodies* (1997) she challenges the widespread belief that 'able-bodiedness' and 'disability' are 'self-evident physical conditions'. Instead, she explores how the 'physically disabled body' becomes 'a repository for social anxieties about such troubling concerns as vulnerability, control, and identity' (1997, p. 6). Her objective is to remove the disabled body from medical discourse and recast disabled people as a disadvantaged minority in the tradition of American writings. She demonstrates how there are hierarchies of embodiment which decide valued and devalued identities: 'In this economy of visual difference, those bodies deemed inferior become spectacles of otherness while the unmarked are sheltered in the neutral space of normalcy' (ibid., p. 8). To explore this hierarchy or difference, it is necessary to deconstruct, not simply analyse, notions of what is regarded as deviant and also what is deemed normal. In this regard, there are many similarities between the social meanings attributed to female bodies and those assigned to disabled bodies (ibid., p. 9) – both are seen as deviant and inferior, denied full participation in economic and public life, and contrast to the (male/'able-bodied') norm. This presumes a normative body hierarchy, in which some bodies are perceived 'as ugly, disgusting, or degenerate' (Young, 1990, p. 11).

Garland-Thomson further illustrates the body's historical journey in the context of a detailed study of 'freakery', or 'cultural spectacles of the extraordinary body', which flourished into the early twentieth century. She argues that 'enfreakment' (Hevey, 1992) has a cultural significance in the way in which it stylizes, silences, differentiates and distances bodily difference: 'By constituting the freak as an icon of generalized embodied deviance, the exhibitions also simultaneously reinscribed gender, 'race', sexual aberrance, ethnicity, and disability as inextricable yet particular exclusionary systems legitimated by bodily variation' (Garland-Thomson, 1996, p. 10).

The impairment/disability debate

Shelley Tremain (2005b) argues that the importance of the Foucauldian concept of 'bio-power', or 'bio-politics', cannot be overstated in the analysis of disability. This refers to the medical technologies and associate discourses that emerged in the latter half of the eighteenth century to govern and regulate individuals and populations that

> caused the contemporary disabled subject to emerge into discourse and social existence. Among the items that have comprised this expansive apparatus are asylums, income support programmes, quality of life assessments, workers' compensation benefits, special education programmes, regimes of rehabilitation, parallel transit systems, prostheses, home care services, telethons, sheltered workshops, poster child campaigns, and pre natal diagnosis. (Tremain, 2005b, p. 5)

The post-structuralist assault on the social model of disability is particularly evident in the writings of Tremain (2002, 2005b), Shakespeare and Watson (2001) and Shakespeare (2006). While it is acknowledged that the social model has proved invaluable in mobilizing the disabled people's movement and has opened up new areas of academic enquiry, especially in the UK, it is now considered to have outgrown its usefulness within disability studies.

The crux of this critique hinges on the impairment–disability distinction upon which the social model rests. For post-structuralists this distinction is not tenable as it represents nothing less than a new impairment–disability dualism synonymous with a modernist world view. Hence, in concert with the individualistic medical view of disability, the social model explains disability as a universal construct that has generated a totalizing historical meta-narrative that excludes important dimensions of disabled people's lived experience and knowledge. Further, as impairment and disability are structurally determined and reified by the social forces of capitalism and industrialization, the social model/oppression theory of disability is open to accusations of reductionism (Shakespeare and Watson, 2001).

Therefore such accounts are said to be unable to accommodate the historical, local and situational contingencies that influence interpretations of 'impairment' and 'disability', as the global experience of disabled people is too complex to be accounted for by a single unitary theory. Influenced by the growing rejection of essentialist distinctions between the biological and the social – sex/gender in feminist writings (Butler, 1990) and male/female in 'queer' theory' (Seidman, 1994) – the impairment/disability dichotomy is rejected on the grounds that impairment is not a pre-social or pre-cultural biological concept because 'the words we use and the discourses we deploy to represent impairment are socially and culturally determined. There is no pure or natural body existing outside of discourse. Impairment is only ever viewed through the lens of disabling social relations' (Shakespeare, 2006, p. 35).

Clearly poststructuralist writers have replaced material or 'biological essentialism' with 'discursive essentialism'. Here the 'body becomes nothing more than the multiple significations that give meaning . . ., a surface to be written on, to be fabricated by regimes of truth' (Hughes and Paterson, 1997, pp. 333–4). Moreover, as both impairment and disability are social constructs, 'it is difficult to determine where one ends and the other starts', because 'disability is a complex dialectic of biological, psychological, cultural and socio-political factors which cannot be extricated except with imprecision' (Shakespeare and Watson, 2001, p. 22). Further, in *Disability Rights and Wrongs*, Shakespeare (2006) provides a strident attack on the social model of disability, Britain's disabled people's movement, and Disability Studies in the UK. The social model is said to be an outdated ideology because of the distinction between impairment and disability and its emphasis on barrier removal. The disabled people's movement is accused of being unrepresentative of the disabled population as a whole. Disability Studies is criticized for its failure to concentrate on subjective meanings and the nature of impairment, the prevention and minimization of impairment, the strengths and weaknesses of the National Health Service, and the barriers that cause and exacerbate impairment – such as poverty, for example (2006, p. 40).

In doing so, Shakespeare utilizes post-modernist arguments in support of a critical realism perspective as advocated by Simon Williams (1999), which he maintains is 'the most helpful and straightforward way of understanding the social world, because it allows for this complexity' (Shakespeare, 2006, p. 54). This standpoint enables him to justify his newly found allegiance to the ICF and the relational understanding of disability as favoured by the Nordic countries. However, he fails to address Williams's assertion that a critical realist approach runs in marked contrast to recent developments in disability theory and the developments in post-modernist thinking as a basis for health-care policy for the twenty-first century:

> Whatever the outcome, a critical realist position is, I venture, an eminently preferable basis, given the shifting sands of postmodernism and the pitfalls of overly social models of illness and disability, upon which to fashion both medical sociology and emerging forms of health care 'fit' for the 21st century. As for postmodern prayers and the endless process of becoming 'Other', the only truly satisfactory answer and ethical response, I suggest, . . . is as follows: real bodies, real selves; real lives, real worlds. (Williams, 1999, p. 815)

Further, in his advocacy of the relational model of disability, Shakespeare acknowledges that it has not had a major practical impact on disability policy in Nordic countries (2006, p. 26). In these states, welfare and educational policies continue to rely on medical and psychological interpretations and labels. Moreover, research is often focused on defining impairment-specific populations of disabled people, such as people with 'learning disabilities', for example, rather than oppression or discrimination (Tøssebro and Kittelsaa, 2004). For Shakespeare, discrimination and oppression are less evident in Nordic states on account of their 'historically generous' welfare policies (2006, p. 26). Notably, evidence to the contrary for Sweden is provided by Elaine Johansson (Inclusion Europe, 2008).

In summary, while post-structuralist accounts have reaffirmed the importance of cultural responses to disability, their arguments sidestep the material reality of impairment and provide little or no insight into how the problem of disablism might be resolved in terms of policy or politics. Indeed, the 'biographical disruption' (Bury, 1982, 1997, 2001) of a sudden spinal cord injury that results in paralysis cannot be explained away with reference to discourse alone. Moreover, if the post-structuralist denial of the body and agency are taken to their logical conclusion, then disability activism and politics are inconceivable: 'Impaired people might as well lie down to the discrimination and exclusion that disables their lives' (Hughes, 2005, p. 90). Further, because both 'impairment' and 'disability' are determined by socially produced discourses, it is certainly possible to determine where impairment ends and disability begins, even if this is 'accomplished with imprecision' (Rapley, 2004, p. 67). Furthermore, to an extent no longer as true of gender and 'race', as the following chapters show there is substantial evidence that disability is widely regarded as 'natural' difference and inferiority and a source of wide-ranging exclusion from mainstream society.

Bringing impairment back in

Although advocates of a social barriers approach to disability are clear about the significance of separating the different worlds of impairment and disability (UPIAS, 1976a, 1976b; Oliver, 1990, 1996a; Finkelstein, 1996, 2002), a growing number of disabled people have voiced their doubts about this strategy (Abberley, 1987; Tremain, 2002; Shakespeare and Watson, 2001; Shakespeare 2006). This has been emphasized most vividly by disabled feminist writers, who link the exclusion of impairment from a social model approach with a general criticism of disability theory for ignoring personal experience (Morris, 1991). Advocates such as Liz Crow (1992), Sally French (1993, 2004), Mairian Scott-Hill (2004) and Tom Shakespeare (2006) argue that the 'social model of disability' must acknowledge that impairment is part of the experience of disability, and further that, even when social barriers are removed, some impairments will continue to exclude disabled people from specific activities.

Those who assert the importance of the conceptual distinction between impairment and disability respond that 'bringing impairment in' clouds both the crucial question of causality and the source of disability discrimination and prejudice, as well as obscuring the most appropriate targets for political action (Finkelstein, 1996; Oliver, 1996a, 2004). They acknowledge that impairments have diverse origins – such as disease, accident and injury – and that disabled people, like non-disabled people, experience illness at various points in their lives. In such cases, medical and rehabilitative interventions are quite appropriate. Far from denying the 'reality' of impairment and its impact on disabled people's lives, the emphasis on separating impairment and disability is a pragmatic attempt to identify and address issues that can be changed through collective action rather than medical or other professional treatments. Oliver argues that the social model is not and never was conceived as a comprehensive theory of disablement, nor as an attempt to deal with the personal restrictions of impairment, but rather an explicit focus on the environmental and social barriers that constitute disability as defined by the UPIAS (Oliver, 1996a, 2004). This introduces a distinction between the 'private' and 'public' domains and an outcome of gendered relations concomitant to capitalist industrial development (Walby, 1990, 1997).

From a materialist feminist perspective, Carol Thomas argues that a focus on personal experiences need not be 'politically diversionary or provide sustenance to the reviled "personal tragedy" approach to disability' (Thomas, 2007, p. 72). Rather, it opens the possibility of exploring the consequences of 'impairment effects' and 'disablism' within the 'private domains' of everyday life. These include experiential accounts of sexual relations (Shakespeare et al., 1996; McCarthy, 1999), family relations (Read, 2000), parenting (Olsen and Clarke, 2003) and childhood (Robinson and Stalker, 1998). Moreover, studies of the lived experience of impairment and the psycho-emotional consequences of coming to terms with both impairment and disability are a growing feature of disability studies analyses of the process of disablement. This has added weight to those who would argue for a more inclusive, 'relational' or 'all-round' approach to the study of the 'lived experience' of disablement and a reappraisal of the meaning of disability which would have the added advantage of connecting with those people with impairments or chronic illnesses, 'old and young', who do not identify as 'disabled' and 'refuse to recognize disabled signifiers in their own lives' (Thomas, 2007, p. 177). Inevitably, however, such arguments underpin the views of those who promote

an 'embodied rationale' in support of the traditional medical sociological view that disability is a restricted activity caused mainly
by impairment or 'chronic illness' (Williams, 1999; Bury, 2001), as
discussed in chapter 3. In so doing, they fuel support for a more
'enlightened guardianship' approach to disability politics and policy
which effectively allows politicians, policy-makers and bureaucrats to
vacillate between medical and political solutions to the process of disablement (Dartington et al., 1981), illustrated by Harlan Hahn's (2002)
discussion of judicial responses to disability discrimination cases in
American law courts referred to in chapter 2.

Review

This chapter has focused on the emergence of disability theory. The
generation of social political understandings of disability, in particular, the concept of independent living and the social model of
disability, has generated new ways of conceptualizing the complex
process of disablement. Indeed, their impact in focusing attention
on social barriers within both the disabled and the academic communities is not in doubt and forms the entry point into chapter
5. But different theoretical and political emphases have emerged.
Whereas some writers have argued for a materialist approach, which
highlights structural factors in the social creation of disability and
dependency, others have championed accounts which privilege personal experience. Of particular note is the recent post-modernist
turn in theorizing disability, calling for a reappraisal and integration
of the insights and work of medical sociologists on chronic illness.
While such diversity is to be expected and welcomed, given the recent
growth of interest in disability issues within mainstream sociology
and social science generally, they should not detract from their policy
implications and the pressing need for barrier removal in order to
enable people with accredited impairments to achieve meaningful
independent living.

    With this in mind, the next chapter turns from these conceptual
and theoretical debates to consider disabled people's experience of a
broad range of social disadvantages and discrimination which apply
throughout the life course across a range of areas, and central to their
struggle to achieve a lifestyle exemplified by the notion of independent living.

CHAPTER
5
Social Exclusion and
Disabling Barriers

Campaigns by disabled people since the 1960s have highlighted their wide-ranging social exclusion and denial of basic citizenship rights. Disabled writers, such as Frank Bowe (1978) in *Handicapping America*, presented a vivid picture of the negative experiences of disabling social and environmental barriers. He identified six key areas of concern: the built environment, public attitudes, education, the labour market, the law and personal relations. While a few academic studies recognized these economic and social disadvantages (Albrecht, 1976; Blaxter, 1976; Townsend 1979), it was not until the 1990s that disability (disablism) gained broad-based recognition as a significant source of social inequality.

This chapter examines the diverse structural and cultural barriers to disabled people's participation in mainstream society. It starts by reviewing the emergence of a welfare state since the 1940s and social policies directed specifically at disabled people. The changing economic, social and political context since the mid-twentieth century provides the backcloth to addressing social exclusion. Subsequent sections document the form and character of social barriers experienced by disabled people in major areas of everyday life, such as education, employment, financial circumstances, the built environment, housing and transport, and leisure. Research studies and official statistics alike provide compelling evidence of major differences in the life chances of disabled people compared with the rest of the population and also of the interaction of disability and other social divisions. Over the last decade the divide has narrowed slightly, but a major question mark remains against New Labour's ambition that, 'By 2025, disabled people in Britain should have full opportunities and choices to improve their quality of life and will be respected and included as equal members of society' (Cabinet Office, 2005, p. 12).

Disability policy and the welfare state

With the growth of industrial capitalism, the situation of those unable to secure a place in the paid labour market worsened with the decline in the family-based system of production and alternative means of support. Central and local state administration became increasingly important sources of financial and other support as well as social control. Deborah Stone details the trajectories of disability policy in America, Britain and Germany in terms of the search for a balance between two distributive systems: one based on work, the other on need. The 'fundamental' dilemma (1985, p. 18) confronting policy-makers was how redistribution by the state based on need (for social service and welfare support) can be accomplished without undermining the principle of distribution according to participation in the economic system of production.

Historically, the state has regarded non-participation in the labour market with considerable suspicion. With industrialization, an orthodox medical profession assumed a crucial role in distinguishing 'genuine' claimants on the basis of proven 'sickness' and 'disability' and the associated entitlement to certain 'privileges and exemptions' (Stone, 1985, p. 21). Stone argues that medical management of the disability category became indispensable 'as an instrument of the state in controlling labour supply' (ibid., p. 179) and in facilitating dominant class interests. In Britain, the Poor Law Amendment Act of 1834 exemplified the utilitarian foundations of state policy, reinforced by assumptions that personal inadequacy or unwillingness to work threatened labour discipline.

In order to discourage the poor from seeking public assistance, only indoor relief in the workhouse was provided, and then under conditions designed to deter anyone from extending their stay any longer than absolutely necessary. This enforced institutionalization became the favoured policy for dealing with 'infirm' and 'incapacitated' individuals, although it was justified as an enlightened option by the state and voluntary organizations alike. Disabled children and older people were mostly represented as part of the 'deserving poor', but expectations of a less harsh institutional regime, compared to that which dealt with their 'undeserving' counterparts, were rarely fulfilled, and there was a general stigmatization of recipients of social welfare (Humphries and Gordon, 1992; Borsay, 2005).

At the start of the twentieth century, amidst growing concerns about working-class radicalism and poverty and the high levels of sickness and impairment among potential military conscripts, the Liberal government initiated a series of health and welfare policy reforms. These upheld an 'individualistic' explanation of poverty and concentrated on a 'residual' solution (Titmuss, 1958), whereby the state provided a basic 'safety net' for those lacking any support. State benefits were set at a subsistence level to encourage recipients to seek paid employment. The political wisdom endured that welfare assistance encouraged individual dependence and militated against private initiative, hard work and thrift, thus increasing the burden on the productive members of society.

This residual approach prevailed until the 1940s, when a 'post-war settlement' between capital and labour produced wide-ranging institutional reforms. The blueprint for increased social welfare intervention was the Beveridge Report (Beveridge, 1942). It targeted the elimination of the 'five giants' – want, disease, ignorance, squalor and idleness – as necessary to advance equality and social integration: 'What matters is that there is a general enrichment of the concrete substance of civilized life, a general reduction of risk and insecurity, an equalization between the more and the less fortunate at all levels' (Marshall, 1950, p. 56). This 'welfare state' strategy underpinned policies for the National Health Service (NHS), universal and free primary and secondary education, compulsory insurance for all individuals in paid work against unemployment and old age, various non-contributory benefits for those not insured, family and child support, and an expansion in local authority house building. Notwithstanding the significant growth of the public sector, social policy measures also reinforced 'voluntary, charitable, informal and other forms of private welfare' (Ginsburg, 1992, p. 3).

Overall, these reforms represented a compromise between three overlapping 'welfare settlements': political-economic, social and organizational (Clarke and Newman, 1997, pp. 1–8). At the political-economic level, government policy-making in the early post-1945 years was rooted in a Keynesian approach to macro-economic policy that emphasized state management of supply and demand. This was reinforced by a commitment to full employment to cement working-class support while also maximizing tax revenues and reducing claims for welfare benefits (Lowe, 1993). The overall design of social policy entailed a national pooling of risk that underpinned the political and ideological claims for a progressive, social democratic welfare state. It became the litmus test of a civilized society by guaranteeing the basic needs of all citizens, irrespective of their ability to pay (Marshall, 1950). However, in practice, the welfare reforms represented a compromise between a citizenship that was 'state-guaranteed' and 'market-driven' – that is, related to economic participation (Clarke and Newman, 1997, p. 1).

The 'social' settlement that informed welfare state measures incorporated specific notions of family, work and nation (Williams, 1992, pp. 211–12). 'Family' and 'work' presumed the 'norm' of a wage-earning male maintaining other family members. This, in turn, established groups of dependants, including children, older people and married women, plus those in ill-health or who had a diagnosed impairment (Clarke and Langan, 1993, p. 28). In a similar way, the design of the welfare state was geared to 'the British Race and British ideals' and ignored minority ethnic groups. The effect of these exclusionary assumptions was to 'naturalize' (that is, confirm and reinforce) social divisions, not only of gender and 'race' but also 'the distinction between the able-bodied and the "handicapped" ' (Clarke and Newman, 1997, p. 4).

The third of the welfare state settlements was 'organizational'. It comprised 'a commitment to two modes of co-ordination: bureaucratic administration and professionalism' (Clarke and Newman, 1997, pp. 4–8). Public service norms and values in administration reinforced claims that the new system would be more impartial and even-handed in the way it dealt with the different sections and interests in the population. The bureaucratic adherence to agreed rules and regulations in administering social welfare policy and programmes complemented claims to professional expertise and neutrality. The professions gained further state backing and authority in identifying social problems and implementing policy responses. This also enhanced their occupational control and autonomy in the day-to-day delivery of services. This was most evident in professional influence within the National Health Service, and to a lesser extent, in education and the personal social services.

The basic structure and principles of the welfare state remained broadly intact until the 1970s. At that time, a global economic crisis triggered calls to curtail public expenditure and intervention. The election in 1979 of a Conservative government, headed by Margaret Thatcher, signalled a shift away from the political-economic settlement of the 1940s. This paralleled a similar political advance of the 'radical right' in the United States with the election in 1980 of Ronald Reagan as president. The policies of the welfare state were now identified as a primary cause of rather than the solution to major economic and social problems. This produced calls to restructure or 'roll back' the state, reduce taxation, and introduce market forces or quasi-markets into the delivery of welfare services as a way of enhancing their efficiency and effectiveness. The encouragement of private sector involvement in central social policy areas such as health and pensions, education and home ownership illustrated a general retrenchment of state-provided welfare.

The political barometer swung towards market-driven citizenship. This 'neo-liberal' agenda extended to criticism of public sector monopolies and their underlying (bureaucratic) norms and values as inefficient and ineffective. Instead, the Conservative government advocated the virtues of market competition and developed a mixed economy of welfare, with the introduction of commercial sector management techniques into the public sector as well as embarking on a policy of privatization. An associated feature was an enhanced role for 'consumers' by encouraging more choice and user involvement in service organization and delivery. Needless to say, the changing welfare-state policy context presented new opportunities and constraints for disability policy and politics.

In response, a new wave of political campaigns focused on the threatened cut-backs in state welfare provision. Activists argued that institutional and professional power in the design and implementation of social policies reflected and exacerbated social inequalities rooted in, for example, patriarchy and racism (Williams, 1993). These protests extended to a rising militancy among disabled people challenging their 'second-class' status. Their demands centred on achieving a reasonable and appropriate level of welfare benefits and improved service support, ranging from technical aids and adaptations to housing, and less enforced reliance on the informal support of family and friends (Davis, 1981; DeJong, 1981). Criticism ranged from the administration of eligibility and assessment criteria to the inappropriate and excessive surveillance and regulation of their lives by medical practitioners and allied health and social service staff (see chapters 6 and 7).

Social exclusion, disability and New Labour

Since the 1990s, and particularly in the policy statements of the New Labour government elected in 1997, the term 'social exclusion' has moved centre stage. This emulates similar trends in other parts of Europe, North America and Australasia (Byrne, 2005). Its current usage covers 'the dynamic process of being shut out, fully or partially, from any of the social, economic, political or cultural systems which determine the social integration of a person in society' (Walker and Walker, 1997, p. 8). It encompasses those individuals or groups who are 'cut off from the mainstream of opportunities society has to offer' (Giddens, 1998, p. 103).

Ruth Levitas (1998) outlines three main discourses around social exclusion: the traditional redistributionist argument of the social democratic left; the dependency/moral underclass emphasis illustrated in many neo-conservative writings, such as Thatcher in the UK and Reagan in the USA; and the social integrationist discourse that reformulates Émile Durkheim's (1984) emphasis on the centrality of

Table 5.1 A conceptual matrix of poverty and social exclusion

	Static outcome	Dynamic process
Income	Poverty	Impoverishment
Multidimensional	Deprivation	Social exclusion

Source: Adapted from Vleminckx and Berghman 2001, table 2.1

work and social order in modern societies. She argues that the New Labour government articulated a mixture of dependency and social integrationist discourses. Yet, while dismissive of the divisive and 'uncaring' policies of Thatcherism, New Labour retained most of its neo-liberal, anti-collectivist and globalizing agendas and downplayed capitalism as a major source of social inequalities (Fairclough, 2000; Byrne, 2005).

New Labour defined social exclusion as 'a short-hand label for what can happen when individuals or areas suffer from a combination of linked problems such as unemployment, poor skills, low incomes, poor housing, high crime environments, bad health and family breakdown' (DSS, 1999, p. 23). The policy aim was to reduce poverty and welfare dependency, particularly by increasing the proportion of people in paid employment, while also emphasizing individual responsibility and mandatory requirements to make the most of the greater number of opportunities provided (Giddens, 1998; Jordan, 1998). New Labour sponsored the modernization of public sector service organization and delivery and increased involvement from the voluntary and private sectors as well as individual social and political participation, while extending anti-discrimination legislation. It also encouraged new hybrid forms of 'work'.

A central task for empirical researchers is to identify the main dimensions to inequality of opportunity in order to assess changing patterns of social exclusion. As an illustration, Koen Vleminckx and Jos Berghman (2001) outline a conceptual matrix that incorporates, first, a distinction between level of income (relative poverty or deprivation) and a multifaceted concept (covering not simply income but other valued goods, opportunities and rights); and, second, a division between static outcomes and a dynamic process, with a time element (table 5.1). What they term 'social exclusion' is multidimensional and dynamic. It extends beyond the paid labour market to cover social participation in such areas as the built environment, housing and transport, leisure, family life and social relationships. This accords with New Labour's focus on multiple and fluid forms of participation (Byrne, 2005).

Substantive inequalities identified for improvement comprise consumption (income and wealth, access to services, housing, transport and the built environment), production (employment and education) and social interaction (social and political participation and leisure) in line with disabled people's own expressed priorities and 'capabilities' or 'actual freedoms' to 'appear in public without shame; to participate in the life of the community; to move around freely, etc.' (Raveaud and Salais, 2001, p. 59). This emulates demands that research should recognize the possibility of national and cultural injustices, or what Nancy Fraser (1997, 2000) terms 'maldistribution and misrecognition', while examining how socio-economic location interacts with other lines of social division.

Education

With the growth of industrialization and a complex division of labour, schemes for the formal education of children gathered momentum in Western societies. Schools acquired particular significance in providing the basic discipline and training in readiness for work and maintaining social order generally (Bowles and Gintis, 1976). Additionally, through the nineteenth century, a distinctive system of segregated schooling for disabled children took root (Winzer, 1993), with 'special schools' for 'crippled' and 'physically defective' children, including the 'Blind and Deaf' and 'educationally backward', continuing to multiply in the early twentieth century. Dominant class interests expected such schools would instil moral virtues and lessen the demands for welfare support from local authorities and the state (Humphries and Gordon, 1992).

In Britain, the 1944 Education Act outlined the first radical break with this separate ('special') schools policy. Local education authorities (LEAs) were required to deliver education according to 'age, aptitude and ability', as long as the schooling of non-disabled pupils was not disrupted. In practice, this became the pretext for expanding special school places for children with impairments (Tomlinson, 1982). Until 1971, responsibility for these schools rested with the Department of Health and Social Security (DHSS). This reinforced a medicalized approach to disabled pupils' education that emphasized individual pathology and psychological testing of intelligence, with children separated into categories of inferiority such as 'subnormal' and 'maladjusted' (Apple, 1990; Barton, 1995).

In the mid-1980s, the Office of Population Censuses and Surveys (OPCS) estimated that two-thirds of disabled children under sixteen living in residential homes and over a third of those living in private households had attended a special school (Meltzer et al., 1989). A decade later, political and educational support began to dissipate amidst growing concerns that the segregated system was harmful to disabled children's future prospects. A government-sponsored inquiry, chaired by Lady Mary Warnock (1978), advocated situating special provision within mainstream schools. It distinguished three main forms of integration: *locational* – special units or classrooms on the same site as an 'ordinary' school; *social* – co-location complemented by social interaction; and *functional* – 'special needs' children join their peers on a part- or full-time basis. Its recommendations informed the 1981 Education Act which also required LEAs to assess children with an accredited impairment and produce a Statement of Educational Needs (SEN). By 2006–7, 2.8 per cent of pupils in the UK were classified as SEN, but in special schools this figure rose to 95 per cent (DfES, 2007).

Subsequent education acts were more ambivalent about promoting inclusion: the introduction of a national curriculum in 1988 suggested that disabled children would no longer be denied access to 'core' subjects, but the traditional preoccupation with individual (within-child) limitations endured (Florian et al., 2004). Again, there was an extension of market competition into the allocation of public funding, with examination results interpreted as a key performance indicator in constructing school 'league tables'. This fuelled school opposition to inclusion, on the grounds that disabled children achieved lower exam results, while making higher demands on teaching resources. The DfEE (1997) endorsed the 1994 UNESCO Salamanca World Statement on Special Needs Education, which advocated the inclusion of children with special educational needs in mainstream schools and closer links between the sectors. The proportion of all children attending special schools, which rose to just under 1 per cent at the start of the 1980s, declined slowly to 0.8 per cent (Norwich, 1994; Rustemier and Vaughan, 2005; DfES, 2007), while the number of special schools fell from 1,830 in 1990–1 to 1,391 in 2006–7 (DfES, 2007). Moreover, these figures masked considerable variation, with segregation increasing slightly in a third of LEAs in England (Rustemier and Vaughan, 2005).

One significant outcome of special schools is the divide in educational outcomes. National surveys report that over 25 per cent of disabled adults have no qualifications, more than twice the non-disabled adult rate (Grewal et al., 2002; ONS, 2006). This gap is particularly stark for people with learning difficulties and for mental health system users (Jacobsen, 2002; Meltzer et al., 2002). Special schools entered 27 per cent of their pupils for five or more GCSE examinations, compared with 92 per cent of fifteen-year-olds nationally, and just 8 per cent attain one of the top three grades (A–C), compared with 79 per cent overall (DfES, 2007). While special school results have improved over the last decade (G. Thomas, 1997), the average exam points score of 50 compares very unfavourably with the 361 average for all schools (DfES, 2007). Moreover, children rated as SEN in mainstream schools are more than twice as likely as special school pupils to take GCSE or GNVQ exams (Audit Commission, 2002a).

A further hurdle for disabled and SEN pupils is the dominance of a standards agenda and of examination assessment criteria that prioritize outcomes over process issues and disregard the appropriateness of the curriculum design for all children (Hall et al., 2004; Ofsted, 2004; QCA, 2004). For critics, attempts 'to safeguard the "integrity" of qualifications and protect existing standards' disregard the process of learning-generated barriers for disabled pupils (Miller et al., 2005, p. 70). The dominant discourse emphasizes academic success and 'ableist' values (Benjamin, 2003) and is reinforced by both low levels of accessibility in secondary schools (Audit Commission, 2002a) and restricted opportunities for participation in out-of-school activities (Dockrell et al., 2002; Gray, 2002).

The number of disabled students going into further education after secondary school has increased, although they often experience a separate curriculum and classes, with little allowance for student preferences in their education and skills training. Work placements have been criticized for failing to facilitate the transition to 'qualifications and employment' (Gray, 2002, p. 42) and for resembling 'superior day centres', particularly for students with the label of learning difficulties (Jacobsen, 2002). The emphasis is on low-level 'social training', 'general life skills', and basic numeracy and literacy, together with some impairment-related skills such as lip reading. More positively, since 1990, the number of post-secondary school students in England receiving the Disabled Students Allowance rose sharply to over 40,000 following the removal of means testing and the extension of allowances to part-time and post-graduate students (DfES, 2003). Additionally, the proportion of applicants for university admission reporting an impairment increased from 4 to 5.1 per cent between 2000 and 2004.

Official explanations for this wide gap in educational performance concentrate on the relationship between impairment and SEN. Yet a range of social disadvantages are closely associated with SEN, including social class and ethnicity (Dockrell et al., 2002; Dewson et al., 2004), and many children have more than one impairment and multiple, complex support needs (Cabinet Office, 2005). Other accounts emphasize low expectations among disabled children and teachers, a non-academic curriculum, inadequate facilities and resources, high rates of sickness-absence and a general failure to prepare disabled pupils for the economic and social demands of the post-school environment (Wade and Moore, 1993; Barton, 1995; DRC, 2002). Some critics identify teachers as one of the main 'disabling professions' in industrial societies (Illich et al., 1977): 'It is the professional status of those involved in assessment processes that legitimates the complex procedures which have been developed to exclude or marginalise young people from mainstream education' (Tomlinson, 1996, p. 175). This encourages arguments to replace the emphasis on 'special educational needs' with 'additional support for learning' (Scottish Executive, 2004; Miller et al., 2005) and greater policy attention to social and environmental barriers.

New Labour's measures to overcome child poverty and address the lack of appropriate childcare and pre-school provision have particular significance for disabled children. The equal opportunities path was reinforced by establishing the Learning and Skills Council (LSC) in 2000, while the Special Educational Needs and Disability Act (SENDA) 2001 required schools, colleges and universities to take 'reasonable steps' to counter barriers to effective learning and enhance disabled children's participation in mainstream education. *Removing Barriers to Achievement* championed communities of learners who, regardless of impairment, are enabled to 'learn, play and develop alongside each other' (DfES, 2004, p. 6), while the Disability Discrimination Act 2005 and the Disability Equality Duty increased the inclusionary pressure on educational institutions (CSIE, 2005a, 2005b). Support was made available for closer working arrangements between different types of school, co-location, joint placement of children in special and main-stream contexts, flexible use of specialist staff, disability training for staff in mainstream schools, and closer partnerships with parents (DfES, 2003, 2004).

The existence of special schools remains a divisive issue. A sig-nificant proportion of parents and some disabled children prefer this option. They point to the high levels of social isolation and bul-lying experienced by disabled children in mainstream schools and the more supportive peer culture in special schools (Saunders, 1994; Hendey and Pascal, 2002). The Deaf community has been particularly adamant that Deaf children in mainstream schools become outsid-ers because of the unsympathetic hearing culture, with its reliance on 'high tech' aids and lip reading (Ladd, 1988; Gregory and Hartley, 1991). Deaf parents and their organizations have been notable cham-pions of schools for Deaf children where Sign Language is the medium of instruction and informal interaction, and Deaf culture is emphasized. More generally, advocates of special schools argue that they provide a more accessible environment, appropriate techni-cal aids and equipment, trained and experienced SEN teachers, and a better pupil–teacher ratio. Indeed, New Labour's policy to create educational 'centres of excellence' included the award of 'specialist' status to a number of special schools, thus reinforcing their role with extra funding and a remit to share expertise with their mainstream counterparts.

Opponents of special schools declare that they constitute 'the main channels for disseminating able-bodied/minded perceptions of the world and ensuring that disabled school leavers are socially immature and isolated' (BCODP, 1986, p. 6), and so perpetuate disabled people's subordination. They highlight the benefits of inclusive schooling as part of a wider commitment to social equality and citizenship rights. These encompass fostering friendships between disabled and non-disabled children and helping to remove ignorance and negative stereotypes; providing disabled children with a broader curriculum; promoting access to subject specialist teachers; and offering opportunities to develop self-esteem and confidence (Barton, 1995, p. 31). This represents a continuing debate both about whether the abolition of the special education system will benefit all disabled children and concerning its impact on the mainstream school system.

Financial circumstances

Tackling poverty is a stated goal of governments around the world, and there is widespread acceptance that those unable to meet their material needs experience much higher levels of ill-health, impairment and premature death than the rest of the population (Townsend et al., 1992). Most often the focus is on 'relative' poverty – where household income is either below 60 per cent of the median income or generally indicates a lack of financial resources to meet minimum 'social' necessities and maintain a reasonable living standard, while allowing for changes over time and differences between societies (Townsend, 1979; Mack and Lansley, 1985).

National surveys consistently report the much higher proportion of disabled people at or below the poverty line (Harris et al., 1971a; Martin and White, 1988; Cabinet Office, 2005).

> In general, the greater poverty of disabled people is explained by their uneven or limited access to the principal resource systems of society – the labour market and wage system, national insurance and its associated schemes, and the wealth-accumulating systems, particularly home ownership, life insurance and occupational pension schemes; by the indirect limitation which disability imposes upon the capacities of relatives, pooling personal resources in full or part in the household or family, to earn incomes and accumulate wealth themselves; and by the failure of society to recognise, or to recognise only unevenly

Table 5.2 Quintile distribution of income of working-age adults – disabled and non-disabled, Britain, 2002					
	Bottom quintile	Second quintile	Third quintile	Fourth quintile	Top quintile
1 or more disabled adult(s) (per cent)	28	21	19	17	15
No disabled adult (per cent)	15	14	19	24	28

Source: DWP (2003).

> or fitfully, the additional resources that are required in disablement
> to obtain standards of living equivalent to those of the non-disabled.
> (Townsend, 1979, pp. 734–5)

OPCS survey data from the mid-1980s demonstrated that a disproportionate number of disabled people depended on state benefits as their main or sole source of income. Part of the explanation is that a relatively high percentage of disabled people are over retirement age and only a third are in paid work. Overall, only 19 per cent of non-pensioner disabled adults received an 'above average' income, compared with 42 per cent of the general population (Martin and White, 1988, p. 31).

Recent surveys suggest little has changed, with a poverty rate of 30 per cent for working-age disabled adults – twice the level for non-disabled people – while this gap has widened slightly since the 1990s (Palmer et al., 2007) (see table 5.2). After adjustments for extra impairment costs, half of all disabled adults have incomes below the 'official' threshold for poverty. Among households where someone acquired an impairment, 14 per cent fall below the poverty line, twice the rate for households without a disabled member (Burchardt, 2003a).

Disabled married women are much more likely to experience financial deprivation compared with their non-disabled counterparts: 35 per cent of women with a 'minor' impairment, and 47 per cent of those with the most 'severe' rating, fell below the poverty line compared with 21 per cent of non-disabled women (Townsend, 1979, pp. 733–4). Later studies indicate this gap increases significantly among individuals over sixty years of age. Up to 55 per cent of families with a disabled child, and 27 per cent in households with a disabled adult of working age, fall on or below the poverty line. Only 3 per cent of mothers of disabled children are in full-time employment, compared with 22 per cent of mothers of non-disabled children, while the costs of bringing up a disabled child are three times higher than those for a non-disabled child (Gordon et al., 2000). This leads to a higher likelihood of family separation or breakdown and of a disabled child being placed in residential care (Lawton, 1998; Morris et al., 2002). Hence, the pressure to strengthen policies against child poverty and, specifically, support for disabled children (Cabinet Office, 2005).

A common criticism by disabled people of statistics on their financial position is that they do not take proper account of 'impairment costs'. OPCS examined such expenditure in four areas: capital payments for special equipment; capital payments for 'general' support, such as a washing machine; regular impairment-related expenditure, such as medicines and domestic back-up; and regular payments for an impairment-related component of 'normal' expenditure, such as additional food or transport costs. It calculated these as 8 per cent of average income – but with significant variation related to severity and type of impairment (Martin and White, 1988, pp. 52–4).

This approach was strongly disputed by organizations of disabled people, particularly because it underestimated expenditure on 'one-off' special items by only considering purchases in the previous year, and included data on very few people with a 'severe impairment' (Abberley, 1992). The Disablement Income Group conducted a revised study and concluded that disabled people's average extra weekly expenditure was 58 per cent above OPCS figures (Thompson et al., 1988). Recent research confirms the much higher levels of spending on heating, transport, aids and equipment, diets and other impairment-related costs, and the inadequacy of extra costs benefits (Burchardt and Zaidi, 2003; Tibble, 2005). One study developed a budget standard to represent the 'minimum essential resources' necessary for disabled people's needs (Smith et al., 2004). The researchers calculated that a person with high to medium support needs (mobility and personal) required a budget of £1,513; a person with a hearing impairment £1,336; someone with a visual impairment £632; and a person with low to medium needs £389. The weekly income of a disabled person dependent solely on benefits fell below the level required for an 'acceptable' quality of life by around £200, although the cost of public services received was not taken into account.

How then has social security policy responded? In the mid-twentieth century, the two principal schemes comprised the war disablement pension and benefits provided under the National Insurance (Industrial Injury) Act 1946, for those who acquired an impairment at work, with an individual's functional loss estimated against a non-disabled person of a similar age and sex.

> Rather than depending upon the impact of disablement, an individual's benefit entitlement, and the amount of benefit received, rests crucially on: how the disability occurred, the age when a claim is made, the length of time spent in the UK, ability to work, and whether national insurance contributions have been paid for the required period of time. (Walker and Walker, 1991, p. 25)

It was not until the 1970s that this 'compensation for injury' emphasis was significantly overhauled. A range of new measures included

Table 5.3 Types of social security benefits and tax credits for disabled people	
Benefit features	Examples
Extra costs	
Designed to help towards additional costs of living	Attendance Allowance
	Disability Living Allowance
Earnings replacement	
Designed to provide an income for people unable to work or carry out household duties due to long-term sickness or disability	Incapacity Benefit (Severe Disablement Allowance)
	Jobseeker's Allowance
Means-tested	
Designed to top up income to a minimum level/meet housing costs, often with additional premiums for disabled people	Income Support
	Working Tax Credit (replaced by Disabled Persons Tax credit)
	Housing Benefit
Compensatory	
Designed to compensate people who became disabled as a result of military service or employment	Industrial Injuries Disability Benefit
	War Disablement Pension

Source: Adapted from Cabinet Office, 2005, table 2.1.

a general attendance allowance (a universal benefit for those with a severe impairment and high support needs), a mobility allowance, a non-contributory invalidity pension, and an Invalid Care Allowance (ICA). However, these hardly amounted to a coherent or comprehensive package of disability benefits.

In 1979, the newly elected Conservative government embarked on a wide-ranging review of the social security system as part of its planned restructuring and 'downsizing' of the welfare state and reduction in the 'welfare dependency' culture. Its proposals stressed help for those who wanted to work and for those with the highest support needs (DSS, 1990). Successive governments acknowledged the 'benefits trap', or disincentive to work, because the move into paid employment generates less income than that received from disability benefits – particularly if a person is working less than sixteen hours a week (Noble et al., 1997). This underscored the introduction of Disability Working Allowance (DWA), a means-tested benefit to help people with impairments in low-paid employment, as well as Disability Living Allowance (DLA), a non-contributory, non-means-tested benefit designed to cover some of the extra costs of impairment.

Under New Labour, there have been four main types of benefit for adults of working age with evidence of a limiting long-standing health problem or 'disability' (table 5.3).

The benefits and tax credit system is complicated by its use of five main tests of 'disability':

1 *incapacity for work* (Statutory Sick Pay, Incapacity Benefit and Income Support), based on the 'Own Occupation Test' and the 'Personal Capability Assessment'
2 *needing care and supervision* in performing selected every-day tasks (Disability Living Allowance care component and Attendance Allowance)
3 *unable to walk far* (mobility component of Disability Living Allowance and war pensioner's mobility supplement)
4 *degree of disablement* (Industrial Disablement Benefit, War Disablement Pension and Vaccine Damage Payments)
5 *restricted employment opportunities* (Working Tax Credit disability element) (Cabinet Office, 2005).

Interpretation of these qualifying criteria presents particular diffi-culties for individuals with impairments characterized by fluctuating symptoms and/or their severity, such as mental distress, arthritis and multiple sclerosis.

The total number of people on Incapacity Benefit (IB) – the main out-of-work disability benefit – increased threefold in the twenty-five years after 1979, but declined to 2.68 million in February 2007 following government initiatives to move disabled people into paid work. In 2008, IB was replaced by a new employment support allow-ance, backed by more stringent work capability tests. The emphasis shifted to what people can, rather than what they cannot do, with the abolition of some tests such as not being able to walk more than 400 metres, and more emphasis being placed on IT skills.

The post-1945 introduction of income maintenance benefits for disabled people has not broken the underlying link between disability status and poverty. This adds fuel to debates about the most effective way of supporting disabled people into work, with one estimate that governments allocated almost twenty times as much to social security benefits than to employment policies for disabled people (Berthoud et al., 1993). Such debates underpin the continuing development of 'New Labour' policies to modernize the social security system, with measures targeted at disabled people.

Employment

It is widely accepted that the work we do has a crucial impact on our social and material circumstances and well-being. Yet the historical

Table 5.4 Economic activity and unemployment rates for disabled and non-disabled people in Britain, 1995–2006

Year	Disabled people		Non-disabled people	
	Economic activity rate (per cent)	Unemploy-ment rate (per cent)	Economic activity rate (per cent)	Unemploy-ment rate (per cent)
1999	52.0	10.3	84.6	5.4
2003	53.3	7.8	84.5	4.4
2006	55.3	8.8	84.4	5.0
England, 2006	56.3	8.8	84.2	5.0
Scotland, 2006	50.5	8.7	86.6	5.4
Wales, 2006	48.5	9.8	83.7	5.2

Source: ONS (2006), Labour Force Survey.

experience of disabled people within industrial capitalism has been of significant exclusion from, and marginalization in, the labour market. Through the twentieth century, it was only during wartime that labour shortages forced employers drastically to alter their recruitment practices. Yet with pressure to secure jobs for those returning from military service, disabled people's activity rate returned to its previous levels (Humphries and Gordon, 1992; Thornton and Lunt, 1995). This encouraged suggestions that disabled people comprise part of a 'reserve army of labour' drawn into paid employment at specific times, although a significant minority has little prospect of joining the current labour market (Hyde, 2000; Grover and Piggott, 2005).

Since 1945, the employment rate (i.e. number in paid work) for disabled people has remained well below that for the whole population. In April–June 2006 it was 50.4 per cent, compared with 80.2 per cent among non-disabled people. However, this represents a relative advance since 1999, when the comparable rates were 46.7 and 80.0 per cent. The overall figure also masks considerable variation, falling to 22 to 23 per cent for individuals categorized with a 'mental illness' and 'learning difficulties'. As for the total population, employment rates are linked to the level of educational qualification. They are highest for those with a degree (75.7 per cent compared with 89.8 per cent for non-disabled people), falling to 59.5 per cent and 81.6 per cent for those with a GCSE 'A' level or equivalent, and plummeting to 23.2 per cent (60.1 per cent) for people without any qualifications. Table 5.4 also illustrates marked contrasts in employment rates within Britain (ONS, 2006) – that is, the number employed plus those available for work.

Additionally, disabled people experience relatively higher rates, and longer periods, of unemployment (Martin et al., 1989; ONS, 2006). The divide endures in times of relative economic growth, suggesting that barriers to work are deeply embedded. There is a noteworthy level of 'early retirement' among disabled workers, while unemployment rates among younger disabled people are particularly high (ONS, 2005). However, the gap has narrowed slightly: in 1995–6, the unemployment rates for disabled and non-disabled people were 21.2 and 7.6 per cent respectively, compared with 8.8 and 5.0 per cent in 2006 (Sly et al., 1995; ONS, 2006). Nonetheless, the average annual rate of non-disabled people moving back into employment is six times higher than that for disabled people (Burchardt, 2003b). Similarly, among those employees who acquire an impairment, one in six loses their job within a year (Bardasi et al., 2000; Jenkins and Rigg, 2003).

In the labour market, disabled people experience 'vertical' and 'horizontal' segregation: that is, they are overrepresented in less skilled, part-time work with fewer opportunities for promotion and tend to be congregated in specific sectors or types of work. However, the gap has narrowed since the 1990s, with 25 per cent of disabled people classified as 'managers and senior officials' and in 'professional occupations' compared with 29 per cent of non-disabled people (ONS, 2006). Disabled women experience most restrictions on job opportunities – with a much higher proportion in unskilled or semi-skilled posts, and higher rates of part-time working compared with non-disabled women. The pay gap between disabled people and their non-disabled male and female counterparts has narrowed only slightly, from 84 per cent in the mid-1980s (for males working more than thirty hours a week) to 88 per cent in the early twenty-first century, and from 91 to 96 per cent for disabled female employees (DWP, 2004; ONS, 2006).

Through the twentieth century, governments opted mostly for a minimalist and largely voluntarist approach towards the employment of disabled people, as illustrated by the Disabled Persons (Employment) Acts of 1944 and 1958. The 1944 Act provided for the setting up of a disabled persons' employment register; a nation-wide Disablement Resettlement Service (DRS) with assessment, rehabilitation and training facilities; a specialized employment placement service; a duty on employers of twenty or more workers to employ a 3 per cent quota of registered disabled people; designated employment; and a National Advisory Council and local advisory committees (Thornton and Lunt, 1995). The designated employment scheme for disabled people introduced in 1946 effectively limited its focus to car-park and lift attendants.

In the 1950s, employment policy initiatives concentrated on labour supply (that is, making disabled people more 'employable'). Successive governments disregarded demand-side factors, such as employers' unwillingness to recruit disabled people, with levels consistently below the stipulated 3 per cent quota from 1961. Indeed, this figure fell below 2 per cent in 1975 and plummeted to 0.7 per cent in 1993. Yet there were only ten prosecutions of employers, with the last case in 1975, while the maximum fine set at £100 in 1944 was never increased. In the early 1990s, between 40 and 60 per cent of employers did not have any disabled employees (Honey et al., 1993; Dench et al., 1996). Employers attributed this to the lack of disabled applicants, safety concerns and communication difficulties, and the additional costs disabled employees generated. However, studies indicate a much higher rejection rate for disabled as compared with non-disabled applicants, and little evidence of the claimed cost implications (Graham et al., 1990; Honey et al., 1993; Dench et al., 1996). The quota scheme and system of reserved occupations was overtaken by the Disability Discrimination Act (DDA) 1995. Government policy also shifted from a system of segregated and subsidised sheltered workshops to encourage 'supported placements' in the mainstream labour market.

A series of organizational changes in the employment services focused on improving the assessment and advice given to disabled people and employers – with the DRS evolving into a nation-wide network of semi-autonomous Placing, Assessment and Counselling Teams (PACTs). Additionally, campaigns were mounted to persuade employers of the 'business case' for recruiting disabled staff and to sponsor voluntary codes of 'good practice' for employing disabled people. However, surveys of employer behaviour indicated slow and uneven changes, with a third identifying risks in hiring a disabled person and almost a half suggesting difficulties in retaining an employee 'who became disabled' (Roberts et al., 2004, p. 2). There has been a matching indifference and some hostility among trade unions to employing disabled workers (Oliver, 1990, p. 219).

Government initiatives continued to explore financial incentives for employers to recruit disabled workers. For example, the 'Job Introduction Scheme' enabled employers to receive a grant towards the wages of a disabled worker during a six-week trial period. The cost of making premises accessible was addressed by the 'Access to Work' programme and subsidies for low wages accompanying the introduction of the 'Disability Working Allowance' (DWA) in 1991. The supported employment scheme allowed employers to claim compensation for the lower productivity of employees with 'severe disabilities' (Hyde, 1996).

The passage of the DDA 1995 represented a new policy dimension by including a statutory right to challenge discrimination in the workplace. It covers recruitment, terms of employment, promotion, transfer, training and dismissal, although not work experience or voluntary work. However, discrimination is only illegal if proven 'unreasonable', unlike similar legislation on sex and 'race'. This means that the employer has to make appropriate adjustments to working conditions or physical features that might substantially disadvantage a disabled person, such as accessibility, job restructuring, part-time or modified work schedules, the acquisition or modification of equipment and training materials, and the provision of qualified readers and interpreters. However, the legislation does not require employers to adopt minimum standards (Gooding, 1995), unlike anti-discriminatory legislation in other Western industrialized countries (Quinn et al., 1993; Doyle, 1995, 2008). Moreover, the resort to litigation is costly and time-consuming. Subsequent changes included in the Act extend the legislative remit by placing public authorities under a (statutory) Disability Equality Duty to uphold equal opportunities.

More generally, New Labour's modernizing reforms for the welfare state emphasized 'welfare to work' or 'workfare'. A central objective has been to reduce drastically the number of individuals who do not work and claim welfare benefits. Programmes to increase disabled people's labour market participation have multiplied, with an emphasis on improving 'employability' and in-work support allied to more government-provided training, including the New Deal for Disabled People, Access to Work and Pathways to Work schemes. Rates of job retention and return to work after an enforced break have also been targeted (Kellard et al., 2002; Mercer, 2005). These introduced compulsory work-based interviews with a Jobcentre Plus personal adviser every six months to develop an action plan, access to vocational and NHS rehabilitation support, with financial incentives including work credit payments for those entering work with pay of less than £15,000 per year, and a National Minimum Wage (Cabinet Office, 2005; DWP, 2005). Specific measures were directed at Incapacity Benefit recipients.

The Cabinet Office (2005) set out its long-term aspiration to bring disabled people's employment rate to 80 per cent of the working-age population – in part to offset the effects of a decline in the working-age population. Calculations suggested that this would require an additional 2.5 million disabled people to enter paid work. Such policy initiatives indicate a wider 'recommodifying' of disabled people's labour, either to meet future labour market contingencies or as a means of restricting wage demands (Russell, 2002; Bauman, 2005; Grover, 2003). Others express optimism that the changing nature of work in advanced capitalist society – more flexible working hours, short-term contracts, increased reliance on information technology, home-based working, and an individualized and fragmented workforce – offers particular opportunities for disabled people, although any enhancement is likely to be restricted to the younger, better educated minority. As yet, a marked 'digital divide' inhibits the work progression of many disabled people (Audit Commission, 2004; Pillai et al., 2005, 2007). Furthermore, a specific section of the disabled population of people with the most complex support needs will remain outside the labour market, probably even more isolated (Abberley, 1996; Barnes and Mercer, 2005c).

New Labour policies demonstrate a greater inclination towards re-regulation of the economy rather than massive de-regulation, in line with standard neo-liberal demands. There has also been an increased emphasis on disabled people's rights and some acceptance of a social barriers approach in employment policy-making. Evidence of their effectiveness in changing the employment patterns of disabled people is keenly awaited.

The built environment, housing and transport

Disabled people's lack of access to the built environment, housing and transport is widely documented and changing this is a primary objective in disabled people's struggle for social inclusion.

Physical access

Access surveys demonstrate widespread shortcomings in the degree of physical access to the built environment, ranging from roads and pavements to entering and using public buildings. Nonetheless, the heterogeneity of the disabled population inhibits easy architectural answers (Goldsmith, 1976), with the needs of different groups sometimes in conflict with one another. For instance, dropped kerbs favoured by wheelchair users can be a hazard for people with visual impairments. Ambulant disabled people may require a narrow toilet compartment with rails securely fixed at either side for support, whereas wheelchair users typically need more space to manoeuvre and transfer.

This underscores significant barriers to undertaking routine activities such as shopping, going to work and visiting leisure venues. To gain entry to a building may require ramps and easy-to-open doors, while once inside poor colour-contrast on doors and steps and insufficient lighting make navigation difficult for visually impaired people, while those with hearing impairments often experience communication barriers. Wheelchair users find that circulation areas and corridors often lack adequate turning space, while upper floors are 'out-of-bounds' due to the absence of lifts or accessible toilets (Grewal et al., 2002; DRC, 2003b; Lewis et al., 2004).

The Chronically Sick and Disabled Persons Act 1970 (CSDP) was one of the first initiatives detailing those responsible for public buildings, including schools and universities, to enhance access as far as 'practical and reasonable'. This recommendation applied only to existing buildings where 'substantial improvements' were proposed. The CSDP (Amendment) Act 1976 extended the remit to workplaces. The British Standards Institute *Code of Practice for Access of the Disabled to Buildings* (1979) offered guidance for architects and designers. Nevertheless, few local authorities, property developers or architects took positive action (SJAC, 1979; CORAD, 1982; Imrie and Kumar, 1998).

This persuaded the government to amend the Building Regulations, and Part M came into force in December 1987. This stipulated that all new buildings, including shops, offices, factories and schools, should be accessible in their design and construction to 'people with a physical impairment'. However, it was restricted to the level of entry, and there were additional exemptions, such as listed buildings (Imrie and Wells, 1993; MacDonald, 1995), because of a reluctance to place 'unrealistic burdens' on private businesses (DSS, 1994, p. 36). However, revisions to the Building Regulations in 1999 both extended access provisions throughout a building and added those with sensory impairments to the definition of a disabled person.

The Disability Discrimination Act (DDA) 1995 introduced the legislative requirement that 'reasonable adjustments' be taken to remove the physical barriers facing disabled people, including new development plans. What constitutes a 'reasonable adjustment' remains contentious, and ten years later less than 20 per cent of public buildings in London were rated as mobility-accessible, while 80 per cent of pubs, clubs and restaurants and other leisure venues rated as less than satisfactory (DRC, 2005). Other shortfalls included the lack of accessible toilets, ranging from only 10 per cent in restaurants to 55 per cent of cinemas (Scope, 2004), while one in five 'disabled parking' spaces are occupied by non-disabled drivers (Baywatch Campaign, 2007). Since 2004, the implementation of the DDA physical access provisions and revised Building Regulations increased the pressure to improve access, particularly in leisure and entertainment venues. Even so, implementation is uneven, and a fully accessible physical environment remains a long-term goal.

Housing

'The physical aspects of standardised housing design with steps, stairs, narrow doorways and a lack of space can create a disabling environment in the one place where people normally expect to spend the majority of their time and enjoy the most control over their surroundings' (Pillai et al., 2005, p. 38; Harrison, 2001).

Three quarters of non-disabled people compared with less than two-thirds of disabled people are owner-occupiers, with the latter twice as likely to occupy social housing – rented from a local authority or housing association (ODPM, 2005). In the 1980s, housing associations were encouraged to increase purpose-built accessible housing, but much of this was single-bedroom accommodation based on the erroneous assumption that most disabled people live either on their own or as part of a couple (Stewart et al., 1999). Nevertheless, a current government goal is that everyone should have the opportunity of a decent home at a price they can afford (ODPM, 2005). 'Affordability' is a major issue for many disabled people, with homeless numbers almost doubling in the 1980s, while between 1997 and 2003 there was a 44 per cent increase in the number of homeless households with a disabled member rated as a priority need (ibid.; Mayor of London, 2007).

There is not only a serious shortfall in accessible accommodation but also a mismatch between needs and provision: for example, only a quarter of wheelchair dwellings are occupied by a wheelchair user, and over half of wheelchair users are tenants of non-wheelchair dwellings (Harris et al., 1997, p. 7). A further trend is the increasing local segregation of accessible housing (Stewart et al., 1999; Goodridge, 2004). More generally, local authorities, housing associations and private developers have a poor record in consulting with, and providing information and advice for, disabled people (Bevan, 2002).

A significant proportion of families with a disabled child live in accommodation that does not reach the 'decent homes' standard – warm, weatherproof and with reasonably modern facilities (ODPM, 2005). Hence, the policy priority to raise this figure significantly by 2010 and boost occupants' health and well-being (Oldman and Beresford, 2000; Thomas and Ormerod, 2006; DCLG, 2007). The age of Britain's housing stock – with 60 per cent built before 1964 – exacerbates this shortfall. It has been estimated that by 2020 only 12 per cent of homes in England will have been built to Part M standards (Pillai et al., 2007, p. 10). Additionally, the extension of Part M of the building regulations in 1999 to cover new residential dwellings gave a particular emphasis to 'visitability'. This required new homes to have level entry, front and internal doors of a minimum width, a toilet on the ground or first habitable floor, and accessible positions for switches and sockets. Furthermore, the interpretation and enforcement of Part M regulations by builders and building control officers varies widely, and too often seems no stronger than 'half-hearted' (Imrie, 2003; Pillai et al., 2005).

Making adaptations can be a relatively expensive option in comparison with building an accessible house from scratch (Imrie, 2000, 2006). The complex regulations covering building work inhibit the number of publicly funded adaptations. This bleak picture is reinforced by survey findings that a quarter of households with a disabled person cannot afford major adaptations such as bathroom conversions, extensions and lifts (Heywood, 2001, 2004), despite a rise in the maximum grant to £25,000 for structural adaptations by local authorities under the Disabled Facilities Grant scheme (although this is not means tested for households with a disabled child).

One alternative entails making all housing easily adaptable to the (changing) needs of disabled people over their lifetime – such as the Lifetime Homes standards advocated by the Joseph Rowntree Foundation taskforce (Joseph Rowntree Foundation, 1997). This reduces the cost of making adaptations or enforced moves to more accessible accommodation. In Wales, all housing associations have been required to develop new homes along Lifetime Homes standards since April 2001, while social housing providers must achieve the Welsh Housing Quality Standard by 2012. More radical suggestions to develop 'Smart Homes' technology (integrating various devices and appliances so that an entire home can be controlled centrally) have had little impact on new housing, mainly because of the high costs (Pragnell et al., 2000). These examples illustrate the slow momentum towards more inclusive housing.

Transport

An inaccessible transport system (both public and private) has acted as a major restriction to social inclusion – from getting to work to leisure and socializing (DPTAC, 2002; DRC, 2003a). While specific barriers vary across types of transport and between impairment groups, a general consequence is that disabled people travel a third less than the overall population. As many as 39 per cent of disabled people do not use local buses, and two-thirds do not travel by train or fly. The private car is the most popular form of transport in Britain, yet 60 per cent of households with a disabled member do not have a car, compared with 27 per cent of the total population (DPTAC, 2002; ONS, 2004b). This makes disabled people more dependent on public transport, as well as taxis, despite these being relatively more expensive. With transport an important budgetary item, rising travel costs hit disabled people disproportionately.

The main difficulties identified by disabled people are getting to and from bus stops and stations and on or off buses and trains (Grewal et al., 2002). Although most 'Inter-City' train services are now wheelchair accessible, as measured by door widths and the provision of wheelchair standing spaces, this is not yet the case for local services (DfT, 2004; DPTAC, 2004). On the London Underground, in 2005, 46 per cent of trains and twenty-nine of the 253 stations were 'step free', with plans to raise this to 25 per cent in 2010 and 50 per cent by 2015 (Transport for London, 2005). More recently introduced light rapid transit systems, such as those in Manchester, Sheffield, Tyneside and London Docklands and London Underground's Jubilee Line, have incorporated much improved accessibility.

Bus design has advanced noticeably since the 1990s, with more attention to entrance/exit step heights, doorway widths, handrails, seating, bell-pushes and signage. New technologies (such as digitized speech announcements/information) are now being developed to give information to people with hearing and sight impairments on bus times, routes, numbers and destinations. The national average of wheelchair-accessible buses grew from 30 per cent in 2003 to 39 per cent in 2005, and all London buses became wheelchair accessible in 2006. Long-distance coaches include buffet and toilet facilities, although high-level seating and narrow steps create difficulties for some people.

A further obstacle is the shortage of travel information in accessible formats. This is exacerbated by unhelpful attitudes among staff, with local bus drivers attracting particular criticism. However, accessible information that caters for a variety of support needs is increasing, while staff training now includes disability awareness (DPTAC, 2002). The lack of accessibility and support means that between 20 and 30 per cent of disabled people experience difficulties in such basic activities as getting to a doctor's surgery or hospital, visiting relatives and leisure facilities, and getting to work (DRC, 2003a).

Over 400,000 disabled people participate in schemes sponsored by the independent not-for-profit organization Motability, which provides assistance in purchasing or hiring a car – either to drive, or to use as a passenger. The cost of adapting a car can be significant, with a wheelchair lift around £6,000 (in 2005). The Motability scheme offers support to those who cannot afford to buy an adapted car or powered wheelchair (with over 1.7 million supplied by 2005), but the disabled person must contribute a minimum of £500.

The main alternative systems of accessible transport are 'Dial a Ride' and 'Taxicard' services. The former offers door-to-door services, with users booking their journey in advance, while 'Taxicard' covers locally subsidized taxi services. In practice, funding is grossly inadequate and the service is very limited, even more so in rural areas (Heiser, 1995). Another initiative is the network of local schemes organized by the National Federation of Shopmobility, a charity that provides mobility equipment such as scooters, wheelchairs and power chairs, and sometimes also personal assistance, in shopping centres (DRC, 2003a). The drawback of such 'special needs' transport is that it is often limited in scope, with uncertain long-term resources.

Progress on access is being made, albeit slowly and unevenly (DfT, 2004), while free local bus travel was introduced in 2006. One indicator is that disabled people are now equally divided between those who think recent improvements in public transport have been only 'fair' or 'poor' and others who rate it as 'very good' or even 'excellent' (DPTAC, 2004).

Leisure and social participation

There is a considerable literature illustrating the significance that leisure and consumption have assumed in late-modern Western societies (Tomlinson, 1990), and specifically in respect of the social inclusion of disabled people (Aitchison, 2003). Leisure is now a major industry, while leisure choices have become a crucial marker in terms of social identity, lifestyle and well-being. 'It is in the sphere of consumption – conspicuous leisure on the basis of adequate disposable income – that many will seek to express their sense of freedom, their personal power, their status and aspiration' (Tomlinson, 1990, p. 6).

The traditional perception of leisure as equivalent to 'free time' misrepresents how far social factors impinge on the choice of activities. With a relatively high proportion not economically active, disabled people on average have more 'spare time', but their scope to utilize these opportunities is restricted because of low incomes. Additionally, domestic and personal activities often take much longer, and those employing a personal assistant must devote extra time to managing that support. This severely reduces choice of leisure options and chances to build social contacts and friendship networks (Burns and Graefe, 2007).

Studies conducted in Britain confirm that the home provides a primary location for activities such as watching television and videos, surfing the internet and playing computer games, socializing with friends, listening to the radio and CDs, and reading, as with the overall population (Hogg and Cavet, 1995; Sivan and Ruskin, 2000; CSO, 2007). Yet each of these presents barriers for specific groups of disabled people with distinctive impairment support needs. In addition, participation in outdoor activities – whether going to the countryside, holidaying abroad, or visiting pubs and clubs (dancing), restaurants, theatres and cinemas – is characterized by another set of obstacles, particularly related to the inaccessible physical environment and transport system.

A specific complaint by disabled people in the 1990s was that they were not made welcome in mainstream contexts. Places of entertainment such as cinemas and theatres used health and safety and fire regulations to exclude disabled people with mobility, sensory and communication impairments, demanding that they be accompanied by an 'able-bodied' person or that they phoned first 'to be sure of getting in' (Couch et al., 1989, p. 109). The management at one of the most popular tourist attractions, Madame Tussaud's in London, discouraged wheelchair visitors at busy times. Only 17 per cent of pub buildings in London complied with the mobility standards of the Building Regulations (Audit Commission, 2002b). Such factors restrict overall spontaneity and choice and lead to segregated activities, such as day centres, social clubs and special needs holidays.

Campaigns by disabled people's organizations and traditional charities influenced the passage of the DDA 1995, but its application to leisure access and sports venues had to wait until 2004. Furthermore, service providers found it relatively easy to get round the DDA, arguing, for example, that staff were too busy to ensure the safety of wheelchair users (Cavet, 1998), at least until late 2004, when the law was extended to leisure activities. Even though attitudes towards the inclusion of disabled people were becoming less hostile, levels of accessibility to leisure activities still lagged well behind. Additionally, while disabled people are eligible for vital equipment such as electric wheelchairs and reading aids for use in the workplace, there is no equivalent scheme for statutory authorities to support leisure participation. Despite legislative backing and campaigns led by national organizations, such as the Arts Council (2004), there is low public awareness about disabled people's involvement in leisure (French and Hainsworth, 2001). Even physical education schoolteachers indicated little familiarity with either the ambitions and support needs of disabled pupils or the range of disabling barriers (Taub and Greer, 2000; Simeonsson et al., 2001; Brittain, 2004).

A frequent opinion survey finding is that younger disabled people are dissatisfied with their social lives. Among teenagers and young adults, interests generally shift from activities organized by parents and teachers to peer-group relations and social activities outside the home (Cavet, 1998). Yet disabled teenagers participate less in outdoor activities, and even then they are typically accompanied by other family members (Anderson et al., 1982; Hirst and Baldwin, 1994). A third of young disabled people reported that access difficulties inhibited socializing with their peers, but other reasons were significant, from feeling unwelcome to lacking confidence. This feeds into disabled youngsters' complaints about their isolation and how they are seen by their peers as the person that everyone wants to keep off their team (Jackson, 2002; DRC, 2003b). Surveys also suggest that disabled people have a much greater fear of being harassed in public or becoming a victim of crime (Sobsey, 1994; Cabinet Office, 2005).

The sense of isolation was particularly acute among disabled people with the fewest opportunities for community contacts, such as children who attend special schools (Morris, 1999) and older disabled people living alone. People with learning difficulties are another group identified as lacking routine interaction with non-disabled people, beyond service providers, with a significant minority simply left to 'amuse themselves' (Felce, 2000; Beart et al., 2001; DoH, 2001). For many, leisure activities are located in large, traditional day centres where contact is limited mostly to other people with learning difficulties. Across the disabled population, the leisure sphere seems far less a place of socializing and identity exploration than for non-disabled youth.

These issues are illustrated by a study of individuals, classified as having 'profound and multiple disabilities', occupying residential accommodation in the Netherlands. Questionnaires and activity diaries were used to identify weekend activities (Zijlistra and Vlaskamp, 2005). The most frequently mentioned were audio-visual (listening to music, watching TV or video), physically oriented activities (massage, swimming, 'rough and tumble' play, etc.) and play and games (toys, games, books, playgrounds, etc.). On average, individuals spent 3.8 hours, out of the total nineteen hours available, on leisure pursuits. However, almost all of this time was taken up by audio-visual media and physically oriented activities. The researchers concluded that leisure consists mostly of 'killing time' rather than experiencing 'quality time' (ibid., p. 446). Similarly, studies of people with schizophrenia living isolated lives at home demonstrate an overwhelming resort to passive leisure activities, such as reading, listening to music and watching TV, plus 'doing nothing' and sleeping (Harvey et al., 2006).

The overall pattern suggests that disabled people 'end up consuming segregated leisure in segregated spaces and relate to and engage with the 'mainstream' market in ways that are mediated by impairment and more importantly by material barriers to their participation in cultures of consumption' (Hughes et al., 2005, p. 5). Disabled people are not generally targeted for leisure participation, except for 'special needs' activities items that reinforce their difference from the rest of the population (Murray, 2002). They are also underrepresented in voluntary activities and voluntary organizations (IVR, 2004). Choices about lifestyle are more likely to be made by professionals and/or other 'residential home' staff and directed towards 'organized' as opposed to 'casual' leisure (Cavet, 1998). Indeed, supposed leisure activities often carry barely concealed therapeutic overtones (Fullager and Owler, 1998), with an emphasis on managing 'undesirable' behaviour and keeping people occupied in 'harmless' ways.

Similar experiences and patterns of social isolation are reported by research in America in the mid-1990s. Disabled people express higher levels of dissatisfaction with their social lives, with less contact with friends, neighbours and relatives than non-disabled people. As many as 58 per cent of disabled Americans had not been to a cinema in the previous year, while two-thirds go out to a restaurant less than once a week. Three-quarters had not attended a live music performance and over two-thirds had not attended a sporting event (compared with 43 per cent of non-disabled people). Only 56 per cent of disabled people go food shopping at least once a week compared with 85 per cent of non-disabled Americans (Kaye, 1998).

Over recent years, more weight has been placed on social participation as an element of citizenship, as well as promoting individual and group well-being and positive self-esteem (Cabinet Office, 2005). There is an obvious interrelationship between social and civic participation, with exclusion from one area having a knock-on effect elsewhere. However, there is little evidence that participation in these areas by disabled people, across the life course, is increasing significantly. 'Overall, it seems that those who have most to gain from civic engagement and community participation tend to be the most isolated from it' (Pillai et al., 2005, p. 50).

Review

The studies reviewed provide ample evidence in support of claims that multiple and significant social inequalities exist between disabled and non-disabled people. These patterns amount to systematic and institutional discrimination that spans material circumstances, education, employment and the built environment, including housing and transport, leisure and social participation. They encompass structural factors as well as discriminatory attitudes and practices, and extend from 'public' domains to the more 'private' sphere of family life and leisure, as well as moral issues about what sorts of lives are valued. Research studies further demonstrate how gender, ethnicity and age mediate the impact and experience of disability in specific ways within the disabled population. While there is evidence that the divide between disabled and non-disabled people is narrowing, there are major concerns that the severe economic recession that emerged in 2007 will have a long-term impact on levels of unemployment and lead to substantial cutbacks in social policy expenditure. These outcomes will prove a serious test of the anti-discrimination measures introduced from the Disability Discrimination Act 1995 onwards and the extent to which disabled and non-disabled people experience equal treatment and opportunities.

The political response to the entrenched social exclusion of disabled people over the post-1945 decades has shifted slowly from denial or 'explanation' as the inevitable consequence of impairment. The recent policy rethink is largely attributable to the increase in collective organization and campaigns by disabled people to highlight their experience of exclusionary social barriers. In the next chapter, the discussion moves on to examine where disabled people, adopting a social model approach, have identified the shortcomings of traditional policies and have promoted a distinctive policy emphasis on social inclusion and independent living.

Routes to Independent Living

T HIS chapter explores the trajectory of disability policy against the background of wider shifts in welfare policy, particularly in the post-1945 decades. The historical context for disabled people centres on their experience of continuing and wide-ranging social exclusion (as illustrated in chapter 5). An associated and distinctive policy response has been to place professional service providers in control of disabled people's lives, as is graphically illustrated in the threat of enforced institutional segregation. The failures of such policies have stimulated the collective self-organization of disabled people and campaigns for a radical change in disability policy that offered realistic prospects of 'independent living'.

The discussion begins with a review of the policy and practice of segregating large numbers of disabled people in long-stay institutions and the subsequent moves towards de-institutionalization from the 1960s onwards. While associated with optimistic claims about 'care in the community', the latter's implementation raised basic questions about the nature of the 'community' and the type of 'care' provided for dependent groups.

Over recent decades, government discourse on social care shifted under the influence of new priorities of marketization and modernization. However, the emphasis on 'care' (carers and caring) clashed with disabled people's aims for 'independent living' and 'support' and 'personal assistance'. A number of areas graphically illustrate this 'clash of perspectives': the normalization agenda; the establishment of user-controlled services, such as Centres for Independent/Integrated/Inclusive Living; direct payments to enable service users to buy support assistance rather than rely on local authority services; and user involvement in the organization and delivery of services. In each of these case studies, there is evidence of a noteworthy change in policy rhetoric, although the practical progress towards disabled people's goal of independent living still faces obstacles in its implementation.

The critique of residential institutions

Through the first half of the twentieth century, segregated residential institutions occupied a dominant presence in disabled people's lives. The most cited examples were the large, long-stay hospital institutions for individuals diagnosed as 'mentally ill' or 'mentally handicapped'. With the emergence of the post-1945 welfare state, these were incorporated into the newly created National Health Service and exerted a powerful symbolic influence well beyond the numbers 'put away' (Morris, 1969).

Outside the hospital sector, the 1948 National Assistance Act formally abolished the poor law system and transferred responsibility for the provision of residential accommodation for those 'in need of care and attention which is not otherwise available' (Ministry of Health, 1948, section 21) to local authorities. The Act also allowed delegation of residential provision to the voluntary sector, and this resulted in an enhanced role for charities that reinforced their 'all but unimpeachable' place in British society as benefactors of disabled people (Drake, 1996, p. 150). Most notably, in 1948 Leonard Cheshire Disability built their first residential home for disabled people, and by 1980 this number had expanded to seventy-four containing over 2,000 residents (Evans, 1993; Davies, 2002). The general bias, supported by professional and lay opinion, towards residential 'care', extended to segregated activities in day centres and sheltered workshops. In contrast, there was limited provision of domiciliary services, such as home helps and meals-on-wheels, and of technical aids and equipment. This left most disabled people heavily dependent on their family and friends (Humphries and Gordon, 1992; Drake, 1999).

The official position was that: 'welfare services should . . . ensure that all handicapped persons . . . have the maximum opportunity of sharing in and contributing to the life of the community . . . so that their capacities are realized to the full, their self-confidence developed, and their social contacts strengthened' (Ministry of Health, 1948, para. 60). This produced optimistic claims that the quality of life in institutions was moving from that of 'master and inmate' to something closer to 'hotel manager and his guests' (Ministry of Health, 1950, p. 311). In practice, most people dreaded removal to one of these 'human warehouses' (Townsend, 1962, p. 36). Institutional life was described as akin to 'batch living' with a clear staff–resident hierarchy, where inmates occupied a subsidiary, passive role and status (Goffman, 1961; Townsend, 1962, 1969; Morris, 1969). Residents' lives were strictly regulated. They had little choice in how to occupy their time and were largely isolated from their families and outside community contacts. Medical and nursing treatment was minimal and generally ineffective, with staff occupying a mainly custodial role. Even on its own criteria, the residential institution was found severely wanting (Morris, 1969).

A series of scandals in long-stay 'mental handicap' and 'psychiatric' hospitals confirmed their low public reputation (Martin and Evans, 1984). The horrors identified were not attributable simply to low funding and inadequate staff training, but also to a general presumption that nothing could be done to improve significantly the lives of inmates. Studies of institutions for those labelled as 'mentally handicapped' and 'mentally ill' graphically illustrate how a regime of 'isolation, cruelty and deprivation' overlapped with professional and lay characterizations of inmates as differentiated by 'low intelligence, personal incapacity and deviant behaviour' (Townsend, 1969, p. xxxii).

Moves towards de-institutionalization

The number of people diagnosed as 'mentally ill' and 'mentally handicapped' incarcerated in large, segregated, residential institutions peaked in the 1950s and 1960s in Britain, as in the USA and Scandinavia (Mansell and Ericsson, 1996; Tøssebro et al., 1996). By then, the climate of opinion in these (and other) countries was changing, and there were calls to reduce the inmate population – as recommended in Britain by the Royal Commission on the Law Relating to Mental Illness and Mental Deficiency (1957). There was increasing unfavourable comparison of the record of large, long-stay institutions with the perceived financial, professional and therapeutic advantages of community-based alternatives. Pharmacological innovations seemed to offer effective medical control outside the institution, while psychiatric professionals anticipated greater recognition and status from integration with their medical counterparts in general hospitals. The prospects of reduced financial costs and patient benefits proved an irresistible combination to politicians and policy-makers (Scull, 1984; Busfield, 1986).

De-institutionalization in Britain progressed more slowly than originally planned, but still the number held in psychiatric institutions declined significantly, from 148,000 in 1954 to 96,000 in the early 1980s (Ramon, 1996). In 1969, 58,850 individuals were recorded as living in 'mental handicap' hospitals, while 4,900 were in residential care homes and 24,500 attended adult training centres in the community. By 2000, this hospital population had fallen to nearly 10,000 individuals, compared with 53,400 living in residential care and an estimated 84,000 adults receiving community-based care from social services and in NHS day centres (DoH, 2001, p. 17). In 2007, a decade later than in Norway and Sweden, the decision was made to close the remaining thousand hospital places (Mansell, 2006).

However, the demise of large, long-stay institutions did not herald the end of institutionalized living. National surveys of disabled people in the mid-1980s calculated that 80 per cent of the 422,000 disabled adults above retirement age lived in residential homes and institutions, along with a majority of those individuals diagnosed as having a 'severe' mental illness or a comparable learning difficulty (Martin et al., 1988). In contrast, as many as 40 per cent of specific groups in the 1980s – for example, younger people with learning difficulties – remained living at home, along with a significant majority of disabled children, all largely dependent on their families (ibid., 1988; Smyth and Robus, 1989). Similar patterns endured into the twenty-first century.

In the case of psychiatric hospital bed numbers, these have continued to fall since the 1990s, with a corresponding sharp rise in community placements. Part of the explanation stems from a greater readiness within the psychiatric system to treat people with 'less severe' mental distress in residential settings. However, the number of involuntary psychiatric hospital admissions and specifically forensic beds has also increased, which even triggered suggestions of a counter-tendency indicative of 'reinstitutionalization' (Priebe et al., 2005). This has been fuelled by a resurgence in public fears about the threat posed by mental health patients released into the community, fanned by intense media and political interest (Laurance, 2003), and reflected in proposed legislative restrictions on the rights and liberty of people with severe mental health problems.

Yet the experience of disabled people living in the growing number of smaller, community-based, residential homes suggested that criticism of enforced institutional living was displaced, not overturned. The institutional culture was represented as tolerant of wide-ranging restrictions and abuse and harassment of inmates: 'There are staff who bully those who can't complain, who dictate what clothes people should wear, who switch the television off in the middle of a programme, and will take away "privileges" (like getting up for the day) when they choose' (Hunt, 1966b, p. 154). Such concerns led directly to one of the most cited studies of residential living in the 1960s, by Eric Miller and Geraldine Gwynne – *A Life Apart* (1972). Their research sampled twenty-two voluntary and local authority homes and wards in long-stay hospitals and provided a detailed study of Le Court, the first Leonard Cheshire Disability residential home. The researchers identified two contrasting value positions on institutions: one they label 'humanitarian', the other 'liberal'. These correspond to distinctive regime styles: horticultural and warehousing. Horticultural regimes stress developing an individual's 'unsatisfied drives and

Table 6.1 Comparison of institutional regime practice and independent living values

Institutional regime practice	Independent living values
• Depersonalization, infantalization	• Autonomy/interdependence
• Rigidity of routine, structured living, sparse environment	• Choice
• Block treatment of people; residents seen as a homogeneous group	• Dignity and individual worth
• High levels of staff-determined versus resident-determined behaviour	• Self-determination
• Significant social distance between staff and residents	• Integration
• Imbalance between public and private living	• Privacy
• Low participation within and outside home; marked isolation from community	• Citizenship

Source: Adapted from Peace et al. (1997, p. 45).

unfulfilled capacities' (1972, pp. 86–7) to produce as much autonomy for as long as possible. The aim is to achieve the maximum 'normality', irrespective of the individual's circumstances, without raising unrealistic expectations (see table 6.1).

Miller and Gwynne conclude that: 'The warehousing model represents the conventional approach to residential care and is still to be found in relatively pure form, especially in some medically based institutions'. In contrast, the horticultural model is 'an aspiration rather than a reality', even if 'in some institutions the two models coexist somewhat uncomfortably together' (1972, p. 87). The two models represent mirror images in evaluating the positive potential of equipment aids and technology, engaging in paid work activities, receiving visitors, forging close relationships, and sharing in the home management.

The 'warehousing' approach assumes that inmates 'remain dependent and depersonalized' and discourages attempts 'to display individual needs' other than those which are impairment-related (Miller and Gwynne, 1972, p. 86). It concentrates on prolonging physical life and diversionary and passive activities, while largely denying significant outside social contacts and activities. Many staff felt that warehousing produced low job satisfaction and high turnover, with few opportunities to apply their professional expertise. For most residents, entry into the institution constituted a 'point of no return': 'by the very fact of committing people to institutions of this type, society is defining them as, in effect, socially dead, then the essential task to be carried out is to help the inmates make their transition from social death to physical death' (ibid., p. 89).

Indeed, the lack of appropriate community services left many disabled people with no alternative but an enforced move into residential care. A government-sponsored inquiry (Seebohm, 1968) recommended a major reorganization of local authority social services. In 1969, Alf Morris introduced a private member's bill requiring local authorities to provide disabled people with those services ranked as 'permissive' under the 1948 National Assistance Act. The aim was to expand and upgrade support services for community living ranging from council (public) housing alterations and domiciliary services to leisure facilities. Although described optimistically by one supporter as a 'charter' for disabled people (Topliss and Gould, 1981, p. 30), a watered-down Chronically Sick and Disabled Persons Act (CSDPA) was passed in 1970.

However, with limited funding for local authorities, the CSDPA did not produce the hoped-for advances in support services (Shearer, 1981a, 1981b): 'provision was largely ineffective, uncoordinated and patchy and was meeting the needs of very few disabled individuals' (Fiedler, 1991, p. 86). Disabled people living at home continued to rely heavily on relatives and friends for assistance. What is more, the number of day centres in England and Wales jumped from around 200 in 1959 to over 2,600 in 1976 – a sure indication that 'warehousing' flourished in the segregated and institutional atmosphere of community services (Carter, 1981).

Seeking new routes to inclusion

It was disabled activists in North America who popularized the goal of 'independent living' as central to their campaigns for social inclusion. This represented a radical challenge to the predominant characterization of disabled people as 'dependent' and reliant on others for 'care'. In industrial capitalist societies, dependence also signals a general inferiority, including a lesser moral worth (Oliver, 1990; Leonard, 1997). Disabled people emphasized the goal of exercising a similar pattern of choice and control in their lives to that taken for granted by non-disabled people (Oliver, 1983; Brisenden, 1986, 1989; Bracking, 1993).

The personal tragedy approach was denigrated for sustaining basic weaknesses and failings in mainstream welfare provision:

- low standards, with complaints of lack of respect, neglect and abuse – in the community as well as in residential settings;
- a failure to ensure equal access and opportunities to engage in everyday activities;
- the presumption of service-provider control and user passivity/compliance; and
- a lack of accountability, with little recognition of the rights of service users (Morris 1993b, 1994a).

The enforced dependence on families and/or local domiciliary services often left disabled people 'isolated' or effectively 'institutionalized' in their own homes. Disabled people felt unable to exercise meaningful choices or control in determining service priorities or actual delivery.

> In many areas of their lives, disabled people's experiences do not accord with the lifestyle expectations of their contemporaries. For example, many disabled adults do not have the right to decide what time to get up or go to bed, or indeed who to go to bed with, when or what to eat, how often to bath or even be in control of the times when they can empty their bladders or open their bowels. (Oliver, 1996a, p. 48)

Traditional assumptions about gender and ethnicity further diminished service provision. For example, disabled men are more often allocated service support because they are regarded as more 'helpless' than disabled women (Rae, 1993), while disabled people from minority ethnic groups are thought to require less service support because of the greater involvement of family members (Begum, 1993, 1994b). Similarly biased assumptions are made about age, sexuality and an individual's perceived 'intellectual' or 'cognitive' capacity to make informed (rational) choices in their everyday lives.

Policy directions towards independence

By the 1960s, the case against large, segregated residential institutions was generally accepted, but while the community alternative was broadly agreed it was not clearly formulated.

> To the politician, 'community care' is a useful piece of rhetoric; to the sociologist, it is a stick to beat institutional care with; to the civil servant, it is a cheap alternative to institutional care which can be passed to the local authorities for action – or inaction; to the visionary, it is a dream of the new society in which people really do care; to social services departments, it is a nightmare of heightened public expectations and inadequate resources to meet them. (Jones et al., 1978, p. 114)

New Right Conservative

With the election in 1979 of a 'New Right' Conservative government, headed by Margaret Thatcher, there was a concerted effort to restructure, or 'roll back', the state and revitalize market forces and competition in the delivery of health and social services. A series of reports identified shortcomings in existing community care policies, notably in efficiency and quality standards, for the main priority groups – 'the elderly, mentally handicapped, mentally ill and younger disabled' (Audit Commission, 1986).

The government asked Sir Roy Griffiths (1988) to examine ways forward, and his recommendations informed the White Paper *Caring for People* (DoH, 1989). The overall aim of 'community care' was to promote 'choice and independence' by giving individuals more say 'in how they live their lives and the services they need to help them to do so' (ibid., p. 4). The introduction of market competition into the public sector was expected to deliver better 'value for money' by emphasizing 'economy, efficiency and effectiveness' (Exworthy and Halford, 1999; Sanderson, 1999), the so-called 'holy trinity' of neo-liberalism (Clarke, 2004, p. 132). Competition between service providers was also expected to enhance consumer choice (Griffiths, 1988). In this 'supermarket' model, consumer power derived from increased options to 'exit', that is, shop elsewhere (Hirschman, 1970).

This 'mixed economy of welfare' approach, with quasi-market competition between the public, private and voluntary sectors to enhance individual choice, underscored the National Health Service and Community Care Act (NHSCCA) 1990. Policy guidance for its enactment in April 1993 reiterated the significance of consumer empowerment:

> The rationale for this re-organization is the empowerment of users and carers. Instead of users and carers being subordinate to the wishes of service-providers, the roles will be progressively adjusted. In this way, users and carers will be enabled to exercise the same power as consumers of other services. This redressing of the balance of power is the best guarantee of a continuing improvement in the quality of service. (DoH, 1991, p. 9)

At the same time, new inter-organizational and social partnerships were encouraged (Clarke, 2004), while the expansion of community services blurred the boundary lines between formal and informal 'care', leading to mixed forms (Glendinning et al., 2000a).

The reforms emphasized the role of local authority managers in assessing individual support needs, designing a 'care plan' and, within available resources, purchasing 'packages of care' on behalf of service users. Individual needs and circumstances (functional limitations, family situation and financial resources) became the subject of detailed assessments by social workers and other professionals. Implementation of this plan was monitored and the whole process reviewed (DoH, 1991, p. 41). This reinforcement of managerial and professional control was partly tempered by extending earlier initiatives to listen to the views of service users such as the Disabled Persons (Services, Consultation and Representation) Act of 1986. Furthermore, the Community Care (Direct Payments) Act 1995 finally recognized the merits of 'cash for care' or direct payments, both to reinforce its consumerist agenda and to undermine the traditional structures and interests that control service provision, while the Disability Discrimination Act 1995 introduced new powers to challenge social exclusion.

New Labour

The New Labour government elected in 1997 promised a modernizing 'third way' between Labour's 'old left' and the Conservative 'new right':

> The advent of new global markets, and the knowledge economy, coupled with the ending of the Cold War, have affected the capability of national governments to manage economic life and provide an ever-expanding range of social benefits. We need to introduce a different framework, one that avoids both the bureaucratic, top-down government favoured by the old left and the aspiration of the right to dismantle government altogether. (Giddens, 2000, p. 2)

In practice, important continuities remained with Thatcherism and its neo-liberal project to realign economy, state and society. New Labour's modernization strategy confirmed its broad adherence to the new managerialism of the private sector (DoH, 1998). It promoted 'joined-up' government, and hybrid forms of service provision, involving private and voluntary organizations, were encouraged to take on a larger role in delivering services. Professional 'tribalism' was portrayed as a barrier to organizational efficiency and effectiveness. Greater emphasis was given to new forms of governance while maintaining a definite central steer (Newman, 2001; Clarke, 2004). Thus, the delegation of more operational autonomy to local managers was constrained by maintaining 'arm's length control' with the imposition of strict audit and performance quality targets (Flynn, 1999; Clarke et al., 2000; Powell, 2000). Overall, there has been an elevation of 'pragmatic decision making' (Clarke, 2004, p. 133) – 'what counts is what works' – as a virtue over 'ideological' politics.

The government attempted to rewrite the relationship between the state and its citizens – building on the 1995 Disability Discrimination Act. It sided with 'consumers' over 'producers' and encouraged 'partnerships' and collaboration between user organizations and the voluntary, private and statutory sectors in developing and delivering services (DoH, 1998; Glendinning et al., 2002). New inspection and regulatory bodies were established with responsibilities that included the social services, such as the expanded Commission for Social Care Inspection (CSCI) in 2004. An active and responsible citizen willing to take on greater management of their life was proclaimed. The consultation process was widened (Needham, 2003; Clarke, 2004) and reinforced in a series of legislative interventions, such as the Health and Social Care Act 2001.

New Labour gave fresh momentum to the system of direct payments and extended this to individual budgets in line with its wider endorsement of the principle of 'independent living'. These aims were further highlighted in its Green Paper *Independence, Well-being and Choice* (DoH, 2005a) and the follow-up White Paper *Our health, our care, our say* (DoH, 2006). This was complemented by a broad commitment to a social model approach as the way to improve significantly disabled people's life chances by combating discrimination and social barriers to inclusion (Cabinet Office, 2005).

From normalization to *Valuing People*

In the case of people with learning difficulties, the shifting policy emphasis from long-stay institutions to community-based living is captured in the rise of 'normalization' to challenge the institutionalization of people with the label of learning difficulties and the subsequent moves towards a rights-based approach. The Scandinavian accent on 'normalization' was given its first detailed elaboration by Bengt Nirje, as: 'making available to the mentally retarded patterns and conditions of everyday life which are as close as possible to the norms and patterns of the mainstream of society' (1969, p. 181).

This approach was taken up by Wolf Wolfensberger, an American-trained psychologist, who proceeded to 'North Americanize, sociologize and universalize the Scandinavian formulations' (Wolfensberger, 1980a, p. 7). Normalization fitted with his wider argument that the latent function of the 'human care industry' had been to create and sustain large numbers of dependent and devalued people in order to secure both employment for health and social care staff and profits for private companies. Instead of supporting people with learning difficulties, the welfare system 'discriminates against independence, communality, and non-congregate and non-institutional living' (Wolfensberger, 1989, p. 37).

The starting point for Wolfensberger's (1972, 1980b) approach to normalization was deviance theory, and suggestions that societies face four options in managing deviance: segregation or elimination, which he rejected outright, and prevention or reversal of the condition, which he reformulated. Subsequently, he once more downgraded use of the term 'normalization' in favour of 'social role valorization' and assisting individuals into 'socially valued life conditions and socially valued roles' (Wolfensberger and Thomas 1983, p. 24). This represented a significant break away from the early Scandinavian emphasis on people's rights (Perrin and Nirje, 1989; Brown and Smith, 1992; Race, 1999).

The normalization/social role valorization approach attracted considerable interest and critical debate among professionals, policy-makers and academic commentators. For critics, it concentrated on changing the behaviour and attitudes of marginalized individuals so that they became more like counterparts of 'normal' people, rather than challenging the prevailing ideal of 'normality'. Equally, normalization did little to diminish the impact of professional authority in the lives of disabled people. The emphasis is on consensus and shared values rather than on power relations between professional and client (Chappell, 1992; Walmsley, 1997). Hence, normalization requires the individual to adapt to the norms of society, or struggle 'to compete in the world of the able-bodied and the able-minded' (Walmsley, 1991, p. 227), as if 'the values and norms of behaviour and appearance in society are worth striving for' (Hattersley, 1991, p. 3). Additionally, analyses of normalization largely neglect social difference among people with learning difficulties, such as by gender, age, ethnicity and class (Brown and Smith, 1992). Overall, there is too little attempt to analyse normalization as historically specific, and so address the interaction between economic and cultural forces that precipitate and maintain an experience of poverty, subordination and social exclusion.

In Britain, as elsewhere, government thinking – from *Better Services for the Mentally Handicapped* (DHSS, 1971) to *Valuing People* (DoH, 2001) – shifted from the broad aim of people's lives being as close to 'normal' as possible to a new vision rooted in principles of rights, independence, choice and inclusion (ibid., p. 3). The early experience of de-institutionalization was disappointing. Relocation from hospitals to local communities did not in itself guarantee that marginalized groups such as people with learning difficulties managed to significantly overturn their lack of social integration. Indeed, small-sized accommodation or even family life sometimes demonstrated features more associated with institutionalized regimes (Walker and Walker, 1998; Stevens, 2004).

In practice, a simplified version of normalization took hold as leading 'an ordinary life' (King's Fund Centre, 1980; Race, 1999). The emphasis was on achieving community presence, greater choice and opportunities for personal development, respect and community participation (O'Brien, 1987). Yet, as *Valuing People* (DoH, 2001) acknowledged, formal recognition as a priority group for service support counted for little, while reinvention as consumers in the social welfare marketplace proved no more effective. It was estimated that 20,000 people with learning difficulties received no form of support during the day and were left to their own devices, while use of day centres was often related to the absence of anywhere else to go (Whittaker and McIntosh, 2000; DoH, 2001). The unavoidable conclusion was that 'public services have failed to make consistent progress in overcoming the social exclusion of people with learning disabilities' and, if anything, reinforced segregation (DoH, 2001, p. 19).

In response, *Valuing People* outlined a five-year plan to improve individuals' lives and those of their families, focusing on citizenship rights, social inclusion, choice and opportunities for independence in their daily lives – with many people with learning difficulties not living in their own homes or having a choice over who supports them, and less than 10 per cent in paid employment. In 2005, a follow-up report indicated that there had been uneven progress and that many local authorities were struggling to change service priorities (DoH, 2005b; Cole et al., 2007; DoH, 2007b). Academic research identified continuing slow but variable progress in achieving improved outcomes for people living in different community settings (Cambridge et al., 2001; Kim et al., 2001; Stancliffe et al., 2001; Ware, 2004; Mansell, 2006). Many people with a learning difficulty still play little part in community activities or participate in friendships and wider social networks with non-disabled people (Abbott et al., 2001). The challenge is to avoid re-creating institution-like regimes in small group homes, or even within families (Stevens, 2004; SSI, 2004). The DoH (2007b) decided on another rebranding of policy to stress person-centred planning and integrating the personalization agenda into services for people with learning difficulties.

Government policy for people with learning difficulties offers an easy target for Foucauldian-based suggestions that supported living entails a 'new dispersal of power relations' in keeping with the 'drive to greater efficiency' (Drinkwater, 2005, p. 229; Burton and Kagan, 2006). Conversely, the increasing influence of a rights-based approach has attracted criticism from some service providers and academic researchers on the grounds that it disregards the impact of impairment – as if 'people with intellectual disabilities know what they want and just need services to give it to them' (Mansell, 2006, p. 72), or do not require 'skilled support' in their decision-making (Ware, 2004). The impact of 'anti-discriminatory practice and the promotion of choice and opportunity for people who can express clear intentions' (Mansell, 2006, p. 73) is repudiated as operating against the best interests of people with severe learning difficulties. Parents' groups and disabled people's organizations, albeit for different reasons, campaign for the government to rethink its promotion of an 'independence agenda'.

Care or independence?

The formal interpretation of 'care *in* the community' was that it entailed 'care *by* the community' (DHSS, 1981). In practice, key legislation, continuing through to the NHSCC Act 1990 and associated policy guidelines, left little room for doubt that 'community care' was a euphemism for unpaid female labour, often open-ended in its demands (Finch and Groves, 1980; Graham, 1983). This reinforced broader feminist analyses of the exploitation and oppression of women in industrial capitalist societies. Feminist writers sought to challenge the patriarchal assumptions surrounding 'care' as a natural and pre-eminently female trait, reinforced by familial obligation. This directed women into low-status and unpaid work rather than into a paid career, with greater risk of social isolation. According to Janet Finch, 'the residential route is the only one which ultimately will offer us a way out of the impasse of caring' (1983, p. 16), while Gillian Dalley (1988) similarly championed the merits of residential care, albeit in a form that promoted a 'collective ethos' unlike the typical institutional regime.

These arguments clashed with disabled people's insistence on the inherently oppressive character of the 'care' approach, with its reinforcement of discriminatory stereotypes of disabled people as passive and dependent (Morris, 1991, 1997). The White Paper *Caring for People* (DoH, 1989) was based on a 'false notion': 'The concept of care seems to many disabled people a tool through which others are able to dominate and manage our lives' (Wood, 1991, p. 199). ' "Care in the community", "caring for people", providing services through "care managers" . . . all these phrases structure the welfare discourse and imply a particular view of disabled people' (Oliver and Barnes, 1991, pp. 9–10). Such language sustains assumptions that disabled people are helpless, and things are done to them, 'for their own good' (Hunt, 1966a; Morris, 1993a; Rae, 1993). 'We need to reclaim the words "care" and "caring" to mean "love", to mean "caring *about*" someone rather than "caring *for*", with its custodial overtones' (Morris, 1993b, p. 42). The underlying ideology of the 'care' discourse is 'oppressive and objectifying' (Fine and Glendinning, 2005, p. 602).

At the same time, the dominant discourse disregards the impact of unequal power relations. In contrast, disabled people have consistently pointed to the negative consequences of 'community care' on those involved. It is 'the most exploitative of all forms of so called care delivered in our society today for it exploits both the carer and the person receiving care. It ruins relationships between people and results in thwarted life opportunities on both sides of the caring equation' (Brisenden, 1989, p. 10). In this regard, it is surprising that so much of the feminist literature on 'care' disregards how many disabled women provide unpaid domestic assistance as well as being 'cared for' (Morris, 1991, 1993a; Keith, 1992; Keith and Morris, 1996). Furthermore, most individuals (non-disabled and disabled) experience dependence at some time in their lives, and the divide between 'care' givers and receivers is not as entrenched as sometimes implied.

These issues are graphically illustrated in Gillian Parker's (1993) study of pre-retirement married couples where at least one is a disabled person. The individuals faced many uncertainties in deciding how and when to give and receive support: 'Some spouses found receiving personal care from their partners difficult; but others, particularly men, found the idea of care from an outsider even more so' (1993, p. 21). Coupled with the low availability of social welfare services, this put pressure on the non-disabled partner to give up their paid job to provide the necessary support, resulting in a significant decline in family income. This created additional strains in the couple's relationship, particularly if they had married relatively recently. The impact on women is often greater because they earn less and are discriminated against by the benefits system, while service providers generally give a lower priority to their support needs. Service provision is often arranged in ways that replace the disabled woman's household role instead of enabling her to retain control of domestic routines.

Yet, while the social construction of 'dependency' in old age has attracted critical debate (Townsend, 1981; Phillipson, 1982), disability has largely retained its associations with the 'naturalness' of requiring 'care' and being 'cared for'. In practice, socio-historical and comparative studies demonstrate how notions of care and dependency in respect of people with impairments vary considerably over time and between societies, with varying degrees of interdependency (Ingstad, 2001; Borsay, 2005).

Interdependence does not necessarily entail equality of inputs and outcomes, although it becomes difficult to sustain if one 'side' is perceived as too demanding, or overly dependent. It must still come to terms with the contrasting opportunities and resources to provide 'help' and variety of forms of 'care-giving' linked to the context and participants – such as parent, nurse, friend, son or daughter, residential home worker. Overall, 'care as a practice invokes different experiences, different meanings, different contexts and multiple relations of power' (F. Williams, 2001, p. 468). Moreover, some social relationships comprise both giving and receiving across private/informal and public/formal domains. While interdependence ranks as a political aspiration (from each according to their ability, to each according to their needs), it sits uneasily with the demands and constraints of everyday life in capitalist societies.

One feminist-inspired response has been to explore an 'ethic of care' in which multidimensional forms of exchange are recognized, including care-giving and care-receiving (Tronto, 1993). These entail positive and socially desirable features and socially valued relationships as well as more negative meanings (Sevenhuijsen, 1998, 2000). This variety and indeterminacy reinforce the importance of exploring 'care and caring' in terms of power relations (Kittay, 1999). The power dynamics between carer and disabled person are vividly illustrated in intimate personal care, or 'bodywork' (Twigg, 2000). Inequality of power, and its potential 'abuse', may operate in more than one direction. Some individuals who are being 'cared for' become the dominant party (Lloyd, 2002), while both 'sides' may be constrained by the actions of a third party (such as the local authority or service providers).

One specific reaction to the traditional ideology or discourse of 'care' has led to the rise of organizations of 'carers', such as Carers UK, with an active lobbying and campaigning role, to improve service support and contribute to the costs of 'caring', and so strengthen traditional family values and responsibilities. A series of legislative measures since 1995 has provided carers with an assessment of their support needs separate from those of the disabled person. The National Carers' Strategy reiterates the role of family carers (Lloyd, 2000). Nevertheless, there have been few signs of the main protagonists uniting around common grievances: that inadequate support services are a major factor in creating the demand for unpaid assistance (Parker and Clarke, 2002).

A further instance of the dependency of disabled people is the lay and professional perception of disabled mothers, and of their likely shortcomings and 'care' needs. They felt pressured to demonstrate their capacity as 'good enough mothers' to family and friends, as well as to health and social workers.

> Living with the fear of losing the right to care for their children forces some mothers to go to great lengths to 'present' themselves and their children as managing 'normally' – often at great personal cost in terms of comfort, and emotional and physical well-being. One consequence is that assistance may not be requested when it is needed because the mother feels that her request may be interpreted to mean that she is not capable. (C. Thomas, 1997, p. 635)

Disabled mothers experienced stricter 'surveillance', with a greater threat of a child being taken away and placed 'in care' by the local authority. While disabled women wanted to be regarded as 'good mothers', the professionals tended to regard them as 'being cared for' rather than 'care givers' (Morris, 1991). Where 'help' was offered it was often experienced as 'intrusive and disempowering' (C. Thomas, 1997, p. 640).

The extra pressure and lack of support are important factors in the breakdown of family relationships – the divorce rate among couples with a child with learning difficulties being ten times higher than the national average (McCormack, 1992). Disabled children are more likely to be abandoned by their parents, and they have less chance of being adopted (Burrell, 1989). For some parents, the determination to look after and 'protect' their disabled child may result in jealousy from siblings (Meredith Davies, 1982). Notwithstanding, studies of parents highlight the positive as well as negative experiences (Morris 1992; Mitchell, 1997): while among the 45 per cent who suggest that having a disabled child affected their relationship, responses were divided evenly between those who thought they had been brought closer and those who talked of heightened stress and strains (Smyth and Robus, 1989).

While recognizing that many families still supply 'a safe haven and support base for people with disabilities shunned by social institutions and locked out by discriminatory processes' (Meekosha and Dowse, 1997a, p. 53), the underlying reasons for disabled people's dependency remain unresolved.

User-led organizations: Centres for Independent Living

The radical shift in contemporary disability politics dates from the rise of the Independent Living Movement (ILM) in America, with its emphasis on 'self-empowerment' (DeJong, 1983; Hahn, 1986). This encompassed setting up the first Centre for Independent Living (CIL) in 1972 in Berkeley, California, as a self-help group managed by disabled people. Throughout the late 1960s and early 1970s, with the increasing accessibility of the campus and generally supportive culture, the number of disabled students at Berkeley expanded noticeably. Their experience inspired the development of a CIL in the local community and similar initiatives elsewhere in America (Zola, 1994). Services offered ranged widely, from political and legal advocacy, peer counselling, screening and training personal assistants, and wheelchair repair and ramp construction, to moving into accessible housing.

The US Congress amended the Rehabilitation Act in 1978 to establish 'a programme of Comprehensive Services for Independent Living'. A condition of funding was that disabled people should participate in the CIL's management. By the late 1980s, over 300 CILs had been established across America. These user-led services offered an example of disability praxis – with the integration of a socio-political analysis of disability and practical support for independent living. Besides providing services, they became sites for consciousness-raising and political organization, 'although not all have been unambiguously controlled by disabled people' (Scotch, 1989, p. 394).

In Britain, user-led organizations also vary in their origins, organizational structures and processes, as well as specific service provision. Early pioneers included the Spinal Injuries Association, which was set up in 1974. It developed a range of support services, including personal assistance (Oliver and Hasler, 1987). A pivotal role was played by the Derbyshire Coalition of Disabled People (DCODP), whose members developed an early example of controlled services in the Grove Road integrated housing venture in Sutton-in-Ashfield. This was conceived and developed by disabled people who were living in a residential home. Beginning in 1972, the initiative to relocate into a small block of flats took four years to bring to completion. It comprised three ground-floor properties featuring designs and adaptations now commonly associated with accessible housing. Additionally, three first-floor flats were let to non-disabled families willing to provide support to their disabled neighbours (Davis, 1981). The scheme demonstrated that, over time, people with 'severe' physical impairments could live in a community-based setting, given appropriate backup. Another high point stemmed from the activities of a group of disabled people living in the Le Court Cheshire Home in Hampshire. 'Project 81: Consumer Directed Housing and Care' was set up in 1979 and underpinned an innovative scheme of indirect payments in lieu of institutional services to purchase personal assistance to enable living in the community (Evans, 1993).

These experiences of, and commitment to, user-led services provided the momentum for developing Britain's first two CILs, in Derbyshire and Hampshire, in 1985. These differed insofar as the Derbyshire Centre for Integrated Living (DCIL) opted to deliver a wide range of services supporting inclusive living, while the Hampshire Centre for Independent Living (HCIL) concentrated on personal assistance and training in 'independent living skills'. As organizations *of* rather than *for* disabled people, they gave life to the social model of disability and the positive potential of alternatives to traditional assumptions that disabled people are passive, dependent, 'charity cases' (see table 6.1, p. 131).

DCIL implemented a comprehensive strategy and 'operational framework' for service support based on seven key needs and priorities formulated by disabled people. These were: information (to know what options exist); counselling and peer support (for encouragement and advice from other disabled people); housing (an appropriate place to live); technical aids and equipment (to generate more independence); personal assistance (controlled by the disabled person/ employer); transport (mobility options); and access (to the built environment) (Davis, 1990, p. 7; Davis and Mullender, 1993). Throughout, the priority was to provide appropriate and accountable support as the necessary foundations to enable disabled people to live independently and on equal terms in mainstream society (Oliver, 1990; Morris, 1993b).

While action to promote an accessible transport system and built environment entailed campaigns well beyond local CILs, the other areas specified by DCIL concentrate on the considerable potential for user-led organizations to facilitate inclusion at the individual level. *Access to information* is fundamental to meaningful participation in contemporary society, yet support for disabled people was conspicuously weak. Ken Davis, a disabled activist, took the lead in creating one such user-led service – Disablement Information and Advice Line (DIAL) – in 1976. By 2005 this had grown into a network of 135 local information and advice services. Although some critics have suggested that non-disabled people began to exert too much influence, DIAL UK describes itself as an organization 'run by and for disabled people' (2005, p. 1). The role of *personal assistance* is highly significant, with estimates that 60 per cent of all disabled adults require such support in undertaking personal care, cooking and cleaning, and social and economic participation generally (Martin et al., 1988; Cabinet Office, 2005). A combination of statutory and voluntary services is available, but delivery is far from guaranteed and under continuing threat of financial cut-backs.

Counselling and peer support is also much in demand. Information by itself is not necessarily enabling unless it is linked to knowledge about its use. Hence the significance of advice and counselling services provided by disabled people with similar backgrounds and experiences (DeJong, 1981; Davis, 1990). However, there has been a lack of peer support services and, as with information and advice, there are specific concerns about the absence of support for minority ethnic and other marginalized groups within the disabled population (Barnes, 1995; Moore, 1995).

With respect to *technical aids and equipment*, the OPCS survey concluded that 69 per cent of all disabled adults use some form of special equipment, including wheelchairs, surgical braces, artificial limbs, and aids to help vision (in addition to glasses) and hearing and to control incontinence (Martin et al., 1989). However, there are also clear gaps and unevenness in provision across different impairment groups. There are a number of reasons for this under- or uneven provision. First, information on aids and equipment is not always easy to locate. Second, many disabled people encounter long delays before items are supplied. Third, much of the new equipment supplied by the state sector is simply not good enough or out of date. As a consequence, disabled people sometimes have to resort to charities or the second-hand market for required items (Thomas et al., 1989).

Once meaningful progress has been made towards satisfying these support needs, other 'secondary' priorities come to the fore. In 1989, the Hampshire Coalition of Disabled People formally extended its focus to employment, education and training, income and benefits, and advocacy. Since then, discussion has continued within CILs and the disabled people's movement generally about further service contributions, such as advocacy and peer support, specifically for direct payment users in the employment of a personal assistant (covering central issues such as recruitment, training, employment and payroll), disability equality training, and consumer audit of services (Barnes and Mercer, 2006). The establishment of the National Centre for Independent Living (NCIL) by the British Council of Disabled People ensured a centralized resource of advice and support for user-led organizations.

While the 'take off' for self-organization occurred in the 1970s and 1980s, a further and more substantial expansion had to wait until the 1990s. It was facilitated by the 1990 NHSCC Act and the 1996 Community Care (Direct Payments) Act, while campaigns by activists at the local level encouraged more ambitious plans for user-led organizations (Barnes and Mercer, 2006). Even so, the development of CILs in Britain has not matched the growth achieved in the USA. A major obstacle has been the lack of adequate and sustained statutory sector funding for local user-led organizations. This makes long-term planning very difficult. Indeed, with so much income derived from short-term (service) contracts, organizations become funding-led, competing with other user-led organizations for scarce funding. This makes for partial coverage of users' support needs and for difficult decisions about which services to provide (and up to what level). In such circumstances, it is also difficult to retain experienced staff.

Local authorities seem more persuaded by the cheapest option, but without a level playing field for competition between providers, so that larger, better resourced charities and rebranded organizations not controlled by disabled people are most successful, increasingly displacing established user-led organizations and CILs (D'Aboville, 2005; DoH, 2005a; Barnes and Mercer, 2006; Charity Commission, 2007). The role of user-led organizations remains dependent on acceptance of their strengths in capacity-building and peer support in producing effective services for disabled people. Even so, specific groups within the disabled population, such as people with learning difficulties, mental health system users, older people, black and minority ethnic groups, and carers, are underrepresented in CIL membership and among users.

The Prime Minister's Strategy Unit issued a clear statement of support from New Labour regarding the significance attached to user-led organizations in securing independent living: 'By 2010, each locality (defined as that area covered by a Council with social services responsibilities) should have a user-led organization, modelled on existing CILs' (Cabinet Office, 2005, p. 91). CILs are defined as: 'grassroots organizations run and controlled by disabled people . . . Their aims are to assist disabled people to take control over their lives and achieve full participation in society' (ibid., p. 84; DoH, 2007a). As yet, the infrastructure and resources necessary have not been sufficiently forthcoming to realize the potential of CILs.

Direct payments

A central aim of disabled people's campaigns for independent living has been to enhance their choice and control over service support and remove some of their dependency on family and friends, with personal assistance a primary target. In Britain, a major stumbling block was the National Assistance Act 1948, which prohibited direct funding to individuals to employ a personal assistant. Following a campaign by disabled residents of the Leonard Cheshire Le Court Residential Home, in 1982 the local county council agreed that funding should be made available through a third party – Le Court (Evans, 1993). This enabled disabled residents to move into accessible housing and potentially accommodate a personal assistant. They could also allocate these funds to their preferred support needs. However, uncertainties about the scheme's legality inhibited its transfer elsewhere.

Quite separately, social security changes left many disabled people living at home without entitlement to domestic assistance allowances and at risk of being forced into residential accommodation. This led in 1988 to the establishment of the Independent Living Fund (ILF), with a budget of £5 million. It gave a significant impetus to campaigns for the direct funding of support services. Applications far outstripped government estimates, and the 1990–1 budget escalated to £32 million. The scheme was closed to new applicants in April 1993, but continued for the existing 22,000 recipients (Lakey, 1994; Zarb and Nadash, 1994). At this point, a new Independent Living (1993) Fund was established, albeit with restrictions on who qualified and the level of payments (Kestenbaum, 1993a, 1993b). At the end of 2007 there were 21,054 individuals receiving an ILF grant in the UK – of whom 79 per cent were clients of the original fund (ILF, 2008).

Disabled people's campaigns continued into the 1990s to establish the legality of direct payments from local authorities to purchase packages of care (Kestenbaum, 1993a; 1993b; Morris, 1993a). Research studies indicated that direct payments offered a more cost-effective option than existing arrangements and such schemes were also aligned with the Conservative government's promotion of market competition and consumerism (Zarb and Nadash, 1994). In response, the Conservative government passed the Community Care (Direct Payments) Act 1996, which from April 1997 allowed local authorities to allocate cash to disabled people less than sixty-five years of age to purchase their own support services.

The scheme also fitted with New Labour proposals for promoting responsible, enterprising citizens and forging new partnerships involving the private and voluntary sectors (Cabinet Office, 1999). Eligibility was extended to sixteen- and seventeen-year-olds, and to carers and parents responsible for disabled children, before it became mandatory in 2003 for local authorities to offer direct payments to all eligible adult service users. In England, 48,000 individuals aged eighteen or over received direct payments in late 2007, which represents a 29 per cent increase since 2005–6 (NHS, 2008). However, the total numbers remained small relative to the total disabled population, with, in particular, lower coverage of parents of disabled children, mental health system users and people with learning difficulties, while rates also varied significantly between local authorities (CSCI, 2006).

While there have been calls for more 'systematic comparison of costs and benefits of independent living support options compared with other traditional support in the UK' (Hurstfield et al., 2007, p. 49), there is 'substantial qualitative evidence' that independent living options provide 'significantly more benefits than conventional forms of service provision' (ibid., p. 101) for the individual user. Disabled people receiving direct payments report being less tied to social services, allowing enhanced opportunities and flexibility in how they organize their everyday lives. This greater control allows wider social participation and increased self-esteem (Witcher et al., 2000; Stainton and Boyce, 2004). Many mental health system users feel that this greater personal responsibility facilitates their 'recovery agenda' (Jacobsen and Greenley, 2001; Spandler and Vick, 2006).

How then is the slow growth of direct payments explained? The major obstacles comprise the lack of information provided to potential recipients; low staff awareness (of direct payments, and of the principles of independent living) and uncertainty over central guidelines; a reluctance among managerial and front-line staff to devolve power to users; inter-professional rivalry across the health and social services divide; negative views about the capabilities of potential recipients; inadequate support service for users; overly bureaucratic paperwork; and difficulties with recruiting personal assistants (Hasler et al., 1999; Dawson, 2000; Glendinning et al., 2000a, 2000b; Pearson, 2000; Carmichael and Brown, 2002; Clark and Spafford, 2001; Glasby and Littlechild, 2002; Stainton, 2002; Hasler, 2003a; CSCI, 2004; Ellis, 2007).

Government guidelines allowed local authorities and front-line professionals a degree of discretion in determining access to publicly funded services and benefits (Carmichael and Brown, 2002; Spandler and Vick, 2005; CSCI, 2006; Lomas, 2006; Ellis, 2007). Several commentators apply Lipsky's (1980) notion of 'street-level bureaucracy' to characterize the 'relative autonomy' of front-line practitioners, particularly over 'assessment and care management' (Ellis and Rummery, 2000, p. 107), and concerns over an 'excess of demand over resources, indeterminate objectives and low control over front line discretion' (Ellis, 2007, p. 416). Professional gate-keeping was encouraged by requirements that staff assess and manage risk, particularly the 'willing and able' clause, when processing applications – although action is planned to ensure that the requirement of service user consent (formal mental capacity) is not used inappropriately (Clark and Spafford, 2002; Williams and Holman, 2006). As a result, direct payments have not been generally viewed as a mainstream option that providers would routinely recommend to social care users (Stainton, 2002; Clark et al., 2004; Spandler and Vick, 2005).

Further issues centred on the recruitment and work conditions of personal assistants taken on by disabled user employers. There have been suggestions from disabled people that the employment of a personal assistant brings potential conflicts and contradictions. One source of tension arises where such an employee takes over the role of the disabled spouse (Parker, 1993), and disabled women with a partner sometimes feel that employing a younger, non-disabled female poses a challenge to social and personal relations within the household (Rae, 1993). Additionally, the arrangement of a support package and employment of often more than one personal assistant is a daunting and time-consuming matter, with potential conflicts in interpretation of the 'employer' and 'employee' relationship. Hence, the active involvement of CILs and other user-led organizations in supporting direct payments users/employers, with the NCIL playing a national role in promoting 'good practice' (Hasler and Stewart, 2004; CSCI, 2004).

An added concern, forcibly expressed by some feminist academics and service providers, centres on the way in which direct payments generally entail a shift away from local authority services and 'care' staff to an employment contract between a disabled user and a personal assistant (using the cash provided by the direct payments package). It is argued that direct payments will encourage the growth of a mostly female personal assistant workforce who lack even modest security in the terms and conditions of comparable local authority 'care' workers (Ungerson, 1997a, 1997b, 2004). Besides this, the introduction of the cash nexus into the relationship between disabled user/employer and the personal assistant/employee produces very different ways of defining the boundaries, and so of dealing with often intimate and personal tasks with the encouragement of a degree of friendship or the more impersonal, employer–employee relationship (Watson et al., 2004).

Central government support for the increased uptake of direct payments has been reinforced by adding the proportion of direct payments to calculations of local authority star ratings (Priestley et al., 2007). In addition, direct payments have acquired a new gloss with New Labour's promotion of individualized budgets, self-assessment and management of service support, and the 'In Control' project. This 'personalization' of services is part of a wider attempt to upgrade user priorities relative to service providers (DoH, 2001, 2005a, 2005b, 2007b). It entails pooling resources from a wide range of funding streams, such as to housing, transport, equipment and support services. From 2008, the level of self-directed support became a measure of local authority performance, with further user-centred targets set for 2011. The personalization agenda has the ambitious goal of changing the balance between 'paternalism and consumerism' (Leadbetter, 2004, p. 11). It anticipates the 'co-production' of services as 'dependent users' become 'active participants' in managing their lives (ibid., p. 18), as part of a move to 'self-organising solutions' (ibid., p. 24). It also entails a new organizational logic affecting service providers as much as service users (Kemshall, 2002; Lord and Hutchinson, 2003; Glendinning and Means, 2006).

The direction of New Labour reforms has attracted strong criticism, some of which raises an important question mark against the direction taken in implementing independent living policies. One strand charges that social work under New Labour has become an instrument of risk assessment and management (Jordan, 2000), and that direct payments users have taken on more of the responsibilities and functions of government. 'There is no shift in political power', but rather an enhanced 'managerialization of the self' (Scourfield, 2007, p. 116). This invocation of Foucauldian notions of 'governmentality' and 'techniques of the self' suggests that the discourse of individual autonomy brings new forms of self-regulation. Disability activists are criticized as trapped in 'narratives of achievement' (Spandler, 2004), unable to recognize that, far from being a catalyst for self-determination, direct payments have their basis in consumerism, individual responsibility and enterprise. Rather than promote social justice, direct payments potentially undermine collective service provision and encourage privatization (ibid., p. 196). Critics bemoan the lack of monitoring of support organizations and the under-supply, low pay and low job security of personal assistants, and suggest that direct payments users are actually 'gaining' at the expense of traditional service users (Burton and Kagan, 2006; Ferguson, 2007; Scourfield, 2007).

From the perspective of disabled people's organizations, implementation has been very slow and uneven, and not adequately resourced by central government. The projected policy move from direct payments to 'individual budgets' suggests an extension of the service aim to provide wider support for disabled people in their everyday lives. Yet, while individualized funding and 'cash for care packages' have been introduced in Europe, North America and Australasia, there remains a clear shortfall between disabled people's expectations for independent living and how these schemes have been implemented in practice.

Service user involvement

Historically, disabled people, as with other service user groups, have been denied involvement in the decision-making processes in statutory and voluntary organizations, from planning and assessment to delivery and evaluation (Drake, 1994; Morris, 1994a, 1994b; Robson et al., 1997). However, policy moves towards user involvement gathered ground in the last quarter of the twentieth century. These were more recently reinforced by New Labour's Health and Social Care Act 2001 and subsequent schemes for local user networks to examine health and social care issues.

User involvement draws on two very different ideologies: a *consumerist* approach, sponsored by Conservative and Labour governments, with its embrace of a neo-liberal agenda for more efficient and effective public services through increased market competition, and a *democratic/participatory* standpoint articulated by the disabled people's movement. This democratic approach stressed a 'choice agenda' that embodied citizenship and user rights to participate in public sector decision-making as part of a wider project for the empowerment and social inclusion of disabled people, and to revitalize democratic governance in general (Beresford and Croft, 1993; Wistow and Barnes, 1993; Morris, 1997).

Evidence of the support for user involvement can be gathered from its inclusion in legislation and guidance in almost every area of public policy since the 1990s. The primary targets were the organization and delivery of services at the local level rather than strategic policy-making and service planning. However, the provisions are not prescriptive, and local authorities are left to interpret how they should be implemented. Further uncertainty arises from the failure to distinguish different forms of involvement and participation. For example, a 'ladder of participation' has been identified (Arnstein, 1969) that differentiates between the basic provision of information, through consultation (listening to users of services and taking into account the opinions expressed in decision-making) and joint working, to delegating control to users (for example, over budgets or service provision). The schemes implemented span the high-profile introduction of 'charters' between users and public services, with rights to information, complaint processes and redress, general participation in planning or advisory meetings, and consultation about policy delivery and outcomes, such as surveys, workshops and focus groups (Barnes and Wistow, 1994a, 1994b; Cook, 2002).

The NHSCC Act linked user involvement to a 'quality strategy for social care' and evidence-based practice that highlighted targets, performance indicators and outcome measures, and subsequently was reinforced by standards commissions, such as the Commission for Social Care Inspection (CSCI). However, whether perceived in business/managerial terms or according to professional criteria, quality definition and measurement does not always tally with user knowledge or evaluation criteria (Braye, 2000; Beresford and Branfield, 2006). Consultation exercises indicate that, in the field of social services, users' views on appropriate aims and outcomes do not easily satisfy managerial interpretations of 'evidence-based' good practice (Beresford, 2000; DoH, 2000; Edwards, 2002). For example, disabled people dispute that 'activities of daily living' are valid measures of their 'independence' (Albrecht and Devlieger, 1999).

Despite national government endorsement, local managers and service providers remain suspicious of user participation as a threat to their expertise and authority (Baldock, 2003; Hasler, 2003b; Carr, 2004; Hodge, 2005). For the most part, this has been restricted to expressing views, and, if points of disagreement emerge, users felt that their involvement was increasingly 'managed' (Braye, 2000, p. 23). A frequent user criticism was that their presence and participation were largely tokenistic, with professional and management agendas dominant. Some groups, such as mental health system users, have mobilized to present their views at all levels of health and social care, but, nonetheless, users' experiences are individualized, or managers question how representative they are of other users (Campbell, 2001; Crossley and Crossley, 2001).

These features suggest a 'management-centred' rather than a 'user-centred' form of user participation, where service users' objectives and priorities became the organization's objectives and priorities (Robson et al., 2003). While there are likely benefits from the process of participation itself, most user expectations are invested in the achievement of desired outcomes. That is to say, user involvement is a means to a desired end of greater choice and control over people's lives (Truman, 2005). Too often user participation entails 'being involved in the running of welfare services they might prefer not to receive' (Beresford, 1993, p. 18). In contrast to consumerist ideology, 'survivors of the mental health system are no more consumers of services than cockroaches are consumers of Rentokil' (Barker and Peck, 1987, p. 1; Peck and Barker, 1997).

Disabled people's interest in participation reflects two central and interrelated aims: first, that services facilitate desired outcomes, and, second, that they are organized and delivered in ways that individuals find empowering (Begum and Gillespie-Sells, 1994; Beresford et al., 1997; Turner et al., 2003). Specific concerns about implementation highlighted by service users include 'factors which restrict its quality overall; for example, inadequate funding, narrow eligibility criteria, the use of poor-quality agency staff, inflexibility and being over-bureaucratic, rather than issues which relate narrowly to any individual's experience' (Beresford and Branfield, 2006, p. 439; Branfield and Beresford, 2006). The barriers to user-led involvement stem from 'devaluing of service-user knowledge', 'problems of access and tokenism', hostile 'culture of health and social care organizations', and limited and uncertain resources. More broadly, while the government stressed 'developing effective partnerships', in practice this is organized in ways that make users the marginal 'partner', and there are manifest inequalities in power and resources (Beresford and Branfield, 2006).

In general, statutory authorities appear happier dealing with established voluntary organizations – mostly organizations *for* disabled people – carers' groups and groups of 'carers', and individual disabled people recruited through other channels (Beresford and Campbell, 1994; Bewley and Glendinning, 1994; Evans, 1995; Lindow and Morris, 1995). Non-user-led agencies have often been established longer, are mostly staffed by 'professional' service providers, and are more in tune with organizational systems and accessing funding. Overall, problems arise not so much from overt opposition as from less direct constraints, ranging from not enough time for meaningful discussion and low access to senior staff and preparatory training, to a lack of clear guidelines on conducting business and monitoring outcomes. Users often feel closely regulated in their participation (Fletcher, 1995; Bott and Rust, 1997) and complain that their involvement amounted to little more than a 'tick-box' exercise (Beresford and Branfield, 2006) or, at the other extreme, that the policy process appears so complex and bureaucratic that participation becomes an obstacle course.

Participation in practice often displays a surprising lack of awareness of disabled people's support needs, such as the provision of accessible venues, information and documentation; British Sign Language (BSL) interpreting; paying participants and adequately reimbursing their expenses; the specific difficulties of involving users in rural areas; and the failure to integrate members of minority ethnic groups (Turner et al., 2003). Participatory working provides challenges for those who communicate differently or with complex support needs that are often overlooked, and the low involvement of people with learning difficulties is particularly striking (Cole et al., 2000; Cole et al., 2007). Too often service users felt that the consultation process replicated their wider experiences of institutional discrimination and worsened their already low self-confidence when participating in the public arena.

These points are evident in the Audit Commission's (2003) recommendations for good practice in consulting with service users. The emphasis is on careful planning, with a commitment from individuals at all levels of the organization to prioritizing user concerns (Robson et al., 2003). Moreover, bringing users into the policy process rarely works without wider changes in organizational structures and processes (Carr, 2004; Beresford and Branfield, 2006). Disabled people's organizations have therefore supported appropriate training for service user involvement, such as assertiveness/'speaking up' courses, guidance on decision-making structures, negotiating skills, legal issues and rights under current legislation.

A long-term user demand has been for a shift from service provider-led to user needs-led assessments, so that services do not flow from what is available or thought best by service providers, but from the priorities of the disabled user. The 1986 Disabled Persons (Services, Consultation and Representation) Act included the right to an assessment of needs, and these had to be met by social services departments under the terms of the Chronically Sick and Disabled Persons Act. The Social Services Inspectorate (SSI) agreed that the assessment should be participatory and 'recognise that some users may be the best assessors of their own needs and solutions' in their everyday lives (SSI, 1991, p. 15), yet progress has been slow. Again, 'The goals of empowerment are addressed in the form of self-advocacy through sharing experience, acquiring information, exchanging mutual support and engaging in collective action such as independent evaluation of services' (Clare and Cox, 2003, p. 941).

Yet, the organizational context and broader service environment places constraints on practitioners, both with respect to information collected and the assessment process, from care plans to desired outcomes. Many practitioners bemoan the end of the 'giving and doing' tradition which entrusted social workers to serve the user's interest (Richardson, 2005). They are also reluctant to relinquish their power for interpretation of policy and its implementation (Holland, 2000; Lent and Arend, 2004; Foster et al., 2006). There is an enduring suspicion that service users want as much as they can for themselves while managers and professionals are required to defend the public purse.

Review

Since the middle of the twentieth century there has been a slow but significant increase in social policies directed at disabled people. In large part, this is a response to criticism of the 'naturalization' of disability and its emphasis on an individual's perceived biological 'deficits' as justification for the social exclusion, dependency and control by service providers that characterizes disabled people's everyday lives. The policy emphasis has now shifted to ways of reducing these social and economic inequalities and achieving the full range of state-guaranteed citizenship rights.

Nevertheless, the record of social policy intervention has been disappointing for failing to overturn the marginalization of disabled people. Flagship programmes, such as community care, flattered to deceive. There were definite moves to close the large, long-stay institutions, but concerns multiplied that some of their unacceptable features are replicated in smaller residential accommodation placements. And yet policies for the organization and delivery of social services for disabled people have been constrained by a failure both to counter traditional assumptions that people with impairments needed to be 'cared for' and to generate adequate funding support.

In contrast, campaigns by disabled people's organizations stress the goal of independent living and access to appropriate support services. Disabled people have initiated a range of innovative practical initiatives that include setting up their own Centres for Independent/Integrated/Inclusive Living; persuading local authorities to introduce schemes for 'direct payments', which allowed an important degree of service user control of allocated funding; and demanding meaningful participation in service policy development and delivery. While the central government has stated its intention to achieve equality for disabled people by 2025 (Cabinet Office, 2005), the policy rhetoric has not translated easily into practical policies. Progress has been uneven and piecemeal, so that the goal of independent living remains unfulfilled. This raises important questions about the involvement of disabled people and their organizations in the political process, and these are the primary focus of the next chapter.

FACULTY OF HEALTH + SOCIAL CARE
Library
25 JAN 2011
Campus
Clatterbridge
UNIVERSITY OF CHESTER

CHAPTER 7

Politics and Disability Politics

Previous chapters have documented wide-ranging inequalities between disabled and non-disabled people. A striking feature of the latter decades of the twentieth century was the way in which these injustices generated increasing political activity and protest by disabled people around the world. This has also transformed disability into a major area of concern for both politicians and policy-makers. One significant outcome has been the trend in many liberal or representative democracies to introduce some form of anti-discrimination legislation to protect disabled people (Charlton, 1998; Jones and Marks, 1999; Lawson and Gooding, 2005; Doyle, 2008). A sociological approach brings together two dimensions of 'politics': disabled people's relationship to 'conventional' political institutions and processes, and the emergence of a 'politics of disability'.

The traditional focus for the study of politics comprises the formal institutions and office-holders responsible for the organization and regulation of society. In representative democracies around the world, such as America, Australia, Britain and Japan, these range from parliament to congress, from president to prime minister, and involve both local and national governments, the civil service and sponsored bureaucracies, political parties and pressure groups, and the courts. These exercise varying degrees of power and influence in passing, implementing and interpreting laws and regulations which affect every aspect of our daily lives. In contrast, sociological approaches to politics concentrate on those aspects of social life where there is an imbalance of power between individuals and groups, and where attempts are made to bring about a change in that relationship. This extends the focus way beyond the 'official' institutions of political activity and an exploration of politics as 'what politicians do'. As the contemporary women's movement has argued, the 'personal is political' – in that even the closest personal interactions involve inequalities of power and a struggle for change.

In this chapter, both interpretations of politics will be examined. The first part examines the formal political structures and processes and the diverse barriers to the participation of disabled people. These restrictions have unintentionally precipitated the growth of a disabled people's movement. Claims that this exemplifies a 'new social movement' (Oliver, 1990; 1996a; Shakespeare, 1993; Fagan and Lee, 1997; Lee, 2002) will be explored in the second part of this chapter. The third section will evaluate these arguments with particular reference to the politicization of a disabled identity and its potential as a catalyst for social change. It will be argued that the emergence of the disabled people's movement presents a significant alternative to mainstream approaches, and that it has had an increasing influence on politicians, policy-makers and the population at large. Whether such developments signify the assimilation and effective neutralization of disability politics into the established structures of power or another stage in the struggle for a more equitable society has yet to be determined.

Politics and disabled people

A defining characteristic of representative, liberal democratic societies is 'government of the people, by the people, for the people'. In practice, this means periodic elections for legislative bodies, with 'regular' opportunities to influence elected representatives and political parties through individual contact, pressure groups and public campaigns. Even this implies a degree of public involvement that is rarely achieved.

Political power and influence is distributed unevenly, with some (dominant) groups better placed to secure their interests. While the use of overt political force and control through 'repressive' state institutions remains an option, the achievement of social stability has shifted towards the consensual legitimation of power. Different theoretical traditions highlight power/knowledge relations and discourses (Foucault 1980) or emphasize the achievement of willing consent or ideological hegemony (Gramsci, 1971, 1985), with a prominent role credited to institutions such as schools, the mass media and churches/ religion. A further key element to the legitimation of power relations stems from the rights of individual citizens to participate in political processes in general and the electoral process more specifically. However, these formal entitlements are frequently denied or not adequately sustained by appropriate practical measures (ADD, 2005).

Exclusion in the electoral process

There are several obstacles which may inhibit disabled people from exercising their right to vote. Most basically, some sections of the disabled population are excluded from the electoral register (Enticott et al,, 1992; Scott and Crooks, 2005; Mencap, 2007). The legal constraints have diminished recently relative to social and environmental barriers. For example, Section 4(3) of the British Representation of the People Act 1949 prohibited people resident in institutions for those with a 'mental illness' or 'learning difficulties' from joining the electoral roll. The Representation of the People Act 1983 subsequently allowed 'patients' to vote, but 'only under certain narrowly defined conditions' that were finally repealed by the Representation of the People Act 2000. However, people with learning difficulties have remained liable to disenfranchisement if they are deemed not to satisfy the general principle of 'legal capacity' (Scott and Morris, 2001). Inclusion on the electoral register and subsequent voting is open to influence by the awareness and attitudes of 'care' and electoral staff.

Additionally, some disabled people living at home with their families may not be entered on the electoral register by the head of the household. It is likely that part of the problem, particularly for people categorized as having learning difficulties, stems from the low expectations of family members or from a mistaken belief that people with a learning difficulty, mental illness or emotional distress are not entitled to vote. In an effort to address this problem, the Disability Rights Commission (DRC), abolished in 2006, and the NHS Valuing People support team ran projects for people labelled as having learning difficulties hoping to vote prior to the general election of 2005. Among the resources available were information packs on many local authority websites that were also given to presiding officers (Scott and Crooks, 2005).

Nonetheless, research on participation in the 2005 general election by people defined as having learning difficulties in the East of England found that only 34 per cent of those known to local services were registered to vote, compared with 51 per cent for other voters. The type of residence affected both rates of registration and voting patterns. Significantly, people in 'supported accommodation' (residential, supported or nursing homes) were more likely to be registered than those in private households, but less likely to vote (Keeley et al., 2008, p. 1). Other research suggested that one in five people with a 'learning impairment' thought that staff at polling stations were unhelpful. Concern was also raised that people who had not voted previously were being encouraged to do so under the 'Right to Vote' project, whether they wanted to or not (Scott and Crooks, 2005, p. 36).

Even when disabled people are registered to vote, other major problems arise, particularly regarding physical access (Enticott et al., 1992; Scott and Morris, 2001; Scott and Crooks, 2005; Barnett et al., 2007).

These include transport difficulties in getting to and from the polling station, access to the polling station itself and to the polling booth, and difficulties for some disabled people in marking the ballot slip without assistance. While acknowledging that there has been some improvement over the last decade, a study by Scope, formerly the Spastics Society, on the 2005 general election found that 68 per cent of all polling stations studied had one or more 'serious' access barriers. This represented an improvement of just 1 per cent on the 2001 general election: 30 per cent of polling stations did not display a large print copy of the ballot paper, compared with 38 per cent in 2001, and 32 per cent of polling stations did not provide a tactile voting device to assist visually impaired voters to cast their vote independently (Scott and Crooks, 2005, p. 23). This leaves some disabled people reliant on others for assistance if they want to vote, which may deter their participation.

Some of these problems can be overcome by disabled people voting by post or by proxy, where someone else casts their vote for them. Those wishing to take either of these options must obtain and complete the appropriate form for each election in which they wish to participate. A significant minority (27 per cent) of participants in the Scope survey found the written instructions difficult to follow. Hence the recommendation that: 'To maximise accessibility it is vital that postal voting information and instructions are short, unambiguous and written in Plain English' (Scott and Crooks, 2005, p. 28).

Furthermore, despite long-standing concerns that very little political information is produced in accessible formats, such as Braille, tape, video or symbols, for different sections of the disabled community (Fry, 1987; Ward, 1987; Enticott et al., 1992) improvements over recent elections have been marginal at best. For example, the election manifestos of the three main political parties, Conservative, Labour and Liberal Democrats, in the 2005 general election were written in standard print sizes. There was no mention in these documents that they were available in alternative formats, or that they could be obtained by downloading from the parties' websites (Scott and Crooks, 2005, pp. 42–5).

With the enactment of the Electoral Administration Act 2006 there is a requirement that 'reasonable and practical steps' are taken to ensure that polling stations, along with relevant literature and forms, are accessible to disabled people (with physical and sensory impairments) and those with low literacy skills. This act also removed the common-law impediment to voting on grounds of 'lunacy' and 'idiocy' (Keeley et al., 2008). Nonetheless, a study of the National Assembly of Wales election in 2007 reported that 70 per cent of polling stations did not meet acceptable access standards (Barnett et al., 2007, p. 7).

Furthermore, while those with cognitive impairments should have the same voting rights as their non-disabled peers, this does not apply to people who are considered to be without the 'mental capacity' to decide who to vote for, or who to appoint to cast their proxy vote (Mencap, 2007).

Similar concerns have been expressed in America, where confusion in counting ballot papers in Florida during the 2000 presidential election highlighted significant barriers confronting groups of disabled people in recording their votes. Legal action was also taken against the New York City government by Disabled in Action over inaccessible polling stations. Moreover, similar discriminatory practices are replicated in many other countries: 'It is not just inaccessible polling booths and registration tables, long queues or the lack of tactile ballot papers for blind and partially sighted people, but also because both disabled and non-disabled people often *believe* that disabled people do not have the right to vote' (ADD, 2005, unpaged).

Political parties and pressure groups

Disabled people also experience constraints in becoming active in party politics. First, many local constituency meeting-places and party headquarters are physically inaccessible to people with mobility-related impairments, so that it is hard for them to attend meetings or become party activists. Second, local parties may be reluctant to choose a disabled candidate because of the environmental and social barriers to being fully involved in campaigning and door-to-door canvassing (Oliver and Zarb, 1989). Third, disabled people are rarely encouraged to seek selection as party candidates. This contrasts starkly with initiatives to expand the number of women candidates, especially in constituencies where the party has a chance of winning. The number of MPs with accredited impairments in Britain has risen slightly over recent years, but few of these identify as a disabled person or with the disabled people's movement. Paradoxically, several disabled individuals have been appointed to the unelected House of Lords, where they have pursued a disability rights agenda (Peck, 2007, p. 16).

The relatively low profile of disability issues is further confirmed by their near invisibility in the 2005 general election campaign, and specifically in the manifestos of the main political parties. For example:

> The Labour Party did little to promote its work on the disability rights agenda despite the fact that the Disability Discrimination Act 2005 had just made it into law before the Election was called. Other significant policy work such as the Prime Minister's Strategy Unit Report 'Improving the Life Chances of Disabled People', the reform of social

care to support disabled people in independent living and the establishment of a cross-Government 'Office for Disability Issues' all failed
to form part of the Labour Party's public election campaign. (Scott and
Crooks, 2005, pp. 40–1)

A further avenue for political action by disabled people has been single-issue pressure group activity or campaigns. This form of political
participation has increased dramatically over recent years (McAnulla,
2006). There are now hundreds of such organizations, varying widely
in membership, operating at both local and national levels. But pressure groups vary significantly in their access to, and influence on, the
policy-making process. The more established interest groups within
industrial capitalist society, such as employers' organizations and
trade unions, owe their existence to their central position in relation to capital and the division of labour. This provides them with
economic power and influence, although in contrasting degrees. In
addition, there is another, more pluralistic world of competing interest and voluntary groups (Lloyd, 1993). Since they have a less central
socio-economic location, they tend to exert less influence, although
this varies across campaigns (Barnes and Mercer, 2003).

However, there are significant differences between organizations in
their objectives, leadership and membership. Aside from umbrella or
co-ordinating organizations such as Disabled Peoples' International
(DPI), the American Coalition of Citizens with Disabilities (ACCD) and
the United Kingdom Disabled People's Council (UKDCP), there are
four other categories that may be identified (see box 7.1).

In Britain, as in many other countries, there are economic advantages such as tax concessions for organizations accredited as charities.
Until recently, charities ran the risk of losing their status if they
engaged in overt political activity. It was also illegal for 'beneficiaries'
of such organizations to be members of their management boards
or committees. Hence, it was difficult for disabled people effectively
to control disability charities or for these organizations to engage
openly in political activity (Lloyd, 1993). Yet many established disability organizations have, historically, acted as both charities and
pressure groups. This enabled them to build up close working relationships with politicians and policy-makers, although it gave them
some 'credibility but relatively little power' (Barnes, 1991, p. 218).

Even so, a degree of ambiguity remains about the role of charities
and their political engagement:

> Campaigning by charities to mobilise public opinion to influence
> government policy can arouse strong feelings. On the one hand, many
> people think that charities should be allowed, and indeed have a duty,
> to campaign freely to change public policy on any issue if it is relevant

Box 7.1   A typology of disability organizations

1 Partnership/patronage
Organizations *for* disabled people: charitable bodies; provision of services
(often in conjunction with statutory agencies) and a consultative and advisory
role for professional agencies – e.g. Handicap International, Leonard Cheshire
Disability, Mencap, Rehabilitation International, Scope.

2 Economic/parliamentarian
Primarily organizations *for* disabled people: single issue; undertaking
parliamentary lobbying and research; legalistic bodies – e.g. American
Foundation for the Blind, Centre for Studies on Inclusive Education,
Disablement Income Group, Disability Alliance.

3 Consumerist/self-help
Organizations *of* disabled people: self-help projects; sometimes campaigning
groups, or working in collaboration with local or voluntary agencies – e.g.
Berkeley Centre for Independent Living, Derbyshire Coalition for Inclusive
Living, European Network for Independent Living, National Centre for
Independent Living, Spinal Injuries Association.

4 Populist/activist
Organizations *of* disabled people: politically active groups, often antagonistic to
partnership approach; primary activities focused on 'empowerment', personal
and/or political; collective action and consciousness-raising – e.g. ADAPT
(Americans Disabled for Accessible Public Transport, subsequently renamed
Americans Disabled for Attendant Programs Today), Disabled People's
Direct Action Network, People First, Union of the Physically Impaired Against
Segregation, SPAEN (Scottish Personal Assistants Employers Network).

5 Umbrella/co-ordinating
Organizations *of* disabled people: collective groupings of organizations
comprising consumerist and/or populist groups; rejecting divisions within the
disabled population based on impairment, functional limitation or age; may
function at local, national or international level; primarily political organizations
seeking empowerment of disabled people by a variety of means – e.g. UKDPC
(United Kingdom Disabled People's Council), formerly the British Council of
Disabled People (BCODP), Disabled Peoples' International (DPI), American
Coalition of Citizens with Disabilities.

Source: Adapted from Oliver, 1990, pp. 117–18.

to their work and if they have direct experience to offer. On the other
hand, some argue that such campaigning is a misuse of charity funds,
a misdirection of charities and a misuse of the fiscal concessions from
which charities benefit. (Charity Commission, 1999, p. 12)

Yet, in 2004, the Charity Commission stated that it is legal for charities to campaign openly 'for the rights of people with disabilities and

the elderly', although they are 'restricted in the extent to which they can engage in political activities by the legal rules applying to charities' (2004, p. 5). While there is some concern over how these rules are interpreted among local user-led organizations (Barnes and Mercer, 2006), all the large disability charities now campaign openly on disability issues. This is in marked contrast to the situation in the 1990s.

Until recently, it was not thought as important that disability charities should 'represent' disabled people's interests as that they should 'look after' them. Therefore, the key decision-makers in organizations *for* disabled people were salaried professionals who put forward their own 'expert' views about the needs of their particular 'client group'. When coupled with their fundraising strategies and dependency-creating services, this overtly paternalistic approach served to undermine disabled people's efforts to empower themselves (Oliver and Barnes, 1998; Drake, 1999).

However, a key feature of recent government reforms has been an emphasis on greater user involvement, collaboration, and the promotion of much closer working relationships and partnerships between and with organizations and agencies in the health and social service sectors. This ambition extends to the involvement of organizations representing disabled people (DOH, 2005a). It also incorporates a wider discourse around such terms as 'joined-up' government, 'integrated delivery' and 'seamless' services, which are all deemed part of a wider project to create a 'partnership culture' (Balloch and Taylor, 2001). This raises questions about changes in the state and state governance, and some commentators have suggested that this turn to market-based policies is fracturing established hierarchies between state, welfare institutions and civil society (Clarke, 2004).

While the intention of facilitating more collaboration is generally acknowledged, how far this amounts to a 'partnership' is rather less clear-cut (Glendinning et al., 2002). Certainly there is evidence, when considered alongside the growth in disability activism over recent decades, that these government overtures have had a considerable impact on traditional disability charities. Many of these have actively recruited disabled people on to their management committees and laid claims to be more representative of their disabled members' interests. This includes both adopting the language of rights and collaborating on specific projects with disability organizations controlled and run by disabled people. For instance, RADAR was established in 1977 as the Royal Association for Disability and Rehabilitation. It began as an organization *for* disabled people but is now run *by* disabled people. It represents its members by 'fast tracking' their 'opinions and concerns to policy makers and legislators' and campaigns to promote 'equality for all disabled people' (RADAR, 2005, unpaged).

An example of 'single-issue' pressure group activity in Britain is the Disablement Income Group (DIG), formed in 1965 by two disabled women (Megan du Boisson and Berit Moore) to campaign for a national disability income. Poverty was a major concern for disabled people in the 1960s, and DIG lobbied parliament and organized demonstrations (Campbell and Oliver, 1996). In the following decade, fifty voluntary groups formed a larger umbrella organization known as the Disability Alliance (DA), which has continued to produce a regular flow of reports documenting the link between impairment and poverty, and to improve the living standards of disabled people. It has widened its focus to provide information and advice on the welfare benefits and tax credits systems, while also advising and lobbying members of parliament and peers. More usually, however, single-issue groups have concentrated on impairment-specific concerns. For example, 98 per cent of the Multiple Sclerosis Society's research funding is targeted at research into the cause and cure of the condition, while only 4 per cent is directed at effective service delivery (Multiple Sclerosis Society, 2008, unpaged).

Practical schemes with a 'self-help' philosophy designed to enhance the control of disabled people over their lives have multiplied. An important example is the National Association of Disablement Information and Advice Service – now known as DIAL UK – which was initiated by disabled activists in Derbyshire (Davis and Woodward, 1981). In the 1970s, disabled people identified the lack of useful and accessible information as a major obstacle to developing new services. DIAL Derbyshire began as a telephone advice service run by volunteer disabled residents of Cressy Fields, a residential home and day centre, and received a small grant from Derbyshire County Council. It 'not only contributed to the breakdown in the knowledge monopoly held by professional disability experts but also gave disabled people a deeper sense of the increased choices possible for those wanting to live independently in their own homes in the community' (Finkelstein, 1993a, p. 39). The network of local information and advice services continued to grow, so that by 2005 there were almost 135 local DIALs. Although there have been concerns that it was being taken over by non-disabled professionals, it currently claims that its centres are 'run by and for disabled people' (DIAL UK, 2005, p. 1).

The self-help approach has been increasingly associated with the expansion of user-led voluntary organizations. The pressure for user-led services did not simply emerge from dissatisfaction with traditional provider-led models of service delivery that exhibited low standards of accountability, but was also stimulated by the growing emphasis on citizenship rights and a democratic approach (Beresford and Croft, 1993).

In addition to concerns about resources and the education and training of staff, there is often uncertainty about whether such organizations can pursue both a service provider and campaigning role (Stalker et al., 1999). As Gerben DeJong (1983) suggested with reference to the growth of the Independent Living Movement (ILM) in America, its political trajectory followed a 'natural history' of social protest movements. With the beginnings of acceptance of the grievances and policy recommendations in the corridors of power, disabled people's groups increasingly sought to influence traditional government institutions and processes. This change in political direction was reinforced by the gathering acceptance of disabled people's human and civil rights and the promotion of user involvement in service delivery by politicians and policy-makers. This led some disability activists to argue that, as more and more disabled individuals and agencies become embroiled in the complexities of traditional politics on the one hand and service development and delivery on the other, their priorities change and their radicalism in terms of both political aspirations and activities diminishes (Charlton, 1998). Similar arguments have been expressed about recent developments in the UK and several countries in Europe (GMCDP, 2000; Van Houten and Jacobs, 2005; Barnes and Mercer, 2006; Oliver and Barnes, 2006).

Civil rights and legislation

The political participation of disabled people and their organizations opened up a now obvious gap in the area of civil rights and anti-discrimination legislation. This highlights important contrasts between North American and European political contexts and disabled people's struggles. As noted in chapter 6, the ideological cornerstones of American society – market capitalism, consumer sovereignty, self-reliance and economic and political freedom – were replicated in the approach of the ILM, which stressed civil rights, consumerism, self-help, de-medicalization and de-institutionalization (DeJong 1979a). It opposed the professionally dominated and bureaucratic provision of social welfare services, and their sparseness, while demanding opportunities for disabled people to develop their own services in the marketplace.

When the first Centre for Independent Living (CIL) was set up in 1972 in Berkeley, California, the initiative was taken by disabled university students housed by the university authorities in a local hospital 'for their own good'. Led by Ed Roberts, they rejected this custodial environment and sought a community 'home' where supportive services were provided. The CIL adhered to three guiding principles: disabled people were best qualified to determine their needs and how these should be met; a comprehensive programme of support was required; and disabled people should be integrated as fully as possible into their community (Center for Independent Living, 1982, pp. 250–1). More generally, the ILM advocated distinctive approaches to traditional rehabilitation services in terms of their aims, methods of delivery, and programme management. Client choice and control was accentuated, with peer counselling highlighted and personal care directed by the disabled person, in contrast to traditional professionally dominated modes (DeJong, 1979b).

By way of contrast, in Europe, and particularly in Scandinavian countries, the strategic priority has been to enhance existing state-sponsored welfare systems to meet disabled people's needs. The welfare state is regarded as essential to overcome the perceived short-comings of market provision and heightened barriers experienced by poorer disabled people. As noted earlier, the ILM's approach meant that some groups, such as young white Americans with physical and sensory impairments, were better placed to exploit the possibilities of market competition (Blaxter, 1984; Williams, 1984b).

In Britain, organizations of disabled people mobilized opinion initially against their traditional categorization as a vulnerable group in need of 'care'. They argued for the right to define their own needs and service priorities and against traditional service provider domination. Most notably, the Derbyshire Coalition of Disabled People, now known as the Derbyshire Coalition for Inclusive Living, drew up its own list of seven fundamental needs of disabled people – information, access, housing, technical aids, personal assistance, counselling and transport – that exerted considerable influence in the growth of independent living initiatives across the country (Davis and Mullender, 1993).

A growing impact on the choice of strategies and priorities for the advancement of disabled people's interests has been the struggles around 'rights'. According to T. H. Marshall (1950), civil, political and social rights constitute the basis of modern citizenship. The civil rights emphasis in disability politics took off first in America, where there has been a long tradition of rights-based political campaigns. These were given a considerable reinforcement in the civil rights struggles of the 1960s, which in turn influenced the activities of disabled people's organizations. The American black civil rights struggles, with their combination of conventional lobbying tactics and mass political action, provided a major stimulus to an emerging 'disability rights movement' (Hahn, 1987, 2002; Shapiro, 1993). In contrast, the disabled people's movement in Britain has concentrated on achieving changes in social policy – that is, following a legislative route.

Without a written constitution or human rights legislation (until 1998), and with a greater involvement of national charities in lobbying for 'progressive' legislation compared with the United States, protest campaigns were constrained to follow different political paths (Imrie and Wells, 1993).

Until the mid-1970s, the American disability rights movement was a loosely structured amalgam of grass-roots groups and organizations. For example, Disabled in Action was formed in New York in 1970 with the primary purpose of engaging in political campaigns against the discrimination experienced by disabled people (Scotch, 1988). It adopted direct actions, with demonstrations, sit-ins and protests particularly prominent (Shapiro, 1993). Lobbying within Congress also gathered momentum. Sympathetic legislators in key posts helped insert disability-related provisions into the 1973 Rehabilitation Act. Section 504 is particularly important because, for the first time, it prohibited discrimination against disabled people in any federally funded programme. The act also promoted environmental access, more comprehensive services, employment opportunities, and an increase in the numbers of CILs: 'The enactment of section 504 was brought about largely by the activism of disabled people themselves. A number of sit-ins took place before the appropriate regulations were finally issued. The militancy of these sit-ins . . . vividly contradicted the stereotype of the disabled person as powerless' (Zola, 1983, p. 56).

However, local, state and federal governments were reluctant to implement Section 504, and it took several years of vigorous campaigning by disabled people's groups before it was translated into the necessary policy relations required for its implementation. A key role was played by the American Coalition of Citizens with Disabilities (ACCD), which was formed in 1974, from an existing network of self-help groups, as an organization with over sixty local and national affiliated groups. It was at this time that a tension emerged between those involved in advocacy within the federal and state-level political institutions and processes and those 'outsiders' engaged in grass-roots campaigns (Scotch, 1989; Zola, 1994). Throughout the 1980s, the emphasis on 'mass' political action gave way to a rising tide of judicial actions, with disabled individuals seeking redress for the denial of their constitutional rights. This attracted considerable media attention and heightened public awareness of the struggles for disabled people's rights. It eventually culminated in the Americans with Disabilities Act 1990 (ADA) – the oldest, and generally considered the most comprehensive anti-discrimination legislation in the world (Doyle, 2008).

The ADA's formal objective was to 'mainstream' disabled Americans as fully as 'practicable'. It outlawed discrimination against disabled people in employment, transport and the built environment, state and local government, and telecommunications (Pfeiffer, 1994). Some commentators regarded the ADA as representing a significant shift in the perception and approach to disabled people (Albrecht, 1992). By way of contrast, others expressed concern that it supported traditional analyses and solutions: 'with its culture of individualism, absolute individual rights and a rejection of paternalistic state agencies, the analysis has incorporated individualistic objectives of anti-dependency, empowerment and economic self-sufficiency through remunerative employment' (Bickenbach, 1999, p. 105).

The ADA has encouraged notable improvements in the accessibility of the built environment, but its effects in other areas have been much less than anticipated. An examination of its enforcement by the National Council on Disability concluded that:

> while the Administration has consistently asserted its strong support for the civil rights of people with disabilities, the federal agencies charged with the enforcement and policy development under ADA have, to varying degrees, been underfunded, overly cautious, reactive and lacking any coherent and unifying national strategy. In addition, enforcement agencies have not consistently taken leadership roles in clarifying 'frontier' or emergent issues. (Bristo, 2000, p. 1)

Specific concerns have been expressed about the weaknesses of its monitoring and enforcement provisions and its lack of impact on minority groups within the disabled population. Moreover, the onus is on the disabled person to seek 'reasonable accommodation'. In practice, the overwhelming majority of cases are settled out of court, with 95 per cent of the remainder decided in favour of the employer (Johnson, 1997; National Council on Disability, 2000; Hahn, 2002).

Internationally, the passage of the ADA acted as a beacon to anti-discrimination legislation in other countries through the 1990s, including the Australian Disability Discrimination Act (1992), the inclusion of disability discrimination within a Human Rights Act in New Zealand in 1993 and the (British) Disability Discrimination Act 1995 (DDA) (Doyle, 2008). In all this legal ferment, it is generally overlooked that Canada had included disability as a category entitled to human rights in the Canadian Charter of Rights and Freedoms in 1985. Similar legislative measures are also evident in many poor and 'developing' nations (see chapter 10).

Since the 1970s, British organizations controlled and run by disabled people, such as the Union of the Physically Impaired Against Segregation (UPIAS), the Liberation Network and Sisters Against Disability (SAD) embraced similar goals to those of their American counterparts, with the pursuit of disabled people's rights at centre stage and signs of increasing readiness to combat discrimination.

A key element in these campaigns was the establishment by the Labour government in 1978 of the Committee on Restrictions Against Disabled People (CORAD), chaired by the disabled activist Peter Large. It located the problem of discrimination within a structural and institutional context by focusing on a range of issues, such as access to public buildings, transport systems, education, employment and leisure facilities. It made a number of recommendations, including a call for legislation to secure disabled people's rights (CORAD, 1982). However, Margaret Thatcher's newly elected Conservative government was less than sympathetic. Jack Ashley, a deaf Labour MP, introduced a private member's anti-discrimination bill in July 1982, but it was unsuccessful.

The campaign for anti-discrimination legislation continued. In 1985 the Voluntary Organizations for Anti-Discrimination Legislation (VOADL) Committee – renamed Rights Now in 1992 – was established. This provided an uneasy alliance between organizations controlled and run by disabled people and more traditional organizations for disabled people that had often been lukewarm about civil rights legislation. At the same time, this was also a period of growing politicization among disabled people. A major impetus has been attributed to the 'politicisation and subsequent radicalisation of increasingly large sections of the disabled population' (Oliver and Barnes, 1998, p. 90) as a result of the publication of the BCODP-sponsored *Disabled People in Britain and Discrimination: A Case for Anti-Discrimination Legislation* (Barnes, 1991) and the widening dissemination of Disability Equality Training (DET) – an approach to consciousness-raising based on the social model of disability. The BCODP initiative provided substantive quantitative evidence, based on government statistics, of unequal treatment for disabled people in key areas such as education, employment, benefits, health and social support services, the built environment and leisure. It was disseminated in a variety of accessible formats to disabled people's organizations. By the mid-1990s, all the major political parties acknowledged the need for legislation, and the Conservative government introduced a bill in 1994 that was finally passed as the Disability Discrimination Act 1995 (DDA).

As with the ADA, Britain's Disability Discrimination Act is based on an individual medical approach. The individual complainant must prove that they have an impairment before litigation can begin. It defines discrimination as arising in instances of 'less favourable treatment' without good cause, and where reasonable adjustments are not made. The law provides only limited protection from direct discrimination in employment, the provision of goods and services, and in selling or letting of land. Initially, education and transport were excluded from its provisions. Over 90 per cent of employers were not covered by the act because they employed fewer than twenty people. However, subsequent regulations reduced these exemptions, so that by 1 October 2004 all employers were covered by the DDA (Lawson and Gooding, 2005; Doyle, 2008). Business commentators in Britain expressed concerns that disability rights legislation imposed a financial burden unlike comparable initiatives: 'outlawing discrimination against blacks or women does not cost anything, but outlawing discrimination against disabled people will often involve costs' (*The Economist*, 13 August 1994, pp. 33–4).

In 2001, anti-discrimination law was extended with the introduction of the Special Educational Needs and Disability Act (SENDA). Based again on a traditional individualistic definition of 'disability', it prohibits discrimination against disabled students in schools, colleges and universities and requires the latter to make 'reasonable adjustments' so that such students are not disadvantaged. However, as with the DDA, it is a reactive law that requires individuals to complain before any action may be taken. In 2005, a further amendment to the DDA was added – the Disability Equality Duty (DED). In contrast to previous policies, this is a proactive measure which requires all public institutions to produce a Disability Equality Scheme outlining plans to make the necessary changes in all policy and practices to facilitate disabled people's inclusion. The intention is that these schemes are reviewed and amended every three years until equality is achieved. The task of ensuring that public organizations and institutions fulfil their obligations under the DED (Directgov, 2007a) is the responsibility of the recently established Equality and Human Rights Commission (EHRC).

However, the impact of the DED has been only limited. Research commissioned by the Office for Disability Issues (ODI) on thirty-five public authorities across seven policy sectors – housing, education, health, environment, transport, culture and criminal justice – found that 'mainstreaming of disability issues has been partly achieved in some organisations, while others have a long way to go' (Ferrie et al., 2008, p. 14). The best results were evident in agencies which had actively involved disabled people, as specified by the DED. However, although the production of disability equality schemes, action plans and impact assessments has raised the profile of disability issues, most schemes had a stronger focus on 'either staff or (less often) customers and service users . . ., [and] few succeeded in addressing the needs of both groups to the same extent'. Moreover, there was little evidence of monitoring and evaluation (ibid., p. 17).

Furthermore, on 27 April 2009 the government published a single Equality Bill which, if passed, will bring disability, sex, 'race', age, religion and other grounds of discrimination within one piece of legislation. It is expected to achieve royal assent and become law in spring 2010. There is real concern among disabled people and their organizations that the introduction of this bill marks a significant step backwards in the struggle for equality for disabled people (RADAR, 2009). Bert Massie, a long-time disability rights campaigner, has argued that the new bill will dilute disabled people's rights as it will repeal the DDA and incorporate it into what will become a single Equality Act 2010. The DED will be abolished and replaced by a single Equality Duty. Massie fears that the 'single equalities approach will mean that disabled people are less likely to be involved in policy decisions that effect us' (2009, p. 10).

Moreover, the DDA began life without an enforcement agency to monitor its implementation. This is in marked contrast to the ADA, as well as other British anti-discrimination legislation such as the 1975 Sex Discrimination Act, which was overseen by the Equal Opportunities Commission (EOC), and the 1976 Race Relations Act, covered by the Commission for Racial Equality (CRE). Even so, these bodies have been only marginally effective in combating discrimination. Although formally 'independent', funding and appointments to the EOC and CRE are subject to political approval. Critics have suggested that, as a result, the bulk of their activities have centred on 'education and research' rather than enforcement or addressing the structural disadvantages underlying sexism and racism (Oliver, 1990; Barnes, 1991; Bagilhole, 1997; Harwood, 2006).

The New Labour government set up a Disability Rights Task Force after its election in 1997 and, following its recommendations and intense lobbying, the Disability Rights Commission (DRC) in April 2000 to facilitate 'the elimination of discrimination against disabled people'. Like the EOC and the CRE, the DRC's main activities spanned the production of new codes of practice, the updating of existing ones, the provision of information and advice, conciliation, and research. Initially, the DRC had the power to take up cases on behalf of individuals and organizations, and in its first decade the DDA enabled several thousand people to gain some financial redress at employment tribunals.

> However, only a small percentage of actions which constitute 'discrimination' within the meaning of the Act result in a claim being instituted; the great majority, 4,437 in 2004–2005 . . . of instituted claims are abandoned or fail at tribunal; and the DDA provides no redress at all (except with regard to victimization) for individuals who suffer discrimination, however serious, but who are not deemed to meet the statutory definition of 'disabled'. (Harwood, 2005, unpaged)

This has considerably weakened the impact of the DDA in deterring disability discrimination in employment or in encouraging good practice. Wide employment differences remain between people with and without impairments, instances of discrimination are common, 'and institutional discrimination is apparent in most organizations', including those in the public sector (ibid.).

Furthermore, the DRC closed its case work department in 2005 and, along with the EOC and CRE, was abolished in 2007. They were replaced by the Equality and Human Rights Commission (EHRC), which began operations in October 2007. Government justification for the new body hinges on the assertion that it will bring together 'equality experts' and act as a single source of information and point of contact for individuals and organizations, in order to help 'businesses tackle discrimination by promoting awareness of equality which may prevent court and tribunal cases' and tackle 'discrimination on multiple levels – some people may face more than one discrimination' (Directgov, 2007b, unpaged).

In an associated development, the Equality Act 2006 weakens the rights of individuals seeking legal assistance in discrimination cases. Unlike its predecessors, the EHRC does not have the power to represent an individual's complaint to an employment tribunal (except with reference to discriminatory advertisements and 'instructing or causing someone to discriminate'), nor is it required to consider all applications for assistance. One critic suggests that this 'appears to give the Lord Chancellor excessive power to determine the situations in which the EHRC will be able to support cases under the *Human Rights Act*'. Moreover, government ministers have indicated that they expect the EHRC to use its enforcement powers as rarely as the previous commissions used theirs (Harwood, 2006, p. 8). Furthermore, growing disquiet within the EHRC over its retreat from 'a campaigning strategy for tackling inequality and discrimination to one of "fairness"' has been a contributing factor in the resignation of several commissioners. These included the disabled activist and one-time chair of the BCODP and co-founder of the National Centre for Independent Living (NCIL) Baroness Jane Campbell, Professor Francesca Klug, a human rights academic, and Sir Bert Massie (Oliver, 2009).

In the EU, the European Commission adopted a directive on equal opportunities for disabled people in 1996. This encouraged (but did not require) member states to abandon segregated facilities for disabled people in favour of mainstreaming. In addition, Article 13 of the amended Amsterdam Treaty of 1997 empowered the Commission to 'take action on grounds of disability (along with discrimination on grounds of sex, racial or ethnic origin, religion or belief, age and sexual orientation)' but did not convey new rights to disabled people (Priestley, 2005, p. 22). In October 2003 the Commission agreed to a directive requiring member states to introduce anti-discrimination legislation in a number of areas, including disability, and 2003 was declared the European Year of People witih Disabilities. A European action plan on policies for disabled people followed which emphasized the inclusion of disabled people, reinforced by the introduction in 2010 of a rolling action plan.

> The goal of the action plan is to mainstream disability issues into relevant community policies and develop concrete actions in crucial areas to enhance the integration of people with disabilities . . ., the Commission proposes to reinforce the involvement of stake holders and key players in the policy dialogue in order to bring about far reaching and lasting changes within the economy and society as a whole. (European Commission, 2003, p. 3)

It is important to remember that the European Union is a community of sovereign nation-states and the principle of subsidiarity places substantial limits on social policy implementation. Subsidiarity, as defined in Article 5 of the Lisbon Treaty of 2007, gives member states freedom of action in response to EU directives (Europa, 2008). As a consequence there remains considerable variation in disability policy across Europe, with little evidence of substantial convergence in key ideas and policies (Hivenden, 2003; Priestley, 2005).

The passage of the Human Rights Act 1998, as well as the impact of European Community law, promises a further significant impact on disability politics. One possibility is that it will encourage the disabled people's movement in the UK to move closer towards the profile adopted by its counterparts in Australia and New Zealand, with campaigns for increased civil rights as well as fundamental social changes. There is also likely to be further pressure to conform to international agreements on disability, as happened with the acceptance of the United Nations' *Standard Rules on the Equalization of Opportunities for Persons with Disabilities* (UN, 1993). This document outlines a radical programme for governments to follow in identifying and securing disability rights.

The UN Convention on the Rights of Persons with Disabilities and its Optional Protocol was adopted in December 2006. It was negotiated over eight sessions of an Ad Hoc Committee of the General Assembly from 2002 to 2006 that included representatives of disability organizations and marks the first human rights treaty of the twenty-first century. With fifty articles, the Convention is the most comprehensive document yet produced on the rights of disabled people. Article 1 states that:

> The purpose of the present Convention is to promote, protect and ensure the full and equal enjoyment of all human rights and fundamental freedoms by all persons with disabilities, and to promote respect for their inherent dignity. (UN Enable, 2009a, unpaged)

While it is designed in an international law context, the Convention sets out the duty of nation-states to protect human rights. Once in force, it is legally binding on any country that ratifies it. The Convention came into force in April 2008 and at the time of writing has been signed by 140 countries and ratified by fifty-nine states. Eighty-three have signed the Convention and thirty-seven ratified an optional protocol. The UK signed the Convention and ratified it on 8 June 2009. However, the government has opted out of several parts of the Convention, applying to education, immigration and the armed forces. Disabled people may not therefore have the right to a mainstream education, disabled migrants wishing to stay in or enter the UK may be subject to wider health checks, and disabled people may be barred from working in or for the armed forces (Peck, 2009, p. 7). The USA has neither signed nor ratified the Convention or the protocol (UN Enable, 2009b).

Despite considerable enthusiasm among disabled people's groups on both sides of the Atlantic, there is concern and criticism that the experience of following the legal route has been that it produces long-drawn-out and costly court actions. These downgrade collective political struggles and ignore the social and political location of the legal system. In addition:

> A rights-based approach to legal development has been rejected by many modern critical legal scholars. They raise a number of concerns about rights. These include a misuse and abuse of the concept of rights; the indeterminism of rights; the fact that rights are unstable and context bound; the fact that rights cannot determine consequences; and the fact that rights formalise relationships and thereby separate us from each other. (Jones and Marks, 1999, p. 22)

Overall, the emphasis on claims to human and civil rights using existing legal frameworks has not brought about equality for disabled people. This is because the pursuit of legal protection alone does not overtly challenge the overall political and economic system, and therefore will struggle to effect the radical changes necessary to eradicate structural inequalities (Hahn, 2002).

A new social movement?

While conventional politics remains central to political campaigns by disabled people and their organizations, the failures of pressure group and electoral politics to win significant policy reforms have encouraged a more radical disability politics. This has given rise to suggestions that the disabled people's movement may lay claim to be a 'new social movement' (Oliver, 1990, 1996a) or a 'liberation struggle' (Shakespeare, 1993).

The polarization of 'old' and 'new' forms of social protest runs parallel to claims that there have been major realignments in the late twentieth-century social and economic order which herald the emergence of what has been variously termed, 'post-industrial', 'post-capitalist' or 'post-modern' society (Fagan and Lee, 1997). A shift towards consumption rather than production, consequential changes in the division of labour and social structure, along with deepening social and cultural disorganization and crises in the (welfare) state have all been identified as key features. In turn, changing class configurations and other emerging social divisions and conflicts encouraged new forms of social protest. Marxist expectations of the revolutionary potential of the industrial working class were dashed by its incorporation into welfare capitalism. Some writers on the left transferred their hopes for progressive social change on to a burgeoning range of new protest movements emerging in the 1970s and 1980s that included the women's movement and peace and environmental groups (Touraine, 1981; Scott, 1990).

One of the first exponents of new social movement theory, Alain Touraine (1977, 1981), identified a new core conflict within Western European societies. This was linked to the breakdown of traditional work patterns and class boundaries and the decline of traditional forms of class struggle. Similarly, Alberto Melucci (1980) argued that new or 'contemporary social movements' were indicative of an unprecedented structural transformation which entailed a major realignment of society, the state and the economy. More recently, these themes have been developed with reference to the deteriorating social and economic conditions during the 1980s and their effects on welfare provision and delivery (Williams, 1992; Hewitt, 1993; Taylor-Gooby, 1994).

For Touraine (1981), these 'new' social movements have the potential to transform society as they centre on the very meanings and values that predominate within 'post-industrial' society. Claus Offe (1985) regarded the new forms of social protest as representative of minorities hitherto marginalized by governmental structures and powerful interest groups. These movements are not class-based and celebrate alternative political agendas, such as community action and self-help groups which flourished in urban areas, as well as the national and international civil rights, student action, and women's, environmental and peace movements. Sociological interest also concentrated on emergent and divergent sub-cultural lifestyles and 'alternative' cultural values and meanings. Yet the defining features of new social movements were a source of intense debate. Some commentators stressed their capacity to resist bureaucratic encroachment (Melucci, 1989), along with their expressive politics and allegiance to more direct forms of democracy (Habermas, 1981).

Others queried the claimed disjuncture between 'old'- and 'new'-style politics and protest. There are, for example, close parallels between the women's suffrage movement of the early twentieth century and more recent feminist struggles (Shakespeare, 1993). Indeed, there are examples of disability protest at least from the early decades of the twentieth century. Low pay and poor working conditions prompted the National League of the Blind and the Disabled (NLBD) to mobilize blind workers from around Britain to march to London in 1920, and the NLBD also campaigned against the policies of charities, leading to protest marches in the 1930s and 1940s (Campbell and Oliver, 1996). A similar engagement in political action occurred in the United States over this period (Longmore and Goldberger, 2000).

Nevertheless, Mike Oliver (1990) argues that the disabled people's movement warrants classification as a new social movement, based on the following criteria: (i) it is peripheral to conventional politics; (ii) it offers a critical evaluation of society; (iii) it embraces 'post-materialist' or 'post-acquisitive' values; and (iv) it adopts an international perspective (Oliver, 1996a). However, these qualifying criteria omit the widely noted association between such movements and the 'new middle class' (Touraine, 1981; Scott, 1990) or arguments that they involve a 'celebration of difference' (Young, 1990).

On the margins of conventional politics?

Until recently there were few organizations controlled and run by disabled people, and these exercised little influence on policy-makers. Traditionally, voluntary bodies and charities have dominated how disability is viewed and understood within the corridors of power. Many are concerned only with impairment-specific issues and increasingly with service provision rather than political campaigns and lobbying. Disenchantment with the impact and character of these organizations led to an unprecedented growth in campaigning, self-help and activist groups. The emphasis shifted to self-organization and a commitment to radical political action in order to influence the behaviour of groups, organizations and institutions (Anspach, 1979; DeJong, 1979a):

> Clearly the purpose of disabled people's self-organisation is to promote change: to improve the quality of our lives and promote our full inclusion into society. It does this both through involvement in the formal political system and through promotion of other kinds of political activity. (Campbell and Oliver, 1996, p. 22)

In Britain, new, radical groups emerged in the 1970s. A notable example was the formation of UPIAS in 1974. It comprised a small but influential group of disabled activists located in residential institutions who campaigned for more control over their everyday lives. As in America, such groups continue to provide an important source of ideas and support by promoting disabled people's collective interests, to both statutory agencies and political parties and across local and national levels (Zola, 1983; National Council on Disability, 2000). A further significant development in Britain was the emergence of BCODP as a national umbrella for organizations controlled and run by disabled people. At its first meeting in 1981, it had representatives from only seven national groups, including the British Deaf Association, the NLBD, the Spinal Injuries Association and Gemma (an organization of disabled lesbians and gay men), but BCODP quickly became a national voice of disabled people in the campaign for political rights. In 2007 it represented around seventy user-controlled groups with a total membership in the UK of around 70,000 (BCODP, 2008).

However, disability activists on both sides of the Atlantic expressed periodic concerns about the risk of incorporation. There has been a noticeable movement of disabled activists into the mainstream of politics as governments have placed a higher priority on disability issues. This has entailed more consultation with representatives of disabled people as well as appointing disabled people to government-sponsored organizations (Shapiro, 1993; Barnes and Mercer, 2001; Oliver and Barnes, 2006). Indeed, most disabled people's groups have increasingly taken the path of conventional politics, albeit only after considerable soul-searching:

> To get too close to the Government is to risk incorporation and end up carrying out their proposals rather than ours. To move too far away is to risk marginalisation and eventual demise. To collaborate too eagerly with the organisations for disabled people risks having our agendas taken over by them, and having them presented both to us and to politicians as theirs. To remain aloof risks appearing unrealistic and/or unreasonable, and denies possible access to much needed resources. (Barnes and Oliver, 1995, p. 115)

A radical route to social change

New social movements define themselves in counter-hegemonic terms. A defining feature has been their focus on social exclusion and oppression. The barriers to disabled people's inclusion are embedded in policies and practices based on the individualistic medical approach to disability. The removal of such obstacles involves gaining control over material resources and the range and quality of services. It also requires recognition of the contribution of hostile physical and social environments to the marginalization and powerlessness experienced by disabled people. The aim is that disabled people will be 'consciously engaged in critical evaluation of capitalist society and in the creation of alternative models of social organisation at local, national and international levels, as well as trying to reconstruct the world ideologically and to create alternative forms of service provision' (Oliver, 1990, p. 113).

Those promoting the social model have stressed its radical credentials. Concrete evidence of this is seen in the marked contrast between the traditional, voluntary, paternalistic organizations *for* disabled people of the pre-1970s and the newer more representative organizations established in the last decades of the twentieth century that were controlled *by* disabled people (Barnes and Mercer, 2006). Nevertheless, there are strong differences of interpretation around the social model, and it has been invoked in support of a wide range of initiatives, as with the anti-labelling approaches for normalization and integration. This means that service provision for people with learning difficulties typically remains rooted in a 'care', protection and welfare ethos, even though couched in the language of empowerment and civil rights (DoH, 2001; Stevens, 2004).

A further aspect to the 'new' politics has been its adoption of unconventional political tactics, including demonstrations, direct action and civil disobedience. These attracted particular attention in the United States, where disability protests often took their cue from the actions of other social protest movements of the late 1960s and the 1970s. 'When traditional legal channels have been exhausted, disabled people have learned to employ other techniques of social protest' (DeJong, 1983, p. 12).

This engagement in 'direct action' represents a shift in the balance from 'old'- to 'new'-style political protests and campaigning. A central objective has been to attract maximum publicity, so action is 'often carefully planned to influence opinion-formers, the media etc.' (Shakespeare, 1993, p. 258). Through the 1990s there have been a growing number of demonstrations, for example, in America and Britain against charity shows and telethons (Longmore, 1997). In Britain, this precipitated the end of such events in 1992, while also leading to the formation in 1993 of the Direct Action Network (DAN), which organized over 200 local and national demonstrations within its first five years of existence (Pointon, 1999). These actions continue to pose a high-profile political challenge to orthodox notions of disability and traditional stereotypes of disabled people in terms of passivity, pathology and weakness. It is an opportunity for disabled people to 'do it for themselves' and can be an empowering process for participants, creating a sense of solidarity, purpose and collective strength which enhances and develops the aims of the movement.

Disabled people's groups around the world have emulated each other's tactics and campaigns in employing direct action to invade government buildings and disrupt transportation systems and media events. In America, ADAPT has been in the vanguard of such protests, with demonstrations outside the White House in favour of a national attendant care policy and occupation of the Federal Department of Transportation building to demand more accessible inter-city coaches. In Australia, the prime minister's office in Sydney was occupied in 1997 in protest against budget cuts to the Human Rights and Equal Opportunities Commission (Gleeson, 1999). Similar activities have been reported across much of the 'developing' world (see chapter 10).

Post-materialist values?

Another element claimed as a distinguishing feature of new social movements is their adherence to 'post-materialist' or 'post-acquisitive' values – over those that have to do with income, satisfaction of material needs and social security (Inglehart, 1990). This is apparent particularly in environmental and peace groups, but evidence of this 'value switch' is far from compelling when applied generally to disabled people, women, or black and minority ethnic groups. All these groups have stressed the importance of overturning disadvantages in the distribution of income and wealth, welfare benefits and the labour market. Similarly, the demand for more resources and service support typifies disabled people's demands around the world.

In response, Oliver (1996a, p. 157) reinterprets 'post-materialism' to include counter-cultural shifts, such as are identified in a disability culture (see chapter 8), which has confronted the 'stigmatization of difference' and presented an altogether more positive disabled identity. Other accounts of new social movements stress the tension between what Nancy Fraser (1997) terms a politics of 'distribution' and of 'affirmation'. Certainly, disabled people's protest, as with feminist politics, has committed to a more expressive politics in seeking empowerment and social justice. This links with a cultural politics that challenges disabling stereotypes and the notion of 'able-bodied normality' and finds ways to affirm a positive disabled identity. It is in this sense that the disabled people's movement supplements its concern with social and economic inequalities. Nonetheless, this stance falls short of a comprehensive denial of core capitalist values.

A global phenomenon?

A further key feature in new social movements and the politicization of disability has been their internationalization (Driedger,
1989). Disabled activists formed Disabled Peoples' International
(DPI) in 1981. Its first world congress was held in Singapore in the
following year and attracted 400 delegates from around the world.
They agreed on a common programme: the empowerment of disabled people through collective political action (DPI, 1982). For DPI,
the prerequisite for change lies in the promotion of grass-roots
organizations and the development of public awareness of disability issues. Its slogan, 'Nothing about us without us' (Charlton, 1998),
has been embraced by disabled people's organizations around the
world.

There has also been important sharing of experiences in developing new forms of self-organization. For example, the promotion of
'independent living' has drawn heavily on the American experience.
There are now CILs or equivalent organizations across Europe and in
other industrialized countries, such as Australia, Canada and Japan,
as well as in South America and Africa (Ratzka, 1992). A further
instance of the impact of the disabled people's movement at the
international level is found in the attention given to disability issues
within transnational organizations such as the United Nations, the
International Labour Organization, the International Monetary Fund
(IMF), the World Bank and the World Health Organization (Driedger,
1989; Albert, 2006). Needless to say, considerable variation exists in
the form and character of national disability politics (see chapter
10).

Overall, the disabled people's movement demonstrates both radical
and conventional sides. The balance has varied, and arguably the
number committed to wide-ranging social change has lost ground
to what is the majority standpoint of supporting political involvement in the established political institutions, and of trying to break
down disabling barriers from within the system. Of course, there is no
single 'royal road' to 'independent living' or 'empowerment', and no
set of political tactics or form of self-organization that will suit disabled people living in very different societies and political contexts.
Even within Europe, the approach taken by the disabled people's
movement in individual countries demonstrates considerable variation in their political analyses and strategies. Yet, for most disabled
people, what is important is not whether their struggle is categorized
as either 'new'- or 'old'-style politics but that it sustains and enhances
the extraordinary vitality and impact of disability politics built up
over recent decades.

Identity politics

Initially, disability theorists viewed the politicization of disabled people as a response to their common experience of oppression (Finkelstein, 1980; Oliver, 1983). This provided a unifying group identity and interest while identifying the source of these grievances in the structures and processes of a disabling society. For many disabled people, engaging in collective action was liberating and empowering and a source of positive identity: 'Not only is the fashioning of collective identity an explicitly articulated goal of the politicised disabled people's movement, but the very act of political participation in itself induces others to impute certain characteristics to the activist' (Anspach, 1979, p. 766). Disabled campaigners' protests represent one among several examples of a socially oppressed group asserting its 'cultural and experiential specificity' (Young, 1990, p. 160).

The experience of disabled people was that assimilation was on 'able-bodied terms', and inherently oppressive. Hence, the celebration of difference appeared liberating and empowering. It encouraged disabled people to celebrate what they had been taught to despise. The assertion of a positive cultural identity and a 'politics of difference' has become a favoured political strategy for protest movements. It is not assimilation that is the goal but recognition of difference. Instead of focusing on removing the stigma of being a disabled person or ending institutional segregation, disabled people have sought their own self-definition and an affirmation of their own culture.

Just as 'self-identity' is a central issue in considering the emergence of disability culture (see chapter 8), so too is it at the heart of disability politics. Yet many individuals with an accredited impairment do not 'self-identify' as disabled or get involved in political activity of any kind. For example, disability politics may divide on social class grounds, with the financial and other resources of those in a middle-class position used to mitigate some of the worst effects of disability experienced by poor, disabled people (Russell, 1998). Of course, similar comments can be applied to other contemporary social movements, but disabled people's campaigns demonstrate a significant under-representation of older people (Walker and Walker, 1998), individuals from minority ethnic groups (Vernon, 1999), people with learning difficulties (Chappell, 1997) and mental health system users and survivors (Sayce, 2000). For the disabled people's movement to continue to be an effective force for change, it has to address the reluctance of people with a range of impairments to adopt a 'disabled identity'.

However, while disabled activists sought to establish collective interests and politics, there was a growing support for a transition to an identity politics and a novel 'celebration of difference' (Woodward,

1997). Identity politics 'involves claiming one's identity as a member of a marginalised group as a political point of departure and thus identity becomes a major factor in political mobilization' (ibid., p. 24). This involves separating out one part of an individual's experiences rather than emphasizing interrelationships between different 'identities', or presuming a core over peripheral identities. Disability politics had to focus on ways of celebrating difference without instituting new hierarchies.

This emphasis on a basic disabled identity was now criticized for its essentialism and for being in conflict with an emancipatory politics. Identity becomes 'strategic and positional', and fluid rather than fixed (Hall, 1990). Indeed, no limits were placed on the amount of difference or distinct collectivities that might emerge, in terms of age, gender, 'race' or sexuality, for example, to undercut the claims of a common, disabled group identity. Any political movement based on the notion of identity found itself exposed to charges that it denied 'difference' and was liable to fracture. As the disabled people's movement had already discovered with respect to Deaf people, disabled identities are sometimes contested, but now they were interpreted as altogether more uncertain, fluid and lacking any firm base.

For critics of this 'politics of identity', such as Nancy Fraser (1997, 2000), it signalled a retreat from a vision of a 'just social order', and a shift away from struggles over redistribution to focus on winning 'recognition' of social collectivities in a distinctive cultural political struggle. She argues that, whatever its claims, an essentially 'cultural politics of identity and difference' fails to connect with a 'social politics of justice and equality' (1997, p. 186). For the millions of people in the world experiencing extreme poverty and inequality, the politics of identity offers little vision of social justice. While the politics of recognition has advanced, the politics of redistribution has been in retreat. Fraser advocates instead a 'bivalent' approach to social oppression that integrates the 'social and the cultural, the economic and the discursive' (ibid., p. 5). Their separation is flawed in theory and practice: their simultaneous pursuit does not diminish the radical potential of disability politics. Indeed, the acceptance of cultural differences presumes some foundation of social equality.

Nancy Fraser argues rather for a 'transformative' political project that is allied to 'deconstruction'. This rejects the notion that differences are expressions of human diversity and not to be set within a hierarchy, because it implies that 'anything goes' and that there is no basis for making normative judgements about whether some difference is acceptable or not, whether it is better or worse. The goal of those advocating a disability politics should be to break down the disabled/non-disabled polarity in a way that promotes redistribution in the political economic spheres while also deconstructing disabling culturally valued claims around 'able-bodied normality'.

While for supporters of 'identity politics' the emphasis on 'difference' is the first stage in any cultural revaluation, for critics it is more likely to sustain rather than undermine existing differences. Various strategies have been advanced as ways of achieving collective political action within an acceptance of (some) difference: 'Identities may be supplanted by issues, as substantive campaigns around housing, health, welfare, education, employment, immigration, reproduction and media representations combat the multidimensional oppression matrix' (Humphrey, 1999, p. 175).

Nevertheless, a politics of difference has yet to demonstrate its capacity to sustain a coherent and effective political programme. As Marta Russell argues, the challenge for disability politics is to 'build upon mutual respect and support *without dismissing or diluting difference. For instance, to move beyond ramps, we must first agree that ramps are indisputably necessary.* That would be making a common political "home", blending difference into commonality' (Russell, 1998, p. 233, *emphasis in original*).

Review

The remarkable politicization and mobilization of disabled people and their organizations around the world over recent years has been extraordinarily significant in challenging myths and misconceptions about disabled people's supposed passivity. This mobilization is especially remarkable in light of the fact that it has been achieved with few resources and restricted access to the electoral and political processes. Until the 1990s, disability politics in most Western societies was dominated by professionally led impairment-specific organizations that perpetuated a traditional paternalistic understanding of disability and disabled people. The upsurge of disability activism among grass-roots organizations has had a significant influence on these organizations but also on mainstream political parties, policy-makers and the general population. A significant illustration of this impact is demonstrated by the growth of anti-discrimination legislation in many countries around the world and the growing focus on disability among international organizations as diverse as the World Bank and the United Nations.

While there have been significant advances in placing disability issues firmly on national and international political agendas, this has not generated the changes necessary to bring about a more equitable and just society. Indeed, there are concerns among some disability activists that the assimilation of disability politics into mainstream political agendas will undermine the more radical aims and political struggles by disabled people and their organizations for social justice. Any such trend contradicts claims that the disabled people's movement constitutes a 'new social movement'.

A further issue that generates intense debate is how far disability politics should reflect the wider flow of identity politics and the celebration of difference. This has rightly focused attention on cultural politics, as a form of both domination and resistance, and the significance of attending to diversity among disabled people. What is at risk is that the material bases of economic inequality are set aside or marginalized, along with the goal of political-economic redistribution. These are issues and themes that have an obvious importance for understanding cultural representations of disability – the subject of the next chapter.

Culture, the Media and Identity

$\mathbf{T}$HE significance of culture, in both the domination and emancipation of disabled people, has attracted considerable interest in disability studies. The negative values permeating the wider society and culture have been summarized as a personal tragedy approach that condemns disabled people to an inferior 'life apart'. Disabled people's lives are effectively undermined by the negative reactions to impairment by non-disabled people and in a myriad of forms in the wider culture. Thus, when individual disabled people have the opportunity to reflect publicly on their experiences, the prevalence of negative, disabling stereotypes in everyday life is a continuing theme (Hunt, 1966a; Shearer, 1981a; Campling, 1981). Disabled people in America have advanced parallel concerns (Bowe, 1978; Zola, 1982; Deegan and Brooks, 1985). With the growing politicization of disabled people, there have been increasing calls for a radical reappraisal of the role of the media in particular and the cultural domain more generally in producing and sustaining disability. This has also prompted the search for an alternative disability culture, and the development of disability arts, to challenge mainstream representations and explore a positive, unifying identity.

The twin aims of this chapter are to examine the place of disability in culture and the media, and how disability culture has moved to the centre of the wider disability politics agenda for change. The discussion begins with a brief overview of sociological approaches to culture. Second, it appraises the imagery and representation of disabled people in the media and various art forms, and their potential impact on audiences. Third, there is a review of literature that has adopted a 'cultural studies' perspective, distinguished here by the theoretical influence of post-structuralism (post-modernism). In the final part of the chapter, we observe how disabled people have sought to produce a distinctive disability sub-culture in opposition to the dominant 'ableist' culture, and its relationship to a separate disabled identity or identities, as well as the growth of disability arts.

Sociological approaches to culture

Typically, sociologists have adopted a wide-ranging definition of culture in terms of the symbolic aspects of human society, such as beliefs, rituals, customs and values, as well as patterns of work and leisure, and material goods: 'Culture consists of the values the members of a given group hold, the norms they follow, and the material goods they create' (Giddens, 1989, p. 31).

While values are 'abstract ideals', norms encompass the rules or guidelines of what is acceptable in social life. Culture, then, denotes a 'signifying system' through which practices, meanings and values are 'communicated, reproduced, experienced and explored' (Williams, 1981, p. 13). This diffuse view of culture as a 'way of life' is close to, but distinguished from, the notion of 'society', which refers to a 'system of interrelationships' held in common by those who share a similar culture (Giddens, 1989, p. 32). To become a member of a society, it is necessary to learn, or be socialized into, its cultural assumptions and rules.

Raymond Williams maintained that:

> A culture has two aspects: the known meanings and directions, which its members are trained to; the new observations and meanings, which are offered and tested. These are the ordinary processes of human societies and human minds, and we see through them the nature of a culture: that it is always both traditional and creative; that it is both the most ordinary common meanings and the finest common meanings. (1989, p. 4)

Human cultures set the criteria for, or the boundary lines around, both what is considered 'normal' and typical and what is 'abnormal' or different in an unacceptable way. Analyses of disability in culture bring these issues to the fore by examining the common meanings attached to people with impairments as in some way 'deficient', not quite 'normal' or perhaps not fully 'human'.

The significant variation across cultures in the meaning and representation attached to impairment and disability has already been noted. Sociological accounts of the relationship between society and culture have tended to polarize between idealist and materialist accounts. Among the latter, orthodox Marxist accounts emphasize how in any mode of production an economic base ultimately determines the character of the culture/political superstructure. Such economic or technological determinism has been widely refuted, and in the late 1960s so-called Western Marxism began to attribute a degree of relative autonomy to the cultural domain from dominant interests. In developing more complex accounts of the relations between the material and cultural spheres, the writings of Antonio Gramsci (1971) have exerted a major influence. Most notably, his concept of 'hegemony' addressed the ways in which capitalist domination is achieved not only by coercion, but also by the generation of 'willing consent' of the subordinate population. In this task, the production and consumption of culture, in such institutional arenas as education, the law and art and literature, can be crucial.

A further influential alternative to the orthodox Marxist view is the concept of 'cultural materialism' developed by Raymond Williams (1980, 1981). This offers 'a theory of culture as a (social and material) productive process and of specific practices, or "arts", as social uses of material means of production' (Williams, 1980, p. 243). With an acknowledgement again to Gramsci, institutional arenas such as schools and workhouses, churches and the press, are viewed as part of a material system of production, not 'mere' superstructure. Williams also highlights the economic and political contexts in which culture is produced and 'consumed'. Equally important, cultural forms offer scope for alternative 'oppositional' possibilities, an aspect vividly illustrated in studies of the emergence of sub-cultures as potential counter-hegemonies or sources of resistance to dominant interests, pre-eminently gender, 'race' and ethnicity (Hall and Jefferson, 1976; Hall et al., 1978; Hall et al., 1980).

In the late twentieth (post-modern) century, cultural politics moved centre-stage in the face of the development of a 'new right' hegemony in Britain and America. Stuart Hall (1997) focused pre-eminently on 'cultural representations and signifying practices' and how the media generates and sustains particular images of identity and Otherness – as demonstrated in his analyses of the 'racialized Other'. This approach influenced the new field of 'cultural studies', although, most recently, its theoretical debates have been overtaken by structuralism and post-structuralism, often importantly mediated by feminist interventions. In the case of theorizing disability, the major influence has been Michel Foucault's (1965, 1972) examination of the relationship between changing linguistic-discursive practices, or ways of knowing, and shifts in institutional practices (see chapter 4). Even so, his 'genealogical' studies of knowledge–power relations constitute but one among several dimensions pursued in the contemporary literature on post-structuralism. It is clearly separable, to take one example, from Derrida's emphasis on 'deconstruction' (Milner and Browitt, 2002; Corker and Shakespeare, 2002).

Cultural representations of disability

Historically, across European cultures, there has been a 'fascination with spectacles of difference' (Mitchell and Snyder, 2001, p. 210), and a concentration on 'defective' or 'abnormal' bodies and minds. The 'Otherness' of disabled people has been exploited as a source of 'entertainment' as well as to incite the fears and emotions of the non-disabled population. In ancient Greece and Rome:

> ... it would almost seem as if no fashionable household was complete without a generous sprinkling of dwarfs, mutes, cretins, eunuchs and hunchbacks, whose principal duty appears to have been to undergo degrading and painful humiliation in order to provide amusement at dinner parties and other festive occasions. (Garland, 1995, p. 46)

This public display of bodily 'abnormalities' featured throughout the Middle Ages. Many royal courts in Europe retained people of short stature as 'court jesters', while parents sometimes 'toured the countryside displaying for money recently born infants with birth defects' (Gerber, 1996, p. 43). The public exhibition of the inmates of 'mad-houses' and institutions continued this practice, and by the nineteenth century such displays had developed into staged 'freak shows'. These offered a 'formally organized exhibition of people with alleged physical, mental or behavioural difference at circuses, fairs, carnivals or other amusement venues' (Bogdan, 1996, p. 25). They flourished in Europe and North America into the early decades of the twentieth century, and in the USA were complemented by the so-called ugly laws that placed restrictions on the everyday lives of people whose physical appearance might offend or frighten 'normal' people (Bogdan, 1996; Gerber, 1996).

At the end of the twentieth century, the cultural exclusion of disabled people seemed entrenched and all pervasive:

> The general culture invalidates me both by ignoring me and by its particular representations of disability. Disabled people are missing from mainstream culture. When we do appear, it is in specialised forms – from charity telethons to plays about an individual struck down by tragedy – which impose the non-disabled world's definitions on us and our experience. (Morris, 1991, p. 85)

Contemporary media stereotypes

Over recent decades, the representation of disabled people in the media and other art forms, such as literature, film and photography, reinforces what it means to be a disabled person in this society and rationalizes the treatment of disabled people as 'deficient'. Initially, studies concentrated on the negative imagery surrounding disabled people, but increasing attention has been paid to the processes by which meanings about normality and bodily difference are produced, across different media and cultural forms.

Louis Battye's (1966) study of *Lady Chatterley's Lover* provided one of the first critical analyses of disability in literature, the picture of the paralysed husband, as impotent and signalling lost masculinity. Twenty years later, Ann Karpf (1988) detailed the significance of recurring themes or 'crippling images' in media representations more generally: for example, the fondness for cure stories; the role of charity appeals; the invisibility of disabled people on television; the stereotyped portrayal of disabled characters in screen drama; the under-employment of disabled people in broadcasting. This corresponds to a form of oppression, with disabled people portrayed as weak and unattractive personalities, and with impairment routinely employed as a metaphor for sin or wickedness.

Content analyses of the representation of disabled people give empirical corroboration to this view. For example, Guy Cumberbatch and Ralph Negrine (1992) undertook a six-week monitoring of British television during 1988, using content analysis and group discussions. One striking finding is that disabled people comprised less than 1 per cent of all characters in fictional programmes. Equally noteworthy, disabled people are misrepresented or represented in a partial way, with a narrow range of fictional images that centre on criminality and deviance, or the barely human, powerless and pathetic. The most prevalent storylines involving disabled people focus on medical treatment or cure or on an individual's 'special achievements'. They are not depicted as ordinary members of society, engaged in everyday activities, but are exploited to evoke emotions of pity or fear, or contribute to an atmosphere of mystery, deprivation or menace.

These patterns indicate little media sympathy for recommendations from the Broadcasting Standards Council (BSC) in its Code of Practice that programmes and advertising give a 'fair reflection of the parts played in the everyday life of the nation of disabled people' (BSC, 1989, p. 45). To achieve this would require, first, a shift away from the portrayal of disabled people in factual programmes in a manner which gives non-disabled viewers 'a sense of the superiority of their condition, or the emotional enjoyment of their generous sympathy', and, second, a concerted effort on the part of writers and producers to include more disabled characters, preferably played by disabled actors, in fictional programmes. These characters should be part of 'the drama of life' and not used 'in either a sinister or a sentimental fashion' (Cumberbatch and Negrine, 1992, p. 141).

Research on the US media similarly emphasizes the absence of disabled people and their exclusion from major roles (Zola, 1985). People with impairments are depicted as leading one-dimensional lives: as passive victims, dependent and unproductive. So much of the dramatic focus centres on their interaction with health-care or social welfare professionals. The 'good parts' of ordinary lives – love, romance and sex – are largely absent in disabled character's lives (Hahn, 1989). Nor is there much interest in exploring disabling social barriers. Instead, impairment is characterized as a health issue that requires medical intervention or a personal response to be overcome (Longmore, 1997).

Recent studies indicate relatively little change in TV practice. Fictional programming still represents disabled people mainly in one-dimensional terms, rather than as 'ordinary' people experiencing 'ordinary problems' (Ross, 1997, p. ii). Programme-makers concentrate on 'acceptable' disabled characters, typically wheelchair users, primarily because of the concern to avoid impairments that are thought 'off putting' to a mainstream audience. Factual TV programmes are condemned for the regularity with which non-disabled 'experts' are used to pronounce on the experiences and priorities of disabled people. Documentaries are charged with dwelling excessively on disabled people as either 'tragic but brave' or 'helpless and dependent' (ibid., p. iii). Concern was also expressed about the marginalization of specialist disability programmes into 'ghetto-slots', where their potential impact on mainstream audiences is greatly diminished.

A study monitoring trends in the portrayal in TV programmes of disabled people indicates a 'remarkable stability' over the period from 1993 to 2005 (Cumberbatch and Gauntlett, 2006, p. 12). Disabled people generally occupied 'minor' rather than 'major' roles in fictional programmes. In most cases, the impairment was rated as central or relevant, as opposed to 'incidental', in the portrayal of individual characters. Once again, the lack of representation of disabled people is very evident, with only slightly more than 1 per cent of all (non-news) programmes featuring a disabled person, and 10 per cent including a disabled participant in a lower profile way.

In *Disabling Prejudice* (Sancho, 2003), a large-scale interview and questionnaire survey of disabled and non-disabled people, including media professionals, respondents express a 'high degree of acceptance of the principles for increased inclusion, and positive attitudes towards increased representation of disabled people on television in a wider variety of roles' (2003, p. 8). Conversely, in a range of examples from comedy programmes to adverts, they do not agree about what constitutes 'acceptable' in contrast to offensive representations (ibid., p. 13). Most objections to the involvement of disabled people came from individuals who felt uncomfortable when watching a person with an impairment. Broadcasting professionals reinforced this point, suggesting that a combination of commercial constraints, the structure of the industry and audience prejudices accounted for the continued marginalization of disabled people even more than of women or minority ethnic groups (ibid., p. 14).

Newspaper reporting of disability has attracted similar criticism. Studies organized by the charity Scope in 1990 (Smith and Jordan, 1991), and a decade later (Cooke et al., 2000), conclude that a limited number of themes dominate newspaper coverage, with health, fundraising/charity, and personal/individual interest stories accounting for approximately 35 per cent of the total. Tabloids appear particularly prone to dramatize and sensationalize, and to ignore other aspects of disabled people's experience. However, broadsheets also present a one-sided picture and reinforce a medical approach, as in their preoccupation with negligence claims and legal cases generally. The language used tended to be pejorative and prejudicial, and there was little improvement over the decade. Reporting was not really about disabled people but 'how non-disabled people cope when they encounter a disabled person and their "problems"' (ibid., 2000, p. 6).

Yet there are recent examples of novel and more overtly hostile media representations. These are typically associated with disabled people's participation in political protest campaigns. In Britain, the Direct Action Network (DAN) has been in the vanguard of militant, high-profile direct action. Disabled people have been pictured waving placards, chaining themselves to buses and trains, blocking roads, crawling along the streets, and disrupting charity events such as telethons (Pointon, 1999). This was characterized as 'Sticking two fingers up at the traditional charity-campaign image of disabled people as quietly respectable, submissive types' (Daniel, 1998, p. 22). It diverges markedly from news media portrayals of disabled people as overwhelmed by their personal tragedy, or courageously struggling against the odds. Initially, newspapers and TV seemed bemused and uncertain about what to do, but references to the 'last civil rights battle' were soon mixed with suggestions that such actions threatened to alienate erstwhile (non-disabled) supporters. For example, the broadsheet *Sunday Telegraph* published an article condemning 'the furious Quasimodos' who had defaced part of Downing Street with red paint in an anti-government demonstration (Wilson, 1997).

As with the broadcasting media, the editors of the major national newspapers agreed on a voluntary Code of Practice in 1990 to ensure that disabled people were 'fairly represented' in the press and not exploited for their news potential. Despite this, self-regulation has proven little more than a public relations exercise, as in the appointment of a 'reader's representative' by major newspapers to deal with complaints and push for change. Further criticism from disabled people's organizations has been directed at the Press Complaints Commission, which has been reluctant to exercise its admittedly limited powers. Overall, it has failed to secure a marked improvement in press reporting of disability, and so criticism continues that newspapers are offending needlessly (Cooke et al., 2000).

The portrayal of disabled people in advertising also reinforces negative imagery, with a bias moving between pity and pathetic (Pointon and Davis, 1997). Their cynical exploitation by charities has generated considerable antagonism among disabled people. Nonetheless, Jane Campbell (1990) has detected three main phases in charity advertising: philanthropic ('fundraising garden parties'); 'courageous and exceptional'; and 'look at the ability not the disability'. The latest development implies a shift from a negative focus on impairment to what disabled people can achieve. Against this, the positive aspects are largely interpreted in terms of conforming to 'normal' people's expectations.

This notion of specific images of disabled people attracted a growing volume of research studies in America from the 1970s onwards (Biklen and Bogdan, 1977). Laurie Klobas (1988), for example, identified many examples of distinctive representations on both the small and the large screen. Another landmark was John Schuchman's survey of images of deafness in Hollywood films, in which he concluded: 'Until film makers portray the existence of an active and healthy deaf community, it is improbable that Americans will get beyond the pathological myths that make daily life difficult for disabled individuals' (1988, p. 305). Photography has played a comparable role in the social positioning of individuals/bodies (Berger, 1972). Attempts at positive images too easily slip into 'denial, disavowal or suppression of the struggle and oppression' (Hevey, 1992, p. 103). This is demonstrated in the coverage of President F. D. Roosevelt's mobility impairment, with only a handful of photographs out of 35,000 showing him as a wheelchair user (ibid., p. 102).

The collection *Images of the Disabled, Disabling Images* (Gartner and Joe, 1987) brought together a number of important critiques, exploring the way in which disabled people are objectified by the media. Leonard Kriegel, examining a diverse range of literary sources such as *Lady Chatterley's Lover* and *Moby Dick*, concluded that:

> The world of the crippled and disabled is strange and dark, and it is held up to judgement by those who live in fear of it. The cripple is the creature who has been deprived of his ability to create a self . . . He is the other, if for no other reason than that only by being the other will he be allowed to presume upon the society of the 'normals'. He must accept definition from outside the boundaries of his own existence. (Kriegel, 1987, p. 33)

Paul Longmore illustrates how popular cartoon characters such as Porky Pig and Elmer Fudd carry messages about impairment and identity. He argues that it is the fear of 'disability' which underlies these presentations: 'What we fear, we often stigmatise and shun and sometimes seek to destroy. Popular entertainments depicting disabled characters allude to these fears and prejudices or address them obliquely or fragmentarily, seeking to reassure us about ourselves' (Longmore, 1987, p. 66).

Several reviews of the American media have produced categorizations of the most prevalent media representations of disabled people: pitiable and pathetic; an object of violence; sinister and evil; for atmosphere; a 'super-crip'; an object of ridicule; their own worst and only enemy; a burden; non-sexual; incapable of fully participating in everyday life (Biklen and Bogdan, 1977, pp. 6–9). Even so, disabling stereotypes sometimes include 'diametrically opposed concepts' – as with sexuality, where the range is from asexual or non-sexual to insatiable 'sex degenerates' or 'helpless victims' and 'evil degenerates' (ibid., p. 5). A more recent addition to this list treats disabled people as 'normal'. While this should prove a positive development, the emphasis on 'normality' tends to obscure the need for change: 'if disabled people are viewed as "normal" then there is little need for policies to bring about a society free from disablism' (Barnes, 1992, p. 38).

In a parallel discussion, Clogson (1990) differentiates five key forms of media representation:

1. medical: disability as illness or malfunction;
2. social pathology: disabled people as disadvantaged, needing support;
3. 'super-crip': disabled people as deviants, achieving superhuman feats in spite of impairment;
4. civil rights: disabled people having legitimate grievances, as members of a minority group;
5. cultural pluralism: disabled people as multifaceted, impairments not the only issue.

This list was extended by Haller (1995) to include:

6. business: disabled people as costly to society in general, and especially private/commercial companies;
7. legal: disabled people possessing legal rights;
8. consumer: disabled people as an untapped market.

Within this scheme, models 4, 5, 7 and 8 offer positive representations, but the overwhelming conclusion from this literature spotlights the negative aspects of media images. There was also heightened recognition that disabling stereotypes are mediated and influenced by other social divisions, with a growing research interest in how the cultural representation of disability is 'gendered'.

Gendered stereotypes

In her review of the disabled female in fiction, Deborah Kent suggests that 'Disability seems to undermine the very roots of her womanhood. Not surprisingly, therefore, the disabled women in these works frequently feel inferior to others and regard themselves with loathing' (1987, p. 63). Moreover, authors exhibit less concern with disabled women as subjects, seeking greater control of their lives, than as vehicles or objects: 'In many instances, the disabled woman is little more than a metaphor through which the writer hopes to address some broader theme' (ibid., p. 60).

Jenny Morris argues that, in the gendered imagery of disability, 'the social definition of masculinity is inextricably bound up with a celebration of strength, of perfect bodies. At the same time, to be masculine is not to be vulnerable' (1991, p. 93). For instance, films such as *Born on the Fourth of July* and *Waterdance* had men trying to cope with their loss of masculinity through impairment. The focus is on disabled men, in order to consider the contradiction between masculine potency and disabled impotency – on the presumption that the only thing worse than feeling unloved is to be incapable of making love. Since women are already seen as vulnerable, passive and dependent, there is a narrower artistic focus in portraying disabled women pre-eminently as tragic or saintly figures. While there are images of disabled men as 'super-crips' – characters who triumph over tragedy – there have been only a few examples of disabled women in this category, such as Helen Keller. However, the use of the disabled climber Lisa O'Nion in a Schweppes poster campaign conveys the message that others like her can aspire to overcome their physical limitations.

An associated argument is that the media are generally reluctant to depict disabled women in traditional female roles as wives and mothers (Fine and Asch, 1988). While feminists seek to challenge such gender stereotypes and reject the overwhelming representation of women as occupying conventional domestic positions, disabled women have expressed general support for media images of disabled people in the 'mainstream' roles of wives and mothers, to which they are often denied access. Helen Meekosha and Leanne Dowse add that feminists criticize eroticized images of women but tend to ignore the absence of disabled women, primarily because they are not regarded as sexual beings.

> There are also dangers here of the advertising industry moving from selling the beautiful and sculptured non-disabled body to selling the beautiful and sculptured disabled body. For women with degenerative or acquired disabilities, or illnesses not amenable to physical body

> sculpting, these images can further demoralise and undermine their
> sense of self-worth. (Meekosha and Dowse, 1997b, pp. 97–8)

These examples reinforce two central points: first, the importance
of recognizing the diversity of the disabled population in discussions
of disabling imagery; and, second, the notion of a positive, or a negative, image is complex and contradictory. It is here that an emerging
academic specialism of 'cultural studies' has drawn on wider theoretical debates to take studies of disability, the media and culture in new
directions.

Cultural studies approaches

The descriptions of disability images and content that characterize
so much of the early approaches to understanding disabling representations have recently given ground to a multidisciplinary cultural
studies approach that draws on neo-Marxist, post-structuralist, linguistic and psychoanalytic theoretical influences. This has spawned
a growing literature that engages with specific art-works or texts and
develops detailed, multi-layered readings. In contrast to the mainly
quantitative or classificatory approach, this literature is concerned
with textual critique and looks at qualitative and aesthetic issues.

With some notable exceptions, cultural studies accounts of disability representations have had most impact within the humanities, as
is best illustrated in the American literature. The focus has been on
the role of disability within literature, film and other art forms. This
literature largely disavows a social model distinction between impairment as a property of the body and disability as a social relationship.

A prominent contributor to these debates is Rosemarie Garland-
Thomson, who incorporates forms of literary criticism into her
interrogation of American cultural forms, from the traditional freak
show, through sentimental novels such as *Uncle Tom's Cabin*, to the
contemporary African American fiction of Toni Morrison and Audre
Lorde. Her focus is on impairment: 'To denaturalize the cultural
encoding of these extraordinary bodies, I go beyond assailing stereotypes to interrogate the conventions of representation and unravel
the complexities of identity production within social narratives of
bodily differences' (Garland-Thomson, 1997, p. 5). She draws heavily on
contemporary literary theory, with an emphasis on post-structuralist
arguments, in casting light on the construction of normality, by
examining how 'corporeal deviance' is a 'product of cultural rules'
about 'able-bodiedness': 'Constructed as the embodiment of corporeal
insufficiency and deviance, the physically disabled body becomes a

repository for social anxieties about such troubling concerns as vulnerability, control and identity' (ibid., p. 6). She characterizes disabled bodies as 'extraordinary' rather than 'abnormal', but it is her preoccupation with the individual body, rather than structural and collective forces, that marks a clear difference from most British analyses of disability and culture.

The value of feminist disability theory derives from its capacity to unravel issues of human diversity, materiality of the body, and multiculturalism – that is, 'How these different representational systems 'mutually produce, inflect, and contradict one another' (Garland-Thomson, 2006a, p. 258). Disability is a concept, like gender, that pervades all aspects of culture: 'its structuring institutions, social identities, cultural practices, political positions, historical communities, and the shared human experience of embodiment' (ibid., p. 259). In summary, feminist disability studies 'reimagines disability', locating its 'significance in interactions between bodies and their social and material environments (Garland-Thomson, 2005, p. 1558).

Martin Norden's (1994) comprehensive chronology of disability in film extends the 'image of' approach to the portrayal of social groups in exact social contexts. He shows how, from the earliest days of cinema, stereotypical and distorted representations of disability were the norm – as conveyed in Thomas Edison's short film *Fake Beggar* (1898). As a visual medium, cinema used pictures to reveal character, so it became automatic to represent emotional cripples as physical cripples. Additionally, the new technology offered the opportunity for trick photography to represent miracle cures. The cinema also inherited the voyeuristic traditions of the freak show, typified by Cecil B. DeMille's assertion that 'affliction is more saleable' (quoted in ibid., p. 71).

Norden traces the development of a range of stereotypes – Elderly Dupe, Saintly Sage, Obsessive Avenger, Sweet Innocent, Comic Misadventurer, Tragic Victim, Noble Warrior. Each, he suggests, is characterized by the isolation experienced by the disabled character: 'We might argue that the movie industry has created physically disabled characters primarily to serve the needs of a society long committed to stifling and exploiting its disabled minority' (Norden, 1994, p. 314). That said, he detected positive changes of this imagery as it evolved from the early exploitative phase (1890s–1930s), through the explorative phase (1930s–1970s), to the incidental phase (1970s to present). Nevertheless, even in contemporary films the old stereotypes still surface. While Norden makes connections to broader social, economic and political developments (for instance, the return of disabled veterans from war), he concentrates primarily on psychoanalytic explanations. This focus on the subconscious domain is evident in studies of the disabled 'other', and the perceived fear and dread that some impairments generate (of debility, dependency and mortality) among 'able-bodied' people (Shakespeare, 1994; Davis, 1997; Garland-Thomson, 1997). A major influence is Freud's location of the ego in bodily concerns, parallels being drawn between castration with other (symbolic substitute) losses such as a limb or sight (Marks, 1999; Wilton, 2003).

A different interpretation is advanced by the British critic Paul Darke based on a detailed analysis of disability in such films as *The Elephant Man* (Darke, 1994). This underpins his concept of 'Normality Drama', which he describes as a genre that uses abnormal/impaired characters to deal with a perceived threat to the dominant social hegemony of normality (Darke, 1998). He rejects the psychoanalytical approach taken by Norden and criticizes attempts by disabled critics to propose positive images, suggesting this fails to capture the totality and significance of disability within films. For Darke, normality drama spotlights the cultural rationalization of the social disablement of individuals with an impairment.

The cultural studies approach is similarly active in wider artistic and historical studies. For instance, Lennard Davis (1995) traces the development of the lexicon of disability, and particularly the social construction of 'normalcy' in the mid-nineteenth century. He argues for analyses of the construction of disability and its perceived opposite, able-bodied 'normality'. He also extends this critical analysis to literary texts not focused on disability, concluding that: 'One can find in almost any novel . . . a kind of surveying of the terrain of the body, an attention to difference – physical, mental and national' (ibid., p. 48).

The pre-eminent literary interest is the way in which '[d]isability lends a distinctive idiosyncrasy to any characters that differentiate themselves from the anonymous background of the norm' without exploring its 'social or political dimensions' (Mitchell, 2002, p. 16). The graphic phrase 'narrative prosthesis' is introduced to indicate how disability has been used as a 'crutch on which literary narratives lean for their representational power, disruptive potentiality, and social critique' (ibid., p. 17). A parallel conclusion applies in film, theatre and painting. Disability is used as a metaphor for wider 'ills' in social groups, or society more generally. 'Literary portrayals of disabled bodies move between the specificity of a character's overriding identifying feature and the larger concerns of social disorder' (Garland-Thomson, 1997, p. 25). The 'bodies of the severely congenitally disabled have always functioned as icons upon which people discharge their anxieties, convictions, and fantasies' (ibid., p. 56). Indeed, the TV soap opera has recently been castigated as 'the

ultimate freak show' (Wilde, 2004, p. 369), with a 'preference for characters who are caricatures of normality' (ibid., p. 357), while disabled
male viewers have great difficulty in identifying with disabled characters – perhaps understandable given the stress on 'failed masculinity'
(ibid., p. 368).

> Whether a culture approaches the body's dynamic materiality as a
> denigrated symbol of earthly contamination (as in early Christian
> cultures), or as a perfectible *techné* of the self (as in ancient Athenian
> culture), or as an object of social symbolism (as in the culture of the
> Renaissance), or as a classifiable object of bodily averages (as in the
> Enlightenment), or as specular commodity in the age of electronic
> media (as in postmodernism), disability inaugurates the need to inter-
> pret human differences both biological and imagined. (Mitchell, 2002,
> p. 17)

A provocative portrayal of the entrenched divide between the
disabled and non-disabled worlds is conveyed in a short story by H. G.
Wells published in 1904 that tells of a man called Nunez who falls off
a mountain into an isolated valley populated entirely by people with
congenital blindness. He presumes wrongly that, 'in the Country of
the Blind, the One-eyed Man is King' (Wells, 1979, p. 129). In practice,
the community treats Nunez as a curiosity and finally as an alien presence and threat to their way of life as blind people. Moreover, unlike
most 'imperial' fiction, the civilizer is snubbed and the disabled
inhabitants celebrate the virtues of 'darkness' over those of 'truth'
and 'civilization'.

David Hevey, in *The Creatures Time Forgot* (1992), combines an aesthetic and theoretical analysis of bodily representation with a broader
concern with the social context and political significance in his study
of charity advertising. He demonstrates how charities 'market' their
express impairment focus in ways that parallel the 'branding' of
commercial organizations and their products. The role of charity
adverts is to promote the organization and its approach to impairment in order to secure public donations. This involves presenting
a stark image of impairment/disability, usually in black and white,
which centres on the physical flaw. The purpose is to evoke fear and
sympathy in the viewer. Charity advertising is described as 'the visual
flagship for the myth of the tragedy of impairment' (1992, p. 51), and a
very influential component in the cultural construction of disability:
'It represents the highest public validation of the isolation of disabled
people. It presents a solution to the "problem" of disablement by a
disguised blaming of the victim. It fails to find a solution because it is
itself the problem' (ibid.).

The role of charity imagery in the lives of disabled people has been
equated with the role of pornography in women's oppression. In both

cases, the imagery serves to subordinate the objectified subject of the image. The focus is on the body, and most usually certain parts or deficiencies (the breasts/impairment). The viewer is manipulated into an emotional response (desire/fear). In both cases, the conditions of production of the image are outside the control of the subject and involve wider meanings and power relationships (Shakespeare, 1994; Garland-Thomson, 2002). More problematic is whether such imagery actively creates social oppression or, rather, reflects existing inequalities in power relations.

This discussion of charity advertising raises the issue of changing representation: many cultural studies approaches to disability focus on historical images, where the stereotypical or manipulative treatment of disabled people is at its most extreme. Contemporary films and advertisements have begun to use more complex and subtle images. For example, some charities have adopted a more political approach: recent campaigns by Scope focus on prejudice and discrimination as constitutive of disability, while not jettisoning entirely an individual approach. Again, advertisements by Mencap, a charity for people with learning difficulties, have also sought a new image, replacing its tearful 'Little Stephen' logo with a more positive representation stressing citizenship and social rights. This transition has thrown up several dilemmas: 'the difficulty of changing image and focus within a conservative organisation; the tensions between the level of empowerment sought by those in the disability movement and that which the charity proposes; the inadequate representation of real images in a desire to market attractive pictures' (Corbett and Ralph, 1994, p. 11).

It is the cultural representation of the impaired body as much as the image of the disabled person which is of primary concern. This is captured in the representation of disabled sexuality by advertisers and other producers of cultural images as exotic and erotic (Garland-Thomson, 2002, 2006a) and comprises one of several overlapping modalities (wondrous, sentimental, exotic and realistic) that frame the cultural production of disability. These contrasting forms of visual representation jostle for position in late capitalism. The aim is to scrutinize how these images 'create or dispel disability as a system of exclusions and prejudices' or challenge disabling social and attitudinal barriers and prejudices (2002, p. 75). Contributors to these debates are divided on their conclusions about charity advertising. While some argue that charity approaches are inherently oppressive, no matter what image is employed, others stress possibilities for complex, diverse and contested meanings in their representation of disability.

A precise interest is provided by both the processes of objectification that disabling images reveal and the use of the notion of 'otherness' to explain these representations. Several suggest that disabled people are 'dustbins for disavowal': that non-disabled people's anxieties and denials regarding the body and its limitations are projected onto disabled people through artistic and media imagery (Hevey, 1992; Shakespeare, 1994; Wendell, 1996; Garland-Thomson, 2002). Yet, broad differences remain between the cultural studies approach to disability representation and the more politically based explanations of disabling imagery advanced by critics within disability studies. As Susan Wendell argues, while culture has a central role in constructing impairment/disability, it is very misleading to

> confuse the lived reality of bodies with cultural discourse about and representation of bodies, or that deny or ignore bodily experience in favour of fascination with bodily representations . . . I do not think my body is a cultural representation, although I recognise that my experience of it is both highly interpreted and very influenced by cultural (including medical) representations. (1996, p. 44).

For the most part, cultural studies approaches informed by post-structuralism emphasize the links between corporeal diversity, cultural meanings, and differential privilege, status and power, while social model accounts have concentrated on the ways in which cultural representations reinforce disabling social relations and are related to the underlying materiality of the oppression of disabled people. While cultural forms should not be dismissed as merely ideological reflections of underlying social relations, their key role in perpetuating disabling attitudes and prejudices endures.

Overall, the 'cultural studies' approach offers a theoretically complex analysis, exploring the relationship between impairment and disabling representations. The fascination with unravelling the structures which generate particular readings of media products and practices is driven by the assumption that subjectivity is conferred on the reader/viewer by the structure of the text/film. Additionally, this presumes that a specific 'narrative' locks the reader into an 'able-bodied' view of 'normality' and disabled people without examining either how this process unfolds or its 'effects' from the perspectives of the reader/audience.

Media effects

An often-neglected aspect in this field is 'media effects'. The general presumption of studies of disability and culture is that the preponderance of media imagery is disabling and has a consequential effect on its audience. With so little exposure to contrary messages, this conclusion reinforces a 'hypodermic syringe' model in which the 'naturalness' of disability is generated or at least confirmed by the media. Most direct evidence of the effects of media representation comes from charity advertising, where the success of campaigns in generating income and volunteers has been documented (Williams, 1989; Hevey, 1992). Nonetheless, not all such campaigns fulfil their objectives, and this has led to considerable debate about the potential for dissimilar readings of media representation and the general susceptibility of audiences to media messages.

Equally significant, the notion of an 'inert' or 'passive' audience has been widely disputed. The 'uses and gratifications' approach argues that people actively interpret media materials in accordance with their own needs (McQuail, 1972; Blumler and Katz, 1974). Others utilize Gramsci's notion of hegemony to analyse how the media 'manufacture consent' to the dominant order while acknowledging that its messages may be 'read' in contrary ways, at least by different audiences or in different contexts (Hall et al., 1978). One suggestion is that the impact of the media is less pronounced in changing people's views than in confirming existing opinions. People look at the media having already been socialized in a variety of ways, and often with clear views about individual topics.

This emphasis on an 'active audience' is yet to be fully investigated in the context of the media and disability – because the transparency of media messages is stressed. Yet arguably polarized interpretations are common, as highlighted in Tom Shakespeare's (1999) review of film representations. Is Tod Browning's 1932 classic horror film *Freaks* a breakthrough in disability representation or a 'misplaced' attempt to 'humanize the freaks'? (Snyder and Mitchell, 2001, p. 380). To suggest that audiences can be active, and negotiate their own meaning, does not leave the media without any impact. In research conducted by the Glasgow Media Group, the opportunities for audience 'resistance' are highlighted at the same time as the media are seen as of primary importance in shaping or reinforcing people's views on key social issues, including disability (Philo, 1990, 1996).

In the case of 'mental illness', media coverage has been described as formative, not least because of the repeated association drawn in headlines with unprovoked violence, and how such negative storylines far outnumber more positive reports (Philo, 1996, p. 112). This had a 'major impact' on audiences, with consequential harmful effects on the users of mental health services and their social relationships. Again, studies of the media and HIV/AIDS report considerable media influence on public opinion. Public attitudes were noticeably affected by information, phrases and images that had their inspiration in media reports, including such key themes as the 'ravaged' face of AIDS; the difference between 'guilty' and 'innocent' victims;

and the association with 'unnatural' sexual practices (Kitzinger, 1993). Again, the impact of the media cannot simply be derived from a content analysis but has to be located within people's prior beliefs, which enable certain images to take hold more easily while other messages are rebuffed or reinterpreted. Such research also highlights the under-theorization of the processes of constructing disabling images:

> Models tend to be static and do not necessarily reflect contradictory representations and change over time. They help us 'fit' media stories into boxes, but do not necessarily aid in a more complex analysis of the processes involved in disability construction. Thus overall, the variety of elements of media analysis necessary to understand disability cannot be reduced to a simple categorisation of content, but require a complex sensitivity to multiple dimensions of the process. (Meekosha and Dowse, 1997b, p. 95)

Towards a disability culture?

In the 'cultural politics' of the 1960s and 1970s the development of a 'counter-hegemony' to the personal tragedy approach was a key element in disabled people's struggles. Given that the dominant culture is suffused with negative images of disability, the way forward was defined in terms of developing positive disabled identities, values and representations of living with an impairment. So what are the key issues arising from the attempts by disabled people to produce an alternative culture, or a sub-culture, in opposition to, or separate from, the mainstream culture?

In North America, the emergence of a disability consciousness may be traced from the 1960s and 1970s (Bowe, 1978; Brown, 1997). Autobiographical accounts flourished, and, while many concentrated on a conventional 'living with my impairment' approach, there were notable exceptions, such as Irving Zola's (1982) account of his personal and intellectual journey in rethinking disability and his own identity. *The Disability Rag*, initiated in 1980 by the Centre for Accessible Living in Louisville, Kentucky, became the unofficial newspaper of the Independent Living Movement. Disability awareness extended to the production of novels, comedy, songs, poetry, drama, paintings and sculpture. These conveyed an emerging sense of group identity and common interests (Saxton and Howe, 1988; Davis, 1995; Hirsch, 1995; Tremain, 1996).

Parallel trends in Britain include the first appearance of a television programme – entitled *Link* – in 1975 specifically for, and increasingly produced by, disabled people, as well as a range of newsletters and magazines by disabled people and groups. This was matched by a remarkable growth in contributions from disabled poets, musicians, artists and entertainers (Morrison and Finkelstein, 1993). *In From the Cold*, the magazine produced by Britain's Liberation Network of Disabled People, was published between 1981 and 1987. *Coalition*, the magazine of the Greater Manchester Coalition of Disabled People (GMCDP), appeared in 1986 and *DAIL* (Disability Arts in London) magazine a year later. The number of conferences, exhibitions, workshops, cabarets and performances has continued apace (Pointon and Davies, 1997; Shape, 2008). However, funding difficulties have been a constant concern: for example, the demise of *DAIL* magazine in 2007 was a result of Arts Council grant cutbacks, although it was replaced by an *Art Disability Culture* online journal in 2008. A worsening economic climate now jeopardizes the activities of even established local groups because of major uncertainties over long-term finance.

By the early 1990s, a 'disability culture movement' was emerging in the USA, as in other Western industrialized societies, with a growing input into disability rights protests (Shapiro, 1993; Longmore 1995; Brown, 1997). Yet not all commentators acknowledged the existence of a unique disability culture. Susan Wendell concluded that 'It would be hard to claim that disabled people as a whole have an alternative culture or even the seeds of one' (1996, p. 273). Lois Bragg (cited in Peters, 2000, p. 584) similarly insisted that claims of a disability culture fail to meet basic qualifying criteria: namely, a common language, historical lineage, cohesion, political solidarity, acculturation from an early age, generational/genetic links, and pride in difference. Moreover, she is not alone in identifying Deaf culture as the major exception: 'The D/deaf community apart, there is no unifying culture, language or set of experiences; people with disabilities are not homogeneous, nor is there much prospect for trans-disability solidarity' (Bickenbach, 1999, p. 106).

More typically, Simi Linton maintains that disabled people, at least in America, have 'solidified' as a group, whose cultural heart lies in 'the creative response to atypical experience, the adaptive manoeuvres through a world configured for non-disabled people. The material that binds is the art of finding one another, of identifying and naming disability in a world reluctant to discuss it' (Linton, 1998b, p. 5). Susan Peters also concludes that disability culture is alive and vibrant. It is held together by shared values of 'radical democracy and self-empowerment', as well as 'identity, voice, justice and equality' (2000, p. 593). She denies concerns that the emphasis on diversity undermines a coherent and unifying disability culture on the grounds that difference is a source of strength and allows people to generate new forms of solidarity. This provides an 'individual hybrid consciousness which maintains tactical solidarity while not being swallowed up by universal cultural patterns and norms' (ibid., p. 585).

A necessary feature of a disability culture identified by many disability activists has been to present a positive image of impairment. This is highlighted in John Swain and Sally French's (2000) advocacy of an 'affirmation model' of disability that contradicts the passivity and marginalization of individuals with an impairment central to the personal tragedy approach. Instead, the affirmation model stresses the divide between disabled and non-disabled people in the meanings and responses to impairment, and seeks to validate these experiences:

> Non-disabled people can generally accept that a wheel-chair user cannot enter a building because of steps. Non-disabled people are much more threatened and challenged by the notion that a wheel-chair user could be pleased and proud to be the person he or she is. (2000, p. 570)

This affirmative stance is distanced from the 'orthodox' social model approach (see chapter 2) in its assertion that 'pain and chronic illness' are 'neither impairments nor restricted to the experiences of disabled people' (ibid., pp. 571–2). More substantively, it comprises a positive self-identity created by disabled people themselves. The affirmative approach promotes the aim of disabled people determining their own 'lifestyles, culture and identity', with disabled people asserting the 'value and validity of life as a person with an impairment' (ibid., p. 578). This 'signifies ownership of impairment' (ibid., p. 579).

This approach has obvious parallels with claims associated with other marginalized social groups who, for example, proclaim that 'black is beautiful' or that they are 'glad to be gay'. Yet, equivalent assertions around 'disability pride' and the 'celebration of difference' are problematic for some disabled people. This is particularly the case for those individuals with impairments that are debilitating and painful or may result in premature death. Even if it is accepted that the main determinants of disabled people's quality of life are social, not medical, not all disabled people feel comfortable with Jenny Morris's generalized optimism that 'We can celebrate, and take pride in, our physical and intellectual differences, asserting the value of our lives' (1991, p. 189). Those dissenting from this declaration are more ambivalent towards impairment: equally stressing the value of people with impairment, while refusing to glorify incapacity (Shakespeare, 2006).

The notion of a separate disability culture is also contested by groups uneasy with their designation as people with impairments, such as mental health system survivors and people with learning difficulties. In the case(s) of d/Deaf people, an important distinction is drawn between people with a hearing impairment – who may be described as deaf or hard of hearing – who have often acquired or developed hearing loss, and are not native users of British Sign Language (BSL), and those people with congenital hearing impairment who have grown up in a BSL environment, typically with Deaf parents or other relatives. It is apposite to speak of the latter group as constituting a Deaf culture, on the basis of a shared language, history and other interests. It may extend to specific hearing individuals who are the children of Deaf adults and have acquired sign language and other aspects of Deaf culture (Davis, 1995; Corker, 1998).

By identifying as a cultural or linguistic minority, Deaf people make an analogy with minority ethnic groups, who are excluded on similar grounds. Furthermore, their rejection of being labelled as having an impairment underpins their resistance to medical treatments such as cochlea implants, which may restore a degree of hearing to some people, and to genetic screening of a foetus for genes causing a hearing impairment. Conversely, Deaf people might potentially exploit genetic knowledge to produce a child with a hearing impairment. From this standpoint, a Deaf identity and interest justifies a refusal to assimilate into a wider disability culture.

> Basically D/deaf people whose first language is BSL should be seen as a linguistic minority ... our schools go back to the 1790s and our clubs to the 1820s. Our language is much older. D/deaf people marry each other 90% of the time, 10% have D/deaf children. Our customs and traditions have been passed down the ages and these, together with our values and beliefs, constitute our culture ... the whole definition of culture is so much wider than the one the disability movement is espousing. (Paddy Ladd, quoted in Campbell and Oliver, 1996, p. 120)

Nevertheless, there are many people with a hearing impairment who neither identify with Deaf culture nor use sign language and do not regard themselves as part of the broader disabled population, although this may result in being marginalized by both Deaf culture and the dominant hearing culture (Corker, 1997).

In general terms, disability culture has a more secure base where it emerges from common experiences, such as separate schooling, welfare and rehabilitation services. Examples include agencies for 'blind' people (Scott, 1969), day and training centres for people with learning difficulties, and people with a mobility impairment in rehabilitation units (Oliver et al., 1988; Morris, 1989). This shared socialization may stimulate a sense of group identity and interests. Certainly, the contemporary origins of the disability protest in Britain lay in actions taken by a group of disabled people at the Le Court Cheshire Home in Hampshire, while its American counterpart gathered fresh momentum from the shared experience of disabled veterans of the Vietnam War.

However, it is debatable whether these are sufficiently long-lasting and intensive to generate a sense of a common identity and shared culture. Indeed, reports from disabled users of day centres often suggest entrenched divisions, such as between younger and older individuals, rather than a sense of collective interest. The routine experience is of differentiation into impairment groups, often with a further categorization by level of 'severity'. Disabled people experience a 'felt stigma' (and 'enacted stigma') or internalized oppression (Scambler and Hopkins, 1986; Mason, 1990). This denotes feelings of inadequacy, self-doubt, worthlessness and inferiority. Yet most people acquire their impairment as adults and after they have assumed an 'able-bodied' identity, intertwined with other social divisions such as gender, social class and ethnicity. Any biographical disruption (Bury, 1991) associated with acquiring an impairment requires a complex series of realignments. In comparison, for those growing up with impairment through the formative years of childhood and adolescence, the overwhelming stance of mainstream culture is to accentuate the negative qualities of being a disabled person (Anderson et al., 1982; Hirst and Baldwin, 1994; Hughes et al., 2005).

A novel macro-account, located in the advent of a late modern or post-modern society, suggests significant consequences for the growth and sustainability of a disability culture. Most specifically, the rise in self-reflexivity and enhanced flexibility and fluidity associated with post-modern society and culture facilitates opportunities for choice of self-identity, or encourages multiple and changing or 'liquid' identities (Giddens, 1991; Bauman, 2000). Arguably, important obstacles still confront attempts by disabled people to accomplish a new identity. 'Contemporary divisions in social identity arise out of the expansion of retail capital, the growth of mass markets and the increasing commodification of experience' (Hughes et al., 2005, p. 5). Yet the structures and processes that exclude disabled people from the sphere of production also limit their lifestyle consumption and so narrow their possibilities for accomplishing a new, positive identity. Disabled people are not targeted or differentiated as a consumer group, except by social welfare and educational services (Morris, 2002; Abbott et al., 2001; Hughes et al., 2005, p. 9). They are marginalized mostly by a discourse centred on healthy minds and bodies, and choices about lifestyle and leisure are more likely to be made by professionals, or other 'care' staff, and geared to 'therapeutic' and surveillance goals (Cavet, 1998; Fullager and Owler, 1998). Such exclusion from the mainstream may of course generate its own search for alternatives – or disability sub-cultures.

Disability arts

In Britain, one of the main arenas where a positive cultural conception of disability is now fostered is disability arts (Swain and French, 2000; Arts Council England, 2003). Traditional paternalistic attitudes have dominated what have been regarded as appropriate activities for disabled people in special schools, day centres and other specialist institutions. Disabled people are thought incapable of communicating their feelings and values through the arts, except perhaps as a means of individual therapy, as part of a process of rehabilitation or for fundraising purposes, such as charity Christmas cards. Such an approach tends to individualize arts involvement. While there is a place for art therapy, the politicization of disabled people has transformed the potential of arts involvement to an arena of cultural politics. This shift is captured in the crucial distinction drawn between 'disabled people doing art' and the more overtly political 'disability arts'. Instead of accepting the presumption of perpetual infantilization and passivity, a reflective and active orientation is encouraged.

The emergence of a disability arts movement marks a key stage in the transition towards political awakening and an explicit and positive disabled identity: 'disability arts would not have been possible without disability politics coming along first. It's what makes a disability artist different from an artist with a disability' (Sutherland, 1997, p. 159). Disabled people began to demand a new relationship to art and culture. Disability art is not simply about disabled people obtaining access to the mainstream of artistic consumption and production. It is the development of shared cultural meanings and collective expression of the experience of disability and struggle. This entails using art to expose the discrimination and prejudice disabled people face and to generate group consciousness and solidarity. In Britain, as in America, it comprises magazines, film festivals and a variety of individual and group performers (Brown, 1997). Disability comedy, music and sculpture have the potential to be as empowering as involvement in direct political action:

> Arts practice should also be viewed as much as a tool for change as attending meetings about orange badge provision . . . Only by ensuring an integrated role for disability arts and culture in the struggle can we develop the vision to challenge narrow thinking, elitism and dependency on others for our emancipation. To encourage the growth of a disability culture is no less than to begin the radical task of transforming ourselves from passive and dependent beings into active and creative agents for social change. (Morrison and Finkelstein, 1992, unpaged)

The disability arts movement encompasses several interrelated dimensions. First, it argues for disabled people to have access to the

mainstream of artistic consumption and production. Yet, by search-
ing for an alternative to mainstream arts provision, its originators
intended that it be much more than this. Therefore, second, disability
arts action explores the experience of living with an impairment.
Third, and most crucially, it offers a critical response to the experience of social exclusion and marginalization. This entails using
culture and the media to expose the discrimination and prejudice
disabled people face, and to generate a positive group consciousness
and identity. 'Introducing disabled people to the social role of artistic
creativity and opening a debate about disability culture is a dynamic
way of assisting disabled people to challenge their assumed dependency and place in mainstream society' (Morrison and Finkelstein,
1993, p. 127).

Disability arts seek to be educative, expressive and transformative.
They emphasize the potential of cultural action as a progressive,
emancipatory force at both individual and social levels. The focus on
oppression and injustice provides the rationale for a diverse array
of cultural interventions in which subversive representations or
performances illuminate and resist discriminatory barriers and attitudes. Where the audience consists primarily of non-disabled people,
some disabled artists make a deliberate tactic of 'outing' impairment, often their own, in an attempt to counter social conventions
that impairment is something best kept hidden. For some people the
shock value of a public display of impairment in disability arts is a
catalyst to make a non-disabled audience question its negative and
discriminatory standpoint. All the same, there is an uncertain boundary line between confronting disability and encouraging voyeurism
or pathologizing impairment.

Traditionally, the relationship between disability and culture has
focused on celebrated artists with an impairment and how this was
in varying degrees 'overcome' (such as Beethoven and his deafness)
or which became the means for intense, creative activity (as with Van
Gogh and his 'madness'). While impairment may on occasion add
to the appeal of a specific individual, many artists with an impairment have denied or ignored its impact on their lives, or reacted
in a personal rather than a political way – for example, musicians
Ray Charles, Ian Dury, Evelyn Glennie, Jacqueline du Pré and Hank
Williams. This diverges fundamentally from the notion of disability
arts, which stresses the importance of the arts in developing disability
cultural (and by inference political) identity and action:

> Disability arts also provides a context in which disabled people can
> get together, enjoy themselves and think in some way about issues of
> common concern. But it goes deeper than that, as disability culture
> really does offer people a key to the basic process of identifying as a

disabled person, because culture and identity are closely linked concepts. (Vasey, 1992b, unpaged)

The aim is to overturn the negative cultural stereotypes surrounding people with impairments and transform the whole 'cultural-valuational structure' (Fraser, 1995, 1997).

As yet, the majority of disabled people have a marginal involvement with disability arts, a conception of cultural action that owes much to playwrights such as Berthold Brecht and to educationalists such as Paolo Freire. It has also been given a radical imprint as a 'politics of signification', in which subversive representations or performances seek to dispute discriminatory barriers and attitudes. 'Disability Art, in attempting to create a culture of disabled people revelling in opposition to the dominant hegemonies of normality oppression, went further than being a mere rupture; it undermined the core values and revealed the processes of mainstream cultural construction' (Darke, 2003, p. 138).

It is a sign of the maturity and confidence of the disabled people's movement that it can celebrate difference, with individuals working together to create images of their own choosing. This is very evident in the lively debates conducted in the disability arts magazines on these and other issues. Against this, mainstream arts have remained largely aloof from or disinterested in disability, while disabled people have been largely excluded from arts training. There are fears that disability art and culture will be assimilated into mainstream culture and neutralized. This has been reinforced by the increasing reliance on public and private grants to support disability artists and the potential diminution in its radical edge.

Of course, a key objective for disabled people is to develop their own cultural forms, in environments which they control, as has been the case with disability arts. It is for this reason that the disability community has started to support and nurture its own artists and to provide opportunities to experiment and develop the necessary experience and confidence (Cribb, 1993). One difficulty has been to avoid imposing a non-disabled view of quality: it is vital to recognize the process on which people are engaged, the struggle against barriers involved in getting there, and the context in which work is presented (Pick, 1992).

A more general question posed about disability arts since the 1990s is whether the promotion of a disability culture and identity is achievable or perhaps counter-productive given the contemporary emphasis on diversity and difference. The emergence of social protest in the 1960s and 1970s was characterized by calls for the recognition of social differences and advocating social justice for marginalized groups based around gender, 'race' and ethnicity. For some, this heralded a period of what has been described in North America and Europe as 'identity politics'. Against this, Iris Young differentiates between a 'politics of difference' and 'identity politics'. Social groups should be defined in terms of 'a relational rather than a substantialist logic', since groups as such do not have identities, but rather 'individuals construct their own identities on the basis of social group positioning' (2000, p. 82). This is reinforced by the separation of cultural and structural social groups. While ethnicity provides a cultural identity of shared attributes, disability, gender and 'race' are more like social class in that they involve 'structural relations of power, resource allocation, and discursive hegemony' (ibid., pp. 82-3). Besides this: 'Structural social groups are constituted through the social organization of labour and production, the organization of desire and sexuality, the institutionalized rules of authority and subordination, and the constitution of prestige' (ibid., p. 94). This view is echoed by Simi Linton, who argues that, as disabled people, 'We are all bound together, not by this list of our collective symptoms but by the social and political circumstances that have forged us as a group' (1998a, p. 4).

The preoccupation with distinctive attributes of identity threatens endless fragmentation as new identities are 'discovered'. From a post-structuralist perspective, the search for a single, defining identity is dismissed as a remnant of modernist discourses. Lennard Davis (1999) attributes identity politics to changes in late twentieth-century society and the rise of neo-liberalism. Its main dimensions include a lost universality, an unleashing of subjectivity, growing multinational immigration, a disintegration of family and community life, and rampant marketization. It is not practicable to build a political project on the diversity of contemporary identity groups, and Davis derides these (human rights) struggles for offering little prospect of radical change. He also insists that current assertions of a disabled identity are liable to prove 'oppressive' (2001, p. 535), and argues instead for disabled people to be in the vanguard of moves towards a post-identity world – what he terms 'dis-modernism'.

This critique has been widened into a rejection of the 'essentialist assumptions' of disability culture that lead to a central 'paradox' and 'reinforce its marginalized status': 'How can we claim unity without falling into the same exclusionary practices that have served to create our divisive identifications in the first place?' (Galvin, 2003, pp. 675–6). The strategic aim follows post-structuralist feminist criticism of the 'reification' of gender and identity (Butler, 1990) by challenging the assumption that disabled people exhibit the same embodied identity.

Awareness of a 'mixed heritage in privilege and subjugation'

(Galvin, 2003, p. 682) means prioritizing diversity and, following Foucault, that disability politics must map out more positive ways of identification 'from beyond the categorisations which are responsible for our marginalisation' (ibid., p. 683). The aim is to move beyond a shared history of 'being' into a freer world of 'becoming' (Hall and du Gay, 1996; Woodward, 1997). Rose Galvin expresses optimism that a revived emphasis on impairment (*contra* the social model) will galvanize disability politics and prove a unifying force. At present, disability culture, by not highlighting different psychological, emotional and bodily experiences, excludes 'a great many people who would otherwise identify as disabled and subscribe to a collective notion of empowerment' (Galvin, 2003, p. 680). In contrast to Young's (2000) emphasis on a structural social group analysis, this resurrects a cultural or self-help group focus located in specific illness conditions that have demonstrated little potential for an alternative disability culture. Those of a more 'traditional' approach will wonder where this leaves a strategy for collective political action and disability politics.

Review

The significance of the cultural domain, or the relationship between culture and society's material base, has been central to debates in social theory. While there has been a tendency to polarize idealist/culturalist and materialist accounts, this risks encouraging determinist explanations rather than exploring the complex interplay of these domains. The cultural representations of disabled people are not necessarily one-dimensional or controlled exclusively by the pre-eminent material interests in non-disabled society. That is not to deny that the preponderance of images generated within the cultural domain contribute massively to the production of maintenance of a personal tragedy approach.

Historically, stereotypical images of disability have been generated across the diverse range of cultural industries. The common-sense assumptions of passivity and dependence are consistent and reinforcing across everyday life. These make a crucial contribution to the overall marginalization of disabled people within mainstream society. While audiences of the mass media and other cultural forms should not be regarded as cultural dupes who are unable to filter or disallow its disabling images and stereotypes, the sheer volume and consistency of disabling images is a barrier not experienced by many other disadvantaged minorities.

Most recently, public sensitivity to prejudicial images has gained ground, with disabled people contesting the dominant meanings of disability and seeking to produce new images and cultural forms that reflect their experiences, values and demands for social justice. However, amidst post-structuralist claims of a growing dissolution of identities and an emphasis on the diversity of the disabled population, the possibilities of establishing a vibrant disability sub-culture and a 'cultural politics' of opposition to the disabling society seem compromised. Yet, more optimistic contributors to disability arts argue that culture provides a crucial arena for protest and securing new values and identities, as with disability arts. They celebrate instead the potential for using culture to critique dominant forms of cultural representation and production as well as develop positive alternatives to disabling society:

> The very fact that previous representations of disability have been narrow, confused and unimaginative leaves the way open for disabled writers and film makers. What we can produce can blow the past away. (Sutherland, 1993, p. 8)

Disability and the Right to Life

Iɴ many Western societies, ideas and beliefs about perceived impairment and assumed biological and social inferiority are used to legitimate selective abortion, the withholding of life-saving medical treatments, and 'mercy killing'. The eugenic 'solution' is as powerful today as it was in the ancient world of Greece and Rome and has been given a significant impetus by recent developments in biotechnology and genetic medicine. Changing morality has intertwined with changing medical knowledge and technology to throw up new variants of old ethical dilemmas for those involved in genetic engineering, prenatal screening and selective abortion, definitions of 'death', quality of life/death, and rationing of medical resources. Yet the 'disability' dimension to these issues has only been made explicit since the 1980s. This has become a major concern for disabled activists, their organizations and wider society in view of their claims to equal status and citizenship.

Most significantly, it has been disabled activists and writers who have taken the lead in challenging 'taken-for-granted' assumptions that an impairment greatly reduces a person's quality of life and devalues them as a human being. In this chapter, we examine the key debates and concerns raised by these issues. First, we begin with a discussion of ethics and euthanasia. This is followed by an examination of the influence of eugenics in Western culture. The third section reviews recent innovations in biotechnology and genetic medicine. In the final part of this chapter we consider debates concerning the form and impact of life and death decisions at the beginning and end of life.

Ethics, euthanasia and rights

Contemporary attitudes to death and dying are quite distinct from those of our ancestors. Throughout most of human history coming to terms with death was commonplace. Infant mortality was an everyday occurrence: consequently newborn infants often remained unnamed until they had survived for at least one or two years (Singer, 1993). Moreover, in many poorer countries in the modern world, life expectancy is often uncertain, as those who survive infancy frequently encounter poor nutrition, disease, accidents, violence and natural disasters such as drought and famine (Coleridge, 1993). But economic, social, scientific and technological developments and medical advances have led to rising expectations of longevity. This is especially evident in wealthy industrialized societies, where a greater influence over the process of death and dying is more widely available. Hence, with so much more expectation of death occurring in later adult years, death from any other causes is much more difficult to comprehend, especially when it occurs in childhood or early adulthood. Further problems arise when it is evident that an individual or group has the power to decide when and how other people should die; this has an increasing significance for disabled people and their families (Rock, 1996; Shakespeare 1995, 2006, 2009; Campbell, 2006, 2009).

Adrienne Asch (2001) maintains that the negative view of disability widely held in Western culture is founded on two erroneous assumptions: first, the presence of impairment and disability equals a tragic and disruptive state; and, second, it is automatically associated with a life of isolation, poverty and powerlessness. She contends that the basis of these views rests primarily within the medical model of disability, which equates 'disability' with disease and a 'departure from a desired state of health', and the activities of the medical profession, who are increasingly responsible for making life and death decisions. Consequently, over recent years the ethics of such decision-making has come under growing scrutiny and generated considerable debate. This is largely on account of changing perceptions of disability and the growing demand for meaningful and enforceable equal rights for disabled people (McLean and Williamson, 2007).

Ethics and morality

At the general level, ethics represent a set of moral principles or codes of behaviour. However, morality is a highly contested concept. Although they are commonly associated with religious teachings and traditional claims about declining moral standards, it is evident that ethics and moral principles vary according to time and place. Historically, religion has been particularly influential in determining what is right and what is wrong in Europe and most countries across the world. For many people therefore life was the product of divine intervention, and human behaviour was preordained by God and therefore uncontentious (Singer, 1993). With the onset of modernity and 'post-modernity' and, particularly, secularization, industrialization, urbanization and globalization, a demand has been generated for a new morality and ethics that cater for a society composed of fragmented individuals living in different economic and social contexts with diverse aims, needs and functions (Bauman, 1993, p. 6).

Given the increasing diversity that characterizes most technologically developed post-millennium societies, it is perhaps inevitable that the basis upon which ethical decisions are made should appear to have widespread appeal. Therefore ethics are not something that can be understood only in the context of religion. Nor can they be an intractable set of principles that are not subject to interpretation. Therefore ethics must not be viewed as theoretically justifiable but useless in practice. The whole purpose of ethical decision-making is to guide practice. Finally, ethics must not be perceived as simply relative or subjective if they are to have any meaning at the general level (Singer, 1993).

This raises an immediate but important question: how do ethical decisions and debates differ from non-ethical debates and controversies? According to Peter Singer, in *Practical Ethics* (1993), living by ethical standards is linked to belief systems and values. People must believe that their actions are *right* and are justified. However, justification must not be based on self-interest alone: 'Self interested acts must be shown to be compatible with more broadly based ethical principles if they are to be ethically defensible, for the notion of ethics carries with it something bigger than the individual' (1993, p.10). Moreover, throughout modern history, philosophers have promoted the notion that ethical values and codes are justifiable only on the basis that they are somehow universal. These include theologians, Enlightenment thinkers and contemporary theorists with widely differing standpoints. Recent examples are the existentialist thinker Jean-Paul Sartre (1995), the political philosopher John Rawls (1999) and the critical theorist Jürgen Habermas (1976). It is notable, however, that for post-modernists the notion of a universal ethics is both unacceptable and unrealistic because '[h]uman reality is messy and ambiguous' (Bauman, 1993, p. 32) – notwithstanding that there are some moral principles that do have an apparent widespread appeal and it is notable that, in order to retain their general utility, these ethical precepts and moral values must be suitably ambiguous and subject to interpretation. This is particularly the case in respect of disability and medical or health-care ethics.

Medical ethics and euthanasia

Medical ethics involve questions about what ought and ought not to be done within the practice of medicine:

> These questions may well involve a wide range of people – not just the
> doctor but the nurse, patient, relative, and beyond them, members
> of the community, and are invariably raised in situations of extreme
> moral stress, where, often for the first time, individuals are involved in
> decisions of life and death. (Palmer, 1999, p. 17)

Interest in medical and health-care ethics has increased significantly
in recent years. This is largely a result of the unprecedented technological innovations that have taken place in medicine over the last
half-century, which have given doctors the ability to keep people alive
in circumstances where they would previously have died. These developments have also generated particular moral questions which are
not easily resolved.

According to Sheila McLean and Laura Williamson, medical and
other forms of practical ethics share an avowed 'commitment to
support the well-being of human beings' (2007, p. 37). This aim is
frequently couched in the language of fundamental principles such
as 'human dignity', 'the sanctity of life' and 'respect for persons'. In
spite of the seemingly apparent benefits that may be drawn from
recourse to such fundamental precepts in discussions of impairment and disability, there are several issues and concerns that must
be considered. First, while these principles may be used to express a
common commitment to human well-being, they can also be interpreted differently to allow each principle to foreground slightly
different viewpoints to ensure the value of human existence. Second,
such principles are so central to debates in medical ethics that they
are often invoked by those on opposite sides of the same debate (ibid.,
p. 36). Not surprisingly, this situation is of major concern to disabled
activists and writers, as it raises serious questions about the use of
medical ethics in debates about the right to life of people with impairments. This is because hitherto the 'mainstream bioethics agenda'
appears to be concerned primarily with preventing disabled people
being born or with 'killing them off as soon as possible' rather than
providing an ethical justification for their meaningful inclusion into
everyday life (Bickenbach, 2001b, p. 49).

The complexity of interpretation within medical ethics can be best
explained with reference to the ways in which key principles such
as 'human dignity', 'sanctity of life' and 'respect for persons' can
be interpreted differently. The first, 'human dignity', is generally
understood to mean that humans are of special 'worth' or 'value'. It
is associated with 'efforts to protect human dignity with initiatives to
safeguard traits which are seen as characteristically human' (McLean
and Williamson, 2007, p. 38). This concept is invoked in various
ethical, legal and policy statements, notably the *Charter of the United
Nations* (UN, 1948a) and the *Universal Declaration of Human Rights* (UN,

1948b). The latter states that all people have access to basic rights that protect their dignity and well-being, including 'the right to life, liberty and security of person' (Article 3).

The emphasis on human dignity in these two documents represents a direct response to the systematic abuse and murder of people with impairments and members of 'inferior races' by doctors and medical researchers before and during the Second World War, especially in Japan and Nazi Germany (Burleigh, 1994; Gallagher, 1995; Kevles, 1985). It is therefore not surprising that subsequently:

> a variety of documents and other statements emanating from a range of sources have emphasised the importance of building on the UN's commitment to human dignity to help ensure that biotechnology developments and healthcare support do not denigrate the value (dignity) of human life. (McLean and Williamson, 2007, p. 40)

This is especially important given that many of the issues arising within the context of biomedicine that refer to the concept of human dignity revolve around the treatment people with impairments receive in medical and 'health-care' institutions at the beginning and end of life. For example, advances in medical technology, such as pre-natal screening, may be interpreted as either a safeguard or a denial of human dignity. Advocates maintain that, by helping to reduce the number of children born with genetic disease and impairments, they assure the dignity of life by improving human health and eliminating suffering at the general level. Also they may be perceived as respecting the dignity of those already born by 'respecting their reproductive liberty' (ibid., p. 41).

Furthermore, speaking at the annual meeting of the European Society of Human Reproduction and Embryology, Professor Bob Edwards said that the increasing availability of prenatal screening gave parents a moral responsibility not to give birth to disabled children and that: 'Soon it will be a sin for parents to have a child that carries the heavy burden of genetic disease. We are entering a world where we have to consider the quality of our children' (cited in Rogers, 1999, p. 28).

By way of contrast, others have argued that recent developments in preventative medicine that promote the reduction of genetic diversity among people also undermine the value of human dignity and diversity. For instance, the United States Conference of Catholic Bishops was concerned that genetic technology could be used by politicians and policy-makers to sanction abortion and unwanted sterilization in order to control populations and to 'prevent the birth of people who might become a welfare "burden"' (USCCB, 1996, p. 2). This is a view largely shared by organizations controlled and run by disabled people. For example, Disabled Peoples' International (DPI) posed the question: 'How can we live with dignity in societies that spend millions on genetic research to eradicate disease and impairment but refuse to meet our needs to live dignified and independent lives? We cannot. We will not. The genetic threat to us is a threat to everyone' (DPI, 2000, p. 4). In addition, appeals to human dignity are often found in debates associated with the end of life. It is frequently argued that human dignity is commensurate with voluntary euthanasia. Euthanasia means 'a gentle and easy death', but the term is increasingly used to refer to the killing of people who are viewed as 'incurably ill and in great pain or distress, for the sake of those killed and in order to spare further suffering or distress' (Singer, 1993, p. 175). Voluntary euthanasia is carried out at the request of the person who is killed, and is now often linked to assisted suicide.

Voluntary euthanasia is legal in the Netherlands, Belgium, Switzerland and the American states of Oregon, Washington and Montana, but not in the UK. Most of the groups campaigning for a change in the law support the principle of voluntary euthanasia. In the long-running disputes over assisted suicide and voluntary euthanasia there are frequent reminders of the need to protect human dignity. Among those who argue that human dignity is supported by mercy killing are organizations such as the Voluntary Euthanasia Society, the human rights organization Liberty, and Dignity in Dying. The stated aim of the last-named is 'to secure the right of everyone to be able to die with dignity at the end of their life' (Dignity in Dying, 2006). Conversely, some religions view euthanasia as an assault on human dignity. The Catholic Church, for example, maintains that it is a 'violation of the divine law, an offence against the dignity of the human person, a crime against life and an attack on humanity at the beginning and at the end of life' (cited in McLean and Williamson, 2007, p. 43).

Indeed, debates on voluntary euthanasia clearly indicate that the principle of human dignity may be invoked to support or denigrate a whole range of human behaviour. Consequently, concerns arise about its usefulness with reference to medical ethics generally (Macklin, 2003) and with regard to people with accredited impairments at the beginning and end of life in particular. This is because most life and death decisions are made in hospitals and health-care environments in which the rationing of medical resources is increasingly important and assumptions about disabled people's poor quality of life predominate. Furthermore the recourse to human dignity in the justification for euthanasia is often linked to notions of autonomy, rationality and freedom of choice. But such arguments are difficult to sustain when normative communication or rational thought processes are difficult to identify or evaluate, as in the case of unborn or newly born babies and people with 'severe' and multiple impairments. Here, the value or worth (dignity) may be even more difficult to discern.

Additionally, where human beings are deemed incapable of understanding the choice between life and death, non-voluntary euthanasia may be considered appropriate. For Peter Singer, those people unable to give consent include 'incurably ill or severely disabled infants and people who through accident, illness or old age have permanently lost the capacity to understand the issues involved without having previously requested or rejected euthanasia in these circumstances' (1993, p. 177). He also suggests that euthanasia should be considered involuntary when the person killed is capable of consenting their own death but does not do so; either because she or he is not asked or because she or he is asked and chooses to go on living.

Moreover, the principle of sanctity of life is equally vague in debates around euthanasia and disabled people. As with the concept of human dignity, the notion of sanctity of life suggests that human life is unique and should be revered for its own sake. This idea is rooted in religious teachings and the conviction that human life is sacred and a 'divine gift from God'. This association with religious beliefs has linked the sanctity of life to the notion of vitalism, a philosophical position that maintains that human life should be 'preserved at all costs' (Keown, 2002, p. 39). Such a position lends considerable strength to those who argue against discrimination on the grounds of impairment in life or death decisions at any stage in the life course. Such a position would deem it unethical to abort an unborn child once impairment had been detected or to withhold medical treatment to those people diagnosed as terminally ill, whether through accident, illness or old age.

It is noteworthy that such an absolutist position would demand the abolition of abortion for whatever reason and also the continued supply of medical resources to people with incurable conditions, regardless of age, severity and prognosis of their condition, and irrespective of their wishes. Consequently it would result in the denial of a woman's right to choose to terminate an unwanted pregnancy, but also threaten to disempower those disabled and non-disabled people who may wish to make decisions about how to end their lives. It can also be argued that the application of such a policy would put a considerable strain on medical resources, which would have important negative implications for the rest of society. As one commentator put it:

> What is the point of keeping a road accident victim on a life-support system for years on end? What is the value of providing for the care of a paralysed person who will always require care and attention simply to stay alive in the technical sense? Why should we go to the

expense of adapting our local library so that one or two people in wheelchairs can have access? Surely it is better to kill (sorry, allow to die) infants with congenital malformations since we can predict that the 'quality of life' for such children will be impoverished? (Thomas, 1982, p. 17)

Conversely, alternative interpretations of the principle of sanctity of life assert that life need not be sustained at all costs. The Catholic Church, for example, widely perceived as opposed to assisted suicide, acknowledges that when death is imminent medical interventions may be withheld if they 'would only secure a precarious and burdensome promulgation of life, as long as the normal care due to the sick person in similar cases is not interrupted. In such circumstances the doctor has no reason to reproach himself with failing to help the person in danger' (SCDF, 1980, p. 4). Others interpret the sanctity of life principle in terms of valued human characteristics that go beyond simply biological existence. That is, they accord value to such traits as rationality and free choice. Like human dignity, the sanctity of life serves as a substitute for other more specific concepts and precepts.

In common with the concepts of human dignity and sanctity of life, the notion of respect for persons points to the conviction that individuals are valuable and should be treated in a manner that respects or promotes this value. McLean and Williamson (2007) suggest that the principle of respect for persons provides a meaningful and practical way forward in ethical debates about impairment, disability and life and death decisions. They maintain that the rightness of actions may be judged by determining whether the same decision can be made universally by all persons without its resulting in a self-defeating outcome. In this context the principle of respect for persons is presented as universally acceptable as it accommodates the contemporary values of autonomy, consent and human rights. Arguments in favour of voluntary euthanasia to end assumed intolerable suffering may be one example.

This argument is premised on the assumption that all individuals are sentient, self-aware, rational beings that have the 'capacity to choose, to make and act on [their] own decisions' (Singer, 1993, p. 99). Therefore it would not be universally acceptable to abort an unborn infant or assist a person to die unless it can be shown that such actions are taken only in particular circumstances – notably, if the persons concerned appear to lack, or are unlikely to acquire or regain, the necessary 'capacities for action' (McLean and Williamson, 2007, p. 50). From this perspective those individuals judged to be incapable of decision-making cannot be considered autonomous. 'In particular, only a being who can grasp the difference between dying and continuing to live can autonomously choose to live' (Singer, 1993, p. 99).

The problem with this position is that people with apparent 'severe' or 'multiple' impairments or a 'terminal' illness are particularly vulnerable to the assumptions of others that they are incapable of making their own decisions. As Carolyn Ells points out, several factors can contribute to such assumptions:

> Because authority in health care contexts depends in part on competence, an incorrect assessment of competence contributes to the failure to recognise authority. For example, communication barriers, caused either by physical processes (e.g. aphasia), attitudinal processes (e.g. bias), or confounding conditions (e.g. depression), may suggest the presence of incompetence and non-authority when someone is actually competent and has authority. (Ells, 2001, p. 605)

It is important to remember here that doctors and health-care professionals do not operate in isolation. Their activities must be contextualized within socio-political and cultural environments that historically have to a greater or lesser degree perpetuated the view that people with accredited impairments are a burden to themselves, their families and society at large.

Disability and eugenics

The word 'eugenics' was first coined by Francis Galton, a cousin of Charles Darwin, to refer to the 'science of improvement of the human germ plasm through better breeding'. In pursuit of this goal, Galton distinguished a positive and a negative approach. Positive eugenics referred to policies and practices that were designed to encourage 'so called good stock to breed'. By way of contrast, negative eugenics applied to policies and actions designed to prevent 'the mentally and morally unfit from breeding' (Kerr and Shakespeare, 2002, p. 8).

Scientific legitimacy for such ideas was provided by post-Enlightenment thinkers such as Thomas Malthus, Herbert Spencer and Charles Darwin. In his *Essay on the Principle of Population*, first published in 1798, Malthus noted that the population across Europe was growing rapidly and that, if unchecked, would outstrip natural resources and the food supply. The inevitable outcome, he believed, would be famine, disease and war unless people exercised 'moral restraint' and had fewer children (Wrigley and Souden, 1986). Spencer claimed that over time there is a tendency towards 'the 'survival of the fittest' and he maintained that, if left to compete among themselves, the most intelligent, ambitious and productive people would win out. He endorsed a fiercely competitive world of free market economics in the belief that, as the fittest survived, society would undergo steady improvement (Andreski, 1975).

These ideas, coupled with Darwin's theory of natural selection as evolutionary progress in *The Origin of Species* ([1859] 1996), gave authority to a common belief that the capacity for rational judgement, moral behaviour and business acumen and enterprise was not equally distributed throughout the human population. Prominent figures in late nineteenth-century social science detailed their conviction that certain groups in society, including criminals, non-white 'races' and even women, had limited intelligence and therefore a reduced capacity for rational thought and moral conduct (Dickens, 2000). Such views provided the foundations for an ideology that: 'allayed the qualms of the rich about not helping the poor by telling them that the latter's sufferings were the inevitable price of progress which could only occur through the struggle for existence ending in the survival of the fittest and the elimination of the unfit' (Andreski, 1975, p. 26). Social Darwinists classified disabled people with 'severe' impairments as 'mutants' (Radford, 1994). The spectre of 'race degeneration' was further fostered by Dr John Langdon Down's 1866 classification of the 'Mongolian idiot' as a throwback to a non-Caucasian type (Gould, 1980). Defective bodies and minds were perceived as 'dangerous' and 'threatening' to the rest of society. Eugenicists also highlighted links between intellectual and physical deficiency and a range of social evils such as crime, vagrancy, alcoholism, prostitution and unemployment (Kevles, 1985). Consequentially all forms of physical, sensory and cognitive impairment were identified as a threat to social progress.

> We civilised men, on the other hand, do our utmost to check the process of elimination; we build asylums for the imbecile, the maimed, and the sick; we institute poor-laws; and our medical men exert their utmost skill to save the life of everyone to the last moment . . . Thus the weak members of civilised societies propagate their kind. No one who has attended to the breeding of domestic animals will doubt that this must be highly injurious to the race of man. (Darwin, 1922, p. 136)

Several eminent statisticians, among them Galton, Pearson and Fisher, promoted eugenic applications for 'improving the human race'. Initially, the merger between statistics and biology promised a science of the average effects of the laws of heredity (Abrams, 1968, p. 89), but this interpretation of 'normality' gave way to the idea of ranking, with those deviating from the norm located on a hierarchy from higher to lower scores. This is vividly illustrated in the case of Intelligence Quotient (IQ) tests and scores. IQ tests originated in the work of the German psychologist William Stern and were developed by Alfred Binet and Théodore Simon in the 1920s to measure children's cognitive ability and functioning. The results were quickly linked to misplaced moral judgements of superior and inferior 'intellectual' functioning. Early scientific interest concentrated on distinguishing between 'mental deficiency' and 'normality', but the application of a normal distribution curve and new tests, such as the Binet–Simon scale, led to the identification of 'mildly retarded' and 'moron' categories. Statistical theories reinforced a deterministic account of intelligence, 'race' and human evolution (Tomlinson, 1982).

Policies espousing 'social hygiene' gained ground across Europe and North America. These ranged from segregation in institutions to state- and medically sponsored schemes for sterilization and abortion. Such practices had a particular appeal in America on account of the unprecedented levels of immigration from European states and other parts of the world in the first decades of the twentieth century. From 1915 to 1918, Dr Harry Haiselden, a Chicago surgeon, gained national notoriety by allowing the deaths of at least six infants he diagnosed as 'defectives'. Seeking publicity for his efforts to eliminate those considered 'unfit', he displayed the dying infants to journalists and wrote a book-length series about them for the Hearst newspapers. His campaign was front-page news for several weeks. He also wrote and starred in a film entitled *The Black Stork* that fictionalized an account of his cases. In the subsequent debate hundreds of Americans took a public stand. A majority of those quoted in the press opposed preserving the lives of 'defectives'. They included a public health nurse, Lillian Wald, the family law pioneer Judge Ben Lindsey, the civil rights lawyer Clarence Darrow, the historian Charles A. Beard, and even the disabled campaigner for blind and deaf people Helen Keller (Pernick, 1997, p. 89).

The American eugenic movement supported a very diverse range of activities, among them advanced statistical analyses of human pedigrees and 'better baby contests' modelled on rural livestock shows. American eugenics equated fitness with beauty. 'An attractive appearance goes hand in hand with health', explained the film *The Science of Life*, a twelve-reel survey of high-school biology distributed by the US Public Health Service between 1922 and 1927. The film urged the women of tomorrow to develop strength and beauty through vigorous exercise and selectively highlighted the 'repulsive ugliness of the "unfit"' (Pernick, 1997, p. 94). Also promoted were compulsory sterilization of criminals and 'the retarded' and selective ethnic restrictions on immigration. These were all aimed at 'improving human heredity' (ibid., p. 90).

In 1938, thirty-three American states had a law allowing the forced sterilization of women with diagnosed intellectual impairments. However, in Nazi Germany during the 1930s and 1940s an altogether more systematic and extensive extermination programme was introduced against those considered 'unworthy of life'. These policies had their roots in the work of German eugenicists such as the biologist

Ernst Haeckel, who argued that many common impairments, such as schizophrenia, depression and epilepsy, were inherited. He insisted that society was not bound under all circumstances to prolong life 'even when it becomes utterly useless' (cited in Kerr and Shakespeare, 2002, pp. 22–3). Such assertions were supported by numerous German scholars in prestigious universities. The German Society for Racial Hygiene won support from all political parties, including the Social Democrats. But policy revolved mainly around positive eugenics until the early 1920s and the radicalization of German politics in the aftermath of Germany's defeat in the First World War (Burleigh, 1994).

In 1920, Karl Binding, a lawyer, and Alfred Hoche, a psychiatrist, published the book *Allowing the Destruction of Life Unworthy of Living*. In it they challenged values such as the 'sanctity of life' and recourse to irrational emotions such as pity and paternalism as justifiable responses to impairment and disability. Instead they focused on the economic burden posed by impairment and the logic of 'mercy killing' for disabled people. Three groups of people were singled out for such treatment: first, terminally ill or 'mortally wounded' individuals who expressed the desire to die; second, 'incurable idiots', regardless of whether the 'idiocy' was congenital or acquired, who were considered 'a terrible heavy burden upon their relatives and society as a whole' and 'a travesty of real human beings, occasioning disgust in everyone who encounters them'; and third, 'mentally healthy people who had been rendered unconscious through accident or illness and would be 'appalled' at their condition in the event of their regaining consciousness. Others were encouraged to anticipate their wishes on their behalf (Burleigh, 1994, pp. 17–18).

Binding and Hoche proposed several ways of conducting euthanasia – these included legislative protection for doctors against the possible objection of relatives – and pointed to the additional benefits that the killing of defectives might offer in terms of opportunities for medical research. Binding proposed various procedures in order to implement 'mercy killing' for 'defectives', such as 'permitting committees' composed of lawyers and physicians who would be obliged to keep records. The possibility of error was brushed aside: 'What is good and reasonable must happen despite every risk of error . . . humanity loses so many of its members on account of error, that one more or less hardly counts in the balance' (cited in Burleigh, 1994, p. 18). These arguments were welcomed by many doctors, half of whom joined the Nazi Party (Gallagher, 1995).

Adolf Hitler was an admirer of the Spartan policy of euthanasia for 'sick, weak and deformed children'. In the Greek city of Sparta, where racial homogeneity was highly prized and where the principle of eugenics was strictly upheld, 'the abandonment of deformed and sickly infants was actually a legal requirement' (Garland, 1995, p. 14). Throughout the 1920s and 1930s the Nazi propaganda machine promoted eugenic imagery representing disabled people in the media as 'useless eaters' and 'life unworthy of living'. One example is the film *I Accuse*, directed by Wolfgang Liebeneir. The film tells the story of how two doctors love a woman. She marries one and later falls ill with multiple sclerosis and asks her husband to kill her. He refuses, so she appeals to her former lover, who agrees and fulfils her request. A trial follows but the case is dismissed (Burleigh, 1994, p. 210). Moreover, the film was widely distributed across German-speaking nations. It also 'picked up an award at the Venice Binnale' and 'enjoyed immense popularity, by January 1945 it had been seen by 15.3 million people' (ibid., p. 216).

Germany's Law for the Prevention of Hereditary Diseased Progeny was 'presented to the German Cabinet on 14th July 1933 and published on the 26th July, six days after the signing of the Concordat with the Vatican' (Burleigh, 1994, p. 42). Between then and 1 September 1939, German doctors sterilized approximately 375,000 people to prevent the birth of children with a range of hereditary conditions. Hitler secretly ordered the adult euthanasia programme to begin in September 1939, though it was never a formal law or government order because 'mercy killing' was technically against the law at that time. There was also concern that such a policy might generate opposition. This led to the murder of over 270,000 disabled people regarded as 'travesties of human form and spirit' (ibid., p. 194).

Although Nazi Germany provides undoubtedly the most extreme example of eugenic practices, it is notable that for much of the twentieth century eugenic or 'population policies' were applied in several other European countries and the USA against people regarded as biologically inferior (Kevles, 1995). These policies mostly took the form of enforced sterilization of 'feeble minded' women. Racism led to black women being grossly overrepresented among the 60,000 people forcibly sterilized in American states between 1907 and 1960. In the Scandinavian countries politicians and policy-makers introduced compulsory sterilization laws because they were concerned that the emerging welfare state would encourage the 'unfit' to reproduce and reduce the quality of the 'national stock'. In Sweden alone, 63,000 people, 90 per cent of them women, were sterilized between 1934 and 1975. Norway, a much smaller country, sterilized 48,000 people in the same period (Giddens, 2006, p. 263).

British and Dutch policy-makers adopted strategies of mass institutionalization until the late 1960s and 'voluntary' rather than compulsory sterilization. Nonetheless, in the post-1945 period sterilization for women termed 'handicapped' or 'mentally subnormal and sexually vulnerable' was common and supported by politicians and the general public. Between April 1968 and 1969, for example, '10,545 women were sterilised during abortions in the UK' (Kerr and Shakespeare, 2002, p. 73).

Largely as a consequence of these policies, the concepts of eugenics and Social Darwinism became widely discredited among politicians and policy-makers (Dickens, 2000). Yet, despite substantial evidence to the contrary (Gallagher, 1995), 'modern day eugenicists' (Goble, 2003, p. 48) argue that it was not scientists and doctors but politicians and policy-makers who were responsible for the oppressive policies and practices of the past. Such arguments enabled scientists and doctors to utilize eugenic arguments in the rhetoric surrounding recent developments in biotechnology and biomedicine (Kerr and Shakespeare, 2002; Goble, 2003).

Disability and biotechnology

It is suggested that we are now living in the 'century of the gene' and that current and future developments in biotechnology will have as significant an impact on the global economy, politics and culture as did the recent advances in information technology (Kerr and Shakespeare, 2002). In areas such as agriculture and medicine, unsubstantiated claims are made for genetic technologies in terms of eradicating famine, eliminating poverty and reducing disease and increasing longevity. In the interests of the 'common good', it is claimed that this revolutionary new science will enable us to take control of our 'evolutionary destiny' (Goble, 2003, p. 46). There is, however, growing concern about the use and control of these technologies, particularly with regard to genetically modified crops and their impact on the environment. Environmental activists warn that, although genetic modification may have some benefits, the risks involved are difficult to calculate as, once released into the environment, genetically modified organisms 'may set off a string of knock on effects that will be difficult to monitor and control' (Giddens, 2006, p. 963).

Similar concerns are expressed by disabled activists and their organizations regarding the claims made by advocates of biomedicine as a solution to the problem of disability. Their fears revolve around the frequently repeated assertion that the recent advances in biotechnology or 'new genetics' will enable doctors to identify and eradicate impairment and disease – all of which reinforces the traditional individualistic biological determinist explanation for disablement; threatens eugenic elimination of impairment; 'undermines the authenticity of disabled lives; and reinforces the hegemony of biomedicine over disability' (Shakespeare, 1995, p. 24).

It is claimed that medical science is more than ever poised to engage in wide-ranging preventive intervention (Hood, 1992). It is not simply the rights of disabled people that are at issue. Genetic medicine may soon be able to decipher the very structures and functions of the genes that form the building-blocks of individual human development – what are called genetic markers. This will, it is argued, facilitate the identification and modification of those genes which make an individual most susceptible to those conditions which result in perceived impairment – whether physical, sensory or intellectual. New techniques such as genetic reimplantation and screening will be able to offer prospective parents the embryo of their choice and, by implication, the opportunity to reject any which might manifest a perceived impairment, irregularity or imperfection. It may also soon be possible for 'corrective' gene therapy to 'normalize' what is regarded as 'abnormal'.

Such claims rest on the assertion that genes provide the biochemical information that governs the development and functioning of the cells that make up the human body. Deoxyribonucleic Acid, or DNA, is the genetic material and code that lies at the core of a single cell. DNA is divided into functional units known as genes. According to the British Medical Association Steering Group on Human Genetics, 'Genes provide the instructions for our development from a fertilised egg (oocyte) to a fully grown adult and continue, throughout our lives, to provide the information necessary for everyday maintenance and functioning of our bodies' (BMA, 1998, p. 46). Since Francis Crick and James Watson explained the structure of DNA and its links with heredity in 1951, interest in mapping the human genome has increased apace among doctors, politicians and policy-makers in many nations across the world. As a consequence there has been a proliferation of public and private organizations involved in genetic research. Notable examples are the American Human Genome initiative, based on $5.3 million worth of private and university pilot projects, and the French Généthon: Centre de recherche sur le génome humain, initiated by the privately organized Centre for the Study of Human Polymorphism in alliance with a private sector AFM – Association Française contre les Myopathies, and funded by telethons (Kerr and Shakespeare, 2002, p. 86).

These initiatives are based on the assertion that it is now possible to select those characteristics that we value and select out those that we do not. This has generated two strategies. The first, gene therapies, represents attempts to neutralize negative or disease-generating characteristics and enhance the effects of health-promoting ones by the manipulation of genetic material. The second approach warrants the identification of genetic markers of disease and impairment so that women at risk of carrying an infant with an impairment can be identified and screened (Goble, 2003, p. 47).

However, there are questions about the efficacy of the curative approach associated with gene therapies. The promise is that, by cracking the genetic code, we can manipulate genes in order to eradicate hereditary impairments. This argument downplays the fact that all human characteristics are 'polygenic, and therefore not even genetically understood, let alone subject to manipulation' (Kevles, 1985, p. 298). Further problems arise with reference to stem-cell drug therapies designed to neutralize the effects of defective genes. The claims of advocates of these treatments have been seriously undermined by recent concerns about both conflicts of interest arising from researchers' vested interests and ownership of shares in the companies involved in the development of these techniques. For example, Anne Kerr and Tom Shakespeare report that, in 1999, the *Washington Post* cited several cases of researchers failing to report the deaths of volunteers in gene therapy trials to the American National Institute of Health, as required by federal law: 'An inquiry by Congress revealed that this practice was widespread' (2002, p. 92).

Genetic screening takes many forms, but the most common in the UK and USA is prenatal screening, which is widely available and especially to families with a history of conditions such as cystic fibrosis, Huntington's disease and Duchenne muscular dystrophy. While there is widespread consensus that such conditions are undesirable, the promise of genetic medicine is that it gives us the possibility of selecting those characteristics that we view as valuable and eliminating those that we do not. Moreover, some behavioural geneticists claim that it is possible to identify genetic markers responsible for particular behavioural traits such as homosexuality, intelligence, alcoholism, depression and criminality. The implications for our understanding of what it means to be human, and what form of 'difference' is socially acceptable, are profound. Although the research on which such claims are based remains highly contentious and uncertain, it raises further the spectre of 'designer babies' whereby doctors and prospective parents are able to cherry-pick a much wider range of traits than at present.

Not that innovations in genetic medicine, by themselves, guarantee the means of eradicating disablement, since the majority of impairments are acquired well after birth – through working conditions, accidents, violence, and the ageing process. Indeed, the world is experiencing an unprecedented 'elder explosion'. This is most evident in wealthy 'industrialized nations', where families have fewer children and people live longer than in poorer countries. In these societies, the proportion of the population in the age groups approaching or reaching retirement age grew from 8 per cent in 1950 to 14 per cent in 1998, and is expected to reach 25 per cent in 2050. In the second half of the twenty-first century 'the developing nations will follow suit, as they experience their own elder explosion' (Giddens, 2006, p. 197). Unprecedented environmental changes, with significant air and water pollution, signal new health hazards which will increase the prevalence of impairment. The sharp divide which formally exists between 'disabled' and 'non-disabled' people does not tally with the actual distribution of impairment:

> The idea that physicality involves impairment and increasing impairment, and ultimately death may not seem positive, but a view of life which embraced that fact would be healthier, would probably lessen prejudice against disabled people and older people, and would certainly involve doctors radically altering their view of their role, and of what it is to be human. (Shakespeare, 1995, p. 28)

Despite the challenge to traditional negative assumptions surrounding impairment and disability by disabled people and their organizations, ignorance and prejudice remain widespread. The origins of such beliefs lie primarily in individualistic medical conceptions of impairment as disease and a radical departure from the desired state of health and well-being (Goble, 2003), Hence, a life with impairments is generally assumed to be one of isolation, poverty and powerlessness. Consequentially these are conditions that most people would choose to avoid both for themselves and for their families. It is the prevalence of such views that has served to fuel the growing ethical, biomedical and legal support for the euthanasia of unborn infants, young children and adults with 'terminal illness' and 'severe' impairments.

Life and death decisions

Abortion and infanticide

Since the 1960s, there has been a general trend in Western societies towards the legalization of abortion on broad social grounds. It has been stimulated by a shift in moral views which has coincided with a period of social and sexual liberation and change. However, if abortion is accepted, is it the woman's right to decide? Are there other extenuating or special circumstances to be considered? The solution arrived at in the 1967 Abortion Act in Britain was that 'A pregnancy may be lawfully terminated if continuance would culminate in harm to the pregnant woman, or if there is substantial risk that if the child were born it would suffer from such physical or mental abnormalities as to be seriously handicapped.' Moreover, the extraordinary pace of technological innovation has greatly increased medicine's ability to identify impairments in the unborn child or 'foetus'. Diagnostic procedures such as amniocentesis and ultrasound scanning have all gained widespread usage. Their impact is evidenced in Britain by the decline in births of children with spina bifida by up to three-quarters in the last twenty years. As Alison Davis argues: 'Once handicap has been detected, abortion is not only seen as acceptable, but is often positively encouraged' (1989, p. 83).

While it is illegal to abort a foetus on the grounds of its sex or 'race', termination because of anticipated impairment is permissible. Present legislation states that abortion is permitted up to twenty-four weeks of pregnancy, except in cases where serious 'handicap' is detected. This is when the 'third semester' baby may still be in the womb, but is sentient and has a good chance of survival (Shakespeare, 2006, p. 95). From a legal perspective the 'right to life becomes meaningful on live birth'. At this point the baby is considered a person with human rights (McLean and Williamson, 2007, p. 65). However, these rights are not extended to an infant with an accredited impairment. Consequently late abortion after twenty-four weeks warrants 'infanticide on the grounds of impairment', because an induced birth after this time period will produce a viable baby that can survive with appropriate medical care. It is at this point that decisions about whether the infant should live or die are made and whether post-natal support is provided or withheld (DPI, 2000, p. 7). In 2006, 2,036 abortions were legally carried out in England and Wales under ground E (DoH, 2007c, p. 18), which means that there was 'a substantial risk' that the baby when born would be 'seriously handicapped'.

It may be argued that the clause allowing late abortions was introduced to accommodate the small number of cases where the newborn infant was considered likely to die during or shortly after birth. Yet there is growing evidence that the law is widely exploited and that children with relatively minor conditions that are easily treatable, such as club feet, webbed fingers and cleft palate, are killed (Rogers, 2006). Indeed, in a ten-year period from 1982/3 to 1992, the birth rate for babies born with cleft palate fell from 820 to 464 and with talipes from 2,041 to 747 (Alderson, 2001). Recent statistics suggest that, in just one area of England, over 100 infants were aborted for similar minor treatable conditions (Templeton, 2007, unpaged). Notably in 2004 a baby was aborted at twenty-eight weeks after scans showed it had a cleft palate. Joanna Jepson, a curate who had had this condition as a child, tried to ensure criminal charges were brought against the two doctors responsible, but the case was dismissed (Grear, 2004).

Moreover, women frequently come under considerable professional and family pressure to have an abortion where an impairment is identified (Davis, 1989; Morris, 1991; C. Thomas, 1997, 1999). Richard Light suggests a possible cause: 'There is a particularly high incidence of death amongst disabled children which appears to reflect the still prevalent assumption that disabled lives are "not worth living", such that newborn children with impairments are denied medical treatments or simply left to die' (2002, p. 13). But it is important to distinguish between arguments that recommend abortion on the grounds that life as a disabled person is not worth living and those that hinge on the difficulties associated with bringing up a disabled child. An infant with an impairment may place an excessive burden on the mother and the family – in terms of both additional time needed to support the child and the financial and emotional resources that must be devoted to its well-being – with a consequent deterioration in the quality of family life and relationships. Parents may believe that a disabled child may have a detrimental influence on their partnership and/or a negative impact on their other children. They may be concerned about the financial implications of bringing up a disabled infant, especially if it means giving up work to care for the child. Moreover, those who choose not to terminate a pregnancy where impairment is present may find themselves denigrated as socially irresponsible (Thomas, 1999, 2007; Shakespeare, 2006).

The difficulties parents face when making such decisions are compounded further by the intensifying marketization of health and welfare support services and by the growing media emphasis on preventative measures in the pursuit of a healthy lifestyle. Biogenetic information is generally considered distinct from other data, as it is unique to the individual and highly predictive. Therefore it is of particular value to the vested interests of third parties such as insurance companies, health services and employers. This is because people with a genetic disposition to long-term illness or impairment are considered a greater financial risk than those without, and as a consequence may be refused health insurance, expensive medical treatments and employment (Asch, 2001).

In order to prevent such discriminatory action, both the 1997 UNESCO Declaration on the Human Genome and Human Rights, and the Council of Europe's Convention on Human Rights and Biomedicine prohibit the disclosure of genetic information without consent. Nevertheless opposition to these measures remains high, for example, from the Association of British Insurers. In England, there are no privacy laws, and insurance companies can ask for access to people's medical records for policy assessments. They argue that genetic data are no different from other information such as medical tests and family histories that people have to provide when applying for health or life insurance. They are concerned both that people at risk of contracting inherited illnesses and impairments are far more likely to take out health and life insurance policies than those not at risk and that those with a low risk of genetic disorders are less likely to pay for health insurance (Kerr and Shakespeare, 2002, p. 147).

The birth of a child with an impairment is widely regarded as a tragic and negative event which changes significantly the lives of other family members. There is a widespread lay concern that the baby should be 'all right'. Parents of a child (likely to be) born with an impairment experience a mixture of emotions, including shock, guilt, shame and helplessness. Micheline Mason, a disabled woman, remembers professional intervention in the following way:

> My father and mother, like so many other people, had very little experience of disability or of disabled people. They believed most of what they were told, at first anyway. They were told that I would always be severely 'handicapped'. That I would become increasingly deformed as a result of numerous fractures. That I would always be dependent on them, and that I would be wanted only by them. (Mason, 1992, p. 113)

This raises serious questions about the ability of doctors and related professionals to offer parents an 'unbiased' choice on whether to abort an unborn child if impairment is detected. To make an informed choice, prospective parents need full access to all information. This should cover the actual condition diagnosed and the lives of those individuals and their families who live with it. However, concerns have been raised about the context in which such information is provided, its content, and the attitudes of those charged with the responsibility of providing it (Shakespeare, 2006). While the increase in prenatal screening procedures has successfully reduced the incidence of infant mortality, it has been likened to a conveyer belt. Consequentially choice is undermined (Morris, 1991; Thomas, 1999; Kerr and Shakespeare, 2002; Solberg, 2009).

Social and psychological research indicates that the content and availability of adequate information on prenatal screening available to pregnant women is variable in both quality and availability. Information about the main point of the screening process and the conditions it is designed to detect are often inadequate. For example, comprehensive information about Down's syndrome, spina bifida and other conditions detectable through prenatal screening procedures is rarely available. Early screening may be implemented for the medical benefit of the unborn child. The 'neck fold' which is a marker for Down's syndrome may also indicate other anomalies that are associated with heart disease which may be treatable. 'With a legitimate therapeutic focus, controversial aspects such as selection and negative attitudes to disabled people are downplayed' (Solberg, 2009, p. 200). Moreover, while there are many people working in maternity services that are non-directive and pro-choice, many take the opposite view, and prejudice exists. There is ample evidence from around the world that many professionals are directive and believe that women have a duty to have tests and consent to terminations when impairment is detected (Shakespeare, 2006).

The ethics and politics of prenatal screening are indeed complex. This was especially evident in a RADAR (the disability network) survey of disabled people and their families' views about genetic medicine conducted in 1999. For instance, some, who were opposed to abortion generally, argued that it might be justifiable when prenatal screening detects impairment. Others, who expressed disquiet about such procedures, were anxious that their concerns should not be used to challenge a 'woman's right to choose' and to terminate a pregnancy. Perhaps unsurprisingly, however, the main concern of the respondents to the RADAR survey was that prenatal screening and similar procedures would be used to question the quality of life of disabled people (RADAR, 2006). Certainly many disabled people are acutely aware of a general public hostility towards individuals with impairments. The person with spina bifida or cerebral palsy is made to feel devalued or threatened by societal readiness to allow abortion on these grounds. It is hard to justify equal rights to those alive while denying such rights to the new generation of disabled people: 'For if it is decided that it is both right and proper to kill someone because they have a particular condition, why should others with that same condition be accorded rights simply because they are older?' (Davis, 1989, p. 83).

Voluntary and involuntary euthanasia

For many disabled people, recent debates about how and when to end life because of impairment and disability are especially poignant as they appear to threaten directly their very existence – possibly even more so than biogenetic medicine and prenatal screening (Shakespeare, 2006). These concerns have intensified over recent years as the euthanasia debate has assumed a particularly high profile in many Western societies. The American state of Oregon legalized voluntary euthanasia or assisted suicide with Measure 16, establishing the Death with Dignity Act in 1994. Two years later Australia's Northern Territories introduced the Rights of the Terminally Ill Act, which allowed four terminally ill people to administer lethal injections to end their lives. The legislation was overturned in 1998. However, after thirty years of not bringing charges against those responsible for 'mercy killing', voluntary and non-voluntary euthanasia was legalized in the Netherlands in 2002. Belgium followed suit that same year (Priestley, 2003), Washington in 2008 and Montana in 2009.

There has been a concerted campaign over recent decades to introduce similar legislation in the UK, led by the Voluntary Euthanasia Society, now known as Dignity in Dying. The campaign is bolstered by the support of high-profile public figures such as Chris Woodhead, formerly head of the government's Office for Standards in Education (Ofsted) and regular columnist for the *Sunday Times*, and John Humphrys, the highly respected BBC broadcaster and journalist, both of whom have written articles in national newspapers supporting the case for assisted suicide (Disability Now, 2009; Lawson, 2009; Humphrys, 2009). Furthermore, notwithstanding that there is clear opposition to this campaign within the international disabled people's movement by organizations such as America's Not Dead Yet and DPI, attitudes to the issue within the disabled population as a whole are said to be divided – see, for example, the debate between Jane Campbell (2009) and Tom Shakespeare (2009). The growing moral dilemma for doctors and society generally is heightened by recent technological and clinical advances that have greatly extended the capacity of medicine to keep people alive in otherwise fatal circumstances. Yet despite pressure from many of its members, the British Medical Association (BMA) remains opposed to moves to allow doctors actively to hasten death. At its conference in July 2005 the BMA voted to drop its long-standing opposition to legalize assisted suicide. The motion was overturned at the 2006 meeting (McLean and Wiliamson, 2007). In July 2009 the Royal College of Nursing dropped its opposition to the concept of assisted suicide.

However, in cases where the prognosis is that the quality of life is considered intolerable, doctors may collude with patients and/or their families and agree that nothing more should be done to prolong life. It is notable that some advocates of the legalization of assisted suicide also advocate the legalization of involuntary euthanasia. They maintain that when doctors withdraw life-sustaining treatment from patients diagnosed as in a 'permanently vegetative state' they are effectively practising euthanasia: 'Doctors may not want to admit this and couch their decisions in terms such as "alleviating suffering" but withdrawal of life saving sustaining treatment from severely incompetent patients is morally equivalent to active euthanasia' (Doyal, cited in BBC News 24, 2006, p. 1). The movement for the right to a painless and dignified death has been given further impetus by a series of high-profile legal cases in which disabled people have fought for the right to choose when and how they die. Two key claims have been significant: the right to assisted suicide, and the right to die by refusing medical treatments. Following a period of deteriorating physical abilities and paralysis due to motor neurone disease, Diane Pretty sought assurance that her husband should be allowed to help her die without fear of prosecution when she felt life was no longer bearable and was unable to kill herself. Her application was rejected in the English courts and the European Court of Human Rights on the grounds that 'her legal rights to dignity of life did not extend to choosing death with dignity'. In response she travelled to Switzerland, where assisted suicide has been legal since 1941. Another important case concerns a paralysed woman known as Miss B, who relied on a ventilator to breathe. In March 2002 she won the legal right to end her life by claiming the right to refuse 'unwanted medical treatment' (Priestley, 2003, p. 173). The two cases are significant as they suggest that the claim to a natural death without medical intervention is more 'socially acceptable' than those which bring about an unnatural death by assisted suicide.

In response to these overtures, Lord Joffe has introduced several bills into the House of Lords to legalize assisted suicide in Britain. The Assisted Dying for the Terminally Ill Bill mandated assisted suicide by doctors under specific circumstances. Its supporters claimed that, as mercy killing is common in the UK, it should be accepted and regulated, notwithstanding that a survey of 857 doctors who had attended 22,588 deaths found that none of those deaths occurred through assisted suicide. Only 0.6 per cent were attributed to voluntary euthanasia and a similar figure as a consequence of involuntary euthanasia (Seale, 2006). Also the Joffe bill did not include legislation to cover voluntary or involuntary killing. It would therefore have provided no regulation or control in these cases (RADAR, 2006, p. 8). This is especially important for disabled and older people, as the bill specifically targeted the 'terminally ill'. Indeed, many disabled people live full and productive lives with conditions termed 'terminal illness'. Conditions such as cystic fibrosis, muscular dystrophy, multiple sclerosis, motor neurone disease and HIV/AIDS, for example, are all currently incurable and may result in what is widely considered a 'premature death' (Shakespeare, 2006, p. 124). An amendment to the Coroners and Justice Bill put forward before the House of Lords on 7 July 2009 by Lord Falconer, the former Labour lord chancellor, which would, if passed, have effectively decriminalized assisted suicide, was defeated on a free vote by 194 to 141 (Hansard, 2009, 634).

What particularly concerns many disabled people is the way in which calculations are made about the quality of people's lives. As an illustration, health economists have explored the production of

Table 9.1 Arguments for and against assisted suicide	
For	Against
If people have a right to life and self-determination, then surely they should have the right to make their own choices and choose to die.	Although suicide may not be illegal, every effort is made to discourage non-disabled people from attempting it. Yet those with terminal illness are permitted or encouraged to do so.
If it is no longer a crime for people to commit suicide, then those who are unable to do so themselves should have the necessary support.	As assisted suicide is not legal for non-disabled people, to legalize it for disabled people is overtly discriminatory and a clear indication of a double standard.
People in the late stages of terminal illness experience severe pain and therefore may wish to avoid any further suffering.	Palliative care is extremely effective and should be available to everyone. However, it is not available widely enough to allow people the opportunity to live their last days painlessly and peacefully.
Doctors assist people to die now, but it is often difficult to decide whether the patient has requested it or not. It is important, therefore, to regulate the system to eliminate abuse.	Regulation would not eliminate abuse. It is extremely difficult for people to make a rational decision about their future when they have been told that they are going to suffer and die in pain. Regulation would leave no room for a changing prognosis.
Relatives may often have to watch a loved one suffer extreme physical pain and suffering and occasionally put themselves at risk of prosecution for 'mercy killing'.	The legalization of assisted suicide would compound the existing pressures on disabled people to consider themselves an emotional and financial burden to their families and friends, and in so doing would compound their disadvantage.

Source: Adapted from RADAR (2006, pp. 25–7)

a QALY (quality-adjusted life years) measure whose intention is to allow comparison of treatments for different conditions (Culyer et al., 1972). Four aspects of life quality have been stressed: physical mobility; capacity for self-care; freedom from pain and distress; and social adjustment. While it is emphasized that these are social judgements, they provide a mechanism by which doctors can judge a person's quality of life, whether or not they would benefit from medical interventions, and whether the resources are available to keep them alive.

What is especially alarming is that such judgements allow doctors to deny medical treatments to those who need and want them, if they feel that they are not in the 'patient's' best interests. Inevitably this is of major concern to many people living with terminal illness. The case of Leslie Burke, a man with a degenerative condition known as cerebella ataxia, illustrates the point well. The condition usually leads to a situation where the individual concerned will lose the ability to do anything for themselves, including the ability to communicate, but will still remain cognitively fully aware until death. Concerned that doctors may decide to withdraw artificial nutrition and hydration if he was hospitalized and unable to feed himself or speak, Burke challenged doctors' right to withdraw treatment in the law courts to avoid the horror of dehydration while still fully conscious. Initially the court ruled in Burke's favour. But this ruling was overturned following a later appeal by the General Medical Council. Hence: 'doctors cannot be forced to provide treatment against their clinical judgment about whether or not it is appropriate, or in the patient's interests, to provide it. Thus, even if the patient wishes treatment, doctors cannot be made to offer it' (McLean and Williamson, 2007, p. 124).

A further example of what some consider a growing and worrying trend in social attitudes to euthanasia for disabled people is reflected in the apparent leniency with which the law courts respond to those responsible for the 'mercy killing' of disabled relatives. For instance, in 2005 a British man killed his ten-year-old son by smothering him with a pillow. The boy was a wheelchair user with Hunter syndrome. The boy's father was given a two-year suspended sentence for manslaughter due to 'diminished responsibility' (RADAR, 2006, p. 13).

The arguments for and against assisted suicide are summarized in table 9.1.

Review

Historically, idealized assumptions about the biological characteristics of what is and what it is not considered to be human have dominated Western cultures. This has led to various social divisions and associated oppressions on the grounds of gender, 'race', ethnicity, sexual preference, age and, latterly, impairment and disability. Increasingly over the last century there has been a formal recognition in most Western states that such differences are a welcome characteristic of a healthy and civilized society and, therefore, should be welcomed and celebrated. To this end various legislative measures have been introduced to eradicate oppression in all its forms.

Such measures are founded on various ethical and legal principles intended to protect the interests of all members of society, and particularly those at most risk of having their interests denied. But, as this chapter has indicated, these precepts are subject to interpretation and operate within an economic and cultural environment in which prejudice and ignorance about impairment and disability still predominate. The end result is that the decision to eradicate those considered unworthy of life and/or an economic and social burden to themselves, their families and the state remains largely unchecked. It is evident in the rhetoric surrounding recent developments in biotechnology, the policies and practices of those charged with life and death decisions at the beginning and end of life, and the general view that living with impairment is no life at all – as exemplified in the leniency accorded those responsible for the mercy killing of disabled relatives. Taken together, these tendencies serve only to reinforce the traditional personal tragedy view of impairment and disability and, in so doing, undermine disabled people's calls for effective political and social change with which to bring about a more equitable and just society.

Disability and Development: Global Perspectives

T HE discussion thus far has concentrated on disability issues in industrialized, predominantly Western societies. In this chapter, we explore approaches to impairment and disability in 'developing', 'poorer' or 'underdeveloped' (sometimes called 'transitional') countries, which contain the majority of the world's population. Their experiences illuminate the dynamics of industrial capitalism and the escalating economic and technological processes and structures of globalization that, since the late twentieth century, are widely believed to have hastened the creation of 'one world'. This background provides a distinctive dimension to analyses of disability and impairment in poorer countries, where this is increasingly viewed as a development issue. It also raises important questions about the relevance of Western approaches to theorizing and challenging disability.

The chapter begins by outlining the international context with the development of industrial capitalism and globalization and their impact on poorer countries over recent decades. Second, the discussion elaborates the diversity of approaches to impairment and disability in non-Western countries. The third section examines the relationship between disability, poverty and economic development and also wider social and environmental barriers to social inclusion, with a specific look at education. Fourth, we examine the growing international focus on disability, including policy initiatives from the United Nations, the World Bank and the World Health Organization, as well as non-governmental organizations. Finally, the spotlight turns to the politicization of disabled people in poorer countries and the emergence of 'alternative' services and support programmes, notably community-based rehabilitation (CBR), in order to promote change.

Disability, industrialization and globalization

A global perspective on political economy is our starting point for exploring disability in poorer countries. In Western industrialized countries, economic development is equated with overall social and human progress. From the dominant, 'neo-liberal' standpoint, such growth depends on the replacement of 'traditional' political, cultural and legal customs, values and institutions with 'modern' or Western alternatives (Hoogvelt, 1976; Hout, 1993).

However, terms such as 'developed' and 'developing' obscure the ways in which richer industrialized countries have been actively engaged in the 'underdevelopment' of the rest of the world. They deflect consideration of how a core of powerful capitalist states emerged to dominate and exploit the majority of poorer countries and their populations at the periphery of this world economic system, with production, trade and the financial system geared primarily to 'First World' interests – akin, for some, to the class relations and inequalities between the bourgeoisie and proletariat central to Marxist class analysis (Frank, 1975; Wallerstein, 1979). The actions of industrialized nation-states in maintaining their economic, political and cultural interests overlap with the expansion of international capital and large multinational corporations (Hoogvelt, 1997; Allen and Thomas, 2000).

The globalization of industrial and financial capitalism over the last two decades has hastened the imposition of a capitalist world order. These trends are exemplified by the dramatic expansion of transnational corporations such as Coca-Cola, General Motors and Exxon, which have become richer than many of the countries where the bulk of the world's population live. Their impact is reinforced by the much greater interconnectedness of individuals and groups within economic, political and cultural structures and processes, particularly following the rapid internationalization of information and communication technologies (Held et al., 1999; Bisley, 2007).

While there are competing interpretations of the outcome of these trends, most commentators argue that, with the advent of the global economic system, nation-states have been relegated to the position of less significant economic or political players. Globalization is also held responsible for generally widening the gap between richer and poorer countries. Even if the consequences are not necessarily one way, or certain in their effects, they are associated with a general worsening of the inequalities between richer and poorer countries. According to some estimates, the gap between the world's richest and poorest nations in 1820 was approximately three to one, but widened with the growth of international capitalism, so that by 1992 the difference had multiplied to a staggering seventy-two to one (Giddens, 2001, p. 70). Currently, over a billion people are forced to exist on less than US 1$ a day (UNDP, 2005), graphically highlighting the disparity in wealth between the 'developed' and the 'developing' world. The odds are heavily stacked against a poor country achieving significant and sustained economic growth in an international world economic and political system effectively directed by industrialized economies and associated dominant institutions such as the International Monetary Fund and the World Bank.

While the gap has lessened in some countries, with improved levels of literacy, malnutrition, infant mortality and life expectancy, international indices of human development mostly suggest that, since the 1990s, 'the overall rate of convergence is slowing – and for a large group of countries divergence is becoming the order of the day' (UNDP, 2005, p. 25). In social policy terms, concerns about the consequences of globalization revolve on how large, multinational companies exert considerable leverage over national governments by threatening not to locate in countries where the costs of production (from wages and taxation), that sustain a social welfare system, are relatively higher (Held et al., 1999; Holden and Beresford, 2002). This implies that the negative results of globalization include external constraints on any efforts by poorer countries to build the welfare services so important to the life chances of many disabled people.

Nevertheless, drawing a line between richer and poorer countries conveys neither the contrasts in the level of economic development nor the scale of poverty among and within 'developing' countries (Ncube, 2006). Moreover, a general designation as a 'developing' or 'poorer' world country can be very misleading, as the case of India illustrates. It ranks in the top ten of industrialized countries, is a global leader in information technology, but also contains one-third of the world's poorest people, with poverty being a way of life in many villages in rural areas. Indeed, vast differences between the circumstances of the poor, located in traditional village communities and increasingly in large urban slums, and wealthy, privileged elites appear across Africa, Asia and Latin America. Again, some countries are more accurately categorized as transitional (whether industrializing or, for example, exploiting financial services and natural resources), while others remain largely traditional, non-industrialized, small-scale rural societies.

What, then, is the relationship between global capitalism and the production and experience of impairment and disability in poorer countries? Recent studies have been central in contesting the short-comings so evident in much of the Western literature on this subject. These display a tendency towards the 'anecdotal' and the 'impressionistic' (Miles, 1983) and tend towards overwhelmingly negative accounts (Kisanji, 1995) that converge on the 'restrictions' imposed by traditional attitudes and values and other 'myth making' (Ingstad, 1999, p. 757). This is then used to justify Western interventions about how to advance the interests of disabled people (Barnes and Mercer, 2005a; Sheldon, 2005).

One alternative is to regard disability as a 'development issue shared by north and south' (Coleridge, 1993, p. 65). Nonetheless, some materialist accounts taking this approach may be criticized as 'politically naïve' (Gleeson, 1997, p. 197), and as imposing a set of Western-based assumptions about the theory and practice of impairment and disability in developing countries. It is worth mentioning, but hardly surprising, that disabled people's organizations around the world do not generally adopt an overtly materialist analysis or anti-capitalist political stance. It is imperative to explore materialist analyses of the impact of uneven economic development and poverty while locating these within specific social, political and cultural contexts. A robust political economy approach suggests a close relationship between disability and uneven economic development, without descending into a simple determinist position or presuming an unproblematic embrace of a social model approach by disabled people in poorer countries.

In summary, it remains unproven, and a research issue, 'whether the transplant of Western-evolved disability discourses into non-Western contexts works for or against the lives of individual disabled people' (Stone, 1999d, p. 146).

Comparative perspectives on impairment

The value of a comparative perspective on disability and impairment is that it both challenges common-sense assumptions about what is 'normal' in bodily terms and attempts to 'universalize' Western beliefs and practices. To understand the significance of impairment and how and why certain individuals and groups are labelled 'abnormal' or 'incompetent', and therefore associated service and policy provision, it is necessary to explore these issues within specific contexts. Much anthropological effort has been invested in exploring cross-cultural approaches and the extensive variation in ways of perceiving the individual, including the biological constitution of the body and allied understandings of health, impairment and disability. Studies also illustrate how the contemporary Western perspective on impairment in biomedical and individualistic terms is peculiar to its philosophical and historical traditions (Miles, 1995, 2006).

A particularly instructive set of contemporary anthropological studies is contained in Benedicte Ingstad and Susan Reynolds Whyte's (1995) collection *Disability and Culture*. This concentrates on small-scale communities based in rural areas and offers ample evidence of the relationship between perceived impairment and wider social roles and participation. In the Tuareg, for example, these include 'old age and immaturity (making one physically dependent), illegitimate birth (making one socially anomalous), and ugliness (rendering it difficult to marry)' (Ingstad and Whyte, 1995, p. 6). Moreover, the assumed 'defects' that mark individuals out as unacceptably different encompass features that other cultures disregard or believe of little consequence, such as freckles, small or flabby buttocks, and protruding navels (ibid.). Although most cultures have notions of a 'normal' or 'ideal' body–mind, and what constitute acceptable individual attributes, these vary markedly. What counts as an 'impairment' and what is reckoned an appropriate social response is far from universal: 'The disfiguring scar in Dallas becomes an honorific mark in Dahomey' (Hanks and Hanks, 1948, p. 11).

Again, the separation of body and mind that became a characteristic feature of Enlightenment thinking in Euro-American societies has little resonance in many non-Western countries. For instance, in Chinese cultures, the mind, heart and body are regarded as indistinguishable, while illnesses and impairments are conceived as signs or products of imbalances within or between the constituent realms of the total body–mind system. Moreover, the body–mind is viewed as part of a wider constellation involving lineage, family, community, country, nature and cosmos. This has important implications for the ways in which people with impairments are perceived and treated by family and community members within Chinese society (Stone, 1999c).

Religious ideas have often been accorded a crucial role in determining what is deemed socially acceptable. However, there is no consensus among major religions such as Buddhism, Hinduism and Islam on the 'correct' way to regard impairment. In societies where these religions are pre-eminent, impairments are widely regarded as 'misfortunes, sent by deity, fate, karma; and often associated with parental sin' (Miles, 1995, p. 52). As with Christianity, this emphasis on the ways of understanding and responding to misfortune through individual acceptance and spiritual salvation produces very different social responses to the individual with an impairment and their family (Charlton, 1998). Such ideas and practices may be particularly strong in traditional, rural-based societies (Scheer and Groce, 1988; Ingstad and Whyte, 1995).

According to Mary Douglas (1966), responses to perceived physical, sensory or cognitive difference involve deep-seated psychological . fears of 'anomaly'. This denotes a connection between perceptions of impairment and a non-human 'liminal' status. Cultures deal with assumed ambiguity either by attempting to control it in some way or by adopting it as ritual. Douglas examines traditional, small-scale cultures such as that of the Nuer, who treat 'monstrous' births as baby hippopotamuses accidentally born to humans. The Nuer's response is to return them to 'the river where they belong' (ibid., p. 39). This interpretation illustrates the dilemmas of establishing the level of infanticide between societies. Nancy Scheper-Hughes adds further examples of 'crocodile infants', 'poor little critters', in north-east Brazil, and Irish 'changelings', and concludes that: 'The sickly, wasted, or congenitally deformed infant challenges the tentative and fragile symbolic boundaries between human and non-human, natural and supernatural, normal and abominable' (1992, p. 375).

The Masai people of Kenya generally view congenital impairments as caused by 'nature' or 'God' (and witchcraft) and not as a source of individual blame. The Songye people of Zaire distinguish three categories of abnormal children: ceremonial, bad and faulty. 'Ceremonial' children, for example those born feet first, or with the umbilical cord round the neck, are marked in a positive way. 'Bad' children are not regarded as human beings, but as supernatural, from the anti-world of sorcerers, and include albino, dwarf and hydrocephalic children. 'Faulty' children – for example those with polio, cerebral palsy, club feet – have an indeterminate status. Still, the emphasis is not on improving their situation but on interpreting the fault. Potential sources are: the physical environment (failure of parents to respect food or sex taboos); family members (bad relationships leading to sorcery); ancestors (lack of respect); or divine intervention (Ingstad and Whyte, 1995).

Cultural practices also diverge in the interpretation of behavioural misdemeanours, and whether these are due to moral failings or form the basis for cognitive or intellectual impairment. Indeed, tolerance of 'mental incompetence' varies greatly, even between the Islamic Bedouin and Islamic Pakistan (Miles, 1992; Bazna and Hatab, 2005). Equally, there is no consistent support for claims that the less technologically advanced the society, the more its population integrates people with cognitive impairments (Edgerton, 1967).

In Songye and Masai cultures, and also that of the Punan Bah (of Central Borneo), people with impairments are not regarded as a distinct group, but are distinguished according to the explanation and implications of the condition. Among the Punan Bah, people with physical impairments are not separated from the household, and share in production and consumption with the family. Most impairments, unlike ugliness, are not stigmatized. Similarly, in the Masai: 'Physically impaired persons marry, become parents, and participate in all communal activities to the best of their abilities' (Talle, 1995, p. 69). Even so, different cultures create their own complex hierarchies to locate individuals. Ida Nicolaisen (1995) identifies notions of 'humanity' and 'personhood' as vital concepts. Among the Punan Bah, a relatively narrow set of conditions, including epilepsy, 'madness' and severe birth defects, denote a non-human status that warrants social exclusion. The notion of 'personhood' is used to distinguish between specific roles, rankings and expectations. Whereas in most Western societies personhood is equated with paid employment, in China it has been traditionally linked to marriage, parenthood and producing a son to continue the family lineage (Stone, 1999c).

In many traditional societies, such as the Masai and Punan Bah, the primary 'disabling' condition is the failure to have children, with parenthood the key to adult status. Those without children of their own, including people with impairments, are sometimes given children by other members of their family, so that they can acquire full (adult) status. Among the Songye, a disabled woman may not marry, but can conceive a child, living with her parents until the child can perform household tasks. In contrast: 'physical and mental capacities are not culturally constructed as differences having implications for a person's fulfilment in life' (Talle, 1995, p. 70).

How, then, is this ample evidence of substantial variation between traditional societies explained? Jane Hanks and L. Hanks (1948) ground this diversity in divergent economic or material conditions. They argue that a primary constraint is the level of economic stability and viability of the society – that is, the demand for different types of labour, the amount of surplus generated, and how it is distributed. In turn, this is affected by social structure – whether it is hierarchical or egalitarian, how achievement is defined, perceptions of age and sex, its relations with neighbouring societies, its aesthetic values, 'and many more functionally related factors' (ibid., p. 13). Across societies, the range of social status of people with physical impairments stretches from 'pariah', because the individual is deemed an economic or moral liability or threat, through 'limited participation', where the individual is granted selected social or other concessions, to 'laissez-faire', where some people enjoy opportunities to acquire prestige and wealth.

One basic issue that has received rather little examination is the effect of the spread of industrial capitalism on traditional approaches to impairment and disability. The suggested impact on the Punah Bah economy and culture of Central Borneo has been dramatic (Nicolaisen, 1995). The arrival of international logging companies has curbed the local economy and brought very different approaches to work and wage labour that conflict with established understandings of personhood and the status of people with accredited impairments. Furthermore, smaller family units have been replacing the typical extended household, leading to a greater dependence of people with an impairment on non-family sources. Traditional belief systems are being challenged. Overall, 'capitalist' values are beginning imperceptibly to 'permeate Punan Bah view of themselves and the world' (ibid., p. 54). In a similar fashion, the exposure of Masai society to market forces has led to a shift from established patterns of residence to one-family households and has undermined traditional community support networks of mutual aid and co-operation for people with impairments (Talle, 1995), while Susie Miles (1996) concludes from studies of southern Africa that mothers of disabled children and disabled women are particularly vulnerable. This process has been heightened by the growing influence of 'scientific medicine' and the Western mass media in promoting a novel understanding of 'able-bodied normalcy' (Coleridge, 1993; Charlton, 1998). The interdependence of cultural and material factors is graphically illustrated – with outcomes that transform the link between impairment and disability.

Impairment: patterns and social origins

Considerable caution must be used when interpreting cross-national data on the prevalence of 'impairments' because the collection and processing procedures vary significantly, with some countries relying on professional diagnoses and others on survey questionnaire responses, sometimes constrained by their links with eligibility for welfare benefits and services (UN, 1990). Notwithstanding these major concerns about the validity and reliability of official statistics, the international league tables based on criteria similar to those expounded in the *ICIDH* (WHO, 1980) indicate that the measured prevalence of impairment is generally lower than that for 'disability' or functional limitations. 'Among the 55 nations impairment rates varied between 0.2 per cent to around 6 per cent, whilst disability rates varied from approximately 7 per cent to 20.9 per cent' (Ingstad, 2001, p. 773).

These surveys demonstrate that most of the world's population with impairments live in the poorer nations of the majority world. The British government's Department for International Development (DfID, 2000) suggests that nearly three-quarters of disabled people live in developing countries, although the incidence of both reported impairment and 'disability' is generally higher in wealthier nations (UN, 1990). There are several possible reasons for this pattern. First, in richer societies the longer life expectancy and much larger proportion of people over the age of fifty are linked directly with higher (age-related) rates of impairment. Second, these countries have more extensive health and support services, which typically produce a higher survival rate among people born with impairments and those who acquire them later in life. Thus, over recent decades in South Africa, a spinally injured white person was ten times more likely to survive into late middle age than a black person with a similar condition. Third, some conditions such as dyslexia are classified as an impairment in highly industrialized economies, although in more rural majority world countries these are often not considered a 'functional limitation' and therefore not recorded as an impairment to anything like the same degree (Coleridge, 1993).

The main causes of 'chronic diseases and long term impairments' in poorer countries are poverty, inadequate sanitation, poor diet and bad housing (WHO, 2001b). For example, over 100 million people in these countries have acquired impairments because of chronic malnutrition. Every year 250,000 children lose their sight through a lack of vitamin A that is usually provided by the regular intake of green vegetables. Perhaps as many as 800 million people acquire a cognitive/intellectual impairment due to a lack of iodine in their diet (Stone, 1999b, p. 5). Specific diseases once common but now rarely recorded in developed countries remain widespread and in some cases are increasing in other parts of the world. More than 30 per cent of the population in some villages in Zaire are affected by 'river blindness' (Coleridge, 1993). In addition, there were over 100,000 new cases of polio in 'developing' countries in 1994 (Stone, 1999b, p. 5). In India, the prevalence of polio and blindness is at least four times higher among people who are below the poverty line compared with those who are above it (Ghai, 2001, p. 29).

A fuller set of likely 'causes' extends to specific cultural practices (such as female genital mutilation), natural disasters (earthquakes, floods), and the effects of economic development (industrial accidents and pollution) (Baird, 1992). Some estimate that over 100 million females in Africa acquire an impairment as a result of genital mutilation (DfID, 2000, p. 5), while disabled girls and women experience being 'left marginalised, neglected and are often considered a burden' (ibid., p. 5). A vicious downward spiral sets in, with the negative consequences of impairment, disability and poverty reinforcing each other.

Civil wars, often fanned by the international arms trade, have caused an unprecedented growth in the number of civilians and military personnel with impairments. In Cambodia, an estimated 100,000 people lost limbs as a direct result of the combatants' use of landmines (UNESCO, 1995). In Rwanda, a dramatic rise in the number of people with impairments is attributed to its violent civil war. In such conflicts, a strategy of maiming rather than killing people was sometimes pursued, because 'disabled people remain far more visible than the dead' (Coleridge, 1993, p. 107) and diminish economic and psychological resistance.

Overall, international data suggest that up to one half of the world's impairment is directly or indirectly linked to poverty (DfID, 2000). These data indicate the high proportion of impairment in developing countries that is preventable: 'as far as the majority of the world's disabled people are concerned, impairment is very clearly, primarily the consequence of social and political factors, not an unavoidable "fact of nature"' (Abberley, 1987, p. 11). The reality for poorer people is a broad range of unhealthy or risky living conditions – inadequate shelter, water supply and sanitation; unsafe traffic and working conditions; absence and inaccessibility of timely and adequate health care and rehabilitation (as a result of environmental and/or monetary barriers); restricted access to education and employment; and exclusion from social and political life, including physical barriers (Handicap International, 2006, p. 66). This shifts the policy emphasis to a wide-ranging attack on poverty and malnutrition and the lack of sanitation and drinking water, as well as seeking improvements in the wider social environment, notably social welfare benefits and support services, and striving for greater political stability and security (Charlton, 1998; DfID, 2000).

The lack of government funding in poorer countries to counter impairment represents a major obstacle. It is worsened by the policies of international financial institutions such as the World Bank and the IMF that force governments to cut back on public services to pay off enormous international debts. With access to medical and rehabilitation services often dependent on an individual's ability to pay, this poses large problems for disabled people and their families. There is also a severe shortage of trained medical personnel that is exacerbated by the active 'poaching' of qualified staff by richer nations, without financial compensation for poorer countries to educate and train new staff. As a result, only 1 per cent of disabled people in 'developing' nations have access to any form of rehabilitation or impairment-related services (WHO, 2001b).

In comparison, in richer countries, the idea of prevention has become a contested issue among disabled people's groups, where it is sometimes equated with policies on eugenics, euthanasia, selective abortion and attempts to deny the right to life. Moreover, a disproportionate amount of resources, both financial and human, are invested in expensive medical interventions that 'will benefit only a relative minority of the world's population' (WHO, 2001b, p. 15). Whereas lifestyle choices such as diet, lack of exercise, consumption of alcohol and smoking are ranked as significant causes of impairments in wealthier nations, around three-quarters of India's 60 million disabled people live in areas where public amenities such as clean water, electricity, sanitation and medical services are often absent (Ghai, 2001). The lack of adequate public health and other medical facilities and medical services has a further impact. Hence, the demand for a wider public debate in developing countries about the proper balance of investment between high-technology medical intervention, public health measures and action to overturn social and environmental barriers.

Poverty, disability and social exclusion

As discussed in chapter 5, poverty is best understood as a complex system of social exclusion, comprising formal income and employment, food and housing, transport that extends to participation in health and education, family life and social relationships. Individuals experiencing poverty are more likely to acquire an impairment, and then to be excluded from society (see figure 10.1). Individuals and families become trapped in a set of mutually reinforcing disadvantages. The causes of disadvantage for disabled people are manifested in exclusionary attitudes and prejudice, but are more deeply rooted in structural inequalities and social processes. According to recent estimates, disabled people comprise around 15 to 20 per cent of the poor in developing countries (Elwan, 1999; UNDP, 2005).

Consider the example of India, where almost a third of the world's 'absolute poor' live. This level of poverty applies where people do not have sufficient resources to support a minimum of health and efficiency. Furthermore, 'while 46 per cent of India's people survive in absolute poverty . . . about two thirds are "capability poor", i.e. they do not receive the minimum level of education and health care necessary for functioning human capabilities' (Mabub ul Huq, quoted in Shariff, 1999, p. 45). One study in the province of Tamil Nadu found that impairment/disability affects one-third of the rural population (Erb and Harriss-White, 2002). Throughout India, disabled people are overrepresented among those people who are unemployed and have little formal education, as well as those subjected to high levels of abuse and social exclusion more generally.

It is little surprise that surveys of people in developing countries stress that an impairment would make their everyday experience even more acute: 'Being disabled, for example blind, crippled, mentally impaired, chronically ill' are major worries (UNDP, 1997, p. 17). The scale of the divide is vividly demonstrated by calculations that in some poorer countries, 90 per cent of those with an impairment die before they reach the age of twenty, and the same percentage of children with 'mental impairments' do not live beyond their fifth birthday (UNESCO, 1995). Children with an impairment are more likely not simply to die younger, but to be exposed to malnutrition,

Source: Adapted from DfID (2000, figure 2).

Figure 10.1   Linkages between poverty and disability

to experience little (if any) formal education, and to have little prospect of finding regular, paid employment – or, at most, to experience
low pay and underemployment (Handicap International, 2006). This
amounts to a cycle of disability and poverty, outlined in figure 10.1,
which leaves disabled people severely disadvantaged and excluded
from everyday life.

The transitional process with the shift to industrial production
(from agrarian economies) and to living in large, urban centres generates a further set of obstacles for many disabled people. In Malaysia,
for example, the impact of the built environment and transport
system on families, including employment of women, means that
disabled people have far fewer opportunities for recruitment or
retention in the paid labour market (Jayasooria et al., 1997). These
difficulties often have their roots in lower levels of education and
qualifications. Even in work, disabled people typically earn less than
their non-disabled counterparts. Special vocational workshops have
been a feature of disabled people's employment, along with subsidies
to encourage employers to take on disabled workers. The International
Labour Organization has also promoted anti-discrimination legislation in the workplace, although its effects have been lessened because
a high proportion of those disabled people in work are located in the
informal sector and subsistence agriculture.

Disabled people must also confront formidable barriers in respect of an inaccessible built environment, housing and transport systems. These are graphically illustrated in the densely populated and rapidly expanding cities of the majority world. They constitute a general deterrence to the integration of disabled people into everyday life. In addition, there is little short-term prospect of moving significantly towards satisfying such needs for accessibility because overall standards are so low, and again there is little funding available for such projects. According to a disabled commentator:

> In all my travels, Bangkok, where 40 percent of the Thai people live, is the hardest city to get around. Although the actual structural inaccessibility (lack of ramps, curb cuts, elevators) is more or less the same throughout the Third World, the streets of Bangkok are almost impossible to cross . . . Bangkok is a wheelchair user's nightmare. Jakarta and Bombay are close runners-up. (Charlton, 1998, p. 106)

Additionally, there are acute shortfalls in appropriate social welfare support systems, ranging from the lack of personal assistance schemes to the basic resources of organizations that have service responsibilities for disabled people. This extends to serious deficits in equipment, aids and accessible technology, such as brailling machines and computers, wheelchairs and prostheses. A specific issue for people with hearing impairments is the general absence of sign language interpreters in many countries, stretching from Thailand to Uganda and Venezuela (Katsui, 2006). Often where basic support items are available disabled individuals cannot afford to buy them, while alternatives, for example to assist mobility, are often inadequate and sometimes degrading.

The marginalization and powerlessness experienced by disabled people living in isolated rural areas and urban slums applies across so many parts of Africa, Asia and Latin America. When juxtaposed with the lack of the most basic medical and rehabilitation treatments and support systems, 'the problems of inequality and injustice are so massive as to appear unmanageable' (Ghai, 2001, p. 29). In a similar vein, a Brazilian disabled activist argues that disabled people are reduced to living in a 'pitiful condition', and forced to exist as 'outcasts deprived of social life, dignity, and citizenship' (Rosangela Bieler, quoted in Charlton, 1998, p. 19).

The harsh reality is that few poorer countries have the resources to sustain anything like an adequate welfare safety net for the most disadvantaged groups in the population. It has been calculated that only about 2 per cent of disabled people in low- and middle-income countries have access to disability-related support (Katsui, 2006). Hence, the likelihood of large-scale improvements being achieved is remote exactly because the disabling barriers are so extensive and entrenched and the resources to fund the necessary changes so limited (Charlton, 1998).

A further feature of social exclusion in poorer countries (as in their richer, industrialized counterparts) is the way in which poverty interacts with other social divisions. Research studies document the multiple oppressions of people on the basis of poverty, gender and disability (Boylan, 1991; Driedger et al., 1996; DfID, 2000). For instance, disabled women are widely regarded as experiencing specific barriers that clearly set them apart even from disabled men in most developing countries (Driedger, 1991; Miles, 1996; UN ESCAP, 2003). While socio-cultural practices vary considerably between societies, most demonstrate 'additional' limits on disabled women's access to education, employment and health services. Traditional gender roles (as wife and mother, for example) may enhance or reduce the consequences of poverty and disability (particularly if these roles cannot be performed as expected).

> Women in many parts of India are routinely fed last and least. Not only is there overwhelming evidence of differential food intake, but there is also evidence that girls are given poorer quality medical care . . . girls are admitted to hospital less often than boys are, and when admitted are often in a dangerous condition. (Ghai, 2001, p. 30)

Disabled women often encounter particular difficulties in accessing culturally appropriate services (Coleridge, 2000). This also holds back their representation in organizations of disabled people, although it has led to groups of disabled women setting up organizations to promote their specific interests.

Case study of education

Education is frequently presented as a means of addressing the problem of poverty and a route to social inclusion. Yet, in some developing countries, disabled children, particularly girls, are more likely to be denied formal education (UNESCO, 1995; UN ESCAP, 2003). Again, the transfer of the types of schooling and skills favoured in Western societies may prove more exclusionary or less relevant to disabled people's needs (Kalyanpur, 1996; Miles, 1996). For example, it tends to promote specific social and economic competence skills that lead to the labelling of some children as 'educationally backward' or having 'learning difficulties'. This results in their marginalization, even from contexts where numeracy and literacy skills may not be as vital to an individual's life chances (Kalyanpur, 1996; Ingstad, 2001).

> In fact, wealthier nations have arguably created greater, more insurmountable obstacles to inclusion because of their relatively vast material resources. In the South, by contrast, the rehabilitation and special needs industry is much smaller and less powerful, and human

resources can be harnessed to bring about inclusion. Here, implementation of inclusive education may simply involve the positive reinforcement of well-established, community-based and inclusive attitudes and practices. (S. Miles, 1999, p. 76)

In a reaction against the segregated residential approach of special schools promoted by Western educators and charities, and increasingly criticized in their own countries, there was a policy shift towards advocacy of 'inclusive education'. International initiatives played a prominent part, particularly the *Salamanca Statement and Framework for Action on Special Needs Education* (UNESCO, 1994). Subsequent studies further focused on the continuing exclusionary barriers facing disabled children, with rates very high among those labelled as having learning difficulties (UNESCO, 1995). The denial of the human rights of disabled children was acute, as 30 to 40 per cent of 'out of school' children have an impairment, and 80 per cent of this latter group live in poorer, developing countries (UNESCO, 2006, 2007a, 2007b). In some of these countries, the likelihood of attending a primary school is two to three times lower for disabled children. Reports monitoring the Education for All (EFA) initiative launched by UNESCO in 1990 calculate that only 10 per cent of disabled children receive a school education (UNESCO, 2006, 2007a). However, there is a strong argument that the cost–benefits of educating a disabled child are relatively higher (for the child and society in general) compared with non-disabled children (Jonsson and Wiman, 2001).

Even so, according to Michael Miles (2003), much inclusive education is a barely refurbished version of special education, with disabled children used as 'guinea pigs' to encourage all schools down the inclusionary path without providing any extra resources. He illustrates this point with an example from China, where sizeable progress has been made towards inclusion, reinforced by basic policy indicators of school attendance, but some of the evidence supporting these claims looks more dubious, with disabled children sometimes listed on the school register but not always attending on a regular basis. That acknowledged, the extremely low school attendance among disabled children is generally identified as a significant issue, with fewer than 5 per cent actually completing primary school (Peters, 2003, p. 12).

Since the 1990s, the rhetoric and vocabulary of inclusive education have gained international usage, although its implementation varies markedly between countries. Researchers note important examples of developing countries moving down this path, including Laos, Ghana and South Africa, although 'no country, developed or developing, has implemented a fully inclusive educational system' (Jonsson and Wiman, 2001, p. 15). This means that its radical philosophy has not been adequately tested, whether in developing or developed countries

(Ainscow et al., 2006). Equally, some argue that the advancement of the EFA in general and inclusive education in particular represents an extraordinary uphill struggle given the lack of adequate funding and other resources. This is particularly evident in poorer nations, where there is an acute shortage of trained teachers and other educational resources (Dube, 2006b). Others insist the struggle must continue because the EFA programme exemplifies a commitment to social justice and equality, with its broad emphasis on access to learning through to general skills and knowledge acquisition (Miles and Ahuja, 2007).

Internationalization of disability policy

The politics of disability have acquired a place on the international political agenda much more quickly in the last three decades than seemed possible fifty years ago. The growing international interest in disability issues can be traced back to the 1970s and the UN's *Declaration on the Rights of Mentally Retarded Persons* (1971) and the *Declaration on the Rights of Disabled Persons* (1975). These were followed by the UN's designation of 1981 as the International Year of Disabled Persons and 1983–92 as the Decade of Disabled Persons. Nonetheless, since the 1990s, anti-discrimination legislation for disabled people has been enacted in a growing number of countries around the world. Another decisive initiative was the United Nations' *Standard Rules on the Equalization of Opportunities for People with Disabilities* (UN, 1993). This comprises twenty-three rules to facilitate full participation and equality for 'persons with disabilities' and covers aspects of daily living, including awareness raising, medical and support services, education, employment, leisure and cultural activities.

While these initiatives indicate widespread agreement that disability is a 'development issue' (Baylies, 2002, p. 728), what is noteworthy is the way in which a human rights emphasis has come to the fore. The *Universal Declaration of Human Rights* (UN, 1948b) specified disability as a dependent status beyond individual control that justifies a right to a degree of security. Critics charged that it largely failed to address the specific needs of disabled people, who were 'buried in the general category of vulnerable groups' (Coleridge, 2006, p. 23). Subsequently the World Programme of Action Concerning Disabled Persons (UN Enable, 1982) and the *Standard Rules on the Equalization of Opportunities for People with Disabilities* (UN, 1993) signal a shift towards inclusion, with pressure from Disabled Peoples' International a primary factor. Increasingly, disability is approached as a consequence of failures by society to accommodate to impairment, with the creation of social and environmental barriers. The flow of international initiatives recognizing the social exclusion of disabled people continues unabated, examples being the African Decade of Disabled Persons (2000–9), the European Year of People with Disabilities (2003), the Asian and Pacific Decade of Disabled Persons (1993–2002), and the Arab Decade of Disabled Persons (2003–12).

Hitherto, international organizations had been resolutely committed to a biomedical classification that has universal applicability, and thus allows a relatively easy transfer between richer and poorer countries (WHO, 1980, 2001a; Üstün et al., 2001). A clear recognition of the need for a change in approach led to the WHO's refurbishment of the *ICIDH* and the introduction of a revised taxonomy and definition of disability – the *International Classification of Functioning, Disability and Health* (*ICF*). This initiative (WHO, 2001a) has been associated with an 'environmental turn' in international disability policy (Tøssebro, 2004). The new discourse around participation complements a rights approach and an explicit link to the *Standard Rules*, as does the emphasis on environmental factors.

Nevertheless, the apparent radical thrust of these initiatives sits uncomfortably with the continuing influence of conventional individualistic notions of disability and medical rehabilitation in policy implementation at the local level (Barnes and Mercer, 2003, 2005a). This is particularly evident in the difficulties associated with implementing the *ICF* in developing countries. Conflict points include its bases in a universal language of disability that is not readily accepted at the local level; the emphasis on individual functional limitations; the lack of development of participation; and the absence of a comprehensive tool for measuring the outcomes of policy action – whether barriers or facilitating factors (Baylies, 2002; Kalyanpur, 2008).

Similarly, international agencies have all highlighted the links between disability and poverty, but this has been slow to translate into participatory programmes (Albert, 2005, 2006). Thus, the poverty reduction strategy promoted by the IMF categorizes disabled people and the chronically sick as not economically active but as 'objects of charity' (Coleridge, 2006, p. 22), and therefore they are denied participation in the development process. Still, the policy rhetoric of international agencies has shifted notably over the last decade, not least because of a growing pressure from disabled people's organizations. In this vein, the DfID (2000) report on poverty and disability emphasizes the requirement for an integrated approach that links measures to break down exclusionary barriers, changes in attitudes, prevention and rehabilitation, while also empowering disabled people (as indicated in figure 10.1). Furthermore, the World Bank 'offers a practical guide to integrating social analysis and disability-inclusive development into sector and thematic projects and programs' (2007, p. 1). This spells out the message that poverty and disability are closely intertwined, with specific examples of the implications for disabled people being raised by the United Nations' 'Millennium Development Goals' (ibid., p. 4).

Needless to say, the impact of such guidance is heavily dependent both on the local and national contexts and on available funding and resources (drawing on a variety of public, private and voluntary sector sources). Indeed, the World Bank has attracted censure for not providing more support for developing countries adopting an inclusionary approach to disability, such as South Africa and Uganda (Yeo, 2005). Most recently, the descent into a world-wide economic recession in 2007–8, mounting alarm about environmental crises such as global warming, rising threats to national and international security, and continuing population expansion ensure continuing heavy demands on economic and financial resources.

The links between poverty and disability and disability as a human rights issue are now well-established themes, and the UN, World Bank and European Commission all sing from the same liberal song sheet. But evaluators argue that what is lacking is a clear translation of the broad diagnosis of the relationship between poverty and disability into practical policies supported by disabled people. Having trawled through international documents, Bill Albert confides that: '[f]inding out precisely what official policies were was difficult' (2005, p. 133). Some documents, such as *Disability, Poverty and Development* (DfID, 2000), achieved a wide audience but had no official government backing. Moreover, the literature contains no agreed definition of disability. Many national governments and international organizations still use the *ICIDH* (WHO, 1980) as their baseline. While the Nordic countries have gone further than most in arguing for policy action on disability and development linked to the UN *Standard Rules*, 'what the human rights approach means in practice remains at best ambiguous' (Albert, 2005, p. 137). Similar anxieties surround the international development policies of governments across North America and Europe. This raises doubts about the depth of the formal commitment to disability on the 'official' development agenda, and is ominously reinforced by the lack of progress in advancing gender rights, even though this has had perhaps even more prominent national and international support than disability.

Bolivian case study

What are the bases, then, for this gap between the grand international policy statements and their translation into practical initiatives within developing countries? A fundamental issue is the commitment of international NGOs to pushing forward inclusionary policies and generally supporting disabled people in their political struggles.

It is instructive, therefore, to examine the experience of individual countries to contextualize and illustrate the issues involved. Here, we use an illuminating case study by Rebecca Yeo and Andrew Bolton (2008) that reviews how disability policies and activities by NGOs influence the lives and aspirations of ordinary disabled people in Bolivia. In their study, Yeo and Bolton conducted focus groups and individual interviews with disabled people and officials from local and national authorities and NGOs. Their report reinforces the general portrayal of the experiences of disabled people in poorer, developing countries, with widespread discrimination in life chances, including employment, transport, education and health services. The authors provide graphic illustrations of the dilemmas of ordinary working people trying to make a living in an economic system that offers little recognition of the rights or support needs of disabled people. The problems experienced in the use of transport frequently attract disapproval from disabled people. A specific target is bus drivers, who often refuse to pick up disabled passengers. From a bus driver's point of view, there is no economic incentive: they are paid by results, and the extra time and perhaps space required in taking a disabled passenger is not compensated by the bus company. Another example of exclusion is where families move to the city or abroad to get work. Disabled members tend to be left behind, thus reinforcing their separate status and reliance on others to survive. For many living in the rural areas, even basic survival is difficult in terms of obtaining adequate food, shelter and clothing.

Yet, while formally providing support for disabled people, the relationship with NGOs is often described as difficult. As far as disabled people are concerned, these organizations have a rather narrow set of priorities: rehabilitation, the prevention of impairments, and family attitudes towards disabled members. Contrasts are also drawn between organizations for and of disabled people. While several governmental and non-governmental organizations set up projects for disabled people, very few of these are actually led and controlled by disabled people, or involve disabled people in their activities and plans beyond a fairly superficial level. Additionally, NGOs have a bad record in employing disabled people, except at the lowest levels of the organization. Given their poverty and general marginalization in society, disabled people consider any support is better than nothing, but it is far from being what they really want. Moreover, disabled people cannot afford to alienate those working for NGOs, although too often these seem 'beholden to their national and international funders' (Yeo and Bolton, 2008, p. 102).

Finding employment or other source of income is very difficult, but essential given the lack of social welfare benefits and services. A sizeable proportion of disabled people said that they have to resort to begging. For their part, employers justified not employing disabled people in terms of their inability to do a proper day's work. A large organization for people with a visual impairment was recruiting more people to train as teachers of blind people, but did not seek out blind people to undertake this work (Yeo and Bolton, 2008, p. 16). In general, official employment quotas are not met, even in NGOs, and where disabled people are employed it is typically in the lowest paid positions. There is also a tendency to recruit non-disabled foreigners rather than disabled Bolivians.

The claim by NGO representatives to be alleviating poverty is rather weakened by the difficulties in identifying practical measures introduced to achieve this goal. Officials responded to questions about measures taken to address poverty by describing their funded projects, such as providing a Western-trained doctor or medical mission, irrigation system or school. However, some recognize that these schemes are directed more at the symptoms of poverty than at its root causes (Yeo and Bolton, 2008, p. 86). Even so, international NGOs generally did not view the answer to endemic poverty in terms of supporting attempts to build a stronger disabled people's movement. As a result, despite the sometimes substantial funding available to international and national sources, many Bolivians held NGOs in low regard, charging that they were not sufficiently committed to overturning the status quo on disability.

Disabled people identify a range of alternative ways forward: greater progress on social inclusion, more involvement in and control over the activities of organizations by disabled people, and stronger legislation to outlaw discrimination. Yeo and Bolton conclude that 'disability issues cannot be tackled in isolation' (2008, p. 98), and that the experience of systemic discrimination must be addressed. There is a general feeling that 'NGOs should make it clear where their basic allegiances lie – with their funders in rich countries, or with marginalized and oppressed people' (ibid., p. 101). It is also essential that disabled people have a greater say in policy change, setting the priorities, and monitoring their implementation and outcomes.

This Bolivian case study is representative of a growing interest in the capacity-building potential of disabled people's organizations in poorer, developing countries (Stone, 1999a; Albert, 2006). All too often, governments have adopted a disability policy, perhaps under pressure to conform to practice elsewhere, but without the resources or commitment to implement radical changes.

Disability activism: mobilizing for change

As in richer, industrialized countries, the experience of social exclusion over recent decades has been accompanied by a growing politicization of disabled people. International contacts in the 1980s had a particularly galvanizing effect on many disabled activists and disability organizations. The emerging conflicts between old and new disability politics became very apparent at the meeting of Rehabilitation International in 1980 in Singapore. Dissident disabled representatives left to set up what became the Disabled Peoples' International (DPI). As Joshua Malinga from Zimbabwe commented: 'When I went to Singapore I was a conservative, but when I returned I was very radical' (quoted in Charlton, 1998, p. 133).

One yardstick of the politicization of disability in poorer, developing countries is the extent and forms of self-organization by disabled people. As in developed countries, there have been debates about the way forward for disabled people's organizations, such as divisions between single and cross-impairment groups; an exclusive focus on impairment and disability; local or national groups; and a divide between organizations for and of disabled people (Charlton, 1998). There are also familiar constraints (particularly the lack of resources), but also specific possibilities, as opened up by the internationalization of disability politics, and increased pressure by organizations such the UN to address disability inequalities. This has facilitated the involvement of disabled people and their organizations in the national and international arenas.

As discussed in chapter 6, over the past two decades there has been a dramatic increase world-wide in organizations controlled and run by disabled people. Local, national and international groups have taken a more prominent and assertive role in generating campaigns, raising awareness of disability issues, and promoting policies to confront disabling barriers (Jayasooria, 2000). The establishment of international networks and newsletters has had an important facilitative role in helping to sustain this process. Examples include the activities of DPI, the international umbrella for national organizations controlled and run by disabled people, and Disability Awareness in Action, a project led by disabled people to promote world-wide networking.

However, there are often significant difficulties in generating and sustaining disabled people's organizations because of the high level of poverty and general lack of resources. As illustrated in Mozambique, in such circumstances it is a notable achievement simply to maintain a presence and even a basic network of disabled people's organizations (Ncube, 2006). Disabled people are faced with extremely hard decisions about their priorities – not least, how far they should try to access funding from richer countries and (international) NGOs. There is unease about becoming overly dependent on donor organizations or governments for funding such that their political aims are comprised. As illustrated in the Bolivian case study above, this is too often distributed on terms set by outsiders, so that participation of local people is frustrated or directed in ways that do not fit with their priorities, so leading to 'a markedly unequal and disempowering relationship' (ibid., pp. 155–6).

The growth of organizations of disabled people, as opposed to those largely controlled by non-disabled people, gathered momentum through the last decades of the twentieth century. This trend drew inspiration from the development of the Independent Living Movement in North America and led to schemes in different parts of the world. For example, early contacts between disabled activists in the USA and Japan led to the establishment in 1986 of the first Independent Living Centre in Asia (Hayashi and Okuhira, 2001). Their number expanded remarkably, so that by 2006 there were around 130 such centres in Japan (JIL, 2006). Equally noteworthy, this initiative generated a lot of interest in promoting similar schemes and good practice more widely in non-Western contexts across South and South-East Asia. This led to regional training programmes, including one in Japan that recruits disabled people from surrounding countries. A specific aim has been to develop policies and practices for independent living that recognize the significance of distinctive local and national social and cultural contexts (UN ESCAP, 2006).

Another illustration of disabled people's organizations working together to influence international policy is the role of the International Disability Caucus in advancing the disability rights agenda at the United Nations. It was an active participant in the development of the UN Convention on the Rights of Persons with Disabilities (2006), with activists providing evidence of violations of the human rights of disabled people and their families (see chapter 7). These and other initiatives, such as that on the Disability Awareness in Action Human Rights Database, reinforced the argument that disabled people required the protection that a UN convention might help to support (Hurst and Albert, 2006). More generally, disability rights campaigns have begun to influence government policy across developing countries.

A specific issue is how to take advantage of changing international opinion on disability. There is a divergence of opinion on the relative benefits of the differing forms of international involvement. Joseph Walugembe and Julia Peckett (2005) argue from their experience in Uganda that direct assistance from international development agencies has made an important difference to the organizational resources and impact of disabled people's organizations. In 1987, local groups formed an umbrella organization – the National Union of Disabled Persons of Uganda – and lobbied to be included in the political process. In 1995, the overhaul of the constitution provided an opportunity for innovative proposals to 'mainstream' disability, leading to the introduction of a range of legislation. Furthermore, disabled people were allocated five representatives in parliament, one of whom must be a woman (Dube, 2006a). In South Africa, disability activism and organization drew more on its experiences of political struggles against apartheid. Lobbying from disabled people's organizations after the African National Congress came to power in 1994 led to the inclusion of disabled people in a Bill of Rights and the acceptance of an integrated disability strategy by the national government in 1997, with parallel versions agreed at the provincial level. This has been reinforced by a range of measures targeted at specific areas, such as employment-equity quotas, disability welfare benefits, and inclusive education. In addition, the Office on the Status of Disabled People has been established within the presidency and at provincial levels (Dube, 2006b). This model for locating disability issues at the heart of the government has been championed across other African countries.

However, policies for social inclusion demonstrate uneven success in their implementation. Funding and resources for disability initiatives compete with huge demands on governments generally to address poverty, promote economic growth and reduce overall social inequality. In response, there have been moves by small groups of disabled people to generate their own initiatives, notably work schemes to obtain an income (Charlton, 1998; Werner, 2005). The Self-Help Association of Paraplegics (SHAP) in South Africa provides one such example. It was established in 1982 as an organization to challenge disabling attitudes and barriers. A small manufacturing workshop employing only disabled people was set up in 1983 and subsequently extended its activities by prioritizing contracts and tenders for disabled people. SHAP also widened its activities beyond providing employment to include support in such areas as education, transport, peer support and sport. Its experience has encouraged other self-help organizations in South Africa to follow its lead (Nkeli, 1998). Nonetheless, as in most developing countries, the level of disabled people's employment in the public sector remains well below the target figure. Overall improvements are slow to appear, while the vast majority of disabled people experience little improvement in their life chances and languish on the margins of society (Hurst and Albert, 2006).

Community-based rehabilitation

One area where there has been substantial policy activity in recent years, with financial and other support from richer, industrialized countries, has been in the area of community-based rehabilitation (CBR). This was conceived and championed by the WHO with the aim of making basic 'disability and rehabilitation' services (from an *ICIDH* perspective) available to local communities in developing countries. It took root in the 1980s with an emphasis on action by local communities rather than external institutions (Freire, 1970), sustained by the involvement of local people (with suitable training) and its claims to be cost-effective. The aim was to generate a range of 'working partnerships between local communities, disabled people and their families, governments and rehabilitation professionals' (Lang, 1999, p. 131). Primarily Western or Western-trained professionals (planners, implementers, evaluators and specialist rehabilitation staff) were attached to CBR programmes with the support of international funding, networks, training manuals and programmes, conferences and journals (Helander, 1993; Stone, 1999b; Hartley, 2002, 2006).

CBR programmes quickly expanded, but so too did the criticism. The main concerns comprise the failure to engage fully with local communities and disabled people; an overreliance on medical rehabilitation, rather than social and economic factors; a simplistic notion of the 'community'; an appropriate balance of community and institutional services; and assumptions that CBR is a 'cheap option' (Lang, 1999; Albert, 2006). In response, efforts have been made to produce a more comprehensive approach that includes education, vocational training and social rehabilitation, and also espouses a definite human rights orientation towards disabled people and community empowerment.

Attempts to integrate the medical and social models have been promoted by the WHO with an obvious eye to disparaging comments about CBR practice and its outcomes. Again, the lack of rigorous evaluation does little to assuage anxieties that the empowerment of disabled people has not moved forwards as anticipated (Lang, 2000). NGOs span a wide range, from large bilateral funding agencies such as Oxfam, Save the Children and World Vision through to organizations operating solely at the local (village) level that are not sufficiently large players to warrant NGO status. The number of NGOs in OECD countries doubled between the 1980s and 1990s (ibid.), and this has increased dependence on their funding of projects and activities as ways of bringing local people out of poverty. Nevertheless, there have been signs of a shift in the form of intervention favoured by NGOs, or at least in the rhetoric that underpins community-based development.

There has been considerable debate about the character and effectiveness of CBR. For its detractors, early CBR projects represented updated but poorly disguised versions of what colonizing countries have been attempting to do over the last two centuries. Many CBR projects have been rightly condemned for being, at best, well meaning but ill-conceived and, at worst, ideologically and culturally biased with a concealed political agenda (Thomas and Thomas, 2002) – 'an updated, less obviously imperialistic, version of what missionaries were doing in the 1890s' (Stone, 1999b, p. 8). The intention underpinning CBR was that disadvantaged and dependent groups such as disabled and other poor people should be supported by charitable fundraising and private donations. In some countries, this coincided with the traditions of alms-giving in religions such as Islam and Hinduism. Such ideas have continued to characterize and envelop services for disabled people in developing countries and help to explain why so many governments are reluctant 'to commit to full responsibility for disabled citizens' (Ingstad, 2001, p. 778).

There has been a gradual and uneven shift towards a social rather than a medical approach and the integration of disability issues into the development process (Jones, 1999; Liton, 2000). A major criticism has been that CBR programmes have been planned without sufficient opportunities for local communities to express their own needs and priorities. Thus, CBR has been described as akin to externally directed 'community therapy' (Thomas and Thomas, 2002), with relatively passive 'beneficiaries' (Wirz and Hartley, 1999). Volunteers with the requisite skills and available time are in short supply, and David Werner (2005), a strategic figure in promoting village-level rehabilitation knowledge and practice, has repeatedly warned that CBR risks being undermined by the lack of full-time, trained local workers. In particular there is a marked shortage of female staff, which tends to inhibit the participation of disabled women in CBR programmes in some cultures (Thomas and Thomas, 2002). These problems are compounded because too many of the foreign CBR staff have been trained to act as professional experts, often with a 'special needs' orientation towards disabled people, something that contradicts the formal philosophy of inclusive service support and fails to recognize local people's expertise (Wirz and Hartley, 1999). Such shortfalls help explain why CBR is charged with not delivering the anticipated tangible long-term benefits for disabled people, their families or local communities (Stone, 1999b; WHO, 2001b).

Conversely, it is important to note exceptions where progress has been accomplished in forging meaningful participation and partnerships. In a study of the involvement of rural disabled people in participatory rural appraisal methods, Steve Harknett (2006) describes how, in a village community in Cambodia, disabled people with no familiarity of development projects gained invaluable experience and confidence from their participation. A particular feature was the way in which individual disabled people became recognized locally as 'high-profile' actors in this process. This was possible because one of the largest NGOs working in this part of Cambodia made concerted efforts to involve disabled people from the outset in a meaningful way. All participants reported enthusiasm and tangible gains from this process, although doubts have surfaced about how far the goals of local planning and partnerships have been assimilated by NGO staff. There was evidence, for example, from subsequent projects in other villages that NGO staff did not continue with the same participatory practices.

Over time, those implementing CBR have begun to give more credence to social, political and cultural contexts in the development of local communities, something clearly lacking in its early days (Coleridge, 1999, 2006). While these local contexts are changing to a greater or lesser degree, they remain central to reinforcing power differentials and interests.

> Some development planners tend to regard culture . . . as an impediment to 'development', but any development interventions which do not engage at a significant not just superficial level with the local cultural context are bound to be short lived. What is true for development generally is even more true of community level disability programmes because disability is defined by culture, and without an awareness of how disability is perceived in the target culture a disability programme does not stand much chance of being relevant or sustainable. (Coleridge, 2000, p. 21)

Too often, traditional cultural values, processes and institutions are viewed as the antithesis of modernization, or simply as an ideological obfuscation (Sheldon, 2005). In practice, the importation of Western approaches to disability and impairment to poorer countries is often unthinking and unhelpful in understanding disabled people's experiences and priorities (Stone, 1999a). 'So when human rights are talked about in a strictly Islamic country like Afghanistan, who is *entitled* to set the agenda?' (Coleridge, 2000, p. 25). There is no globalized disability identity and culture. As the case of Afghanistan illustrates, a traditional culture and history of resistance to externally imposed change – whether emanating from the East or West – is not going to acquiesce easily when confronted by very different ideas and practices around disability and development. It 'provides a dramatic illustration of why culture matters' (ibid., p. 29). Development plans are initiated by outsiders, who also control their direction. A CBR 'conflict zone' is identified where 'local concepts of disability, culture, poverty, the nature of CBR, and local social values meet' (ibid., p. 34).

Since the mid-1990s, the primary sponsors of CBR programmes have given an increasing priority to the involvement of disabled people at all levels and contexts (Thomas and Thomas, 2000; Hartley, 2002, 2006). This spans ambitious schemes to encourage self-help groups of disabled people to generate and control the identification of priorities and ways of dealing with them. A World Bank-financed initiative – the Veluga project in Andhra Pradesh, one of the poorest states in India – has attracted a lot of interest, and similar schemes have subsequently been established in Cambodia and Bangladesh (Takamine, 2006). The emphasis is on small self-help groups of people with diverse impairments who devise ways of generating income, savings and loans to fund, for example, schemes in such areas as rehabilitation, appropriate transport and housing. This offers a stark contrast to usual rehabilitation practice, where community projects have developed piecemeal and become increasingly dependent on external sources for funding and other resources.

Another noteworthy trend has been the increased input from national governments, with Norway and Sweden in the vanguard of those who have become prominent donors. Despite disquiet about the continuity of funding and whether any strings are attached, their involvement has sometimes helped change the CBR focus on short-term, small-scale operations driven by a predominantly medical model of disability to larger, longer-term strategies addressing the sources of social exclusion. Equally significant, there has been growing recognition that disabled people, their families and key representatives of local communities must be meaningfully involved at every level and stage in the planning and implementation of CBR projects. There is less agreement about whether disabled people should have separate programmes or be integrated into the wider community rehabilitation process (WHO, 2001b; Werner, 2005). There is a continuing debate about whether CBR has proved a relatively less expensive option or has achieved this only by restricting its support to specific groups. Notwithstanding such doubts about its practice, the orientation of CBR philosophy has shifted markedly towards more emphasis on 'community development and the promotion of equal rights' (Ingstad, 2001, p. 786).

Review

The production of impairment and disability is inseparable from the extreme levels of poverty and inequality in developing countries and the wider background of capitalist industrialization and globalization. Notwithstanding this basic pattern, the form and level of impairment and disability are mediated significantly by social, cultural and political conditions and contexts. Not only are there considerable contrasts both in people's understandings of what constitutes an impairment and their appropriate socio-cultural responses, but broadly defined social causes account for around a half of all impairment. The linkages between poverty and disability encompass outcomes such as limited access to education, employment, food and housing, and public health and health care, and reduced social, civil and political rights. A cycle of poverty and disability sets in, with cumulative and reinforcing disadvantages and inequalities.

Over recent decades, there has been a growing internationalization of disability politics and policies. Pressure has built up on governments around the world to address the social exclusion and the lack of basic human rights of disabled people. Action relied heavily on funding and inputs from donor countries and international aid organizations and charities, with community-based rehabilitation projects prominent. Yet, the historical record is of the relative lack of positive changes in the lives of disabled people and poor communities. This offers a salutary lesson about the pitfalls of *ad hoc*, short-term experiments in social reform that are not adequately resourced, although there is intense competition for material support. Too often projects do not emerge organically from the communities they are designed to enhance, but remain largely under the direction of external, professional 'experts'.

A powerful stimulus to changing 'official' thinking has been the actions of poor and disabled people establishing their own organizations, campaigning for social justice, equality and self-empowerment, and highlighting the consequences of disabling social and environmental barriers. This politicization and articulation of broader strategies has been pursued despite the endless pressure for survival among so many poorer and disabled people. Nonetheless, it is vital that disabled people maintain a critical approach to Western theories and policies. Ideas about what is best for a particular country must not be imposed by outside 'experts', whether non-disabled or disabled. A disability rights agenda has yet to nullify the impact of vast material differences between countries. Hence, the need to explore more fundamental changes in the relationship between poorer countries and the capitalist world order to achieve the goals of disabled people.

References

Abberley, P. (1987) The concept of oppression and the development of a social theory of disability, *Disability, Handicap and Society*, 2(1): 5–19.

Abberley, P. (1992) Counting us out: a discussion of the OPCS disability surveys, *Disability, Handicap and Society*, 7(2): 139–55.

Abberley, P. (1993) Disabled people and 'normality', in J. Swain, V. Finkelstein, S. French, and M. Oliver (eds), *Disabling Barriers – Enabling Environments*. London: Sage, pp. 107–15.

Abberley, P. (1995) Disabling ideology in health and welfare: the case of occupational therapy, *Disability & Society*, 10(2): 221–32.

Abberley, P. (1996) Work, utopia and impairment, in L. Barton (ed.), *Disability & Society: Emerging Issues and Insights*. London: Longman, pp. 61–79.

Abberley, P. (2002) Work, disability, and European social theory, in C. Barnes, M. Oliver and L. Barton (eds), *Disability Studies Today*. Cambridge: Polity, pp. 120–38.

Abbott, D., Morris, J., and Ward, L. (2001) *Residential Schools and Disabled Children: Decision-making and experiences*. York: Joseph Rowntree Foundation.

Abrams, P. (1968) *The Origins of British Sociology 1834–1914*. Chicago: University of Chicago Press.

Abu-Habib, L. (1997) *Gender and Disability: Women's experiences in the Middle East*. Oxford: Oxfam.

ADD (2005) *Election Monitoring and Disabled People's Right to Vote*. Frome: Action on Disability and Development. Available at: www.add.org.uk/downloads/Election%20Monitoring.pdf (accessed 10 March 2008).

Ahmad, W. I. U. (ed.) (2000) *Ethnicity, Disability and Chronic Illness*. Buckingham: Open University Press.

Ainscow, M., Booth, T., and Dyson, A. (2006) *Improving Schools, Developing Inclusion*. Abingdon: Routledge.

Aitchison, C. (2003) From leisure and disability to disability leisure: developing data, definitions and discourses, *Disability & Society*, 18(7): 955–69.

Alaszewski, A., Alaszewski, H., and Potter, J. (2004) The bereavement model, stroke and rehabilitation: a critical analysis of the use of a psychological model in professional practice, *Disability & Rehabilitation*, 26(18): 1067–78.

Albert, B. (2005) Finally included on the disability agenda? A review of official disability and development policies, in C. Barnes and G. Mercer (eds), *The Social Model of Disability: Europe and the Majority World*. Leeds: Disability Press, pp. 131–47.

Albert, B. (ed.) (2006) *In or Out of the Mainstream? Lessons from research on disability and development cooperation*. Leeds: Disability Press.

Albrecht, G. L. (ed.) (1976) *The Sociology of Physical Disability and Rehabilitation*. Pittsburgh: University of Pittsburgh Press.

Albrecht, G. L. (1992) *The Disability Business: Rehabilitation in America*. London: Sage.

Albrecht, G. L., and Devlieger, P. J. (1999) The disability paradox: high quality of life against all odds, *Social Science & Medicine*, 48(8): 977–88.

Albrecht, G. L., Seelman, K. D., and Bury, M. (eds) (2001) *Handbook of Disability Studies*. London: Sage.

Alderson, P. (2001) Some unanswered questions, in L. Ward (ed.), *Considered Choices? The new genetics, prenatal testing and people with learning disabilities*. Kidderminster: BILD, pp. 63–71.

Allen, T., and Thomas, A. (eds) (2000) *Poverty and Development into the 21st Century*. Milton Keynes: Open University in association with Oxford University Press.

Anderson, E. M., Clarke, L., and Spain, B. (1982) *Disability in Adolescence*. London: Methuen.

Anderson, R., and Bury, M. (eds) (1988) *Living with Chronic Illness: the experience of patients and their families*. London: Unwin Hyman.

Andreski, S. (ed.) (1975) *Herbert Spencer*. London: Nelson.

Anspach, R. (1979) From stigma to identity politics: political activism among the physically disabled and former mental patients, *Social Science & Medicine*, 13A: 765–73.

Apple, M. (1990) *Ideology and Curriculum*. 2nd edn, London: Routledge.

Arksey, H. (1994) Expert and lay participation in the construction of medical knowledge, *Sociology of Health & Illness*, 16(4): 448–68.

Arksey, H. (1998) *RSI and the Experts: The construction of medical knowledge*. London: UCL Press.

Armstrong, D. (1980) Madness and coping, *Sociology of Health & Illness*, 2(3): 293–316.

Armstrong, D. (1983) *Political Anatomy of the Body: Medical knowledge in Britain in the twentieth century*. Cambridge: Cambridge University Press.

Armstrong, D. (1984) The patient's view, *Social Science & Medicine*, 18(9): 737–44.

Armstrong, D. (1987) Bodies of knowledge: Foucault and the problem of human anatomy, in G. Scambler (ed.), *Sociological Theory and Medical Sociology*. London: Tavistock, pp. 59–75.

Armstrong, D. (2005) The myth of concordance: response to Stevenson and Scambler, *Health*, 9(1): 23–7.

Arney, W. R., and Bergen, B. J. (1983) The anomaly, the chronic patient and the play of medical power, *Sociology of Health & Illness*, 5(1): 1–24.

Arnstein, S. (1969) A ladder of citizen participation, *Journal of the American Institute of Planners*, 35: 216–24.

Arts Council England (2003) *Celebrating Disability Arts*. London: Arts Council England.

Arts Council England (2004) *Action for Access*. 2nd edn, London: Arts Council England.

Asch, A. (2001) Disability, bioethics and human rights, in G. L. Albrecht, K. D. Seelman and M. Bury (eds), *Handbook of Disability Studies*. London: Sage, pp. 297–327.

Audit Commission (1986) *Making a Reality of Community Care*. London: HMSO.

Audit Commission (2002a) *Special Educational Needs: A mainstream issue*. London: Audit Commission.

Audit Commission (2002b) *Equality and Diversity*. London: Audit Commission.

Audit Commission (2003) *Human Rights: Improving public service delivery*. London: Audit Commission.

Audit Commission (2004) *Assistive Technology: Independence and well-being*. London: Audit Commission.

Bagilhole, B. (1997) *Equal Opportunities and Social Policy*. London: Longman.

Baird, V. (1992) Disabled lives: difference and defiance, *New Internationalist*, 233(July) [special issue]. Available at: www.newint.org/issue233/liberation. htm (accessed 14 April 2006).

Baldock, J. (2003) On being a welfare consumer in a consumer society, *Social Policy and Society*, 2(1): 65–71.

Ballard, K., and Elston, M. A. (2005) Medicalisation: a multi-dimensional concept, *Social Theory & Health*, 3(3): 228–41.

Balloch, S., and Taylor, M. (2001) Introduction, in S. Balloch and M. Taylor (eds), *Partnership Working: Policy and practice*. Bristol: Policy Press, pp 1–14.

Bardasi, E., Jenkins, S., and Rigg, J. (2000) *Disability Work and Income: A British perspective*. Working Paper no. 2000-36. Colchester: Institute for Social and Economic Research, University of Essex.

Barker, I., and Peck, E. (1987) *Power in Strange Places*. London: Good Practices in Mental Health.

Barker, R. G., Wright, B. A., and Gonick, M. R. (1953) *Adjustment to Physical Handicap and Illness: A survey of the social psychology of physique and disability*. Bulletin 55. New York: Social Science Research Council.

Barnes, C. (1990) *Cabbage Syndrome: The social construction of dependence*. Lewes: Falmer Press.

Barnes, C. (1991) *Disabled People in Britain and Discrimination*. London: Hurst, in association with the British Council of Organizations of Disabled People.

Barnes, C. (1992) *Disabling Imagery and the Media: An exploration of media representations of disabled people*. Belper: British Council of Organizations of Disabled People.

Barnes, C. (1995) *From National to Local: An evaluation of national disablement information providers services to local disablement information providers*. Derby: British Council of Organizations of Disabled People.

Barnes, C. (1996) Foreword, in J. Campbell and M. Oliver, *Disability Politics: Understanding our past, changing our future*. London: Routledge, pp, ix–xii.

Barnes, C. (2000) A working social model? Disability, work and disability politics in the 21st century, *Critical Social Policy*, 24(4): 441–58.

Barnes, C., and Mercer, G. (eds) (1996) *Exploring the Divide: Illness and disability*. Leeds: Disability Press.

Barnes, C., and Mercer, G. (eds) (1997) *Doing Disability Research*. Leeds: Disability Press.

Barnes, C., and Mercer, G. (2001) The politics of disability and the struggle for change, in L. Barton (ed.), *Disability, Politics and the Struggle for Change*. London: David Fulton, pp. 11–23.

Barnes, C., and Mercer, G. (2003) *Disability: An introduction*. Cambridge: Polity.

Barnes, C., and Mercer, G. (eds) (2005a) *The Social Model of Disability: Europe and the majority world*. Leeds: Disability Press.

Barnes, C and Mercer, G. (2005b) Understanding disability: towards an international perspective, in C. Barnes and G. Mercer (eds), *The Social Model of Disability: Europe and the majority world*. Leeds: Disability Press, pp. 1–16.

Barnes, C., and Mercer, G. (2005c) Disability, work and welfare: challenging the social exclusion of disabled people, *Work, Employment & Society*, 19(5): 527–45.

Barnes, C., and Mercer, G. (2006) *Independent Futures: Creating user-led disability services in a disabling society*. Bristol: Policy Press.

Barnes, C., and Oliver, M. (1995) Disability rights: rhetoric and reality in the UK, *Disability & Society*, 10(1): 111–16.

Barnes, C., and Roulstone, A. (2005) Work is a four letter word: disability, work and welfare, in A. Roulstone and C. Barnes (eds), *Working Futures: Disabled people, policy and social inclusion*. Bristol: Policy Press, pp. 315–29.

Barnes, C., Mercer, G. and Shakespeare, T. (1999) *Exploring Disability: A sociological introduction*. Cambridge: Polity.

Barnes, C., Oliver, M., and Barton, L. (2002) Introduction, in C. Barnes, M. Oliver and L. Barton (eds), *Disability Studies Today*. Cambridge: Polity, pp. 1–18.

Barnes, M., and Shardlow, P. (1996) Identity crisis: mental health user groups and the 'problem of identity', in C. Barnes and G. Mercer (eds), *Exploring the Divide: Illness and disability*, Leeds: Disability Press, pp. 114–34.

Barnes, M., and Wistow, G. (1994a) Learning to hear voices: listening to users of mental health services, *Journal of Mental Health*, 3(5): 525–40.

Barnes, M., and Wistow, G. (1994b) Achieving a strategy for user involvement in community care, *Health & Social Care in the Community*, 2(6): 347–56.

Barnett, E., Scott, R., and Morris, G. (2007) *Polls Apart Cymru 2007*. London: Scope Cymru.

Barrett, M. (1981) *Women's Oppression Today: Problems in Marxist feminist analysis*. London: Verso.

Barton, L. (1995) Segregated special education: some critical observations, in G. Zarb (ed.), *Removing Disabling Barriers*. London: Policy Studies Institute, pp. 27–37.

Barton, L. (ed.) (2001) *Disability, Politics and the Struggle for Change*. London: David Fulton.

Battye, L. (1966) The Chatterley syndrome, in P. Hunt (ed.), *Stigma: The experience of disability*. London: Geoffrey Chapman, pp. 2–16.

Bauman, Z. (1990) *Thinking Sociologically*. Oxford: Blackwell.

Bauman, Z. (1993) *Postmodern Ethics*. London: Routledge.

Bauman, Z. (2000) *Liquid Modernity*. Cambridge: Polity.

Bauman, Z. (2005) *Work, Consumerism and the New Poor*. 2nd edn, Buckingham: Open University Press.

Baxter, C., Poonia, K., Ward, L., and Nadirshaw, Z. (1990) *Double Discrimination: Issues and services for people with learning difficulties from black and ethnic minority communities*. London: King's Fund Centre.

Baylies, C. (2002) Disability and the notion of human development: questions of rights and responsibilities, *Disability & Society*, 17(7): 725–39.

Baywatch Campaign (2007) *Baywatch Survey Results*. Available at: www.baywatch-campaign.org/LatestNews.asp?ItemId=24 (accessed 12 January 2008).

Bazna, M. S., and Hatab, T. A. (2005) Disability in the Qu'ran: the Islamic alternative to defining, viewing and relating to disability, *Journal of Religion, Disability & Health*, 9(1): 5–27.

BBC News 24 (2006) 'Legalise euthanasia', says expert. Available at: http://news.bbc.co.uk/1/hi/health/5056326.stm (accessed 8 January 2008).

BCODP (1986) *Disabled Young People Living Independently*. London: British Council of Organizations of Disabled People.

BCODP (2008) Who are we? UK Disabled People's Council (formerly the British Council of Disabled People). Available at: www.bcodp.org.uk/index/shtml (accessed 18 January 2008).

Beart, S., Hawkins, D., Stenfert Kroese, B., Smithson, P., and Tolosa, I. (2001) Barriers to accessing leisure opportunities for people with learning difficulties, *British Journal of Learning Disabilities*, 29(4): 133–8.

Beck, U. (1992) *Risk Society: Towards a new modernity*, trans. M. Ritter. London: Sage.

Beck, U. (2000) *The Brave New World of Work*, trans. P. Camiller. Cambridge: Polity.

Becker, H. (1963) *Outsiders: Studies in the sociology of deviance*. New York: Free Press.

Begum, N. (1992) Disabled women and the feminist agenda, *Feminist Review*, 40(spring): 70–84.

Begum, N. (1993) Independent living, personal assistance and black disabled people, in C. Barnes (ed.), *Making our own Choices: Independent living, personal assistance and disabled people*. Belper: British Council of Organizations of Disabled People, pp. 51–4.

Begum, N. (1994a) Mirror, mirror on the wall, in N. Begum, M. Hill and A. Stevens (eds), *Reflections*. London: Central Council for Education and Training in Social Work, pp. 17–36.

Begum, N. (1994b) Optimism, pessimism & care management: the impact of community care policies, in N. Begum, M. Hill and A. Stevens (eds), *Reflections*. London: Central Council for Education and Training in Social Work, pp. 143–59.

Begum, N. (1996) General practitioners' role in shaping disabled women's lives, in C. Barnes and G. Mercer (eds), *Exploring the Divide*. Leeds: Disability Press, pp. 157–72.

Begum, N., and Gillespie-Sells, K. (1994) *Towards Managing User-Led Services*. London: Race Equality Unit.

Begum, N., Hill, M., and Stevens, A. (eds) (1994) *Reflections*. London: Central Council for Education and Training in Social Work.

Bell, C. (2006) Introducing white disability studies: a modest proposal, in L. Davis (ed.), *The Disability Studies Reader*. 2nd edn, London: Routledge, pp. 275–82.

Bellaby, P. (1990) What is genuine sickness? The relation between work discipline and the sick role in a pottery factory, *Sociology of Health & Illness*, 12(1): 47–68.

Benjamin, S. (2003) What counts as success? Hierarchical discourses in a girls' comprehensive school, *Discourse*, 24(1): 105–18.

Beresford, P. (1993) A programme for change: current issues in user involvement and empowerment, in P. Beresford and T. Harding (eds), *A Challenge to Change: Practical experience of building user-led services*, London: NISW, pp. 9–29.

Beresford, P. (2000) What have madness and psychiatric system survivors got to do with disability and disability studies?, *Disability & Society*, 15(1): 167–72.

Beresford, P. (2002) Thinking about 'mental health': towards a social model, *Journal of Mental Health*, 11(6): 581–4.

Beresford, P. (2005) Social approaches to madness and distress: user perspectives and user knowledges, in J. Tew (ed.), *Social Perspectives in Mental Health*. London: Jessica Kingsley, pp. 32–52.

Beresford, P., and Branfield, F. (2006) Developing inclusive partnerships: user-defined outcomes, networking and knowledge – a case study, *Health & Social Care in the Community*, 14(5): 436–44.

Beresford, P., and Campbell, J. (1994) Disabled people, service users user involvement and representation, *Disability & Society*, 9(3): 315–25.

Beresford, P., and Croft, S. (1993) *Citizen Involvement: A practical guide for change*. Basingstoke: Macmillan.

Beresford, P., and Wallcraft, J. (1997) Psychiatric system survivors and emancipatory research: issues, overlaps and differences, in C. Barnes and G. Mercer (eds), *Doing Disability Research*. Leeds: Disability Press, pp. 67–87.

Beresford, P., Croft, S., Evans, C., and Harding, T. (1997) Quality in personal social services: the developing role of user involvement in the UK, in A. Evers, R. Haverinen, K. Leichsenring, and G. Wistow (eds), *Developing Quality in Personal Social Services: Concepts, cases and comments*, Vienna: European Centre, pp, 63–80.

Berger, J. (1972) *Ways of Seeing*. London: BBC and Penguin.

Berger, P. (1963) *Invitation to Sociology. A Humanistic Perspective*. New York: Anchor Books.

Berger, P., and Luckmann, T. (1967) *The Social Construction of Reality: A treatise in the sociology of knowledge*. Harmondsworth: Penguin.

Berkowitz, E. (1987) *Disabled Policy: America's programs for the handicapped*. Cambridge: Cambridge University Press.

Berthoud, R., Lakey, J., and McKay, S. 1993: *The Economic Problems of Disabled People*. London: Policy Studies Institute.

Bevan, M. (2002) *Housing and Disabled Children: The art of the possible*. Bristol: Policy Press.

Beveridge, W. H. (1942) *Social Insurance and Allied Services*, Cmd. 6404. London: HMSO [Beveridge Report].

Bewley, C., and Glendinning, C. (1994) *Involving Disabled People in Community Care Planning*. York: Joseph Rowntree Foundation and *Community Care* magazine.

Bhaskar, R. (1998) *The Possibility of Naturalism: A Philosophical Critique of the Contemporary Human Sciences*. 3rd edn, London: Routledge.

Bhugra, D., and Bhui, K. (1999) Racism in psychiatry: paradigm lost – paradigm regained, *International Review of Psychiatry*, 11: 236–43.

Bhui, K., Stansfield, S., Hull, S., Priebe, S., Mole, F., and Feder, G. (2003) Ethnic variations in pathways to and use of specialist mental health services in the UK: systematic review, *British Journal of Psychiatry*, 182(February): 105–16.

Bickenbach, J. E. (1999) Minority rights or universal participation: the politics of disablement, in M. Jones and L. A. B. Marks (eds), *Disability, Divers-ability and Legal Change*. The Hague: Kluwer Law International/ Martinus Nijhoff, pp. 101–15.

Bickenbach, J. E. (2001a) Disability human rights, law, and policy, in G. L. Albrecht, K. D. Seelman and M. Bury (eds), *Handbook of Disability Studies*. Thousand Oaks, CA.: Sage, pp. 565–84.

Bickenbach, J. E. (2001b) Disability studies and bioethics: a comment on Kuczewski, *American Journal of Bioethics*, 1(3): 49–50.

Bickenbach, J. E. 2009: Disability: non-talent and distributive justice, in K.

Kristiansen, S. Vehmas and T. Shakespeare (eds), *Arguing about Disability: Philosophical Perspectives*. London: Routledge, pp. 105–23.

Bickenbach, J. E., Chatterji, S., Badley, E. M., and Üstün, T. B. (1999) Models of disablement, universalism and the international classification of impairments, disabilities and handicaps, *Social Science & Medicine*, 48(9): 1173–87.

Biddle, B. J., and Thomas, E. J. (eds) (1966) *Role Theory: Concepts and research*. New York: Wiley.

Biklen, D., and Bogdan, R. (1977) Media portrayals of disabled people: a study of stereotypes, *Interracial Books for Children Bulletin*, 8(6/7): 4–7.

Birenbaum, A. (1970) On managing a courtesy stigma, *Journal of Health and Social Behaviour*, 11(3): 196–206.

Bisley, N. (2007) *Rethinking Globalization*. Basingstoke: Palgrave Macmillan.

Bissell, P., May, C. R., and Noyce, P. R. (2004) From compliance to concordance: barriers to accomplishing a re-framed model of health care interactions, *Social Science & Medicine*, 58(4): 851–62.

Blaxter, M. (1976) *The Meaning of Disability*. London: Heinemann.

Blaxter, M. (1984) Letter in response to Williams, *Social Science & Medicine*, 17(15): 104.

Bloch, M. (1965) *Feudal Society*, trans. L. A. Manyon, vol. 1. London: Routledge & Kegan Paul.

Bloor, M. J. (1976) Professional autonomy and client exclusion: a study in ENT clinics, in M. Wadsworth and D. Robinson (eds), *Studies in Everyday Medical Life*. London: Martin Robertson, pp. 52–68.

Bloor, M. J., and Horobin, G. (1975) Conflict and conflict resolution in doctor/patient interactions, in C. Cox and A. Mead (eds), *A Sociology of Medical Practice*. London: Collier Macmillan, pp. 271–84.

Blumer, H. (1969) *Symbolic Interactionism: Perspective and method*. Englewood Cliffs, NJ: Prentice-Hall.

Blumler, J., and Katz, E. (eds) (1974) *The Uses of Mass Communications*. Beverly Hills, CA: Sage.

BMA (British Medical Association) Steering Group on Human Genetics (1998) *Human Genetics: Choice and responsibility*. Oxford: Oxford University Press.

Bogdan, R. (1996) The social construction of freaks, in R. Garland-Thomson (ed.), *Freakery: Culture spectacles of the extraordinary body*. New York: New York University Press, pp. 23–37.

Bogdan, R., and Biklen, D. (1977) Handicapism, *Social Policy*, March/April: 14–19.

Bogdan, R., and Taylor, S. J. (1975) *Introduction to Qualitative Research Methods: A phenomenological approach to the social sciences*. New York: Wiley.

Booth, T. (1985) *Home Truths*. Aldershot: Gower.

Booth, T., and Booth, W. (1994) *Parenting under Pressure: Mothers and fathers with learning difficulties*. Buckingham: Open University Press.

Borsay, A. (2005) *Disability and Social Policy in Britain since 1750*. Basingstoke: Palgrave Macmillan.

Botelho, L. A. (2004) *Old Age and the English Poor Law, 1500–1700*. Woodbridge: Boydell Press.

Bott, S., and Rust, A. (1997) Involving physically disabled users in service planning and delivery: Shropshire as a case study, *Research Policy and Planning*, 15(2): 38–42.

Bowe, F. (1978) *Handicapping America*. New York: Harper & Rowe.

Bowles, S., and Gintis, H. (1976) *Schooling in Capitalist America*. London: Routledge & Kegan Paul.

Boylan, E. (1991) *Women and Disability*. London: Zed Books.

Boyle, G. (2005) The role of autonomy in explaining mental ill-health and depression among older people in long-term care settings, *Ageing & Society*, 25(5): 731–48.

Bracking, S. (1993) An introduction to the idea of independent/integrated living, in C. Barnes (ed.), *Making our own Choices*. Derby: British Council of Organizations of Disabled People, pp. 11–14.

Branfield, F., and Beresford, P. (2006) *Making User Involvement Work: Supporting user networking and knowledge*. York: Joseph Rowntree Foundation.

Brattgard, S.-O. (1974) Social and psychological aspects of the situation of the disabled, in D. M. Boswell and J. M. Wingrove (eds), *The Handicapped Person in the Community: A reader and sourcebook*. London: Tavistock in association with Open University Press, pp. 7–9.

Brault, M. (2008) *Americans with Disabilities: 2005*. Current Population Reports, P70-117. Washington, DC: US Census Bureau.

Braye, S. (2000) Participation and involvement in social care: an overview, in H. Kemshall and R. Littlechild (eds), *User Involvement and Participation in Social Care*. London: Jessica Kingsley, pp. 9–28.

Bredberg, E. (1999) Writing disability history: problems, perspectives and sources, *Disability & Society*, 14(2): 189–201.

Breslin, M. L., and Yee, S. (eds) (2002) *Disability Rights Law and Policy: International perspectives*. Ardsley, NY: Transnational.

Brisenden, S. (1986) Independent living and the medical model of disability, *Disability, Handicap & Society*, 1(2): 173–8.

Brisenden, S. (1989) A charter for personal care, in Disablement Income Group, *Progress London*, no. 16, pp. 9–10.

Bristo, M. (2000) Letter of transmittal, in National Council on Disability, *Promises to Keep: A decade of federal enforcement of the Americans with Disabilities Act*. Washington, DC: National Council on Disability.

Brittan, A., and Maynard, M. (1984) *Sexism, Racism and Oppression*. Oxford: Blackwell.

Brittain, I. (2004) The role of schools in constructing self-perceptions of sport and physical education in relation to people with disabilities, *Sport, Education and Society*, 9(1): 75–94.

Broom, D. H., and Woodward, R. (1996) Medicalisation reconsidered: toward a collaborative approach to care, *Sociology of Health & Illness*, 18(3): 357–78.

Brown, H., and Smith, H. (eds) (1992) *Normalisation: A reader for the nineties*. London: Tavistock/Routledge.

Brown, P., and Zavestoski, S. (eds) (2005) Social Movements in Health. Oxford: Blackwell.

Brown, S. E. (1997) 'Oh, don't you envy us our privileged lives?' A review of the disability culture movement, *Disability & Rehabilitation*, 19(8): 339–49.

BSC (1989) *A Code of Practice*. London: Broadcasting Standards Council.

Burchardt, T. (2003a) *Being and Becoming: Social exclusion and the onset of disability*. CASE Report 21. London: ESARC Centre for Analysis of Social Exclusion.

Burchardt, T. (2003b) *Social Exclusion and the Onset of Disability*. York: Joseph Rowntree Foundation.

Burchardt, T., and Zaidi, A. (2003) *Disabled People's Costs of Living*. York: Joseph Rowntree Foundation.

Burleigh, M. (1994) *Death and Deliverance: Euthanasia in Germany 1900–1945*. Cambridge: Cambridge University Press.

Burns, R. C., and Graefe, A. R. (2007) Constraints to outdoor recreation: exploring the effects of disabilities on perceptions and participation, *Journal of Leisure Research*, 39(1): 156–81.

Burr, V. (1996) *An Introduction to Social Constructionism*. London: Routledge.

Burrell, E. (1989) Fostering children with disabilities: the lessons of the last ten years, *Foster Care*, 59(September): 22–3.

Burton, M., and Kagan, C. (2006) Decoding *Valuing People*, *Disability & Society*, 21(4): 299–313.

Bury, M. (1982) Chronic illness as biographical disruption, *Sociology of Health & Illness*, 4(2): 167–82.

Bury, M. (1988) Meanings at risk: the experience of arthritis, in R. Anderson and M. Bury (eds), *Living with Chronic Illness: The experience of patients and their families*. London: Unwin Hyman, pp. 89–116.

Bury, M. (1991) The sociology of chronic illness: a review of research and prospects, *Sociology of Health & Illness*, 13(4): 451–68.

Bury, M. (1996) Defining and researching disability: challenges and responses, in C. Barnes and G. Mercer (eds), *Exploring the Divide*, Leeds: Disability Press, pp. 17–38.

Bury, M. (1997) *Health and Illness in a Changing Society*. London: Routledge.

Bury, M. (2000a) A comment on the ICIDH2, *Disability & Society*, 15(7): 1073–7.

Bury, M. (2000b) On chronic illness and disability, in C. E. Bird, P. Conrad and A. M. Fremont (eds), *Handbook of Medical Sociology*. 5th edn, Upper Saddle River, NJ: Prentice-Hall International, pp. 173–83.

Bury, M. (2001) Illness narratives: fact or fiction?, *Sociology of Health & Illness*, 23(3): 263–85.

Bury, M. (2008) New dimensions of health care organization, in D. Wainwright (ed.), *A Sociology of Health*. London: Sage, pp. 151–72.

Busfield, J. (1986) *Managing Madness: Changing ideas and practice*. London: Unwin Hyman.

Busfield, J. (1988) Mental illness as a social product or social construct: a contradiction in feminists' arguments?, *Sociology of Health & Illness*, 10(4): 521–42.

Busfield, J. (1989) Sexism and psychiatry, *Sociology*, 23(3): 343–64.

Busfield, J. (1996) *Men, Women and Madness: Understanding gender and mental disorder*. London: Macmillan.

Butler, J. (1990) *Gender Trouble: Feminism and the subversion of identity*. London: Routledge.

Butler, R., and Parr, H. (eds) (1999) *Mind and Body Spaces: Geographies of illness, impairment and disability*. London: Routledge.

Byrne, D. (2005) *Social Exclusion*. 2nd edn, Maidenhead: Open University Press.

Cabinet Office (1999) *Modernising Government*. London: Cabinet Office.

Cabinet Office (2005) *Improving the Life Chances of Disabled People: Final report*. London: Cabinet Office. Available at: www.cabinetoffice.gov.uk/media/cabinet office/strategy/assets/disability.pdf (accessed 23 March 2007).

Cambridge, P., Carpenter, J., Beecham, J., Hallam, A., Knapp, M., Forrester-Jones, R., et al. (2001) *Twelve Years On: The outcomes and costs of community care for people with learning disabilities and mental health problems.* Canterbury: Tizard Centre, University of Kent.

Campbell, J. (1990) Developing our image – who's in control? Paper presented at the 'Cap-in-Hand' conference, February. Available at: www.leeds.ac.uk/disability-studies/archiveuk/Campbell/DEVELOPING%20OUR%20IMAGE.pdf (accessed 4 May 2005).

Campbell, J. (2006) Assisted dying: a question of choice? Paper presented at the Centre for Disability Studies, School of Sociology and Social Policy, 15 November. Available at: www.leeds.ac.uk/disability-studies/archiveuk/Campbell/Leeds%20Uni%2015%20Nov%202006.pdf (accessed 26 January 2008).

Campbell, J. (2009) Not in our name: disabled and terminally ill people reject the view that our lives are a tragic burden. We can speak for ourselves – hear us now. *The Guardian*, 7 July. Available at: www.guardian.co.uk/comment isfree/2009/jul/07/assisted-dying-disabled-terminally-ill (accessed 7 July 2009).

Campbell, J., and Oliver, M. (1996) *Disability Politics: Understanding our past, changing our future.* London: Routledge.

Campbell, P. (2001) The role of users of psychiatric services in service development – influence not power, *Psychiatric Bulletin*, 25(March): 87–8.

Campling, J. (1979) *Better Lives for Disabled Women.* London: Virago.

Campling, J. (ed.) (1981) *Images of Ourselves: Women with disabilities talking.* London: Routledge & Kegan Paul.

Carmichael, A., and Brown, L. (2002) The future challenge for direct payments, *Disability & Society*, 17(7): 797–808.

Carr, S. (2004) *Has Service User Participation Made a Difference to Social Care Services?* London: Social Care Institute for Excellence.

Carricaburu, D., and Pierret, J. (1995) From biographical disruption to biographical reinforcement: the case of HIV positive men, *Sociology of Health & Illness*, 17(1): 65–88.

Carter, J. (1981) *Day Services for Adults: Somewhere to go.* London: Allen & Unwin.

Castells, M. (1997) *The Information Age: Economy, society and culture*, Vol. 2: *The Power of Identity.* Oxford: Blackwell.

Cavet, J. (1998) Leisure and friendship, in C. Robinson and K. Stalker (eds), *Growing up with Disability.* London: Jessica Kingsley, pp. 97–110.

CEC (2003) *Equal Opportunities for People with Disabilities: A European action plan.* Brussells: Commission of the European Community, COM (2003) final.

Center for Independent Living (1982) Independent living: the right to choose, in M. Eisenberg, C. Griggins and R. Duval (eds), *Disabled People as Second-Class Citizens.* New York: Springer, pp. 247–60.

Chappell, A. (1992) Towards a sociological critique of the normalisation principle, *Disability, Handicap & Society*, 7(1): 35–51.

Chappell, A. (1997) From normalisation to where?, in L. Barton and M. Oliver (eds), *Disability Studies: Past, present and future.* Leeds: Disability Press, pp. 45–61.

Charity Commission (1999) *CC9 Political Campaigning by Charities.* London: Charity Commission.

Charity Commission (2004) *CC9 Campaigning and Political Activities by Charities.* London: Charity Commission.

Charity Commission (2007) *Stand and Deliver: The future for charities providing public services*. London: Charity Commission.

Charlton, J. I. (1998) *Nothing about Us without Us: Disability oppression and empowerment*. Berkeley: University of California Press.

Charmaz, K. (1980) The social construction of self-pity in the chronically ill, in N. Denzin (ed.), *Studies in Symbolic Interaction*, Vol. 3. Greenwich, CT: Jai Press, pp. 123–44.

Charmaz, K. (1983) Loss of self: a fundamental form of suffering in the chronically ill, *Sociology of Health & Illness*, 5(2): 168–95.

Charmaz, K. (2000) Experiencing chronic illness, in G. L. Albrecht, R. Fitzpatrick and S. C. Scrimshaw (eds), *The Handbook of Social Studies in Health and Medicine*. London: Sage, pp. 277–92.

Clare, L., and Cox, S. (2003) Improving service approaches and outcomes for people with complex needs through consultation and involvement, *Disability & Society*, 18(7): 935–53.

Clark, D., and Seymour, J. (1999) *Reflections on Palliative Care: Sociological and policy perspectives*. Buckingham: Open University Press.

Clark, H., and Spafford, J. (2001) *Piloting Choice and Control for Older People: An evaluation*. Bristol: Policy Press.

Clark, H., and Spafford, J. (2002) Adapting to the culture of user control?, *Social Work Education*, 21(2): 247–57.

Clark, H., Gough, H., and Macfarlane, A. (2004) *It Pays Dividends: Direct payments and older people*. Bristol: Policy Press.

Clarke, J. (2004) *Changing Welfare, Changing States: New directions in social policy*. London: Sage.

Clarke, J., and Langan, M. (1993) The British welfare state: foundation and modernisation, in A. Cochrane and J. Clarke (eds), *Comparing Welfare States: Britain in international context*. London: Sage, pp. 19–48.

Clarke, J., and Newman, J. (1997) *The Managerial State: Power, politics and ideology in the remaking of social welfare*. London: Sage.

Clarke, J., Gewirtz, S., and McLaughlin, E. (eds) (2000) *New Managerialism, New Welfare?* London: Sage.

Clear, M. (ed.) (2000) *Promises Promises: Disability and terms of inclusion*. Leichhardt, NSW: Federation Press.

Clogson, J. (1990) *Disability Coverage in Sixteen Newspapers*. Louisville, KY: Avocado Press.

Cole, A., McIntosh, B., and Whittaker, A. (2000) *'We Want our Voices Heard': Developing new lifestyles with disabled people*. Bristol: Policy Press.

Cole, A., and Williams, V., with Lloyd, A., Major, V., Mattingly, V., McIntosh, B., Swift, P., and Townsley, P. (2007) *Having a Good Day? A study of community-based activities for people with learning disabilities*. Bristol: Policy Press.

Coleridge, P. (1993) *Disability, Liberation and Development*. Oxford: Oxfam.

Coleridge, P. (1999) Development, cultural values and disability: the example of Afghanistan, in E. Stone (ed.), *Disability and Development: Learning from action and research on disability in the majority world*. Leeds: Disability Press, pp. 149–67.

Coleridge, P. (2000) Disability and culture, in M. Thomas and M. J. Thomas (eds), *Selected Readings in Community Based Rehabilitation*, Series 1. Bangalore: Asia Pacific Disability Rehabilitation Journal, pp. 21–38.

Coleridge, P. (2006) CBR as part of community development and poverty reduction, in S. Hartley (ed.), *CBR as part of Community Development: A poverty reduction strategy*. London: Centre for International Child Health, University College, pp. 19–39.

Confederation of Indian Organizations (1987) *Double Bind: To be disabled and Asian*. London: Confederation of Indian Organizations.

Conrad, P. (1975) The discovery of hyperkinesis: notes on the medicalisation of deviant behaviour, *Social Problems*, 23(1): 12–21.

Conrad, P. (2005) The shifting engines of medicalisation, *Journal of Health and Social Behaviour*, 46(1): 3–14.

Conrad, P., and Leiter, V. (2004) Medicalisation, markets and consumers, *Journal of Health and Social Behaviour*, 45(Supplement 1): 158–76.

Conrad, P., and Potter, D. (2000) From hyperactive children to ADHD adults, *Social Problems*, 47(3): 559–82.

Conrad, P., and Schneider, J. (1980) *Deviance and Medicalisation: From deviance to badness*. St Louis: C. V. Mosby.

Cook, D. (2002) Consultation, for a change? Engaging users and communities in the policy process, *Social Policy & Administration*, 36(5): 516–31.

Cooke, C., Daone, L., and Morris, G. (2000) *Stop Press! How the press portrays disabled people*. London: Scope.

CORAD (1982) *Report of the Committee on Restrictions against Disabled People*. London: HMSO.

Corbett, J., and Ralph, S. (1994) Empowering adults: the changing imagery of charity advertising, *Australian Disability Review*, 1: 5–14.

Corbin, J., and Strauss, A. L. (1985) Managing chronic illness at home: three lines of work, *Qualitative Sociology*, 8(3): 224–47.

Corbin, J., and Strauss, A. L. (1988) *Unending Work and Care: Managing chronic illness at home*. San Francisco: Jossey-Bass.

Corbin, J., and Strauss, A. L. (1991) Comeback: the process of overcoming disability, in G. L. Albrecht and J. A. Levy (eds), *Advances in Medical Sociology*, Vol. 2. Greenwich, CT: JAI Press, pp. 137–59.

Corker, M. (1997) Deaf people and interpreting: the struggle in language, *Deaf Worlds*, 13(3): 13–20.

Corker, M. (1998) *Deaf and Disabled, or Deafness Disabled?* Buckingham: Open University Press.

Corker, M., and Shakespeare, T. (2002) Mapping the terrain, in M. Corker and T. Shakespeare, *Disability/Postmodernity: Embodying disability theory*, London: Continuum, pp. 1–17.

Cornwell, J. (1984) *Hard-Earned Lives: Accounts of health and illness from East London*. London: Tavistock.

Couch, G., Forrester, W., and Mayhew-Smith, P. (1989) *Access in London*. London: Nicholson.

Crawford, R. (1977) You are dangerous to your health: the ideology and politics of victim blaming, *International Journal of Health Services*, 7(4): 663–80.

Crawford, R. (1980) Healthism and the medicalisation of everyday life, *International Journal of Health Services*, 10(3): 365–88.

Cribb, S. (1993) Are disabled artists cotton-woolled?, *Disability Arts Magazine*, 3(2): 10–11.

Crossley, M., and Crossley, N. (2001) 'Patient' voices, social movements and the habitus: how psychiatric survivors 'speak out', *Social Science & Medicine*, 52(10): 1477–89.

Crossley, N. (2000) Emotions, psychiatry and social order: a Habermasian approach, in S. Williams, J. Gabe and M. Calnan (eds), *Health, Medicine and Society*. London: Routledge, pp. 277–95.

Crow, L. (1992) Renewing the social model of disability, *Coalition*, July: 5–9.

Crow, L. (1996) Including all of our lives: renewing the social model of disability, in C. Barnes and G. Mercer (eds), *Exploring the Divide*. Leeds: Disability Press, pp. 55–73.

CSCI (Commission for Social Care Inspection) (2004) *Direct Payments: What are the barriers?* London: CSCI.

CSCI (Commission for Social Care Inspection) (2006) *The State of Social Care in England 2004/05*. London: CSCI.

CSCI (Commission for Social Care Inspection) and Health Care Commission (2006) *Joint Investigation into the Provision of Services for People with Learning Disabilities at Cornwall Partnership NHS Trust*. London: Commission for Healthcare Audit and Inspection.

CSIE (2005a) *Segregation Trends: LEAs in England 2002–4*. Bristol: Centre for Studies in Inclusive Education.

CSIE (2005b) *Working for Inclusion in 2005*. Bristol: Centre for Studies in Inclusive Education. Available at: http://uwe.ac.uk/csie05.htm (accessed 10 June 2007).

CSO (2007) *Social Trends 37*. London: Central Statistical Office.

Culyer, A. J., Lavers, R. J., and Williams, A. (1972) Health indicators, in A. Schonfield and S. Shaw (eds), *Social Indicators*. London: Heinemann Educational, pp. 94–118.

Cumberbatch, G., and Gauntlett, S. (2006) *On Screen Representations of Disability*. London: Broadcasting and Creative Industries Disability Network.

Cumberbatch, G., and Negrine R. (1992) *Images of Disability on Television*. London: Routledge.

D'Aboville, E. (2005) Implementing direct payments: a support organisation perspective, in J. Leece and J. Bornat (eds.), *Developments in Direct Payments*. Bristol: Policy Press, pp. 145–8.

Dalley, G. (ed.) (1988) *Ideologies of Caring: Rethinking community and collectivism*. Basingstoke: Macmillan.

Daniel, C. (1998) Radical, angry and willing to work, *New Statesman*, 6 March: 22–3.

Darke, P. (1994) *The Elephant Man* (David Lynch, EMI Films, 1980): an analysis from a disabled perspective, *Disability & Society*, 9(3): 327–42.

Darke, P. (1998) Understanding cinematic representations of disability, in T. Shakespeare (ed.), *The Disability Reader*. London: Cassell, pp. 181–97.

Darke, P. (2003) Now I know why disability art is drowning in the River Lethe (with thanks to Pierre Bourdieu), in S. Riddell and N. Watson (eds), *Disability, Culture and Identity*. Harlow: Pearson Education, pp. 131–42.

Darke, P. (2004) The changing face of representations of disability in the media, in J. Swain, S. French, C. Barnes and C. Thomas (eds), *Disabling Barriers – Enabling Environments*. 2nd edn, London: Sage, pp. 100–5.

Dartington, T., Miller, E. J., and Gwynne, G. V. (1981) *A Life Together: The distribution of attitudes around the disabled*. London: Tavistock.

Darwin, C. (1922) *The Descent of Man and Selection in Relation to Sex*. New York: Appleton.

Darwin, C. (1996) *The Origin of Species*, ed. G. Beer. Oxford: Oxford University Press.

Davies, C. (2002) *Changing Society: A personal history of Scope (formerly the Spastics Society) 1952–2002*. London: Scope.

Davis, A. (1989) *From Where I Sit: Living with disability in an able bodied world*. London: Triangle.

Davis, F. (1961) Deviance disavowal: the management of strained interaction by the visibly handicapped, *Social Problems*, 9(2): 120–32.

Davis, K. (1981) 28–38 Grove Road: accommodation and care in a community setting, in A. Brechin, P. Liddiard and J. Swain (eds), *Handicap in a Social World*. London: Hodder & Stoughton in association with the Open University, pp. 322–7.

Davis, K. (1990) *Activating the Social Model of Disability: The emergence of the seven needs*. Derby: Derbyshire Coalition of Disabled People.

Davis, K., and Mullender, A. (1993) *Ten Turbulent Years: A review of the work of the Derbyshire Coalition of Disabled People*. Nottingham: University of Nottingham Centre for Social Action.

Davis, K., and Woodward, J. (1981) DIAL UK: development of the National Association of Disablement and Advice Services, in A. Brechin, A. Liddiard and J. Swain (eds), *Handicap in a Social World*. Hodder & Stoughton in association with the Open University, pp. 328–32.

Davis, L. J. (1995) *Enforcing Normalcy: Disability, deafness, and the body*. London and New York: Verso.

Davis, L. J. (1997) Introduction, in L. J. Davis (ed.), *The Disability Studies Reader*. London: Routledge, pp. 1–6.

Davis, L. J. (1999) Riding with the man on the escalator: citizenship and disability, in M. Jones and L. A. B. Marks (eds), *Disability, Divers-ability and Legal Change*. The Hague: Kluwer Law International/Martinus Nijhoff, pp. 65–74.

Davis, L. J. (2001) Identity politics, disability and culture, in G. L. Albrecht, K. D. Seelman and M. Bury (eds), *Handbook of Disability Studies*. London: Sage, pp. 535–45.

Davis, L. J. (ed.) (2006) *The Disability Studies Reader*. 2nd edn, London: Routledge.

Dawson, C. (2000) *Independent Success: Implementing direct payments*. York: Joseph Rowntree Foundation.

DCLG (Department for Communities and Local Government) (2007) *English House Condition Survey 2005: Annual report*. London DCLG.

Deegan, M. J., and Brooks, N. A. (eds) (1985) *Women with Disability: The double handicap*. Oxford: Transaction Books.

DeJong, G. (1979a) *The Movement for Independent Living: Origins, ideology and implications for disability research*. Michigan: University Centre for International Rehabilitation, Michigan State University.

DeJong, G. (1979b) Independent living: from social movement to analytic paradigm, *Archives of Physical Medicine and Rehabilitation*, 60: 435–46.

DeJong, G. (1981) The movement for independent living: origins, ideology and implications for disability research, in A. Brechin, P. Liddiard and J. Swain (eds), *Handicap in a Social World*. Sevenoaks: Hodder & Stoughton in association with the Open University, pp. 239–48.

DeJong, G. (1983) Defining and implementing the independent living concept, in N. Crewe and I. Zola (eds), *Independent Living for Physically Disabled People*. London: Jossey-Bass, pp. 4–27.

Dench, S., Meager, N., and Morris, S. (1996) *The Recruitment and Retention of People with Disabilities*. Brighton: Institute for Employment Studies.

Derrida, J. (1990) *Writing and Difference*, trans. A. Bass. London: Routledge & Kegan Paul.

De Swaan, A. (1988) *In Care of the State: State formation and the collectivisation of health care, education and welfare in Europe and America during the modern era*. Oxford: Oxford University Press.

De Swaan, A. (1989) The reluctant imperialism of the medical profession, *Social Science & Medicine*, 28(11): 1165–70.

De Swaan, A. (1990) *The Management of Normality*. London: Routledge.

Dewson, S., Aston, J., Bates, P., Ritchie, H., and Dyson, A. (2004) *Post-16 Transitions: A longitudinal study of young people with special educational needs, wave two*. DfES Research Report RR582. London: DfES.

Dexter, L. A. (1958) A social theory of mental deficiency, *American Journal of Mental Deficiency*, 62(March): 920–8.

DfEE (Department for Education and Employment) (1997) *Excellence for All Children: Meeting special educational needs*, CM 3785. London: HMSO.

DfES (Department for Education and Skills) (2003) *Every Child Matters*, Cm 5860. London: HMSO.

DfES (Department for Education and Skills) (2004) *Removing Barriers to Achievement: The government's strategy for SEN*. London: DfES.

DfES (Department for Education and Skills) (2007) *Education and Training Statistics for the UK, 2007*. London: DfES.

DfID (Department for International Development) (2000) *Disability, Poverty and Development*. London: DfID. Available at: www.dfid.gov.uk/Documents/publications/disabilitypovertydevelopment.pdf (accessed 12 April 2007).

DfT (Department for Transport) (2004) *National Travel Survey, 2002–2004*. London: DfT.

DHSS (Department of Health and Social Security) (1971) *Better Services for the Mentally Handicapped*, Cmnd. 4683. London: HMSO.

DHSS (Department of Health and Social Security) (1981) *Care in Action*. London: HMSO.

DIAL UK (2005) *Annual Report, 2004–05*. Doncaster: DIAL UK.

Dickens, P. (2000) *Social Darwinism*. Buckingham: Open University Press.

Dignity in Dying (2006) *Dignity in Dying: About us*. Available at: www.dignityindying.org.uk/about.html (accessed 23 October 2006).

Dingwall, R. (1994) Litigation and the threat to medicine, in J. Gabe, D. Kelleher and G. Williams (eds), *Modern Medicine: Lay perspectives and experiences*. London: UCL Press, pp. 46–64.

Directgov (2007a) *Disability and the Equality and Human Rights Commission*. Available at: www.direct.gov.uk/en/DisabledPeople/RightsAndObligations/DisabilityRights/DG_10023457 (accessed 4 April 2008).

Directgov (2007b) *The Disability Equality Duty*. Available at: www.direct.gov.uk/en/DisabledPeople/RightsAndObligations/DisabilityRights/DG_10038105 (accessed 4 April 2008).

Disability Now (2009) Editorial: When personal goes public, *Disability Now*, 1.

Dockrell, J., Peacey, N., and Lunt, I. (2002) *Literature Review: Meeting the needs of children with special educational needs.* London: Institute of Education, University of London.

DoH (Department of Health) (1989) *Caring for People.* London: HMSO.

DoH (Department of Health) (1991) *Care Management and Assessment: Managers' guide.* London: HMSO.

DoH (Department of Health) (1998) *Modernising Social Services: Promoting independence, improving protection, raising standards.* London: HMSO.

DoH (Department of Health) (2000) *A Quality Strategy for Social Care.* London: DoH

DoH (Department of Health) (2001) *Valuing People: A new strategy for learning disability for the 21st century,* Cm 5086. London: HMSO.

DoH (Department of Health) (2005a) *Independence, Well-being and Choice,* Cm 6499. London: DoH.

DoH (Department of Health) (2005b) *Valuing People: The story so far.* London: DoH.

DoH (Department of Health) (2006) *Our health, our care, our say: A new direction for community services,* Cm 6737. London: DoH.

DoH (Department of Health) (2007a) *User Led Organisations.* London: DoH.

DoH (Department of Health) (2007b) *Valuing People Now: From progress to transformation.* London: DoH.

DoH (Department of Health) (2007c) *Department of Health Statistical Bulletin: Abortion statistics, England and Wales 2006.* Available at: www.dh.gov.uk/en/Publicationsandstatistics/Publications/PublicationsStatistics/DH_075697 (accessed 23 October 2007).

Douglas, M. (1966) *Purity and Danger: An analysis of the concepts of pollution and taboo.* London: Routledge.

Downes, D., and Rock, P. (1988) *Understanding Deviance: A guide to the sociology of crime and rule breaking.* 2nd edn, Oxford: Clarendon Press.

Doyle, B. (1995) *Disability, Discrimination and Equal Opportunities: A comparative study of the employment rights of disabled persons.* London: Mansell.

Doyle, B. (2008) *Disability Discrimination: Law and practice.* 6th edn, Bristol: Jordans.

DPI (1982) *Disabled Peoples' International: Proceedings of the First World Congress.* Singapore: Disabled Peoples' International.

DPI (1992) *Disabled Peoples' International: Proceedings of the Third World Congress of the Disabled Peoples' International.* Winnipeg: Disabled Peoples' International.

DPI (1994) *Agreed Statement: Human rights plenary meeting in support of European Day of Disabled Persons.* London: Disabled Peoples' International.

DPI (2000) *Disabled People Speak on the New Genetics: DPI Europe position statement on bioethics and human rights.* Available at: http://freespace.virgin.net/dpi.europe/downloads/bioethics-english.pdf (accessed 23 October 2007).

DPTAC (2002) *Attitudes of Disabled People to Public Transport.* London: Disabled Persons Transport Advisory Committee.

DPTAC (2004) *Attitudes of Disabled People to Community Transport.* London: Disabled Persons Transport Advisory Committee.

Drake, R. (1994) The exclusion of disabled people from positions of power in British voluntary organizations, *Disability & Society* 9(4): 461–80.

Drake, R. (1996) A critique of the role of the traditional charities, in L. Barton (ed.), *Disability and Society: Emerging issues and insights.* London: Longman, pp. 147–66.

Drake, R. (1999) *Understanding Disability Policies*. Basingstoke: Macmillan.

DRC (2002) *Disability Rights Commission: Educational qualifications briefing*. London: Disability Rights Commission.

DRC (2003a) *An Overview of the Literature on Disability and Transport*. London: Disability Rights Commission.

DRC (2003b) *Young Disabled People: A survey of the views and experiences of young disabled people in Great Britain*. London: Disability Rights Commission.

DRC (2005) *Shaping the Future of Equality: Discussion paper*. London: Disability Rights Commission.

Driedger, D. (1989) *The Last Civil Rights Movement: Disabled Peoples' International*. London: Hurst.

Driedger, D. (ed.) (1991) *Disabled People in International Development*. Winnipeg: Coalition of Provincial Organizations of the Handicapped. Available at: www.independentliving.org/docs1/dispeopleintldev1.html#anchor2552326 (accessed 3 May 2006).

Driedger, D., and Gray, S. (eds) (1992) *Imprinting our Image: An international anthology by women with disabilities*. Charlottetown, Prince Edward Island: Gynergy Books.

Driedger, D., Feika, I., and Gironbatres, E. (eds) (1996) *Across Borders*. Charlottetown, Prince Edward Island: Gynergy Books.

Drinkwater, C. (2005) Supported living and the production of individuals, in S. Tremain (ed.), *Foucault and the Government of Disability*. Ann Arbor: University of Michigan Press, pp. 229–44.

DSS (Department of Social Security) (1990) *The Way Ahead: Benefits for disabled people*, Cm. 917. London: HMSO.

DSS (Department of Social Security) (1994) *A Consultation on Government Measures to Tackle Discrimination against Disabled People*. Bristol: Enable.

DSS (Department of Social Security) (1999) *Opportunity for All: Tackling poverty and social exclusion*, Cm. 4445. London: HMSO.

Dube, A. K. (2006a) Participation of disabled people in the PRSP PEAP process in Uganda, in B. Albert (ed.), *In or Out of the Mainstream? Lessons from research on disability and development cooperation*. Leeds: Disability Press, pp. 135–49.

Dube, A. K. (2006b) The role and effectiveness of disability legislation in South Africa, in B. Albert (ed.), *In or Out of the Mainstream? Lessons from research on disability and development cooperation*. Leeds: Disability Press, pp. 119–33.

Durkheim, E. (1984) *The Division of Labour in Society*, trans. W. D. Halls. Basingstoke: Macmillan.

DWP (Department for Work and Pensions) (2003) *Households below Average Income*. London: DWP.

DWP (Department for Work and Pensions) (2004) *Family Resources Survey 2003–2004*. London: DWP.

DWP (Department for Work and Pensions) (2005) *Opportunity and Security throughout Life: Five year strategy*. London: DWP.

Edgerton, R. B. (1967) *Cloak of Competence: Stigma in the lives of the mentally retarded*. Berkeley: University of California Press.

Edwards, A. (2002) What is knowledge in social care?, *MCC: Building Knowledge for Integrated Care*, 10(1): 13–16.

Ehrenreich, J. (ed.) (1978) *The Cultural Crisis of Modern Medicine*. New York: Monthly Review Press.

284   REFERENCES

Eide, A. H., and Loeb, M. E. (2006) Reflections on disability data and statistics in developing countries, in B. Albert (ed.), *In or Out of the Mainstream: Lessons from research on disability and development cooperation*. Leeds: Disability Press, pp. 89–103.

Elias, N. (1978) *The Civilising Process*, vol. 1. Oxford: Blackwell.

Ellis, K. (2007) Direct payments and social work practice: the significance of 'street-level bureaucracy' in determining eligibility, *British Journal of Social Work*, 37(3): 405–22.

Ellis, K., and Rummery, K. (2000) Politics into practice: the production of a disabled person's guide to accessing community care assessments, in H. Kemshall and R. Littlechild (eds), *User Involvement and Participation in Social Care*. London: Jessica Kingsley, pp. 97–110.

Ells, C. (2001) Lessons about autonomy from the experience of disability, *Social Theory and Practice*, 27(4): 599–615.

Elston, M. A. (1991) The politics of professional power: medicine in a changing health service, in J. Gabe, M. Calnan and M. Bury (eds), *The Sociology of the Health Service*. London: Routledge, pp. 58–88.

Elwan, A. (1999) *Poverty and Disability: A survey of the literature*. Washington: World Bank. Available at: http://siteresources.worldbank.org/DISABILITY/Resources/280658-1172608138489/PovertyDisabElwan.pdf (accessed 15 May 2008).

Emerson, E. (1992) What is normalisation?, in H. Brown and H. Smith (eds), *Normalisation: A reader for the nineties*. London: Tavistock, pp. 1–17.

Enticott, J., Graham, P., and Lamb, B. (1992) *Polls Apart: Disabled people and the 1992 general election*. London: Spastics Society.

Erb, S., and Harriss-White, B. (2002) *Outcast from Social Welfare: Disability in rural India*. London: Sage.

Europa (2008) *Europa Glossary: Subsidiarity*. Available at: http://europa.eu/scadplus/glossary/subsidiarity_en.htm (accessed 4 April 2008).

European Commission (2003) *Equal Opportunities for People with Disabilities: A European action plan*. Brussels: European Commission, 30 October. Available at: http://eur-lex.europa.eu/LexUriServ/LexUriServ.do?uri=COM:2003:0650:FIN:EN:PDF (accessed 4 April 2008).

Evans, C. (1995) Disability, discrimination and local authority social services, 2: Users' perspectives, in G. Zarb (ed.), *Removing Disabling Barriers*. London: Policy Studies Institute, pp. 116–22.

Evans, J. (1993) The role of centres of independent/integrated living and networks of disabled people, in C. Barnes (ed.), *Making our own Choices*. Derby: British Council of Organizations of Disabled People, pp. 59–64.

Exworthy, M., and Halford, S. (1999) Professionals and managers in a changing public sector: conflict, compromise and collaboration?, in M. Exworthy and S. Halford (eds), *Professionals and the New Managerialism in the Public Sector*. Buckingham: Open University Press, pp. 1–17.

Fagan, T., and Lee, P. (1997) New social movements and social policy: a case study of the disability movement, in M. Lavalette and A. Pratt (eds), *Social Policy: A conceptual and theoretical introduction*. London: Sage, pp. 140–60.

Faircloth, C., Boylstein, C., Rittman, M., Young, M. E., and Gubrium, J. (2004) Sudden illness and biographical flow in narratives of stroke recovery, *Sociology of Health & Illness*, 26(2): 242–61.

Fairclough, N. (2000) *New Labour, New Language*. London: Routledge.

Fawcett, B. (2000) *Feminist Perspectives on Disability*. Harlow: Pearson Education.

Featherstone, M. (1991) The body in consumer culture, in M. Featherstone, M. Hepworth and B. S. Turner (eds), *The Body: Social process and cultural theory*. London: Sage, pp. 170–96.

Felce, D. (2000) *Quality of Life for People with Learning Disabilities in Supported Housing in the Community: A review of research*. Exeter: University of Exeter, Centre for Evidence-Based Social Services.

Ferguson, I. (2007) Increasing user choice or privatising risk? The antinomies of personalization, *British Journal of Social Work*, 37(2): 387–403.

Fernando, S. (2002) *Mental Health, Race and Culture*. 2nd edn, Basingstoke: Palgrave.

Fernando, S. (2003) *Cultural Diversity, Mental Health and Psychiatry*. Hove: Brunner-Routledge.

Ferrie, J., Lerpiniere, J., Paterson, K., Pearson, C., Stalker, K., and Watson, N. (2008) *An In Depth Analysis of the Implementation of the Disability Equality Duty in England*. London: Office of Disability Issues.

Fiedler, B. (1991) Housing and independence, in M. Oliver (ed.), *Social Work: Disabled people and disabling environments*. London: Jessica Kingsley, pp. 86–97.

Finch, J. (1983) Community care: developing non-sexist alternatives, *Critical Social Policy*, 3(9): 6–18.

Finch, J., and Groves, D. (1980) Community care and the family: a case for equal opportunities?, *Journal of Social Policy*, 9(4): 487–514.

Fine, M., and Asch, A. (1985) Disabled women: sexism without the pedestal?, in M. J. Deegan and N. A. Brooks (eds), *Women with Disability: The double handicap*. Oxford: Transaction Books, pp. 6–22.

Fine, M., and Asch, A. (1988) *Women with Disabilities: Essays in psychology, culture, and politics*. Philadelphia: Temple University Press.

Fine, M., and Glendinning, C. (2005) Dependence, independence or inter-dependence? Re-visiting the concepts of 'care' and 'dependency', *Ageing and Society*, 25(4): 601–21.

Finger, A. (1991) *Past Due: A story of disability, pregnancy and birth*. London: Disability Press.

Finkelstein, V. (1980) *Attitudes and Disabled People: Issues for discussion*. New York: World Rehabilitation Fund.

Finkelstein, V. (1991) Disability: an administrative challenge (the health and welfare heritage), in M. Oliver (ed.), *Social Work: Disabled people and disabling environments*. London: Jessica Kingsley, pp. 19–39.

Finkelstein, V. (1993a) The commonality of disability, in J. Swain, V. Finkelstein, S. French and M. Oliver (eds), *Disabling Barriers – Enabling Environments*. London: Sage, pp. 9–16.

Finkelstein, V. (1993b) Disability: a social challenge or an administrative responsibility, in J. Swain, V. Finkelstein, S. French and M. Oliver (eds), *Disabling Barriers – Enabling Environments*. London: Sage, pp. 34–43.

Finkelstein, V. (1996) Outside: 'Inside Out', *Coalition*, April: 31–6.

Finkelstein, V. (1998) Rethinking care in a society providing equal opportunities for all. Discussion paper prepared for the World Health Organization's Disability and Rehabilitation Team. Available at: www.leeds.ac.uk/disability-studies/archiveuk/finkelstein/finkelstein2.pdf (accessed 12 March 2007).

Finkelstein, V. (1999) A profession allied to the community: the disabled people's trade union, in E. Stone (ed.), *Disability and Development: Learning from action and research in the majority world*. Leeds: Disability Press, pp. 21–4.

Finkelstein, V. (2001a) The social model repossessed. Unpublished paper, Centre for Disability Studies, University of Leeds. Available at: www.leeds.ac.uk/disability-studies/archiveuk/finkelstein/soc%20mod%20repossessed.pdf (accessed 12 March 2007).

Finkelstein, V. (2001b) A personal journey into disability politics. Unpublished paper, Centre for Disability Studies, University of Leeds. Available at: www.leeds.ac.uk/disability-studies/archiveuk/finkelstein/presentn.pdf (accessed 12 March 2007).

Finkelstein, V. (2002) The social model of disability repossessed, *Coalition*, February: 12–13.

Finkelstein, V., and French, S. (1993) Towards a psychology of disability, in J. Swain, S. French, C. Barnes and C. Thomas (eds), *Disabling Barriers – Enabling Environments*. London: Sage, pp. 26–33.

Fletcher, S. (1995) *Evaluating Community Care: A guide to evaluations led by disabled people*. London: King's Fund.

Florian, L. (ed.) (2007) *The Sage Handbook of Special Education*. London: Sage.

Florian, L., Rouse, M., Black-Hawkins, K., and Jull, S. (2004) What can national data sets tell us about inclusion and pupil achievement?, *British Journal of Special Education*, 31(3): 115–21.

Flynn, R. (1999) Managerialism, professionalism and quasi-markets, in M. Exworthy and S. Halford (eds), *Professionals and the New Managerialism in the Public Sector*. Buckingham: Open University Press, pp. 18–36.

Foster, M., Harris, J., Jackson, K., Morgan, H., and Glendinning, C. (2006) Personalised social care for adults with disabilities: a problematic concept for frontline practice, *Health & Social Care in the Community*, 14(2): 125–35.

Foster, P. (1989) Improving the doctor/patient relationship, *Journal of Social Policy*, 18(3): 337–61.

Foucault, M. (1965) *Madness and Civilisation: A history of insanity in the age of reason*. London: Tavistock.

Foucault, M. (1972) *The Archaeology of Knowledge*, trans. A. M. Sheridan. London: Tavistock.

Foucault, M. (1976) *The Birth of the Clinic*. London: Tavistock.

Foucault, M. (1979) *Discipline and Punish*. Harmondsworth: Penguin.

Foucault, M. (1980) The eye of power, in *Power/Knowledge: Selected interviews and other writings 1972–1977*, ed. C. Gordon. Brighton: Harvester Press, pp 146–65.

Fox, P. (1989) From senility to Alzheimer's disease: the rise of the Alzheimer's disease movement, *Milbank Quarterly*, 67(1): 58–101.

Fox, R. (1977) The medicalisation and demedicalisation of American society, *Daedalus*, 106(1): 9–22.

Frank, A. G. (1975) *On Capitalist Underdevelopment*. Oxford: Oxford University Press.

Frank, A. W. (1991) *At the Will of the Body: Reflections on illness*. Boston: Houghton Mifflin.

Frank, A. W. (1995) *The Wounded Storyteller: Body, illness and ethics*. Chicago: University of Chicago Press.

Fraser, N. (1995) From redistribution to recognition? Dilemmas of justice in a 'post-socialist' age, *New Left Review*, 212(July–August): 68–93.

Fraser, N. (1997) *Justice Interruptus: Critical reflections on the 'postsocialist' condition.* New York and London: Routledge.

Fraser, N. (2000) Rethinking recognition, *New Left Review* (2nd series), 3(May/June): 107–20.

Freidson, E. (1970a) *Profession of Medicine: A study of the sociology of applied knowledge.* Chicago: University of Chicago Press.

Freidson, E. (1970b) *Professional Dominance.* Chicago: Aldine.

Freire, P. (1970) *Pedagogy of the Oppressed.* Harmondsworth: Penguin.

French, D., and Hainsworth, J. (2001) 'There aren't any buses and the swimming pool is always cold!': Obstacles and opportunities in the provision of sport for disabled people, *Managing Leisure*, 6(1): 35–49.

French, S. (1993) Disability, impairment or something in-between, in J. Swain, V. Finkelstein, S. French and M. Oliver (eds), *Disabling Barriers – Enabling Environments.* London: Sage, pp. 17–25.

French, S. (2004) Can you see the rainbow? The roots of denial, in J. Swain, S. French, C. Barnes and C. Thomas (eds), *Disabling Barriers – Enabling Environments.* 2nd edn, London, Sage, pp. 81–6.

French, S., and Swain, J. (2001) The relationship between disabled people and health and welfare professionals, in G. L. Albrecht, K. D. Seelman and M. Bury (eds), *Handbook of Disability Studies.* London: Sage, pp. 734–53.

Fry, E. (1987) *Disabled People and the 1987 General Election.* London: Spastics Society.

Fujiura, G. T., and Rutkowski-Kmitta, V. (2001) Counting disability, in G. L. Albrecht, K. D. Seelman, and M. Bury (eds), *Handbook of Disability Studies.* London: Sage, pp. 69–96.

Fullager, S., and Owler, K. (1998) Narratives of leisure: recreating the self, *Disability & Society*, 13(3): 441–50.

Gallagher, C., and Laqueur, T. (1987) *The Making of the Modern Body.* Berkeley: University of California Press.

Gallagher, H. (1995) *By Trust Betrayed: Patients, physicians and the licence to kill in the Third Reich.* Arlington, VA: Vandamere Press.

Galvin, R. (2003) The paradox of disability culture: the need to combine versus the imperative to let go, *Disability & Society*, 18(5): 675–90.

Garfinkel, H. (1967) *Studies in Ethnomethodology.* Englewood Cliffs, NJ: Prentice-Hall.

Garland, R. R. J. (1995) *The Eye of the Beholder: Deformity and disability in the Graeco-Roman world.* London: Duckworth.

Garland-Thomson, R. (ed.) (1996) *Freakery: Cultural spectacles of the extraordinary body.* New York: New York University Press.

Garland-Thomson, R. (1997) *Extraordinary Bodies: Figuring physical disability in American culture and literature.* New York: Columbia University Press.

Garland-Thomson, R. (2002) The politics of staring, in S. L. Snyder, B. J. Brueggemann and R. Garland-Thomson (eds), *Disability Studies.* New York: Modern Language Association, pp. 56–73.

Garland-Thomson, R. (2005) Feminist disability studies, *Signs*, 30(2): 1558–87.

Garland-Thomson, R. (2006a) Integrating disability, transforming feminist theory, in L. Davis (ed.), *The Disability Studies Reader.* 2nd edn, London: Routledge, pp. 257–76.

Garland-Thomson, R. (2006b) Ways of staring, *Journal of Visual Culture*, 5(2): 173–92.

Gartner, A., and Joe, T. (eds) (1987) *Images of the Disabled, Disabling Images*. New York and London: Praeger.

Gerber, D. (1996) The careers of people exhibited in freak shows: the problem of volition and valorisation, in R. Garland-Thomson (ed.), *Freakery: Cultural spectacles of the extraordinary body*. New York: New York University Press, pp. 38–53.

Gerhardt, U. (1989) *Ideas about Illness: An intellectual and political history of medical sociology*. London: Macmillan.

Gerschick, T. V., and Miller, A. S. (1995) Coming to terms: masculinity and physical disability, in D. Sabo and D. F. Gordon (eds), *Men's Health and Illness: Gender, power and the body*. London: Sage, pp. 183–204.

Ghai, A. (2001) Marginalisation and disability: experiences from the third world, in M. Priestley (ed.), *Disability and the Life Course*. Cambridge: Cambridge University Press, pp. 26–37.

Giddens, A. (1982a) *Profiles and Critiques in Social Theory*. London: Macmillan.

Giddens A. (1982b) *Sociology: A brief but critical introduction*. London: Macmillan.

Giddens, A. (1989) *Sociology*. Cambridge: Polity.

Giddens, A. (1991) *Modernity and Self-Identity: Self and society in the late modern age*. Cambridge: Polity.

Giddens, A. (1998) *The Third Way: The renewal of social democracy*. Cambridge: Polity.

Giddens, A. (2000) *The Third Way and its Critics*. Cambridge: Polity.

Giddens, A. (2001) *Sociology*. 4th edn, Cambridge: Polity.

Giddens, A. (2006) *Sociology*. 5th edn, Cambridge: Polity.

Gillespie-Sells, K., Hill, M., and Robbins, B. (1998) *She Dances to Different Drums: Research into disabled women's sexuality*. London: King's Fund.

Ginsburg, N. (1992) *Divisions in Welfare: A critical introduction to comparative social policy*. London: Sage.

Glasby, J., and Littlechild, B. (2002) *Social Work and Direct Payments*. Bristol: Policy Press.

Gleeson, B. J. (1997) Disability studies: a historical materialist view, *Disability & Society*, 12(2): 179–202.

Gleeson, B. J. (1999) *Geographies of Disability*. London: Routledge.

Glendinning, C., and Means, R. (2006) Personal social services: developments in adult social care, in L. Bauld, K. Clarke and T. Maltby (eds), *Social Policy Review 18: Analysis and debate in social policy, 2006*. Bristol: Policy Press, pp. 15–32.

Glendinning, C., Halliwell, S., Jacobs, S., Rummery, K., and Tyrer, J. (2000a) Bridging the gap: using direct payments to purchase integrated care, *Health & Social Care in the Community*, 8(3): 192–200.

Glendinning, C., Halliwell, S., Jacobs, S., Rummery, K., and Tyrer, J. (2000b) New kinds of care, new kinds of relationships: how purchasing services affects relationships in giving and receiving personal assistance, *Health & Social Care in the Community*, 8(3): 201–11.

Glendinning, C., Powell, M., and Rummery, K. (eds) (2002) *Partnerships, New Labour and the Governance of Welfare*. Bristol: Policy Press.

GMCDP (Greater Manchester Coalition of Disabled People) (2000) Where have all the activists gone?, parts 1 and 2, *Coalition*, August; October.

Goble, C. (2003) Controlling life, in J. Swain, S. French and C. Cameron (eds), *Controversial Issues in a Disabling Society*. Buckingham: Open University Press, pp. 45–53.

Goffman, E. (1959) *The Presentation of Self in Everyday Life*. Garden City, NY: Anchor Books.

Goffman, E. (1961) *Asylums*. Garden City, NY: Doubleday/Anchor Books.

Goffman, E. (1963) *Stigma: Notes on the management of spoiled identity*. Englewood Cliffs, NJ: Prentice-Hall.

Goldsmith, S. (1976) *Designing for the Disabled*. 3rd edn, London: RIBA.

Gooding, C. (1995) Employment and disabled people: equal rights or positive action, in G. Zarb (ed.), *Removing Disabling Barriers*. London: Policy Studies Institute, pp. 64–76.

Goodley, D. (2000) *Self-advocacy in the Lives of People with Learning Difficulties*. Buckingham: Open University Press.

Goodley, D., and Lawthom, R. (2006) Disability studies and psychology: new allies?, in D. Goodley and R. Lawthom (eds), *Psychology and Disability: Critical introductions and reflections*. Basingstoke: Palgrave Macmillan, pp. 1–15.

Goodridge, C. (2004) *Housing: A contemporary view of disabled people's experience, provision and policy directions*. London: Disability Rights Commission.

Gordon, C. (1966) *Role Theory and Illness: A sociological perspective*. New Haven, CT: College and University Press.

Gordon, D., Parker, R., Loughran, F., and Heslop, P. (2000) *Disabled Children in Britain: A re-analysis of the OPCS disability surveys*. London: HMSO.

Gould, S. (1980) *The Panda's Thumb*. Harmondsworth: Penguin.

Gouldner, A. (1970) *The Coming Crisis of Western Sociology*. New York: Avon.

Graham, H. (1983) Caring, a labour of love, in J. Finch and D. Groves (eds), *A Labour of Love: Women, work and caring*. London: Routledge & Kegan Paul, pp. 13–30.

Graham, H. (ed.) (2000) *Understanding Health Inequalities*. Buckingham: Open University Press.

Graham, P., Jordan, A., and Lamb, B. (1990) *An Equal Chance or No Chance*. London: Spastics Society.

Gramsci, A. (1971) *Selections from the Prison Notebooks of Antonio Gramsci*, ed. and trans. Q. Hoare and G. Nowell-Smith. London: Lawrence & Wishart.

Gramsci, A. (1985) *Selections from the Cultural Writings*, ed. and trans. D. Forgacs and G. Nowell-Smith. London: Lawrence & Wishart.

Gray, D. (2003) Gender and coping: the parents of children with high functioning autism, *Social Science & Medicine*, 56(3): 631–42.

Gray, P. (2002) *Disability Discrimination in Education: A review of the literature on discrimination across the 0–19 age range*. London: Disability Rights Commission.

Grear, A. (2004) The curate, a cleft palate and ideological closure in the Abortion Act 1967: time to reconsider the relationship between doctors and the abortion decision, *Web Journal of Current Legal Issues*, 4(12). Available at: http://webjcli.ncl.ac.uk/2004/issue4/grear4.html (accessed 8 January 2008).

Gregory, S., and Hartley, G. (eds) (1991) *Constructing Deafness*. London: Pinter/Open University.

Grewal, I., Joy, S., Lewis, J., Swales, K., and Woodfield, K. (2002) *Disabled for Life? Attitudes towards, and experiences of, disability in Britain*. London: Department for Work and Pensions.

Griffiths, R. (1988) *Community Care: Agenda for action*. London: HMSO.

Grover, C. (2003) New Labour, welfare reform and the reserve army of labour, *Capital & Class*, 79(spring): 17–23.

Grover, C., and Piggott, L. (2005) Disabled people, the reserve army of labour and welfare reform, *Disability & Society*, 20(7): 705–17.

Grunewald, K. (1974) The guiding environment: the dynamic of residential living, in D. M. Boswell and J. M. Wingrove (eds), *The Handicapped Person in the Community: A reader and sourcebook*. London: Tavistock/Open University Press, pp. 10–15.

Gussow, Z., and Tracy, G. (1968) Status, ideology, and adaptation to stigmatised illness: a study of leprosy, *Human Organization*, 27(4): 316–25.

Gustavsson, A. (2004) The role of theory in disability research: springboard or strait-jacket?, *Scandinavian Journal of Disability Research*, 6(1): 55–70.

Habermas, J. (1976) *Legitimation Crisis*, trans. T. McCarthy. London: Heinemann.

Habermas, J. (1981) New social movements, *Telos*, 49(fall): 33–7.

Haffter, C. (1968) The changeling: history and psychodynamics of attitudes to handicapped children in European folklore, *Journal of the History of Behavioural Studies*, 4: 55–61.

Hahn, H. (1985) Towards a politics of disability: definitions, disciplines and policies, *Social Science Journal*, 22(4): 87–105.

Hahn, H. (1986) Public support for rehabilitation programmes: the analysis of US disability policy, *Disability, Handicap & Society*, 1(2): 121–38.

Hahn, H. (1987) Civil rights for disabled Americans: the foundation of a political agenda, in A. Gartner and T. Joe (eds), *Images of the Disabled, Disabling Images*. New York and London: Praeger, pp. 181–203.

Hahn, H. (1989) Disability and the reproduction of bodily images: the dynamics of human appearances, in J. Wolch and M. Dear (eds), *The Power of Geography*. Boston: Unwin Hyman, pp. 370–88.

Hahn, H. (2002) Academic debates and political advocacy: the US disability movement, in C. Barnes, M. Oliver and L. Barton (eds), *Disability Studies Today*. Cambridge: Polity, pp. 162–89.

Hall, K., Collins, J., Benjamin, S., Nind, M., and Sheehy, K. (2004) SATurated models of pupildom: assessment and inclusion/exclusion, *British Educational Research Journal*, 30(6): 801–17.

Hall, S. (1990) Cultural identity and diaspora, in J. Rutherford (ed.), *Identity: Community, culture, difference*. London: Lawrence & Wishart, pp. 222–37.

Hall, S. (ed.) (1997) *Representation: Cultural representations and signifying practices*. London: Sage, in association with the Open University.

Hall, S. and du Gay, P. (eds) (1996) *Questions of Cultural Identity*. London: Sage.

Hall, S. and Jefferson, T. (eds) (1976) *Resistance through Rituals*. London: Hutchinson.

Hall, S., Critcher, C., Jefferson, T., Clarke, J., and Roberts, B. (1978) *Policing the Crisis*. London: Macmillan.

Hall, S., et al. (eds) (1980) *Culture, Media, Language: Working papers in cultural studies 1972–79*. London: Hutchinson in association with the Centre for Contemporary Cultural Studies, University of Birmingham.

Haller, B. (1995) Rethinking models of media representations of disability, *Disability Studies Quarterly*, 15(2): 26–30.

Haller, B., Dorries, B., and Rahn, J. (2006) Media labelling versus the US disability community identity: a study of shifting cultural language, *Disability & Society*, 21(1): 61–75.

Hamilton, K. W. (1950) *Counselling the Handicapped in the Rehabilitation Process*. New York: Ronald.

Handicap International (2006) *Making PRSP Inclusive*. Munich: Handicap International.

Hanks, J., and Hanks, L. (1948) The physically handicapped in certain non-occidental societies, *Journal of Social Issues*, 4(4): 11–20.

Hansard (2009) Coroners and Justice Bill, *Hansard*, vol. 712, no. 103, 7 July. Available at: www.publications.parliament.uk/pa/ld200809/ldhansrd/lhan 103.pdf (accessed 10 July 2009).

Harknett, S. (2006) Improving participatory appraisal approaches with rural disabled people: a pilot project in Pursat province, Cambodia, in B. Albert (ed.), *In or Out of the Mainstream? Lessons from research on disability and development cooperation*. Leeds: Disability Press, pp. 179–92.

Harris, A., Cox, E., and Smith, C. (1971a) *Handicapped and Impaired in Great Britain, Part 1*. London: HMSO.

Harris, A., Cox, E., and Smith, C. (1971b) *Handicapped and Impaired in Great Britain, Part 2*. London: HMSO.

Harris, J., Sapey, B., and Stewart, J. (1997) *Wheelchair Housing and the Estimation of Need*. Preston: University of Central Lancashire.

Harrison, M., and Davis, C. (2001) *Housing, Social Policy and Difference: Disability, ethnicity, gender and housing*. Bristol: Policy Press.

Harrison, S., and Ahmad, W. (2000) Medical autonomy and the UK state, 1975–2025, *Sociology*, 34(1): 129–46.

Hartley, S. (ed.) (2002) *CBR: A participatory strategy in Africa*. London: UCL Press.

Hartley, S. (ed.) (2006) *CBR As Part of Community Development: As poverty reduction strategy*. London: UCL Press.

Harvey, C., Fossey, E., Jackson, H., and Shimitras, L. (2006) Time use of people with schizophrenia living in North London: predictors of participation in occupations and their implications for improving social inclusion, *Journal of Mental Health*, 15(1): 43–55.

Harwood, R. (2005) *The End of the Beginning: An analysis of the first decade of the Disability Discrimination Act employment provision (1995–2005)*. London: Public Interest Research Unit.

Harwood, R. (2006) *Teeth and their Use: Enforcement action by the three equality commissions*. London: Public Interest Research Unit.

Hasler, F. (2003a) *Clarifying the Evidence on Direct Payments into Practice*. London: National Council for Independent Living.

Hasler, F. (2003b) *Users at the Heart: User participation in the governance and operation of social care regulatory bodies*. London: Social Care Institute for Excellence.

Hasler, F., and Stewart, A. (2004) *Making Direct Payments Work: Identifying and overcoming barriers to implementation*. Brighton: Pavilion.

Hasler, F., Campbell, J., and Zarb, G. (1999) *Direct Routes to Independence: A guide to local authorities' implementation and management of direct payments policy*. London: Policy Studies Institute.

Hattersley, J. (1991) The future of normalisation, in S. Baldwin and J. Hattersley (eds), *Mental Handicap: Social science perspectives*. London: Tavistock/Routledge, pp. 1–11.

Haug, M. (1988) A re-examination of the hypothesis of deprofessionalisation, *Milbank Memorial Quarterly*, 66(Supplement 2): 48–56.

Hayashi, R., and Okuhira, M. (2001) The disability rights movement in Japan: past, present, and future, *Disability & Society*, 16(6): 855–69.

Heiser, B. (1995) The nature and causes of transport disability in Britain and how to remove it, in G. Zarb (ed.), *Removing Disabling Barriers*. London: Policy Studies Institute, pp. 49–63.

Helander, E. (1993) *Prejudice and Dignity: An introduction to community-based rehabilitation*. Geneva: World Health Organization.

Held, D., McGrew, A., Goldblatt, D., and Perraton, J. (1999) *Global Transformations: Politics, economics and culture*. Cambridge: Polity.

Hendey, N., and Pascall, G. (2002) *Disability and Transition to Adulthood: Achieving independent living*. York: Joseph Rowntree Foundation.

Herz, M., Endicott, J., and Spitzer, R. (1977) Brief hospitalisation: a two-year follow-up, *American Journal of Psychiatry*, 134(5): 502–7.

Herzlich, C., and Pierret, J. (1987) *Illness and Self in Society*, trans. E. Forster. Baltimore: Johns Hopkins University Press.

Hevey, D. (1992) *The Creatures Time Forgot: Photography and disability imagery*. London: Routledge.

Hewitt, M. (1993) Social movements and social need: problems with postmodern political theory, *Critical Social Policy*, 13(1): 52–74.

Heywood, F. (2001) *Money Well Spent: The effectiveness and value of housing adaptations*. Bristol: Policy Press.

Heywood, F. (2004) The health outcomes of housing adaptations, *Disability & Society*, 19(2): 129–43.

Hill, M. (1994) They are not our brothers: the disability movement and the black disability movement, in N. Begum, M. Hill and A. Stevens (eds), *Reflections*. London: Central Council for the Education and Training in Social Work, pp. 68–80.

Hill Collins, P. (1990) *Black Feminist Thought: Knowledge, consciousness, and the politics of empowerment*. London: Routledge.

Hirsch, K. (1995) Culture and disability: the role of oral history, *Oral History Review*, 22(1): 1–27.

Hirschman, A. (1970) *Exit, Voice and Loyalty: Responses to decline in firms, organizations and states*. Cambridge, MA: Harvard University Press.

Hirst, M., and Baldwin, S. (1994) *Unequal Opportunities: Growing up disabled*. York: Social Policy Research Unit, University of York.

Hivenden, B. (2003) The uncertain convergence of disability policies in Western Europe, *Social Policy & Administration*, 37(6): 609–24.

Hodge, S. (2005) Participation, discourse and power: a case study in service user involvement, *Critical Social Policy*, 25(2): 164–79.

Hogg, J., and Cavet, J. (eds) (1995) *Making Leisure Provision for People with Profound Learning and Multiple Disabilities*. London: Chapman & Hall.

Holden, C., and Beresford, P. (2002) Globalization and disability, in C. Barnes, M. Oliver and L. Barton (eds), *Disability Studies Today*. Cambridge: Polity, pp. 190–209.

Holland, S. (2000) The assessment relationship: interactions between social workers and parents in child protection assessments, *British Journal of Social Work*, 30(2): 149–63.

Holstein, J. A., and Miller, G. (eds) (1993) *Reconsidering Social Constructionism: Debates in social problems theory*. New York: Aldine de Gruyter.

Honey, S., Meagar, N., and Williams, M. (1993) *Employers' Attitudes towards People with Disabilities*. Sussex: University of Sussex, Manpower Studies Institute.

Hood, L. (1992) Biology and medicine in the twenty-first century, in D. J. Kevles and L. Hood (eds), *The Code of Codes: Scientific and social issues in the human genome project*. London: Routledge, pp. 136–63.

Hoogvelt, A. M. (1976) *The Sociology of Developing Societies*. London: Macmillan.

Hoogvelt, A. M. (1997) *Globalisation and the Postcolonial World: The new political economy of development*. Basingstoke: Macmillan.

hooks, b. (1984) *Ain't I a woman: Black women and feminism*. London: Pluto Press.

Hout, W. (1993) *Capitalism and the Third World: Development, dependence and the world system*. Aldershot: Elgar.

Hughes, B. (2005) What can a Foucauldian analysis contribute to disability theory?, in S. Tremain (ed.), *Foucault and the Government of Disability*. Ann Arbor: University of Michigan Press, pp. 78–92.

Hughes, B., and Paterson, K. (1997) The social model of disability and the disappearing body: towards a sociology of impairment, *Disability & Society*, 12(3): 325–40.

Hughes, B., Russell, R., and Paterson, K. (2005) Nothing to be had 'off the peg': consumption, identity and the immobilisation of young disabled people, *Disability & Society*, 20(1): 3–17.

Humphrey, J. (1999) Disabled people and the politics of difference, *Disability & Society*, 14(2): 173–88.

Humphries, S., and Gordon, P. (1992) *Out of Sight: The experience of disability 1900–1950*. London: Northcote House.

Humphrys, J. (2009) Assisted suicide should be legal, *Daily Mail*, 21 March: 14–16.

Hunt, P. (ed.) (1966a) *Stigma: The experience of disability*. London: Geoffrey Chapman.

Hunt, P. (1966b) A critical condition, in P. Hunt (ed.), *Stigma: The experience of disability*, London: Geoffrey Chapman, pp. 145–59.

Hurst, R., and Albert, B. (2006) The social model of disability: human rights and development cooperation, in B. Albert (ed.), *In or Out of the Mainstream? Lessons from research on disability and development cooperation*. Leeds: Disability Press, pp. 24–39.

Hurstfield, J., Parashar, U., and Schofield, K. (2007) *The Costs and Benefits of Independent Living*. London: Office for Disability Issues.

Hyde, M. (1996) Fifty years of failure: employment services for disabled people in the UK, *Work, Employment & Society*, 10(4): 683–700.

Hyde, M. (2000) From welfare to work? Social policy for disabled people of working age in the United Kingdom in the 1990s, *Disability & Society*, 15(2): 327–41.

ILF (Independent Living Fund) (2008) *User Profile Analysis at 31 December 2007*. Available at: www.ilf.org.uk/home/index.html (accessed 20 March 2008).

Illich, I. (1975) *Medical Nemesis: The expropriation of health*. London: Marion Boyars.

Illich, I., Zola, I. K., McKnight, J., Caplan, J., and Shaiken, H. (1977) *Disabling Professions*. London: Marion Boyars.

Imrie, R. (2000) Disabling environments and the geography of access policies and practices, *Disability & Society*, 15(1): 5–24.

Imrie, R. (2003) Housing quality and the provision of accessible homes, *Housing Studies*, 18(3): 387–408.

Imrie, R. (2006) *Accessible Housing: Quality, disability and design*. London: Routledge.

Imrie, R., and Kumar, M. (1998) Focusing on disability and access in the built environment, *Disability & Society*, 13(3): 357–74.

Imrie, R., and Wells, P. (1993) Disablism, planning and the built environment, *Environment and Planning C: Government and Policy*, 11(2): 213–31.

Inclusion Europe (2008) Country reports: Sweden, in *The Specific Risks of Discrimination against Persons in Situations of Major Dependence or with Complex Needs: Report of a European study*, Vol. 3: *Country Reports*. Brussels: Inclusion Europe. Available at: www.inclusion-europe.org/documents/CNS%20Volume%203.pdf (accessed 20 July 2009).

Inglehart, R. (1990) Values, ideology and cognitive mobilisations in new social movements, in R. J. Dalton and M. Kuechler (eds), *Challenging the Political Order*. Cambridge: Polity, pp. 43–66.

Ingstad, B. (1999) The myth of disability in developing nations, *The Lancet*, 354(9180): 757–8.

Ingstad, B. (2001) Disability in the developing world, in G. L. Albrecht, K. D. Seelman and M. Bury (eds), *Handbook of Disability Studies*. London: Sage, pp. 772–92.

Ingstad, B., and Whyte, S. R. (eds) (1995) *Disability and Culture*. Berkeley: University of California Press.

IVR (Institute for Volunteering Research) (2004) *Volunteering for All? Exploring the link between volunteering and social exclusion*. London: Institute for Volunteering Research.

Jackson, L. (2002) *Freaks, Geeks and Asperger Syndrome: A user guide to adolescence*. London: Jessica Kingsley.

Jacobsen, N., and Greenley, D. (2001) What is recovery? A conceptual model and explication, *Psychiatric Services*, 52(4): 482–5.

Jacobsen, Y. (2002) *Making the Jump: Transition to Work: A guide to supporting adults with learning difficulties make the jump from education to employment*. London: National Institute of Adult Continuing Education.

Jaworski, A., and Coupland, N. (eds) (1999) *The Discourse Reader*. London: Routledge.

Jayasooria, D. (2000) *Disabled People, Citizenship and Social Work: The Malaysian experience*. London: Asian Academy Press.

Jayasooria, D., Krishnan, B., and Ooi, G. (1997) Disabled people in a newly industrialising economy: opportunities and challenges in Malaysia, *Disability & Society*, 12(3): 455–64.

Jeffery, R. (1979) Normal rubbish: deviant patients in casualty departments, *Sociology of Health & Illness*, 1(1): 90–107.

Jefferys, M., Millard, J. B., Hyman, M., and Warren, M. D. (1969) A set of tests for measuring motor impairment in prevalence studies, *Journal of Chronic Diseases*, 22(5): 303–19.

Jenkins, R. (1991) Disability and social stratification, *British Journal of Sociology*, 42(4): 557–80.

Jenkins, R. (ed.) (1998) *Questions of Competence: Culture, classification and intellectual disability*. Cambridge: Cambridge University Press.

Jenkins, S., and Rigg, J. (2003) *Disability and Disadvantage: Selection, onset, and duration effects*. Working Papers of the Institute for Social and Economic Research, no. 18, University of Essex.

Jewson, N. (1974) Medical knowledge and the patronage system in eighteenth-century England, *Sociology*, 8: 369–85.

Jewson, N. (1976) The disappearance of the sick man from medical cosmology 1770–1870, *Sociology*, 10: 225–44.

JIL (2006) *The Japanese Council on Independent Living Centres*. Available at: www.j-il.jp (accessed 4 February 2008).

Johnson, W. G. (ed.) (1997) The Americans with Disabilities Act: social contract or special privilege?, *The Annals*, 549(January): 1–220 [special issue].

Jones, H. (1999) Integrating a disability perspective into mainstream development programmes: the experience of Save the Children (UK) in East Asia, in E. Stone (ed.), *Disability and Development*. Leeds: Disability Press, pp. 54–73.

Jones, K., and Fowles, A. (1984) *Ideas on Institutions*. London: Routlege & Kegan Paul.

Jones, K., Brown, J., and Bradshaw, J. (1978) *Issues in Social Policy*. London: Routledge & Kegan Paul.

Jones, M., and Marks, L. (eds) (1999) *Disability, Divers-ability and Legal Change*. The Hague: Kluwer Law International/Martinus Nijhoff.

Jonsson, T., and Wiman, R. (2001) *Education, Poverty and Disability in Developing Countries*. Available at: http://siteresources.worldbank.org/DISABILITY/Resources/Education/PovJonsson.pdf (accessed 16 May 2008).

Jordan, B. (1998) *The New Politics of Welfare: Social justice in a global context*. London: Sage.

Jordan, B. (2000) *Social Work and the Third Way*. London: Sage.

Joseph Rowntree Foundation (Lifetime Homes Group) (1997) *Building Lifetime Homes*. York: York Publishing Services.

Kalyanpur, M. (1996) The influences of Western special education on community-based services in India, *Disability & Society*, 11(2): 249–69.

Kalyanpur, M. (2008) Equality, quality and quantity: challenges in inclusive education policy and service provision in India, *International Journal of Inclusive Education*, 12(3): 243–62.

Karpf, A. (1988) *Doctoring the Media*. London: Routledge.

Kassebaum, G., and Baumann, B. (1965) Dimensions of the sick role in chronic illness, *Journal of Health and Social Behaviour*, 6(1): 16–25.

Katsui, H. (2006) Human rights and disabled people in the South, in A. Teittinen (ed.), *Vammaisten Ihmisoikeuksista Etäiiä*. Helsinki: Vliopistopaino, pp. 86–119. Available at: www.disability-archive.leeds.ac.uk (accessed 5 June 2008).

Kaye, H. S. (1998) *Is the Status of People with Disabilities Improving?* Abstract 21. San Francisco: Disability Statistics Center, University of California.

Keating, F., and Robertson, D. (2004) Fear, black people and mental illness: a vicious circle?, *Health & Social Care in the Community*, 12(5): 439–47.

Keeley, H., Redley, M., Holland, A. J., and Clare, I. (2008) Participation in the 2005 general election by adults with intellectual disabilities, *Journal of Intellectual Disability Research*, 52(3): 175–81.

Keith, L. (1992) Who cares wins: women, caring and disability, *Disability & Society*, 7(2): 167–75.

Keith, L., and Morris, J. (1996) Easy targets: a disability rights perspective on the 'children as carers' debate, in J. Morris (ed.), *Encounters with Strangers*. London: Women's Press, pp. 89–115.

Kellard, K., Adelman, L., Cebulla, A., and Heaver, C. (2002) *From Job Seekers to Job Keepers: Job retention, advancement and the role of in-work support programmes*.

Department for Work and Pensions, Research Report no. 170. Leeds: Corporate Document Services.

Kelly, M. P. (1992a) *Colitis*. London: Routledge.

Kelly, M. P. (1992b) Self, identity and radical surgery, *Sociology of Health & Illness*, 14(3): 390–415.

Kemshall, H. (2002) *Risk, Social Policy and Welfare*. Buckingham: Open University Press.

Kent, D. (1987) Disabled women: portraits in fiction and drama, in A. Gartner and T. Joe (eds), *Images of the Disabled, Disabling Images*. New York and London: Praeger, pp. 47–63.

Keown, J. (2002) *Euthanasia, Ethics and Public Policy: An argument against legislation*. Cambridge: Cambridge University Press.

Kerr, A., and Shakespeare, T. (2002) *Genetic Politics: From eugenics to genome*. Cheltenham: New Clarion Press.

Kestenbaum, A. (1993a) *Making Community Care a Reality*. Nottingham: Independent Living Fund.

Kestenbaum, A. (1993b) *Taking Care in the Market*. Nottingham: Independent Living Fund.

Kevles, D. J. (1985) *In the Name of Eugenics: Genetics and the uses of human heredity*. New York: Knopf.

Kevles, D. J. (1995) *The Physician: The history of a scientific community in modern America*. New York: Vintage.

Kim, S., Larson, S. A., and Lakin, K. C. (2001) Behavioural outcomes of deinstitutionalisation for people with intellectual disability: a review of US studies conducted between 1980 and 1999, *Journal of Intellectual & Developmental Disability*, 26(1): 35–50.

King's Fund Centre (1980) *An Ordinary Life: Comprehensive locally based residential services for mentally handicapped people*. Project Paper no 24. London: King's Fund Centre.

Kisanji, J. (1995) Attitudes and beliefs about disability, in B. O'Toole and R. McConkey (eds), *Innovations in Developing Countries for People with Disabilities*. Chorley: Liseaux Hall, pp. 51–69.

Kitsuse, J. I., and Cicourel, A. V. (1963) A note on the uses of official statistics, *Social Problems*, 11(2): 131–9.

Kittay, E. F. (1999) *Love's Labour: Essays on women, equality, and dependency*. New York: Routledge.

Kitzinger, J. (1993) Media messages and what people know about acquired immune deficiency syndrome, in Glasgow University Media Group, *Getting the Message*. London: Routledge, pp. 271–304.

Klobas, L. E. (1988) *Disability Drama in Television and Film*. Jefferson, NC: McFarland.

Krause, E. (1977) *Power and Illness: The political sociology of health and medical care*. Oxford: Elsevier.

Kriegel, L. (1987) The cripple in literature, in A. Gartner and T. Joe (eds), *Images of the Disabled, Disabling Images*. New York and London: Praeger, pp. 31–46.

Kurtz, R. A. (1977) *Social Aspects of Mental Retardation*. Lexington, MA: Lexington Books.

Ladd, P. (1988) Hearing impaired or British Sign Language users: social policies and the deaf community, *Disability, Handicap & Society*, 3(2): 195–200.

Lakey, J. (1994) *Caring about Independence: Disabled people and the Independent Living Fund*. London: Policy Studies Institute.

Lamb, B., and Layzell, S. (1994) *Disabled in Britain: A world apart*. London: Scope.

Lamb, B., and Layzell, S. (1995) *Disabled in Britain: Counting on community care*. London: Scope.

Lang, R. (1999) Empowerment and CBR? Issues raised by the South Indian experience, in E. Stone (ed.), *Disability and Development: Learning from action and research on disability in the majority world*. Leeds: Disability Press, pp. 130–48.

Lang, R. (2000) The role of NGOs in the process of empowerment and social transformation of people with disabilities, in M. Thomas and M. J. Thomas (eds), *Selected Readings in Community Based Rehabilitation, Series 1*. Bangalore: Asia Pacific Disability Rehabilitation Journal, pp. 1–20.

Larson, M. (1977) *The Rise of Professionalism*. Berkeley: University of California Press.

Laurance, J. (2003) *Pure Madness: How fear drives the mental health system*. London: Routledge.

Lawson, A., and Gooding, C. (eds) (2005) *Disability Rights in Europe: From theory to practice*. Oxford: Hart.

Lawson, D. (2009) John Humphrys: 'assisted suicide should be legalised', *The Times*, 29 March. Available at: www.timesonline.co.uk/tol/news/uk/health/article5992844.ece (accessed 22 July 2009).

Lawton, D. (1998) *Complex Numbers: Families with more than one disabled child*. York: SPRU.

Layder, D. (1997) *Modern Social Theory*. London: UCL Press.

Leadbetter, C. (2004) *Personalisation through Participation: A new script for public services*. London: Demos.

Lee, P. (2002) Shooting for the moon: politics and disability at the beginning of the 21st century, in C. Barnes, M. Oliver and L. Barton (eds), *Disability Studies Today*. Cambridge: Polity, pp. 139–61.

Lemert, E. (1951) *Social Pathology*. New York: McGraw Hill.

Lemert, E. (1967) *Human Deviance, Social Problems and Social Control*. Englewood Cliffs, NJ: Prentice-Hall.

Lent, A., and Arend, N. (2004) *Making Choices: How can choice improve local public services?* London: New Local Government Network.

Leonard, P. (1997) *Postmodern Welfare*. London: Sage.

Lester, H., and Tritter, J. Q. (2005) 'Listen to my madness': understanding the experiences of people with serious mental illness, *Sociology of Health & Illness*, 27(5): 649–69.

Levitas, R. (1998) *The Inclusive Society: Social exclusion and New Labour*. Basingstoke: Palgrave Macmillan.

Lewis, C., McQuade, J., and Thomas, C. (2004) *Measuring Physical Access Barriers to Services: 'Snapshot' research in 4 town/city centres in Britain*. London: Disability Rights Commission.

Liggett, H. (1988) Stars are not born: an interpretive approach to the politics of disability, *Disability, Handicap & Society*, 3(3): 263–76.

Light, R. (2002) A real horror story: the abuse of disabled people's human rights, *Tribune*, June. Available at: www.daa.org.uk/e_tribune/e_2002_06_hr.htm (accessed 8 January 2008).

Lindow, V., and Morris, J. (1995) *Service User Involvement: Synthesis of findings and experience in the field of community care*. York: Joseph Rowntree Foundation.

Link, B., and Phelan, J. (2001) Conceptualising stigma, *Annual Review of Sociology*, 27: 363–85.

Linton, S. (1998a) *Claiming Disability: Knowledge and identity*. New York: New York University Press.

Linton, S. (1998b) Disability studies: not disability studies, *Disability & Society*, 13(4): 525–41.

Lipsky, M. (1980) *Street-Level Bureaucracy: Dilemmas of the individual in public services*. New York: Russell Sage.

Lister, R. (1997) *Citizenship: Feminist perspectives*. Basingstoke: Macmillan.

Liton, S. A. (2000) Integrating people with disabilities into development programmes: some lessons from Oxfam – Bangladesh, *Asia Pacific Disability Rehabilitation Journal*, 11(1): 34–5.

Littlewood, R., and Lipsedge, M. (1997) *Aliens and Alienists*. 3rd edn, London: Routledge.

Lloyd, L. (2000) Caring about carers: only half the picture?, *Critical Social Policy*, 20(1): 136–50.

Lloyd, L. (2002) Caring relationships: beyond 'carers' and 'service users', in K. Stalker (ed.), *Reconceptualising Work with 'Carers': New directions for policy and research*. London: Jessica Kingsley, pp. 37–55.

Lloyd, M. (1992) 'Does she boil eggs?': Towards a feminist model of disability, *Disability, Handicap & Society*, 7(3): 207–21.

Lloyd, T. (1993) *The Charity Business: The new philanthropists*. London: John Murray.

Locker, D. (1983) *Disability and Disadvantage*. London: Tavistock.

Lomas, A. (2006) Care managers and direct payments, in J. Leece and J. Bornat (eds), *Developments in Direct Payments*, Bristol: Policy Press, pp. 237–49.

Longmore, P. (1987) Screening stereotypes: images of disabled people in television and motion pictures, in A. Gartner and T. Joe (eds), *Images of the Disabled, Disabling Images*. New York and London: Praeger, pp. 65–78.

Longmore, P. (1995) The second phase: from disability rights to disability culture, *Disability Rag and Resource*, 16: 4–11.

Longmore, P. K. (1997) Conspicuous contribution and American cultural dilemmas: telethon rituals of cleansing and renewal, in D. T. Mitchell and S. L. Snyder (eds), *The Body and Physical Difference: Discourses of disability*. Ann Arbor: University of Michigan Press, pp. 134–58.

Longmore, P. K., and Goldberger, D. (2000) The League of the Physically Handicapped and the Great Depression: a case study in the new disability history, *Journal of American History*, 87(3): 888–922.

Longmore, P. K., and Omansky, L. (eds) (2001) *The New Disability History: American perspectives*. New York: New York University Press.

Lonsdale, S. (1990) *Women and Disability*. London: Macmillan.

Lord, J., and Hutchinson, P. (2003) Individualised support and funding: building blocks for capacity building and inclusion, *Disability & Society*, 18(1): 71–86.

Lowe, R. (1993) *The Welfare State in Britain since 1945*. London: Macmillan.

Lupton, D. (1994) *Medicine as Culture*. London: Sage.

Lyotard, J.-F. (1984) *The Postmodern Condition: A report on knowledge*, trans. G. Bennington and B. Massumi. Manchester: Manchester University Press.

McAnulla. S. (2006) *British Politics: A critical introduction*. London: Continuum.

McCarthy, M. (1999) *Sexuality and Women with Learning Disabilities*. London: Jessica Kingsley.

McCormack, M. (1992) *Special Children, Special Needs: Families talk about living with mental handicap*. Wellingborough: Thorson.

MacDonald, R. (1995) Disability and planning policy guidance. Paper for Access Sub-Committee, Oxford City Council, 7 March. School of Planning, Oxford Brookes University.

McIntyre, S. (1977) *Single and Pregnant*. London: Croom Helm.

Mack, J., and Lansley, S. (1985) *Poor Britain*. London: Allen & Unwin.

McKinlay, J., and Arches, J. (1985) Towards the proletarianisation of physicians, *International Journal of Health Services*, 15(2): 161–95.

McKinlay, J., and Marceau, L. (2002) The end of the golden age of doctoring, *International Journal of Health Services*, 32(2): 379–416.

Macklin, R. (2003) Dignity is a useless concept, *British Medical Journal*, 327(7429): 1419–20.

McLean, A. (2000) From ex-patient alternatives to consumer options: consequences of consumerism for psychiatric consumers and the ex-patient movement, *International Journal of Health Services*, 30(4): 821–47.

McLean, C., Campbell, C., and Cornish, F. (2003) African-Caribbean interactions with mental health services in the UK: experiences and expectations of exclusion as (re)productive of health inequalities, *Social Science & Medicine*, 56(3): 657–69.

McLean, S. A. M., and Williamson, L. (2007) *Impairment and Disability: Law and ethics at the beginning and end of life*. London: Routledge-Cavendish.

McQuail, D. (ed.) (1972) *Sociology of Mass Communications: Selected readings*. Harmondsworth: Penguin.

MacRae, H. (1999) Managing courtesy stigma: the case of Alzheimer's disease, *Sociology of Health & Illness*, 21(1): 54–70.

McRuer, R. (2006) *Crip Theory: Cultural signs of queerness and disability*. New York: New York University Press.

Mansell, J. (2006) Deinstitutionalisation and community living: progress, problems and priorities, *Journal of Intellectual & Developmental Disability*, 31(2): 65–76.

Mansell, J., and Ericsson, K. (eds) (1996) *Deinstitutionalisation and Community Living: Intellectual disability services in Britain, Scandinavia and the USA*. London: Chapman & Hall.

Marks, D. (1999) *Disability: Controversial debates and psychosocial perspectives*. London: Routledge.

Marshall, T. H. (1950) *Citizenship and Social Class*. Cambridge: Cambridge University Press.

Martin, J., and White, A. (1988) *OPCS Surveys of Disability in Great Britain: Report 2 – The financial circumstances of disabled adults living in private households*. London: HMSO.

Martin, J., Meltzer, H., and Elliot, D. (1988) *OPCS Surveys of Disability in Great Britain: Report 1 – The prevalence of disability among adults*. London: HMSO.

Martin, J., White, A., and Meltzer, H. (1989) *OPCS Surveys of Disability in Great Britain: Report 4 – Disabled adults: services, transport and employment*. London: HMSO.

Martin, J. P., with Evans, D. (1984) *Hospitals in Trouble*. Oxford: Blackwell.

Måseide, P. (1991) Possibly abusive, often benign, and always necessary: on power and domination in medical practice, *Sociology of Health & Illness*, 13(4): 545–61.

Mason, M. (1990) Internalised oppression, in R. Rieser and M. Mason (eds), *Disability Equality in the Classroom: A human rights issue*. London: Inner London Education Authority, pp. 27–8.

Mason, M. (1992) A nineteen parent family, in J. Morris (ed.), *Alone Together: Voices of single mothers*. London: Women's Press, pp. 112–25.

Massie, B. (2009) 'Equality bill disappointing', says Sir Bert, *Disability Now*, June: 10.

Mathieson, C. M., and Stam, H. J. (1995) Renegotiating identity: cancer narratives, *Sociology of Health & Illness*, 17(3): 283–306.

Mayor of London (2007) *Housing Choice for Disabled Londoners*. London: Greater London Authority.

Mbogoni, M. (2003) On the application of the ICIDH and ICF in developing countries: evidence from the United Nations Disability Statistics Database (DISTAT), *Disability & Rehabilitation*, 25(11): 644–58.

Meekosha, H., and Dowse, L. (1997a) Enabling citizenship: gender, disability and citizenship in Australia, *Feminist Review*, 57(autumn): 45–72.

Meekosha, H., and Dowse, L. (1997b) Distorting images, invisible images: gender, disability and the media, *Media International Australia*, 84(May): 91–101.

Meltzer, H., Gatward, R., Goodman, R., and Ford, T. (2000) *Mental Health of Children and Adolescents in Great Britain*. London: Office for National Statistics.

Meltzer, H., Singleton, N., Lee, A., Bebbington, P., Brugha, T., and Jenkins, R. (2002) *The Social and Economic Circumstances of Adults with Mental Disorders*. London: HMSO.

Meltzer, H., Smyth, M., and Robus, N. (1989) *OPCS Surveys of Disability in Great Britain: Report 6 – Disabled children, services, transport and education*. London: HMSO.

Melucci, A. (1980) The symbolic challenge of contemporary movements, *Social Research*, 52(4): 789–816.

Melucci, A. (1989) *Nomads of the Present: Social movements and individual needs in contemporary society*. London: Hutchinson.

Mencap (2007) *Voting Rights in Political Elections*. London: Mencap.

Mercer, G. (2005) Job retention: a new policy priority for disabled people, in A. Roulstone and C. Barnes (eds), *Working Futures*. Bristol: Policy Press, pp. 107–20.

Meredith Davies, B. (1982) *The Disabled Child and Adult*. London: Balliere Tindall.

Merton, R. K. (1966) Social problems and sociological theory, in R. K. Merton and R. A. Nisbet (eds), *Contemporary Social Problems*. 2nd edn, New York: Harcourt, Brace & World, pp. 775–823.

Merton, R. K., and Nisbet, R. A. (eds) (1966) *Contemporary Social Problems*. 2nd edn, New York: Harcourt, Brace & World.

Michailakis, D. (2002) The systems theory concept of disability: one is not born a disabled person, one is observed to be one, *Disability & Society*, 18(2): 209–29.

Miles, M. (1983) *Attitudes towards People with Disabilities after I.Y.D.P. (1981) with Suggestions for Promoting Positive Changes*. Peshawar, Pakistan: Mental Health Centre.

Miles, M. (1992) Concepts of mental retardation in Pakistan: toward cross-cultural and historical perspectives, *Disability, Handicap & Society*, 7(3): 235–55.

Miles, M. (1995) Disability in an eastern religious context: historical perspectives, *Disability & Society*, 10(1): 49–69.

Miles, M. (2003) *International strategies for disability-related work in developing countries: historical, modern and critical reflections*. Available at: www.independentliving.org/docs7/miles200701.html (accessed 26 October 2007).

Miles, M. (2006) Social responses to disability and poverty in economically weaker countries: research, trends, critique, and lessons not usually learnt. Annotated bibliography of modern and historical material. Available at: www.independentliving.org/docs7/miles200603.html (accessed 26 October 2007).

Miles, S. (1996) Engaging with the disability rights movement: the experience of community-based rehabilitation in Southern Africa, *Disability & Society*, 11(4): 501–17.

Miles, S. (1999) Creating conversations: the evolution of the enabling education network, in E. Stone (ed.), *Disability and Development: Learning from action and research in the majority world*. Leeds: Disability Press, pp. 74–88.

Miles, S., and Ahuja, A. (2007) Learning from difference: sharing international experiences of developments in inclusive education, in L. Forian (ed.), *The Sage Handbook of Special Education*. London: Sage, pp. 131–45.

Miller, E. J., and Gwynne, G. V. (1972) *A Life Apart*. London: Tavistock.

Miller, O., Keil, S., and Cobb, R. (2005) *A Review of the Literature on Accessible Curricula, Qualifications and Assessment*. London: Disability Rights Commission.

Mills, C. W. (1970) *The Sociological Imagination*. Harmondsworth: Penguin.

Milner, A., and Browitt, J. (2002) *Contemporary Cultural Theory*. 2nd edn, London: Routledge.

Minde, K. S., Hackett, J. D., Killov, D., and Silver, S. (1972) How they grow up: 41 physically handicapped children and their families, *American Journal of Psychiatry*, 128(12): 1554–60.

Ministry of Health (1948) *National Assistance Act, 1948, Circular 87/48*, 7 June. London: HMSO.

Ministry of Health (1950) *Report of the Ministry of Health for the Year ended 31 March 1949*, Cmd 7910. London: HMSO.

Mishler, E. G. (1981) Critical perspectives on the biomedical model, in E. G. Mishler, L. A. Singham, S. T. Hauser, R. Liem, S. D. Osherson and N. E. Waxler (eds), *Social Contexts of Health, Illness, and Patient Care*. Cambridge: Cambridge University Press, pp. 1–23.

Mitchell, D. T. (2002) Narrative prosthesis and the materiality of metaphor, in S. L. Snyder, B. J. Brueggemann and R. Garland-Thomson (eds), *Disability Studies: Enabling the humanities*. New York: Modern Language Association of America, pp. 15–30.

Mitchell, D. T., and Snyder, S. L. (eds) (1997) *The Body and Physical Difference: Discourses of disability*. Ann Arbor: University of Michigan Press.

Mitchell, D. T., and Snyder, S. L. (2000) *Narrative Prosthesis: Disability and the dependencies of discourse*. Ann Arbor: University of Michigan Press.

Mitchell, D. T., and Snyder, S. L. (2001) Representation and its discontents, in G. L. Albrecht, K. D. Seelman and M. Bury (eds), *Handbook of Disability Studies*. London: Sage, pp. 195–218.

Mitchell, P. (1997) The impact of self-advocacy on families, *Disability & Society*, 12(1): 43–56.

Moore, N. (1995) *Access to Information: A survey of the provision of disability information*. London: Policy Studies Institute.

Morris, J. (1989) *Able Lives: Women's experience of paralysis*. London: Women's Press.

Morris, J. (1991) *Pride against Prejudice: Transforming attitudes to disability*. London: Women's Press.

Morris, J. (1992) Personal and political: a feminist perspective in researching physical disability, *Disability, Handicap & Society*, 7(2): 157–66.

Morris, J. (1993a) *Independent Lives, Community Care and Disabled People*. Basingstoke: Macmillan.

Morris, J. (1993b) Feminism and disability, *Feminist Review*, 43(autumn): 57–70.

Morris, J. (1994a) *The Shape of Things to Come? User led services*. London: National Institute for Social Work.

Morris, J. (1994b) Community care or independent living?, *Critical Social Policy*, 40(1): 24–45.

Morris, J. (ed.) (1996) *Encounters with Strangers*. London: Women's Press.

Morris, J. (1997) Care or empowerment? A disability rights perspective, *Social Policy & Administration*, 31(1): 54–60.

Morris, J. (1999) *Hurtling into a Void: Transition to adulthood for young disabled people with 'complex health and support needs'*. York: Joseph Rowntree Foundation.

Morris, J. (2002) *Moving into Adulthood*. York: Joseph Rowntree Foundation.

Morris, J. (2004) Independent living and community care: a disempowering framework, *Disability & Society*, 19(5): 427–42.

Morris, J., Abbott, D., and Ward, L. (2002) At home or away? An exploration of policy and practice in the placement of disabled children at residential schools, *Children & Society*, 16(1): 3–16.

Morris, P. (1969) *Put Away: A sociological study of institutions for the mentally retarded*. London: Routledge & Kegan Paul.

Morrison, E., and Finkelstein, V. (1992) Culture as struggle: access to power, in S. Lees (ed.), *Disability Arts in London*, Part 2. London: Shape.

Morrison, E., and Finkelstein, V. (1993) Broken arts and cultural repair: the role of culture in the empowerment of disabled people, in J. Swain, V. Finkelstein, S. French and M. Oliver (eds), *Disabling Barriers – Enabling Environments*. London: Sage, pp. 122–7.

Multiple Sclerosis Society (2008) *Research We Fund by Category*. Available at: www.mssociety.org.uk/research/research_we_fund/ccq_cat_pie.html (accessed 16 June 2008).

Mulvany, J. (2000) Disability, impairment or illness? The relevance of the social model of disability to the study of mental disorder, *Sociology of Health & Illness*, 22(5): 582–601.

Murphy, R. (1987) *The Body Silent*. New York: Henry Holt.

Murray, P. (2002) *Disabled Teenagers' Experiences of Access to Inclusive Leisure*. York: Joseph Rowntree Foundation.

National Council on Disability (2000) *Promises to Keep: A decade of federal enforcement of the Americans with Disabilities Act*. Washington, DC: National Council on Disability.

Navarro, V. (1976) *Medicine under Capitalism*. London: Croom Helm.

Navarro, V. (1978) *Class Struggle, the State and Medicine*. London: Martin Robertson.

Nazroo, J. Y. (1997) *The Health of Britain's Ethnic Minorities*. London: Policy Studies Institute.

Ncube, J. (2006) Capacity building with DPOs in Mozambique, in B. Albert (ed.), *In or Out of the Mainstream? Lessons from research on disability and development cooperation*. Leeds: Disability Press, pp. 150–62.

Needham, C. (2003) *Citizen-Consumers: New Labour's marketplace democracy*. London: Catalyst.

Neubeck, K. J. (1979) *Social Problems: A critical approach*. New York: Random House.

Newman, J. (2001) *Modernising Governance: New Labour, policy and society*. London: Sage.

NHS (2008) *Community Care Statistics 2006–07: Referrals, assessments and packages of care for adults, England*. London: Information Centre.

Nicolaisen, I. (1995) Persons and nonpersons: disability and personhood among the Punan Bah of Central Borneo, in B. Ingstad and S. R. Whyte (eds), *Disability and Culture*. Berkeley: University of California Press, pp. 38–55.

Nirje, B. (1969) The normalization principle and its human management implications, in R. Kugel and W. Wolfensberger (eds), *Changing Patterns in Residential Services for the Mentally Retarded*. Washington, DC: President's Committee on Mental Retardation, pp. 179–95.

Nkeli, J. (1998) How to overcome double discrimination in South Africa. Paper presented at the international conference Legislation for Human Rights, Stockholm, 24 August. Available at: http://independentliving.org/docs1/hr5.html (accessed 15 May 2008).

Noble, M., Platt, L., Smith, G., and Daly, M. (1997) The spread of disability living allowance, *Disability & Society*, 12(5): 741–51.

Norden, M. (1994) *The Cinema of Isolation: A history of disability in the movies*. New Brunswick, NJ: Rutgers University Press.

Norwich, B. (1994) *Segregation and Inclusion: English LEA statistics 1988–92*. Bristol: Centre for Studies on Inclusive Education.

Oakley, A. (1980) *Women Confined: Towards a sociology of childbirth*. Oxford: Martin Robertson.

O'Brien, J. (1987) A guide to life style planning: using the activities catalogue to integrate services and natural support systems, in B. W. Wilcox and G. T. Bellamy (eds), *The Activities Catalogue: An alternative curriculum for youth and adults with severe disabilities*. Baltimore: Paul H. Brookes, pp. 175–89.

ODPM (Office of the Deputy Prime Minister) (2005) *Sustainable Communities: Homes for all – a five year plan*. London: ODPM.

Offe, C. (1985) New social movements: challenging the boundaries of institutional politics, *Social Research*, 52(4): 817–68.

Ofsted (2004) *Special Educational Needs and Disability: Towards inclusive schools*. London: Ofsted.

Oldman, C., and Beresford, B. (2000) Home, sick home: using the housing experiences of disabled children to suggest a new theoretical framework, *Housing Studies*, 15(3): 429–42.

Oliver, J. (1995) Counselling disabled people: a counsellor's perspective, *Disability & Society*, 10(3): 261–79.

Oliver, J. (2009) Equality quango in turmoil as two quit, *The Times*, 19 July. Available at: www.timesonline.co.uk/tol/news/politics/article6719184.ece (accessed 21 July 2009).

Oliver, M. (1983) *Social Work with Disabled People*. Basingstoke: Macmillan.

Oliver, M. (1986) Social policy and disability: some theoretical issues, *Disability, Handicap & Society*, 1(1): 5–17.

Oliver, M. (1990) *The Politics of Disablement*. Basingstoke: Macmillan.

Oliver, M. (1992) Changing the social relations of research production?, *Disability, Handicap & Society*, 7(2): 101–14.

Oliver, M. (1996a) *Understanding Disability: From theory to practice*. London: Macmillan.

Oliver, M. (1996b) A sociology of disability or a disablist sociology?, in L. Barton (ed.), *Disability & Society: Emerging Issues and Insights*. London: Longman, pp. 18–42.

Oliver, M. (2004) The social model in action: if I had a hammer?, in C. Barnes and G. Mercer (eds), *Implementing the Social Model of Disability: Theory and research*. Leeds: Disability Press, pp. 18–31.

Oliver, M., and Barnes, C. (1991) Discrimination, disability and welfare: from needs to rights, in I. Bynoe, M. Oliver and C. Barnes (eds), *Equal Rights for Disabled People: The case for a new law*. London: Institute of Public Policy Research, pp. 7–16.

Oliver, M., and Barnes, C. (1998) *Social Policy and Disabled People: From exclusion to inclusion*. London: Longman.

Oliver, M., and Barnes, C. (2006) Disability politics: where did it all go wrong?, *Coalition*, August: 8–13.

Oliver, M., and Hasler, F. (1987) Disability and self-help: a case study of the Spinal Injuries Association, *Disability, Handicap & Society*, 2(2): 113–25.

Oliver, M., and Zarb, G. (1989) The politics of disability: a new approach, *Disability, Handicap & Society*, 4(3): 221–40.

Oliver, M., Zarb, G., Silver, J., Moore, M., and Salisbury, V. (1988) *Walking into Darkness: The experience of spinal cord injury*. Basingstoke: Macmillan.

Olkin, R., and Pledger, C. (2003) Can disability studies and psychology join hands?, *American Psychologist*, 58(4): 296–304.

Ollman, B. (1971) *Alienation: Marx's conception of man in capitalist society*. London: Cambridge University Press.

Olsen, R., and Clarke, H. (2003) *Parenting and Disability: Disabled parents' experiences of raising children*. Bristol: Policy Press.

ONS (2004a) *Living in Britain: Results from the 2002 General Household Survey*. London: Office for National Statistics.

ONS (2004b) *The Omnibus Survey 2004*. London: Office for National Statistics.

ONS (2005) *Labour Force Survey, April–June, 2005*. Available at www.statistics.gov.uk/StatBase (accessed 10 November 2006).

ONS (2006) *Labour Force Survey, April–June, 2006*. Available at www.statistics.gov.uk/StatBase (accessed 15 November 2006).

Palmer, G., MacInnes, T., and Kenway, P. (2007) *Monitoring Poverty and Social Exclusion 2007*. York: York Publishing Services/Joseph Rowntree Foundation.

Palmer, M. (1999) *Moral Problems in Medicine: A practical coursebook*. Cambridge: Lutterworth Press.

Parker, G. (1993) *With this Body: Caring and Disability in Marriage*. Buckingham: Open University Press.

Parker, G., and Clarke, H. (2002) Making the ends meet: do carers and disabled people have a common agenda?, *Policy & Politics*, 30(3): 347–59.

Parker, R., and Aggleton, P. (2003) HIV and AIDS-related stigma and discrimination: a conceptual framework and implications for action, *Social Science & Medicine*, 57(1): 13–24.

Parkes, C. M. (1975) *Bereavement: Studies of grief in adult life.* Harmondsworth: Penguin.

Parsons, T. (1951) *The Social System.* New York: Free Press.

Parsons, T. (1958) Definitions of health and illness in the light of American values and social structure, in E. G. Jaco (ed.), *Patients, Physicians, and Illness.* New York: Free Press, pp. 165–87.

Parsons, T. (1975) The sick role and the role of the physician reconsidered, *Milbank Memorial Fund Quarterly: Health and Society*, 53(3): 257–78.

Peace, S. M., Kellaher, L. A., and Willcocks, D. M. (1997) *Re-evaluating Residential Care.* Buckingham: Open University Press.

Pearson, C. (2000) Money talks? Competing discourses in the implementation of direct payments, *Critical Social Policy*, 20(4): 459–77.

Peck, E., and Barker, I. (1997) Users as partners in mental health: ten years of experience, *Journal of Interprofessional Care*, 11(3): 269–77.

Peck, S. (2007) A disabled prime minister', *Disability Now*, July: 16.

Peck, S. (2009) Rieser's reservations on ratification, *Disability Now*, April: 7.

Pernick, D. (1997) Defining the defective: eugenics, aesthetics and mass culture in early twentieth century America, in D. T. Mitchell and S. L. Snyder (eds), *The Body and Physical Difference.* Ann Arbor: University of Michigan Press, pp. 89–110.

Perrin, B., and Nirje, B. (1989) Setting the record straight: a critique of some frequent misconceptions of the normalisation principle, in A. Brechin and J. Walmsley (eds), *Making Connections: Reflecting on the lives and experiences of people with learning difficulties.* London: Hodder & Stoughton, pp. 220–8.

Pescosolido, B., Brooks Gardner, C., and Lubell, K. (1998) How people get into mental health services: stories of choice, coercion and 'muddling through' from 'first-timers', *Social Science & Medicine*, 46(2): 275–86.

Peters, S. (2000) Is there a disability culture? A syncretisation of three possible world views, *Disability & Society*, 15(4): 583–601.

Peters, S. (2003) *Inclusive Education: Achieving education for all by including those with disabilities and special education needs.* Washington, DC: World Bank.

Pfeiffer, D. (1994) The Americans with Disabilities Act: costly mandates or civil rights?, *Disability & Society*, 9(4): 533–42.

Pfeiffer, D. (2000) The devils are in the detail: the ICIDH2 and the disability movement, *Disability & Society*, 15(7): 1079–82.

Phillipson, C. (1982) *Capitalism and the Construction of Old Age.* London: Macmillan.

Philo, G. (1990) *Seeing and Believing.* London: Routledge.

Philo, G. (ed.) (1996) *Media and Mental Distress.* London: Longman.

Pick, J. (1992) Why have there been no great disabled artists?, *Disability Arts Magazine*, 2(4): 18–20.

Pilgrim, D., and Rogers, A. (1993) *A Sociology of Mental Health and Illness.* Buckingham: Open University Press.

Pilgrim, D. and Treacher, A. (1992) *Clinical Psychology Observed.* London: Routledge.

Pillai, R., Stanley, K., Bennett, J., Stone, L., and Withers, K. (2005) *Disability 2005: The citizenship of disabled people in Britain in 2005.* London: Institute for Public Policy Research for the Disability Rights Commission.

Pillai, R., Rankin, J., Stanley, K., Bennett, J., Stone, L., and Withers, K. (2007) *Disability 2020: Opportunities for the full and equal citizenship of disabled people in Britain in 2020.* London: Institute for Public Policy Research for the Disability Rights Commission.

Pinder, R. (1996) Sick-but-fit or fit-but-sick? Ambiguity and identity at the workplace, in C. Barnes and G. Mercer (eds), *Exploring the Divide: Illness and Disability.* Leeds: Disability Press, pp. 135–56.

Pointon, A. (1999) Out of the closet: new images of disability in the civil rights campaign, in B. Franklin (ed.), *Social Policy, the Media and Misrepresentation.* London: Routledge, pp. 222–37.

Pointon, A., and Davies, C. (eds) (1997) *Framed: Interrogating Disability in the Media.* London: British Film Institute.

Pothier, D., and Devlin, R. (eds) (2006) *Critical Disability Theory: Essays in philosophy, politics, policy and law.* Vancouver: UBC Press.

Pound, P., Gompertz, P., and Ebrahim, S. (1998) Illness in the context of older age: the case of stroke, *Sociology of Health & Illness,* 20(4): 489–506.

Powell, M. (2000) New Labour and the third way in the British welfare state: a new and distinctive approach?, *Critical Social Policy,* 20(1): 39–60.

Pragnell, M., Spence, L., and Moore, R. (2000) *The Market Potential for Smart Homes.* York: Yorkshire Publishing Services.

Prideaux, S., Roulstone, A., Harris, J., and Barnes, C. (2009) Disabled people and direct payments: conceptualising work and welfare in the 21st century, *Disability & Society,* 24(5).

Priebe, S., Badesconyi, A., Fioritti, A., Hansson, L., Kilian, R., Torres-Gonzalves, F., Turner, T., and Wiersma, D. (2005) Reinstitutionalisation in mental health care: comparison of data on service provision from six European countries, *British Medical Journal,* 15 January: 123–6.

Priestley, M. (ed.) (2001) *Disability and the Life Course: Global perspectives.* Cambridge: Cambridge University Press.

Priestley, M. (2003) *Disability: A life course approach.* Cambridge: Polity.

Priestley, M. (2005) We're all Europeans now: the social model of disability and social policy in Europe, in C. Barnes and G. Mercer (eds), *The Social Model of Disability: Europe and the majority world.* Leeds: Disability Press, pp. 16–32.

Priestley, M., Jolly, D., Pearson, C., Riddell, S., Barnes, C., and Mercer, G. (2007) Direct payments and disabled people in the UK: supply, demand and devolution, *British Journal of Social Work,* 37(7): 1189–204.

Prout, A. (1986) 'Wet children' and 'little actresses': going sick in primary school, *Sociology of Health & Illness,* 8(2): 113–36.

QCA (Qualifications and Curriculum Authority) (2004) *Inclusive Learning: 2002/03 annual report on curriculum and assessment.* London: QCA.

Quinn, G., McDonagh, M., and Kimber, C. (1993) *Disability Discrimination Laws in the United States, Australia and Canada.* Dublin: Oak Tree Press in association with the National Rehabilitation Board.

Race, D. (1999) Historical development of service provision, in N. Malin (ed.), *Services for People with Learning Disabilities.* London: Routledge, pp. 46–78.

RADAR (Royal Association for Disability and Rehabilitation) (2005) *Campaigns.*

Available at: www.radar.org.uk/radarwebsite/tabid/2/default.aspx (accessed 20 September 2007).

RADAR (Royal Association for Disability and Rehabilitation) (2006) *Assisted Dying: The facts*. London: RADAR.

RADAR (Royal Association for Disability and Rehabilitation) (2009) *Policy Briefing: A single equality duty fit for disabled people*. Available at: www.radar.org.uk/radarwebsite/tabid/245/default.aspx (accessed 21 July 2009).

Radford, J. P. (1994) Intellectual disability and the heritage of modernity, in M. Rioux and M. Bach (eds), *Disability is Not Measles: New research paradigms in disability*. North York, Ontario: Roeher Institute, pp. 9–27.

Radley, A. (1989) Style, discourse and constraint in adjustment to chronic illness, *Sociology of Health & Illness*, 11(3): 230–52.

Radley, A. (1994) *Making Sense of Illness*. London: Sage.

Radley, A., and Green, R. (1987) Illness as adjustment: a methodology and conceptual framework, *Sociology of Health & Illness*, 9(2): 179–207.

Rae, A. (1993) Independent living, personal assistance and disabled women, in C. Barnes (ed.), *Making our own Choices: Independent living, personal assistance and disabled people*. Derby: British Council of Organizations of Disabled People, pp. 47–50.

Ramon, S. (1985) *Psychiatry in Britain: Meaning and policy*. London: Croom Helm.

Ramon, S. (1996) *Mental Health in Europe: Ends, beginnings, and rediscoveries*. Basingstoke: Macmillan.

Rapley, M. (2004) *The Social Construction of Intellectual Disability*. Cambridge: Cambridge University Press.

Ratzka, A. (1992) Independent living, in *World Congress III: Disabled people's equalisation of opportunities*. Vancouver: Disabled Peoples' International, pp. 23–5.

Ratzka, A. (2003) *Independent Living in Sweden*. Available at: www.independent living.org/docs6/ratzka200302b.html (accessed 6 April 2005).

Raveaud, G., and Salais, R. (2001) Fighting against social exclusion in a European knowledge-based society: what principles of action?, in D. G. Mayes, J. Berghman and R. Salais (eds), *Social Exclusion and European Policy*. Cheltenham: Elgar, pp. 47–71.

Rawls, J. (1999) *A Theory of Justice*. Rev. edn, Oxford: Oxford University Press.

Read, J. (2000) *Disability, the Family and Society: Listening to the mothers*. Buckingham: Open University Press.

Reeve, D. (2000) Oppression within the counselling room, *Disability & Society*, 15(4): 669–82.

Richardson, L. (2005) User engagement in public services: policy and implementation, *Benefits*, 13(3): 189–97.

Rieser, R. (1990) Internalised oppression: how it seems to me, in R. Rieser and M. Mason (eds), *Disability Equality in the Classroom: A human rights issue*. London: Inner London Education Authority, pp. 29–32.

Rioux, M. H., and Bach, M. (eds) (1994) *Disability is Not Measles: New research paradigms in disability*. North York, Ontario: Roeher Institute.

Rioux, M. H., Crawford, C., Ticoll, M., and Bach, M. (1997) Uncovering the shape of violence: a research methodology rooted in the experience of people with disabilities, in C. Barnes and G. Mercer (eds), *Doing Disability Research*. Leeds: Disability Press, pp. 190–206.

Roberts, S., Heaver, C., Hill, K., Reninson, J., Stafford, B., Howat, N., Kelly,

G., Krishnan, S., Tapp, P., and Thomas, A. (2004) *Disability in the Workplace: Employers' and service providers' responses to the DDA in 2003 and preparation for 2004 changes*. Research Report 202. London: Department of Work and Pensions.

Robertson, S. (2004) Men and disability, in J. Swain, S. French, C. Barnes and C. Thomas (eds), *Disabling Barriers – Enabling Environments*. 2nd edn, London: Sage, pp. 75–80.

Robinson, C., and Stalker, K. (eds) (1998) *Growing up with Disability*. London: Jessica Kingsley.

Robinson, I. (1988) *Multiple Sclerosis*. London: Routledge.

Robson, P., Begum, N., and Locke, M. (2003) *Increasing User Involvement in Voluntary Organisations*. Bristol: Policy Press.

Robson, P., Locke, M., and Dawson, J. (1997) *Consumerism or Democracy: User involvement in the control of voluntary organisations*. Bristol: Policy Press.

Rock, P. (1979) *The Making of Symbolic Interactionism*. London: Macmillan.

Rock, P. J. (1996) Eugenics and euthanasia: a case for concern for disabled people, particularly disabled women, *Disability & Society*, 11(1): 121–8.

Rogers, L. (1999) Disabled children will be 'sin', says scientist, *Sunday Times*, 4 July: 28.

Rogers, L. (2006) Babies with club foot are aborted. *Sunday Times*, 28 July: 15.

Rose, N. (1986) Psychiatry: the discipline of mental health, in P. Miller and N. Rose (eds), *The Power of Psychiatry*. Cambridge: Polity, pp. 43–84.

Rose, N. (1989) *Governing the Soul: The shaping of the private self*. 2nd edn, London: Free Association Books.

Rosenhan, D. (1973) On being sane in insane places, *Science*, 179: 250–8.

Ross, K. (1997) *Disability and Broadcasting: A view from the margins*. Cheltenham: Cheltenham and Gloucester College of Higher Education.

Roth, J. (1963) *Timetables: Structuring the passage of time in hospital treatment*. New York: Bobbs-Merrill.

Roth, J. (1984) Staff–inmate bargaining tactics in long-term treatment institutions, *Sociology of Health & Illness*, 6(2): 111–31.

Roulstone, A. (1998) *Enabling Technology: Disabled people, work and new technology*. Buckingham: Open University Press.

Royal Commission on the Law Relating to Mental Illness and Mental Deficiency (1957) *Report*. Cmnd 169. London: HMSO.

Russell, M. (1998) *Beyond Ramps: Disability at the end of the social contract – a warning from an uppity crip*. Monroe, ME: Common Courage Press.

Russell, M. (2002) What disability civil rights cannot do: employment and political economy, *Disability & Society*, 17(2): 117–35.

Rustemier, S., and Vaughan, M. (2005) *Segregation Trends: LEAs in England 2002–2004*. Bristol: Centre for Studies on Inclusive Education.

Ryan, J., and Thomas, F. (1980) *The Politics of Mental Handicap*. Harmondsworth: Penguin.

Safilios-Rothschild, C. (1970) *The Sociology and Social Psychology of Disability and Rehabilitation*. New York: Random House.

Safilios-Rothschild, C. (1976) Disabled persons' self-definitions and their implications for rehabilitation, in G. Albrecht (ed.), *The Sociology of Physical Disability and Rehabilitation*. Pittsburgh: University of Pittsburgh Press, pp. 39–56.

Sainsbury, S. (1973) *Measuring Disability*. Occasional Papers on Social Administration, no. 54. London: Bell.

Salmon, P., and Hall, G. M. (2003) Patient empowerment and control: a psychological discourse in the service of medicine, *Social Science & Medicine*, 57(10): 1969–80.

Sancho, J. (2003) *Disabling Prejudice: Attitudes towards disability and its portrayal on television*. Available at: www.bbc.co.uk/guidelines/editorial/guidelines/assets/research/disabling_prejudice.pdf (accessed 20 February 2007).

Sanders, C., Donovan, J., and Dieppe, P. (2002) The significance and consequences of having painful and disabled joints in older age: co-existing accounts of normal and disrupted biographies, *Sociology of Health & Illness*, 24(2): 227–53.

Sanderson, I. (1999) Participation or democratic renewal: from instrumental rationality to communicative rationality, *Policy and Politics*, 27(3): 325–42.

Sapey, B. (2004) Impairment, disability, and loss: reassessing the rejection of loss, *Illness, Crisis & Loss*, 12(1): 1–12.

Sartre, J.-P. (1995) *Truth and Existence*, trans. A. van den Hoven. Chicago: University of Chicago Press.

Saunders, S. (1994) The residential school: a valid choice, *British Journal of Special Education*, 21(2): 64–6.

Saxton, M., and Howe, F. (eds) (1988) *With Wings: An anthology of literature by women with disabilities*. London: Virago.

Sayce, L. (2000) *From Psychiatric Patient to Citizen*. Basingstoke: Macmillan.

Sayers, J. (1982) *Biological Politics: Feminist and anti-feminist perspectives*. London: Tavistock.

Scambler, G. (1989) *Epilepsy*. London: Tavistock and Routledge.

Scambler, G. (2002) *Health and Social Change: A critical social theory*. Buckingham: Open University Press.

Scambler, G. (2004) Re-framing stigma: felt and enacted stigma and challenges to the sociology of chronic and disabling conditions, *Social Theory and Health*, 2(1): 29–46.

Scambler, G., and Higgs, P. (1999) Stratification, class and health: class relations and health inequalities in high modernity, *Sociology*, 33(2): 275–96.

Scambler, G., and Hopkins, A. (1986) Being epileptic: coming to terms with stigma, *Sociology of Health & Illness*, 8(1): 26–43.

Scambler, G., and Kelleher, D. (2006) New social and health movements: issues of representation and change, *Critical Public Health*, 16(3): 219–32.

SCDF (Sacred Congregation of the Doctrine of the Faith) (1980) *Declaration on Euthanasia*. Available at: www.vatican.va/roman_curia/congregations/cfaith/documents/rc_con_cfaith_doc_19800505_euthanasia_en.html (accessed 23 October 2007).

Scheer, J., and Groce, N. (1988) Impairment as a human constant: cross cultural and historical perspectives, *Journal of Social Issues*, 44(1): 23–37.

Scheff, T. J. (1966) *Being Mentally Ill*. New York: Aldine.

Scheper-Hughes, N. (1992) *Death without Weeping: The violence of everyday life in Brazil*. Berkeley: University of California Press.

Scheper-Hughes, N., and Lock, M. (1987) The mindful body: a prolegomenon to future work in medical anthropology, *Medical Anthropology Quarterly*, l(1): 6–41.

Schneidert, M., Hurst, R., Miller, J., and Üstün, B. (2003) The role of the environment in *The International Classification of Functioning, Disability and Health* (ICF), *Disability & Rehabilitation*, 25(11/12): 588–95.

Schuchman, J. S. (1988) *Hollywood Speaks: Deafness and the film entertainment industry*. Urbana: University of Illinois Press.

Scope (2004) *Free2pee*. London: Scope.

Scotch, R. (1988) Disability as the basis for a social movement: advocacy and the politics of definition, *Journal of Social Issues*, 44(1): 159–72.

Scotch, R. (1989) Politics and policy in the history of the disability rights movement, *Milbank Quarterly*, 67(Supplement 2, Part 2): 380–400.

Scott, A. (1990) *Ideology and New Social Movements*. London: Unwin Hyman.

Scott, R. A. (1969) *The Making of Blind Men*. London: Sage.

Scott, R., and Crooks, A. (2005) *Polls Apart 4: Campaigning for accessible democracy*. London: Scope.

Scott, R., and Morris G. (2001) *Polls Apart 3: Campaigning for accessible democracy*. London: Scope.

Scott, S. (2006) The medicalisation of shyness: from social misfits to social fitness, *Sociology of Health & Illness*, 28(2): 133–53.

Scott-Hill, M. (2004) Impairment, difference and 'identity', in J. Swain, S. French, C. Barnes and C. Thomas (eds), *Disabling Barriers – Enabling Environments*. 2nd edn, London: Sage, pp. 87–93.

Scottish Executive (2004) *Social focus on disability 2004*. Available at: www.scotland.gov.uk//resfinds/sfod04-05.asp.html (accessed 15 March 2007).

Scourfield, P. (2007) Social care and the modern citizen: client, consumer, service user, manager and entrepreneur, *British Journal of Social Work*, 37(1): 107–22.

Scull, A. (1979) *Museums of Madness*. London: Allen Lane.

Scull, A. (1984) *Decarceration*. 2nd edn, Cambridge: Polity.

Seale, C. (2006) National survey of end of life decisions made by UK medical practitioners, *Palliative Medicine*, 20(1): 3–10.

Seebohm, F. (1968) *Report of the Committee on Local Authority and Allied Personal Social Services*. Cmnd 3703. London: HMSO [Seebohm Report].

Seidman, S. (1994) *Contested Knowledge: Social theory in the postmodern age*. Oxford: Blackwell.

Sevenhuijsen, S. (1998) *Citizenship and the Ethics of Care: Feminist considerations on justice, morality and politics*. London: Routledge.

Sevenhuijsen, S. (2000) Caring in the third way: the relations between obligation, responsibility and care in third way discourse, *Critical Social Policy*, 20(1): 39–60.

Seymour, W. (1998) *Remaking the Body: Rehabilitation and change*. London: Routledge.

Shakespeare, T. (1992) A response to Liz Crow, *Coalition*, September: 40–2.

Shakespeare, T. (1993) Disabled people's self-organisation: a new social movement?, *Disability, Handicap & Society*, 8(3): 249–64.

Shakespeare, T. (1994) Cultural representations of disabled people: dustbins for disavowal, *Disability & Society*, 9(3): 283–301.

Shakespeare, T. (1995) Back to the future? New genetics and disabled people, *Critical Social Policy*, 44(5): 22–35.

Shakespeare, T. (1999) Art and lies? Representations of disability on film, in M. Corker and S. French. (eds), *Disability Discourse*. Buckingham: Open University Press, pp. 164–72.

Shakespeare, T. W. (2006) *Disability Rights and Wrongs*. London: Routledge.

Shakespeare, T. W. (2009) A chance for dignity in dying: Jane Campbell is wrong. Many terminally ill and disabled people want effective assisted dying legislation. *The Guardian*, 7 July. Available at: www.guardian.co.uk/comment-isfree/2009/jul/07/assisted-dying-terminally-ill-disabled (accessed 7 July 2009).

Shakespeare, T., and Watson, N. (1997) Defending the social model, *Disability & Society*, 12(2): 293–300.

Shakespeare, T., and Watson, N. (2001) The social model of disability: an outdated ideology?, in S. N. Barnartt and B. M. Altman (eds), *Exploring Theories and Expanding Methodologies: Where we are and where we need to go*. Amsterdam: JAI, pp. 9–28.

Shakespeare, T., Gillespie-Sells, K., and Davies, D. (1996) *The Sexual Politics of Disability*. London: Cassell.

Shape (2008) *Arts, Access, Action*. Available at: www.shapearts.org.uk/aboutus. (accessed 2 March 2008).

Shapiro, J. P. (1993) *No Pity: People with disabilities forging a new civil rights movement*. New York: Times Books.

Shariff, A. (1999) *India: Human development report: A profile of Indian states in the 1990s*. Oxford: Oxford University Press.

Sharpley, M., Hutchinson, G., Murray, R., and McKenzie, K. (2001) Understanding the excess of psychosis among the African-Caribbean population in England: review of current hypotheses, *British Journal of Psychiatry*, 178(Supplement): s60–s68.

Shearer, A. (1981a) *Disability: Whose handicap?* Oxford: Blackwell.

Shearer, A. (1981b) A framework for independent living, in A. Walker and P. Townsend (eds), *Disability in Britain: A manifesto of rights*. Oxford: Martin Robertson, pp. 73–90.

Sheldon, A. (2004) Changing technology, in J. Swain, S. French, C. Barnes and C. Thomas (eds), *Disabling Barriers – Enabling Environments*. London: Sage, pp. 155–60.

Sheldon, A. (2005) One world, one people, one struggle? Towards the global implementation of the social model of disability, in C. Barnes and G. Mercer (eds), *The Social Model of Disability: Europe and the majority world*. Leeds: Disability Press, pp. 115–30.

Shilling, C. (1993) *The Body and Social Theory*. London: Sage.

Shilling, C. (2003) *The Body and Social Theory*. 2nd edn, London: Sage.

Sieglar, M., and Osmond, M. (1974) *Models of Madness: Models of medicine*. London: Collier Macmillan.

Silverman, D. (1987) *Communication and Medical Practice: Social relations in the clinic*. London: Sage.

Simeonsson, R. J., Carlson, D., Huntingdon, G. S., McMillen, J. S., and Lytle Brent, J. (2001) Students with disabilities: a national survey of participation in school activities, *Disability & Rehabilitation*, 23(2): 49–63.

Singer, P. (1993) *Practical Ethics*. 2nd edn, Cambridge: Cambridge University Press.

Sivan, A., and Ruskin, H. (2000) *Leisure Education, Community Development, and Populations with Special Needs*. Wellingford: CABI.

SJAC (Silver Jubilee Access Committee) (1979) *Can Disabled People Go Where You Go?* London: Department of Health and Social Security.

Sly, F., Duxbury, R., and Tillsley, C. (1995) Disability and the labour market:

findings from the labour force survey, *Labour Market Trends*, December: 439–57.

Smaje, C. (1995) *Health, 'Race' and Ethnicity: Making sense of the evidence*. London: King's Fund Institute.

Smith, B., and Sparks, A. C. (2004) Men, sport and spinal cord injury: an analysis of metaphors and narrative types, *Disability & Society*, 19(6): 613–26.

Smith, G. D. (ed.) (2003) *Health Inequalities: Life course approaches*. Bristol: Policy Press.

Smith, N., Middleton, S., Ashton-Brooks, K., Cox, L., Dobson, B., and Reith, L. (2004) *Disabled People's Costs of Living: 'More than you would think'*. York: Joseph Rowntree Foundation.

Smith, S., and Jordan, A. (1991) *What the Papers Say and Don't Say about Disability*. London: Spastics Society.

Smyth, M., and Robus, N. (1989) *OPCS Surveys of Disability in Great Britain: Report 5 – The financial circumstances of disabled children living in private households*. London: HMSO.

Snyder, S. L., and Mitchell, D. T. (2001) Re-engaging the body: disability studies and the resistance to embodiment, *Public Culture*, 13(3): 367–89.

Snyder, S. L., and Mitchell, D. T. (2006) *Cultural Locations of Disability*. Chicago: University of Chicago Press.

Snyder, S. L., Brueggemann, B. J., and Garland-Thomson, R. (eds) (2002) *Disability Studies: Enabling the humanities*. New York: Modern Language Association of America.

Sobsey, R. (1994) *Violence and Abuse in the Lives of People with Disabilities*. Baltimore: Brookes.

Söder, M. (1999) *Specialpedagogisk forkning mellan det kliniska och det kontextuella*. Bodo: Nordlandsforskning. NF8/99.

Solberg, B. (2009) Prenatal screening for Down syndrome, in K. Kristiansen, S. Vehmas and T. Shakespeare (eds), *Arguing about Disability: Philosophical perspectives*. London: Routledge, pp. 185–202.

Sontag, S. (1991) *Illness as Metaphor and AIDS and its Metaphors*. London: Penguin.

Spandler, H. (2004) Friend or Foe? Towards a critical assessment of direct payments, *Critical Social Policy*, 24(2): 187–209.

Spandler, H., and Vick, N. (2005) Enabling access to direct payments: an exploration of care co-ordinators' decision making practices, *Journal of Mental Health*, 14(2): 145–55.

Spandler, H., and Vick, N. (2006) Opportunities for independent living using direct payments in mental health, *Health & Social Care in the Community*, 14(2): 107–15.

Spector, M., and Kitsuse, J. (1977) *Constructing Social Problems*. Hawthorne, NY: Aldine de Gruyter.

Speed, E. (2006) Patients, consumers and survivors: a case study of mental health service user discourses, *Social Science and Medicine*, 62(1): 28–38.

SSI (Social Services Inspectorate) (1991) *Getting the Message Across: A guide to developing and communicating policies, principles and procedures on assessment*. London: HMSO.

SSI (Social Services Inspectorate) (2004) *All our Lives: Social care in England 2002–2003*. London: Department of Health.

Stainton, T. (2002) Taking rights structurally: disability, rights and social worker responses to direct payments, *British Journal of Social Work*, 32(6): 751–63.

Stainton, T., and Boyce, S. (2004) 'I have my life back': users' experience of direct payments, *Disability & Society*, 19(5): 443–54.

Stalker, K., Barron, S., Riddell, S., and Wilkinson, H. (1999) Models of disability: the relationship between theory and practice in non-statutory organisations, *Critical Social Policy*, 19(1): 5–29.

Stancliffe, R. J., Emerson, E., and Lakin, K. C. (2001) Community living and people with intellectual disability: introduction to Part II, *Journal of Intellectual & Developmental Disability*, 26(1): 5–13.

Starr, P. (1982) *The Social Transformation of American Medicine*. New York: Basic Books.

Stevens, A. (2004) Closer to home: a critique of British government policy towards accommodating learning disabled people in their own homes, *Critical Social Policy*, 24(2): 233–54.

Stevenson, F., and Scambler, G. (2005) The relationship between medicine and the public: the challenge of concordance, *Health*, 9(1): 15–21.

Stewart, J., Harris, J., and Sapey, B. (1999) Disability and dependency: origins and futures of 'special needs' housing for disabled people, *Disability & Society*, 14(1): 5–20.

Stiker, H.-J. (1999) *A History of Disability*, trans. W. Sayers. Ann Arbor: University of Michigan Press.

Stone, D. A. (1979) Diagnosis and the dole: the function of illness in American distributive politics, *Journal of Health Politics, Policy and Law*, 4(3): 507–21.

Stone, D. A. (1985) *The Disabled State*. London: Macmillan.

Stone, E. (ed.) (1999a) *Disability and Development: Learning from action and research on disability in the majority world*. Leeds: Disability Press.

Stone, E. (1999b) Disability and development in the majority world, in E. Stone (ed.), *Disability and Development: Learning from action and research on disability in the majority world*. Leeds: Disability Press, pp. 1–20.

Stone, E. (1999c) Making connections: using stories from China as an example, in E. Stone (ed.), *Disability and Development: Learning from action and research on disability in the majority world*. Leeds: Disability Press, pp. 171–92.

Stone, E. (1999d) Modern slogan, ancient script: impairment and disability in the Chinese language, in M. Corker and S. French (eds), *Disability Discourse*. Buckingham: Open University Press, pp. 136–47.

Strauss, A., L. 1975: *Chronic Illness and the Quality of Life*. St Louis: C.V. Mosby and Co.

Strauss, A. L., Corbin, J., Fagerhaugh, S., Glaser, B.G., Maines, D., Suczek, B., and Weiner, C. L. (1984) *Chronic Illness and the Quality of Life*. 2nd edn, St Louis: C. V. Mosby.

Strong, P. (1979a) *The Ceremonial Order of the Clinic*. London: Routledge & Kegan Paul.

Strong, P. (1979b) Sociological imperialism and the profession of medicine: a critical examination of the thesis of medical imperialism, *Social Science & Medicine*, 13A(2): 199–215.

Stuart, O. (1992) Race and disability: just a double oppression?, *Disability, Handicap & Society*, 7(2): 177–88.

Stuart, O. (1993) Double oppression: an appropriate starting point?, in J. Swain, V. Finkelstein, S. French and M. Oliver (eds), *Disabling Barriers – Enabling Environments*. London: Sage, pp. 93–101.

Sullivan, D. A. (2001) *Cosmetic Surgery: The cutting edge of commercial medicine in America*. New Brunswick, NJ: Rutgers University Press.

Sutherland, A. (1993) Black hats and twisted bodies, *Disability Arts Magazine*, 3(1): 3–8.

Sutherland, D. (1997) Disability arts and disability politics, in A. Pointon and C. Davies (eds), *Framed: Interrogating disability in the media*. London: British Film Institute, p. 159.

Swain, J., and French, S. (2000) Towards an affirmation model of disability, *Disability & Society*, 15(4): 569–82.

Swain. J., French, S., and Cameron, C. (2003) *Controversial Issues in a Disabling Society*. Buckingham: Open University Press.

Swain, J., French, S., Barnes C., and Thomas C. (eds) (2004) *Disabling Barriers – Enabling Environments*. 2nd edn, London: Sage.

Szasz, T. S. (1961) *The Myth of Mental Illness*. New York: Harper & Row.

Szasz, T. S. (1970) *Ideology and Insanity: Essays on the psychiatric duhumanization of man*. Garden City, NY: Anchor Books.

Szasz, T. S. (1983) Mental illness as strategy, in P. Bean (ed.), *Mental Illness: Changes and trends*. Chichester: John Wiley, pp. 93–113.

Szasz, T. S. (1994) Mental illness is still a myth, *Society*, May–June: 34–9.

Szasz, T. S., and Hollender, M. H. (1956) A contribution to the philosophy of medicine, *AMA Archives of Internal Medicine*, 97: 585–92.

Takamine, Y. (2006) *History of the Global Disability Movement*. Okinawa: University of the Ryukyus. Available at: www.jicafriends.jp/leaders/gi2006/training/leader1023am.html (accessed 10 May 2008).

Talle, A. (1995) A child is a child: disability and equality among the Kenya Masai, in B. Ingstad and S. R. Whyte (eds), *Disability and Culture*. Berkeley: University of California Press, pp. 56–72.

Taub, D. E., and Greer, K. R. (2000) Physical activity as a normalising experience for school-age children with physical disabilities: implications for legitimation of social identity and enhancement of social ties, *Journal of Sport & Social Issues*, 24(4): 395–414.

Taylor, S. J., and Bogdan, R. (1989) On accepting relationships between people with mental retardation and non-disabled people: towards an understanding of acceptance, *Disability, Handicap & Society*, 4(1): 21–36.

Taylor-Gooby, P. (1994) Postmodernism and social policy: a great leap backwards, *Journal of Social Policy*, 23(3): 385–404.

Templeton, S.-K. (2007) Babies aborted for minor disabilities, *The Times*, 21 October. Available at: www.timesonline.co.uk/tol/news/uk/health/article2689787.ece (accessed 22 October 2007).

Thomas, A. P., Bax, M. C. O., and Smith, D. P. L. (1989) *The Health and Social Needs of Young Adults with Physical Disabilities*. Oxford: Blackwell Scientific.

Thomas, C. (1997) The baby and the bath water: disabled women and motherhood in social context, *Sociology of Health & Illness*, 19(5): 622–43.

Thomas, C. (1999) *Female Forms: Experiencing and understanding disability*. Buckingham: Open University Press.

Thomas, C. (2004a) How is disability understood? An examination of sociological approaches, *Disability & Society*, 19(6): 569–83.

Thomas, C. (2004b) Developing the social relational in the social model of disability: a theoretical agenda, in C. Barnes and G. Mercer (eds), *The Social Model of Disability: Theory and research*. Leeds: Disability Press, pp. 32–47.

Thomas, C. (2007) *Sociologies of Disability and Illness: Contested ideas in disability studies and medical sociology*. Basingstoke: Palgrave Macmillan.

Thomas, D. (1982) *The Experience of Handicap*. London: Methuen.

Thomas, G. (1997) *Exam Performance in Special Schools*. Bristol: Centre for Studies on Inclusive Education.

Thomas, M., and Thomas, M. J. (2000) *Selected Readings in Community Based Rehabilitation*. Bangalore: Action for Disability.

Thomas, M., and Thomas, M. J. (2002) A discussion of some controversies in community based rehabilitation, *Asia Pacific Disability Rehabilitation Journal*, 13(1): 2–10.

Thomas, P., and Ormerod, M. (2006) *Implementing Decent Homes Standard: How housing associations are addressing accessibility issues*. York: York Publishing Services for Joseph Rowntree Foundation.

Thompson, P., with Buckle, J., and Lavery, M. (1988) *Not the OPCS Survey: Being disabled costs more than they said*. London: Disability Income Group.

Thornton, P., and Lunt, N. (1995) *Employment for Disabled People: Social obligation or individual responsibility*. Social Policy Research Unit, University of York.

Tibble, M. (2005) *Review of Existing Research on the Extra Costs of Disability*. Working Paper no. 21. Leeds: Department for Work and Pensions.

Titmuss, R. (1958) *Essays on the Welfare State*. London: Unwin.

Tomlinson, A. (ed.) (1990) *Consumption, Identity and Style: Marketing, meanings and the packaging of pleasure*. London: Routledge.

Tomlinson, S. (1982) *A Sociology of Special Education*. London: Routledge & Kegan Paul.

Tomlinson, S. (1996) Conflicts and dilemmas for professionals in special education, in C. Christensen and F. Rizvi (eds), *Disability and the Dilemmas of Education and Justice*. Buckingham: Open University Press, pp. 175–86.

Topliss, E., and Gould, B. (1981) *A Charter for the Disabled*. Oxford: Blackwell.

Tøssebro, J. (2004) Introduction to the special issue: understanding disability, *Scandinavian Journal of Disability Research*, 6(1): 3–7.

Tøssebro, J., and Kittelsaa, A. (2004) Studying the living conditions of disabled people: approaches and problems, in J. Tøssebro and A. Kittelsaa (eds), *Exploring the Living Conditions of Disabled People*. Lund: Studentlitteratur, pp. 17–43.

Tøssebro, J., Gustavsson, A., and Dyrendahl, G. (eds) (1996) *Intellectual Disabilities in the Nordic Welfare States: Policies and everyday life*. Kristiansand: Norwegian Academic Press.

Touraine, A. (1977) An introduction to the study of social movements, *Social Research*, 52(4): 749–88.

Touraine, A. (1981) *The Voice and the Eye: An analysis of social movements*. Cambridge: Cambridge University Press.

Townsend, P. (1962) *The Last Refuge: A survey of residential institutions and homes for the aged in England and Wales*. London: Routledge & Kegan Paul.

Townsend, P. (1966) Foreword, in P. Hunt (ed.), *Stigma: The experience of disability*. London: Geoffrey Chapman, pp. vi–viii.

Townsend, P. (1969) Foreword: social planning for the mentally handicapped, in P. Morris, *Put Away: A sociological study of institutions for the mentally retarded*. London: Routledge & Kegan Paul, pp. xi–xxxiii.

Townsend, P. (1979) *Poverty in the United Kingdom*. Harmondsworth: Penguin.

Townsend, P. (1981) The structured dependency of the elderly: creation of social policy in the twentieth century, *Ageing & Society*, 1(1): 5–28.

Townsend, P., Davidson, N., and Whitehead, M. (1992) *Inequalities in Health: The Black Report and the health divide*. Harmondsworth: Penguin.

Transport for London (2005) *Disabled People's Transport Needs*. London: Transport for London.

Traustadóttir, R., and Kristiansen, K. (2004) Introducing gender and disability, in K. Kristiansen and R. Traustadóttir (eds), *Gender and Disability Research in the Nordic Countries*. Lund: Studentlitteratur, pp. 31–48.

Tremain, S. (1996) *Pushing the Limits: Disabled dykes produce culture*. Toronto: Women's Press.

Tremain, S. (2002) On the subject of impairment, in M. Corker and T. Shakespeare (eds), *Disability/Postmodernity: Embodying disability theory*. London: Continuum, pp. 32–47.

Tremain, S. (ed.) (2005a) *Foucault and the Government of Disability*. Ann Arbor: University of Michigan Press.

Tremain, S. (ed.) (2005b) Foucault, governmentality and critical disability theory: an introduction, in S. Tremain (ed.), *Foucault and the Government of Disability*. Ann Arbor: University of Michigan Press, pp. 1–24.

Tremblay, M. (1996) Going back to civvy street: a historical account of the Everest and Jennings wheelchair for Canadian World War II veterans with spinal cord injury, *Disability & Society*, 11(2): 149–69.

Tronto, J. (1993) *Moral Boundaries: A political argument for an ethic of care*. New York and London: Routledge.

Truman, C. (2005) The autonomy of professionals and the involvement of patients and families, *Current Opinion in Psychiatry*, 18(5): 572–5.

Tuckett, D., Boulton, M., Olson, C., and Williams, A. (1985) *Meetings between Experts: An approach to sharing ideas in medical consultations*. London: Tavistock.

Turner, B. (1987) *Medical Power and Social Knowledge*. London: Sage.

Turner, B. (1992) *Regulating Bodies: Essays in medical sociology*. London: Routledge.

Turner, B. (1995) *Medical Power and Social Knowledge*. 2nd edn, London: Sage.

Turner, B. (2001) Disability and the sociology of the body, in G. L. Albrecht, K. D. Seelman and M. Bury (eds), *Handbook of Disability Studies*. London: Routledge, pp. 252–66.

Turner, M., Brough, P., and Williams-Findley, R. B. (2003) *Our Voice in our Future: Service users debate the future of the welfare state*. York: Joseph Rowntree Foundation.

Twigg, J. (2000) *Bathing: The body and community care*. London: Routledge.

UN (1948a) *Charter of the United Nations*. Available at: www.un.org/aboutun/charter/ (accessed 15 October 2007).

UN (1948b) *Universal Declaration of Human Rights*. Available at: www.unhchr.ch/udhr (accessed 5 June 2007).

UN (1971) *Declaration of the Rights of Mentally Retarded Persons*. New York: United Nations.

UN (1975) *Declaration of the Rights of Disabled Persons*. New York: United Nations.

UN (1990) *Disability Statistics Compendium*. New York: United Nations Statistics Office.

UN (1993) *Standard Rules on the Equalization of Opportunities for Persons with Disabilities*. New York: United Nations.

UNDP (United Nations Development Programme) (1997) *Human Development Report 1997*. New York: Oxford University Press.

UNDP (United Nations Development Programme) (2005) *Human Development*

Report: International cooperation at a crossroads. New York: Oxford University Press.

UN Enable (1982) *World Programme of Action Concerning Disabled Persons*. Available at: www.un.org/disabilities/default.asp?id=23 (accessed 15 November 2007).

UN Enable (2009a) *Convention on the Rights of Persons with Disabilities*. Available at: www.un.org/disabilities/default.asp?navid=12&pid=150 (accessed 21 July 2009).

UN Enable (2009b) *Map of Signatures and ratifications*. Available at: www.un.org/disabilities/documents/maps/enablemap16Apr08.jpg (accessed 21 July 2009).

UN ESCAP (2003) *Final Report: UN ESCAP workshop on women and disability*, Bangkok, Thailand, 18–22 August and 13 October. Available at: www.world-enable.net/wadbangkok2003/recommendations.htm (accessed 9 January 2007).

UN ESCAP (2006) *Asian and Pacific Decade of Disabled Persons 1993–2002*. Available at: www.worldenable.net/wadbangkok2003/recommendations.htm (accessed 12 February 2007).

UNESCO (1994) *The Salamanca Statement and Framework for Action on Special Needs Education*. Paris. UNESCO.

UNESCO (1995) *Overcoming Obstacles to the Integration of Disabled People*. London: Disability Awareness in Action.

UNESCO (2006) *EFA Global Monitoring Report 2007: Early childhood care and education*. Paris: UNESCO.

UNESCO (2007a) *EFA Global Monitoring Report 2008: Education for All by 2015. Will we make it?* Paris: UNESCO.

UNESCO (2007b) *Human Rights-Based Approach to Education for All*. Paris: UNESCO.

Ungerson, C. (1997a) Social politics and the commodification of care, *Social Politics*, 4(3): 362–81.

Ungerson, C. (1997b) Personal assistants and disabled people: an examination of a hybrid form of work and care, *Journal of Social Policy*, 29(4): 623–43.

Ungerson, C. (2004) Whose empowerment and independence? A cross-national perspective on 'care for care' schemes, *Work, Employment & Society*, 13(4): 583–600.

UPIAS (1976a) *Fundamental Principles of Disability*. London: Union of the Physically Impaired Against Segregation.

UPIAS (1976b) *Policy Statement*. London: Union of the Physically Impaired Against Segregation.

USCCB (1996) *The Promise and Peril of Genetic Screening*. Washington, DC: United States Conference of Catholic Bishops. Available at: www.nccbuscc.org/shv/screening.htm (accessed 15 October 2007).

Üstün, T. B., Chatterji, S., Bickenbach, J. E., Trotter, R. T., Room, R., Rehm, J., and Saxena, S. (2001) *Disability and Culture: Universalism and diversity*. Seattle: Hogrefe & Huber for the World Health Organization.

Üstün, T. B., Chatterji, S., Bickenbach, J., Kostanjsek, N., and Schneider, M. (2003) The International Classification of Functioning, Disability and Health: a new tool for understanding disability and health, *Disability & Rehabilitation*, 25(11/12): 565–71.

Van Houten, D., and Jacobs, G. (2005) The empowerment of marginals: strategic paradoxes, *Disability & Society*, 20(6): 641–54.

Vasey, S. (1992a) A Response to Liz Crow, *Coalition*, September: 42–4.

Vasey, S. (1992b) Disability arts and culture: an introduction to key issues and questions, in S. Lees (ed.), *Disability Arts and Culture Papers*, Part 1. London: Shape.

Vernon, A. (1999) The dialectics of multiple identities and the disabled people's movement, *Disability & Society*, 14(3): 385–98.

Vleminckx, K., and Berghman, J. (2001) Social exclusion and the welfare state: an overview of conceptual issues and implications, in D. G. Mayes, J. Berghman and R. Salais (eds), *Social Exclusion and European Policy*. Cheltenham: Elgar, pp. 27–46.

Wade, B., and Moore, M. (1993) *Experiencing Special Education: What young people with special education needs can tell us*. Buckingham: Open University Press.

Waitzkin, H. (1983) *The Second Sickness: Contradictions of capitalist health care*. London: Macmillan.

Waitzkin, H. (1984) The micropolitics of medicine: a contextual analysis, *International Journal of Health Services*, 14(3): 339–77.

Waitzkin, H. (1989) A critical theory of medical discourses, *Journal of Health and Social Behaviour*, 30(2): 220–39.

Waitzkin, H., and Waterman, B. (1974) *The Exploitation of Illness in Capitalist Society*. Indianapolis: Indiana University Press.

Walby, S. (1990) *Theorizing Patriarchy*. Oxford: Blackwell.

Walby, S. (1997) *Gender Transformations*. London: Routledge.

Walker, A., and Walker, C. (1991) Disability and financial need: the failure of the social security system, in G. Dalley (ed.), *Disability and Social Policy*. London: Policy Studies Institute, pp. 20–56.

Walker, A., and Walker, C. (eds) (1997) *Britain Divided*. London: CPAG.

Walker, A., and Walker, C. (1998) Normalisation and 'normal' ageing: the social construction of dependency among older people with learning difficulties, *Disability & Society*, 13(1): 125–42.

Wallerstein, I. (1979) *The Capitalist World-Economy*. Cambridge: Cambridge University Press.

Walmsley, J. (1991) 'Talking to top people': some issues relating to the citizenship of people with learning difficulties, *Disability, Handicap & Society*, 6(3): 219–31.

Walmsley, J. (1997) Including people with learning difficulties: theory and practice, in L. Barton and M. Oliver (eds), *Disability Studies: Past, present and future*. Leeds: Disability Press, pp. 62–77.

Walugembe, J., and Peckett, J. (2005) Power struggle, *New Internationalist*, no. 384. Available at: http://newint.org/issue384/power-struggle.htm (accessed 15 May 2007).

Ward, L. (1987) *Talking Points: The right to vote*. London: Values into Action.

Ware, J. (2004) Ascertaining the views of people with profound and multiple learning disabilities, *British Journal of Learning Disabilities*, 32(4): 175–9.

Warnock, H. M. (1978) *Special Educational Needs: Report of the committee of enquiry into the education of handicapped children and young people*. London: HMSO [Warnock Report].

Wates, M., and Jade, R. (eds) (1999) *Bigger than the Sky: Disabled women on parenting*. London: Women's Press.

Watson, N., McKie, L., Hughes, B., Hopkins, D., and Gregory, S. (2004) (Inter)dependence, needs and care: the potential for disability and feminist theorists to develop an emancipatory model, *Sociology*, 38(2): 331–50.

Weber, M. (1948) *The Protestant Ethic and the Spirit of Capitalism*. New York: Free Press.

Weller, D. J., and Miller, P. M. (1977) Emotional reactions of patients, family and staff in acute care period of spinal cord injury, Part 1, *Social Work in Health Care*, 2(4): 369–77.

Wells, H. G. (1979) *The Complete Short Stories of H. G. Wells*. London. Ernest Benn.

Wendell, S. (1989) Towards a feminist theory of disability, *Hypatia*, 4(summer): 10–24.

Wendell, S. (1996) *The Rejected Body: Feminist philosophical reflections on disability*. London: Routledge.

Werner, D. (2005) Community-based rehabilitation in rural India: the strengths and weaknesses of different models, *Newsletter from the Sierra Madre #55*. Available at: www.healthwrights.org/Newsletters/NL55.pdf (accessed 20 March 2007).

Westcott, H., and Cross, M. (1996) *This Far and No Further: Towards the ending of the abuse of disabled children*. Birmingham: Venture Press.

Whittaker, A., and McIntosh, B. (2000) Changing days, *British Journal of Learning Disabilities*, 28(1): 3–8.

WHO (1976) *International Classification of Disease*. 9th revision, Geneva: World Health Organization.

WHO (1980) *International Classification of Impairments, Disabilities and Handicaps*. Geneva: World Health Organization.

WHO (2001a) *International Classification of Functioning, Disability and Health*. Geneva: World Health Organization.

WHO (2001b) *Rethinking Care from the Perspective of Disabled People*. Geneva: World Health Organization. Available at: www.who.int/inf-pr-2001/en/note2001-16.html (accessed 4 August 2007).

WHO (2002) *Towards a Common Language for Functioning, Disability and Health (ICF)*. Geneva: World Health Organization. Available at: www3.who.int/icf/icftemplate.cfm?myurl=beginners.html&mytitle=Beginner%27s%20Guide (accessed 19 February 2007).

Wiener, C. L. (1975) The burden of rheumatoid arthritis: tolerating the uncertainty, *Social Science & Medicine*, 9(2): 97–106.

Wilde, A. (2004) Disabling masculinity: the isolation of a captive audience, *Disability & Society*, 19(4): 355–70.

Williams, F. (1992) Somewhere over the rainbow: universality and diversity in social policy, in N. Manning and R. Page (eds), *Social Policy Review no. 4*. Canterbury: Social Policy Association, pp. 201–19.

Williams, F. (1993) Gender, 'race' and class in British welfare policy, in A. Cochrane and J. Clarke (eds), *Comparing Welfare States: Britain in international context*. London: Sage, pp. 77–104.

Williams, F. (2001) In and beyond New Labour: towards a new political ethics of care, *Critical Social Policy*, 21(4): 467–93.

Williams, G. (1984a) The genesis of chronic illness: narrative reconstruction, *Sociology of Health & Illness*, 6(2): 175–200.

Williams, G. (1984b) The movement for independent living: an evaluation and critique, *Social Science & Medicine*, 17(15): 1000–12.

Williams, G. (1996) Representing disability: some questions of phenomenology and politics, in C. Barnes and G. Mercer (eds), *Exploring the Divide*. Leeds: Disability Press, pp. 194–212.

Williams, G. (1998) The sociology of disability: towards a materialist phenomenology, in T. Shakespeare (ed.), *The Disability Reader: Social science perspectives.*
London: Cassell, pp. 234–44.

Williams, G. (2001) Theorising disability, in G. L. Albrecht, K. D. Seelman and M.
Bury (eds), *Handbook of Disability Studies*. London: Sage, pp. 123–44.

Williams, R. (1980) *Problems in Materialism and Culture*. London: New Left Books.

Williams, R. (1981) *Culture*. Glasgow: Fontana.

Williams, R. (1989) *Resources of Hope*. London: Verso.

Williams, S. (1996) The vicissitudes of embodiment across the chronic illness
trajectory, *Body and Society*, 2(2): 23–47.

Williams, S. (1999) Is anybody there? Critical realism, chronic illness and the
disability debate, *Sociology of Health & Illness*, 21(6): 797–819.

Williams, S. (2000a) Chronic illness as biographical disruption or biographical
disruption as chronic illness? Reflections on a core concept, *Sociology of Health
& Illness*, 22(1): 40–67.

Williams, S. (2000b) Reason, emotion and embodiment: is 'mental' health a contradiction in terms?, *Sociology of Health & Illness*, 22(5): 559–81.

Williams, S. (2003) *Medicine and the Body*. London: Sage.

Williams, S., and Bendelow, G. (1998) *The Lived Body: Sociological themes, embodied
issues*. London: Routledge.

Williams, S., and Calnan, M. (1996) The 'limits' of medicalisation? Modern medicine and the lay populace in 'late' modernity, *Social Science & Medicine*, 42(12):
1609–20.

Williams, V., and Holman, R. (2006) Direct payments and autonomy: issues for
people with learning difficulties, in J. Leece and J. Bornat (eds), *Developments in
Direct Payments*. Bristol: Policy Press, pp. 65–78.

Wilson, A. N. (1997) How not to win friends, *Sunday Telegraph*, 28 December.

Wilson, S. (2003) *Disability, Counselling and Psychotherapy: Challenges and opportunities*. New York: Palgrave Macmillan.

Wilton, R. D. (2003) Locating physical disability in Freudian and Lacanian
psychoanalysis: problems and prospects, *Social and Cultural Geography*, 4(3):
369–89.

Winzer, M. A. (1993) *The History of Special Education: From isolation to integration.*
Washington, DC: Gallaudet University Press.

Wirz, S., and Hartley, D. (1999) Challenges for universities of the North inter-
ested in community based rehabilitation, in E. Stone (ed.), *Disability and
Development: Learning from action and research in the majority world*. Leeds:
Disability Press, pp. 89–106.

Wistow, G., and Barnes, M. (1993) User involvement in community care: origins,
purposes and applications, *Public Administration*, 71(autumn): 279–99.

Witcher, S., Stalker, K., Roadburg, M., and Jones, C. (2000) *Direct Payments: The
impact of choice and control for disabled people*. Edinburgh: Scottish Executive
Central Research Unit.

Wolfensberger, W. (1972) *The Principle of Normalisation in Human Services*. Toronto:
National Institute on Mental Retardation.

Wolfensberger, W. (1980a) A brief overview of the principle of normalization, in
R. J. Flynn and K. E. Nitsch (eds), *Normalization, Social Integration and Community
Services*. Baltimore: University Park Press, pp. 7–30.

Wolfensberger, W. (1980b) The definition of normalization: update, problems, disagreements and misunderstandings, in R. J. Flynn and K. E. Nitsch (eds), *Normalization, Social Integration and Community Services*. Baltimore: University Park Press, pp. 71–115.

Wolfensberger, W. (1983) Social role valorisation: a proposed new term for the principle of normalisation, *Mental Retardation*, 21(6): 234–39.

Wolfensberger, W. (1989) Human service policies: the rhetoric versus the reality, in L. Barton (ed.), *Disability and Dependence*. Lewes: Falmer, pp. 23–42.

Wolfensberger, W., and Thomas, S. (1983) *Program Analysis of Service Systems Implementation of Normalisation Goals: Normalisation and ratings manual*. 2nd edn, Toronto: National Institute of Mental Retardation.

Wood, R. (1991) Care of disabled people, in G. Dalley (ed.), *Disability and Social Policy*. London: Policy Studies Institute, pp. 199–202.

Woodward, K. (ed.) (1997) *Identity and Difference*. London: Sage.

World Bank (2007) *Social Analysis and Disability: A guidance note*. Washington, DC: World Bank.

Wright, B. A. (1960) *Physical Disability: A psychological approach*. New York: Harper.

Wrigley E. A., and Souden, D. (eds) (1986) *The Works of Thomas Robert Malthus*. London: Pickering & Chatto.

Yeo, R.(2005) *Disability, Poverty and the New Development Agenda*. Available at: www.disabilitykar.net/docs/agenda.doc (accessed 15 November 2007).

Yeo, R., and Bolton, A. (2008) '*I Don't Have a Problem, the Problem is Theirs': The lives and aspirations of Bolivian disabled people in words and pictures*. Leeds: Disability Press.

Young, I. M. (1990) *Justice and the Politics of Difference*. Princeton, NJ: Princeton University Press.

Young, I. M. (2000) *Inclusion and Democracy*. Oxford: Oxford University Press.

Zarb, G., and Nadash, P. (1994) *Cashing in on Independence*. Derby: British Council of Organizations of Disabled People.

Zarb, G., and Oliver, M. (1993) *Ageing with a Disability: What do they expect after all these years?* London: University of Greenwich.

Zijlistra, H. P., and Vlaskamp, C. (2005) Leisure provision for persons with profound intellectual and multiple disabilities: quality time or killing time?, *Journal of Intellectual Disability Research*, 49(6): 434–48.

Zola, I. K. (1972) Medicine as an institution of social control, *Sociological Review*, 20(4): 487–504.

Zola, I. K. (1982) *Missing Pieces: A chronicle of living with a disability*. Philadelphia: Temple University Press.

Zola, I. K. (1983) Developing new self-images and interdependence, in N. Crewe and I. K. Zola (eds), *Independent Living for Physically Disabled People*. San Francisco: Jossey-Bass, pp. 49–59.

Zola, I. K. (1985) Depictions of disability – metaphor, message, and medium in the media: a research and political agenda, *Social Science Journal*, 22(4): 5–17.

Zola, I. K. (1991) The medicalisation of ageing and disability, in G. L. Albrecht and J. A. Levy (eds), *Advances in Medical Sociology*, Vol. 2. Greenwich, CT: JAI Press, pp. 299–315.

Zola, I. K. (1994) Towards inclusion: the role of people with disabilities in policy and research issues in the United States – a historical and political analysis, in M. Rioux and M. Bach (eds), *Disability is Not Measles*. North York, Ontario: Roeher Institute, pp. 49–66.

Index

Cabinet Office 64, 98, 109, *111*, 112, 125, 136, 144, 146–7
Cambodia 247, 264–5
Campbell, (Lady) Jane: disability politics 29, 152, 164, 172, 176
    charity advertising 192
    right to life 214, 234–5
Campling, J. 86–7, 185
Canada: Charter of Rights and Freedoms (1985) 168
    CILs 180
capitalism: and disability 73, 78–9, 81–5, 93, 113, 245
    global 239–41, 245
    late capitalism 57, 59, 63–4, 199
    and medicine 57, 60–1
care: agencies 136, 148–9, 154, 206
    approach 93, 127–8, 133–4, 139–42, 166, 178, 206
    feminism 139–42
    informal 100, 102, 128, 133–4, 139–42, 231
    management 139, 148
    packages 147, 150; *see also* community care, health care
carers 56, 102, 127, 134, 139–41, 146–7, 152
Carers UK 141
Caring for People 134, 139
Cartesian dualism 91
cartoons 192
Castells, Manuel 63
Catholic Church 217–18, 220
Central Statistics Office (CSO) 122
Centre for Accessible Living 202
Centre for Independent/ Integrated/ Inclusive Living (CIL) 142–6, 148, 162, 165, 167, 180; *see also* National Centre for Independent Living
Centre for Studies on Inclusive Education (CSIE) 107
cerebral palsy 233, 244
changelings 16, 244
Chappell, A. 75, 137, 181
charity 15–16, 143, 255, 263
    advertising 189, 191–2, 198–9, 201
    organizations 18, 36, 128, 145, *162*, 253, 266
    and disability policy 123, 161–3, 167, 176
    telethons 178, 188–9, 191
Charity Commission 162–3
Charlton, J. 156, 165, 180, 243, 246, 248, 251, 259, 261
Charmaz, K. 52, 54

China: impairment 243, 245; special education 253
Christianity and impairment 15, 198, 243
chronic illness: meanings 51–5, 96
    medical approach 22, 43, 59, 97, 204; narratives 54–5
    and social model 35, 69–70, 204
    social origins 64–5
    stigma 47–51, 55–6, 70
Chronically Sick and Disabled Persons Act (1970) 118, 132, 153
CIL *see* Centre for Independent/ Integrated/ Inclusive Living
citizenship rights 33, 108, 125, *131*, 138, 199
    democratic 150, 157, 160, 164–6
    denied 23, 45, 78–9, 251
    market-driven 101–2
    state-guaranteed 100, 131, 154
civilizing process 16
civil rights: Europe 166, 169, 173, 178
    USA 24–5, 27, 77, 165–8, 174–5
Clarke, J. 100–1, 134–6, 163
class, social 6, 10, 80, 88–90, 175, 206, 210, 210, 240
    dominant 76, 99, 104
    and illness 44, 54, 57
    and disability 26, 36, 47, 85, 106, 137, 181
    middle class 176, 181
    socio-economic factors 20, 48, 64–5, 77, 104, 161
    working-class 57, 99–100, 175
Clogson, J. 193
cochlea implants 205
Coleridge, P. 214, 242, 246–7, 252, 254–5, 264
collective action 96, 154, *162*, 181
commercial interests 62, 102, 190, 193, 198
Commission for Social Care Inspection (CSCI) 135, 147–8, 151
communication impairment 17, 123
community-based rehabilititation (CBR) 75, 239, 262–6
community care 75, 127–9, 132–4, 139, 154; *see also* residential homes
Community Care (Direct Payments) Act (1996) 134–5, 145, 147
compensation programmes 26, 60, 93, 110
competence, social 47, 53, 90, 221, 244, 252
Confederation of Indian Organizations 87

LIBRARY, UNIVERSITY OF CHESTER